A HISTORY OF MURSHIDABAD DISTRICT

A HISTORY OF MURSHIDABAD DISTRICT

(*BENGAL*)

WITH

BIOGRAPHIES OF SOME ITS NOTED FAMILIES

COMPILED AND EDITED BY

MAJOR J. H. TULL WALSH, I.M.S., F.L.S

GYAN

Published by

Gyan Publishing House
5, Ansari Road
Daryaganj, New Delhi-110002
Phone: 011-47034999, 9811692060
E-mail: books@gyanbooks.com

Distribution Network
gyanbooks.com
India, USA, Canada, UK, Australia, France

ISBN : 978-81-212-9834-6 (PB)
First Published, 1903

2nd Impression 2023

Printed at: Gyan Press, Delhi.

A HISTORY OF MURSHIDABAD DISTRICT
Author: MAJOR J. H. TULL WALSH

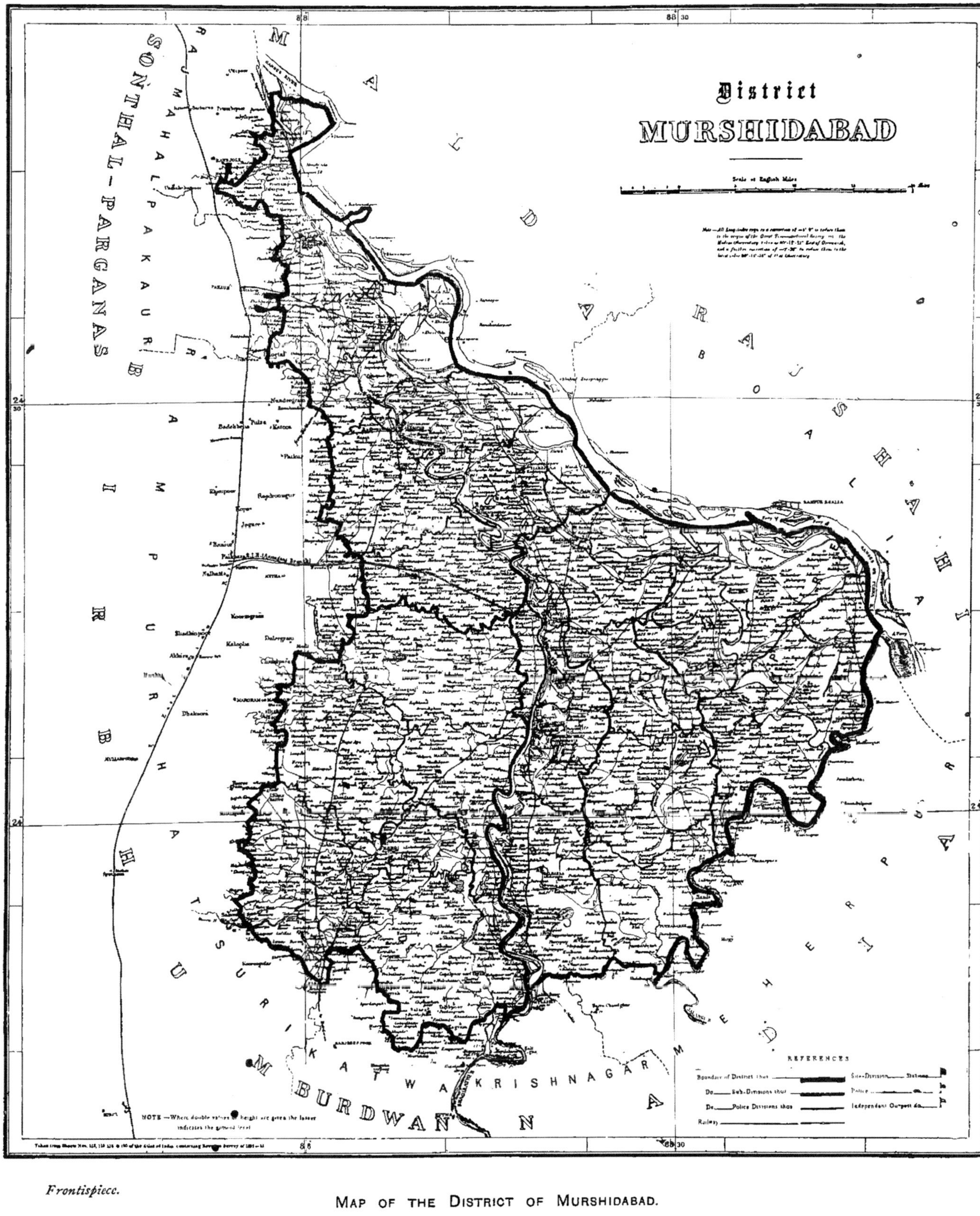

Frontispiece.

MAP OF THE DISTRICT OF MURSHIDABAD.

(*Survey of India—Corrected up to* 1897.)

A HISTORY

OF

MURSHIDABAD DISTRICT

(*BENGAL*)

WITH

BIOGRAPHIES OF SOME OF ITS NOTED FAMILIES

COMPILED AND EDITED BY

MAJOR J. H. TULL WALSH, I.M.S., F.L.S.,

CIVIL SURGEON OF MURSHIDABAD

With Map and Numerous Illustrations

PREFACE.

A FEW words of explanation are necessary as to the origin and object of this work. About two years ago, Colonel T. H. Hendley, I.M.S., C.I.E., Inspector-General of Civil Hospitals, proposed the issue of a "*Medico-Topographical History*" of each district in Bengal. I had collected a large amount of historical material and numerous photographs for that purpose. Much of this material was not required for the work to be edited by Colonel Hendley. He therefore suggested that I might publish it separately by subscription, and obtained sanction. Until I reached England on furlough in June, 1901, I had no opportunity to arrange my notes in a coherent form. Further delay was due to the difficulty of choosing a method of reproducing the illustrations which would be reasonable in price and satisfactory in result. The interest of the Biographies in Part II. lies in the fact that many of the families are connected, more or less, with the history of the district; and many of them owe their possessions, titles, or pensions, to the friendly relations existing between the founders and the Honourable East India Company. Some families have been left out, only because they furnished no replies to my request for information. While Part I. has been compiled from the works mentioned in the Bibliography and information collected in the District, the material in Part II. has been mainly supplied by the families concerned. (The exceptions to this rule are mentioned in the foot-notes.) I have exercised the rights of Editorship where necessary, only to remove irrelevant matter, and to keep down the expense. I here offer my thanks to the Subscribers, and all who have supplied me with material for the Biographies. My thanks are due also to various Government Officers, who furnished information in their respective departments. The Judge and Magistrate of the District kindly allowed me to use any books I required from their official libraries. Many books, maps, and valuable papers were lent to me from the Palace library, by H.H. the Nawab Bahadur of Murshidabad. Indeed, I could hardly have succeeded without his help in that respect, and as a Subscriber. That the work is incomplete, and has other imperfections, I am only too well aware. I can only plead as an excuse that the work was mainly compiled in the few leisure intervals in the busy life of a Civil Surgeon in an Indian District. Where copies or quotations are used, the spelling of the original has been preserved. For the rest uniformity is all that has been attempted. I will here also record my thanks to the Publishers, who have tried to meet my wishes in every way. The Zincographer deserves a word of praise, and it is not his fault that the map (frontispiece) requires good sight, or a magnifying glass. By sacrificing details, larger type could have been used; but I thought it best to have a full map even with very small type.

J. H. T. W.

OLD CATTON,
NORWICH,
July, 1902.

TABLE OF CONTENTS.

PART I.

PART II.

BIOGRAPHIES.

THE HISTORY OF MURSHIDABAD.

PART I.

HISTORY.

THE History of the district of Murshidabad represents the downfall of the Mahomedan Subahs, of Bengal, Behar, and Orissa, who ruled as the Viceroys of the Emperor of Delhi, and the rise of British power and commerce, through a long series of years of fighting and striving, until England had not only ousted all European competitors, but had entirely subjugated a vast and warlike population, from whose rulers they had, at first by favour, and humble petitions, obtained a footing for purposes of trade; and to whom, until after the battle of Plassy, they had paid tribute, as the weaker section. To keep within my special limits I have had to go through a large amount of material, selecting such facts as refer to this district, avoiding prolixity and introducing only such extraneous matter as is absolutely necessary to make the story comprehensible; and I hope, in some degree, interesting. The earliest connection of the Honble. East India Company with this district was marked by the establishment of a factory at Kasimbazar. The factory was situated on the western bank of the river Bhagirathi, and south of the land occupied by the French and the Dutch.* To understand the position of the factory with reference to the topography of the present day, it will be necessary to make a few remarks concerning the alteration which has taken place in the course of the Bhagirathi, or Kasimbazar river, as it was also called in those times. Just above Farashdanga, where the Berhampur town water-works are now situated, the river started to make a loop towards the East, enclosing the then prosperous town of Kasimbazar. Berhampur, with its annex Gorabazar, did not then exist. This condition continued until somewhere about the year 1813, when the Bhagirathi made a straight cut across the loop, thus leaving Kasimbazar and the sites of the French, Dutch, and English factories on the left, or east bank of the river. This change in the river was the cause of the downfall in the trade of the Company and its abandonment of Kasimbazar. I cannot exactly fix the date of the founding of the first factory, for there were two of them, but it was about 1652 or 1653. One, Edward Stephens, formerly second factor at Hughli, was sent to manage affairs at Kasimbazar. He appears to have been a failure, and died deeply in debt in 1654. In 1658 J. Kenns was appointed to manage the factory, and he seems to have been a man of energy and enterprise. In 1661 he reported to the Calcutta Council that the most vendible commodities were gold and silver. The sale of silver, however, would depend somewhat on whether the Dutch received consignments from Japan. The sale was good, since at Muxsudabad, about nine miles away, "there are made several sorts of silver and gold girdles from 10 rupees to 60 rupees." In return, several kinds of silk were obtainable. A public table was to be kept up at the factory, and the work of steward was placed in the hands of one of the younger factors. The second factor was to keep the silk books, and the third was to be warehouse-keeper. A larger factory, on the river bank, was established in 1662, and the Company

* *v.* Orme (42).

were shortly after, in 1663, keeping a fleet of boats on the Kasimbazar river to bring silks and muslins from Kasimbazar to Hughli. This factory was established under the orders of Sir Edward Winter, then President at Madras. The earliest rights of trading were granted by the Emperor, Shah Jehan, through the Subah of Bengal, Nawab Sultan Sujah. The story of Doctor Boughton's connection with this permission is too well known to need more than mention. The Emperor, Shah Jehan, was succeeded in 1660 by the great Emperor Aurungzebe, and Mir Jumlah was Nawab of Bengal, with his capital at Rajmehal. This Mir Jumlah, formerly a general in the army of a brother of Sultan Sujah, had usurped the title, having attacked and seized Rajmehal, and deposed Sultan Sujah. There was considerable friction between the English and Mir Jumlah, but the usurper died somewhere about 1663-4, and better times came with his successor, Nawab Shaistah Khan, a nephew of the beautiful Noor Jehan. In 1672 Shaistah Khan, in return for an annual subsidy of Rs. 3,000, granted a *Firman*, passing all goods free of duty and directing the local *Foujdars* (customs officers) and other officers to assist the factors to recover debts due to them from merchants, weavers, and others with whom they had dealings. The Company's boats were to be allowed to pass along the rivers. The Dutch, who also had a factory at Kasimbazar, were not included in these privileges. It does not appear that the relations between the English and Dutch were very friendly, as the former had not forgotten the massacre of British merchants in Amboyna, in 1623. The men and the times were rough, and we find that in 1676 the Directors of the East India Company found it necessary to send out Mr. Streynsham Master, to inspect the Bengal factories and to inquire into the death of Raghu, Poddar of the Kasimbazar factory, who had been so violently thrashed by the house-broker that he died of his injuries. Kasimbazar was then the headquarters of the silk trade, and President Hedges, as quoted by Wilson,* describes it as "an ordinary Indian town about two miles long with streets so narrow in some places, where markets were kept, that there was barely room for a single palanquin to pass." Hedges relates in his diary that the houses were made of mud dug out close to the house, leaving a hole full of stagnant water, which increased the unhealthiness of the place at certain times of the year." This practice of leaving the hole from which mud for dwellings has been taken, is even now productive of much illness and danger to health, since these pits become the receptacles for refuse, and many things besides water. The soil in the neighbourhood being alluvial was very fertile; all the district round was planted with mulberry for the silkworms. The silk, he says, was yellow, but bleached with a lye made from the ashes of the plantain. Firewood was scarce, and timber dear and bad. As regards this latter condition the country must have improved, as it is fairly well wooded in the present day. To return to Streynsham Master. We find that he arrived at Kasimbazar on the 29th September, 1676, and remained there six weeks. He first inquired into the death of Raghu, Poddar. This man had been placed in custody by the head factor, Mr. Vincent, in order to extract money due from him to the Company. During Mr. Vincent's absence the house-broker, Ananta Ram, had caused Raghu to be severely beaten, with the deplorable result above stated. His death took place the same night. The matter caused great indignation among the natives, and was only hushed up on payment of one thousand rupees to the relatives. The inquiry lasted a fortnight, for Master, as a stranger to the country and language, found it no easy matter to sift the conflicting evidence before him. In the end he could do nothing further than lay down rules for the conduct of the factors, ordering copies of all proceedings to be sent to Fort St. George. On November the 1st, the Council, sitting at Kasimbazar, decided that Hughli was the best place for the residence of the head of the Council of the Bay. They further decided that the Kasimbazar factory ought to be inspected once a year, noting that the expense would be small owing to the convenience of travelling by water. Streynsham Master left Kasimbazar on the 8th November. In the following year, Mr. Vincent was transferred to Hughli as chief of the factories, and the people of Kasimbazar congratulated themselves

* Bibliography (3).

on his departure. He bore a dreadful character, not only on account of the death of Raghu, Poddar, but on account of "diabolical arts with the Bramminees." These appear to have included magic and poison. In this same year, 1677, the Emperor of Delhi removed Shaistah Khan to Agra. Fedai Khan, a foster brother of Aurungzebe, ruled Bengal for a short time, hardly a year, and then died, being succeeded by Sultan Mahomed Azzim, third son of the Emperor. He renewed the privileges granted to the English merchants for a consideration amounting to Rs. 21,000.* Whether his father was dissatisfied with him, or not, is not clear, but for some reason Sultan Mahomed Azzim was recalled in 1679, and Nawab Shaistah Khan again installed as Subahdar of Bengal. In this same year, according to Wilson, Job Charnock,† then at Patna, was made head of the Kasimbazar factory, and second in the Council of the Bay. Charnock was sending off cargoes of saltpetre from Patna and delayed so long in joining his new post, that Streynsham Master censured him and cancelled the appointment, ordering him to Hughli as second factor. An appeal to the Directors brought disgrace on Streynsham Master. The Court said that Charnock had stayed at Patna to attend to the saltpetre, and as they had appointed him to Kasimbazar, to Kasimbazar he should go. He went, and his enemies, Master and Vincent, were dismissed from the Company's service. The year 1680 brought with it a new agreement between the Emperor Aurungzebe and the Company, one not altogether fraught with benefit for the latter. Owing to difference of opinion as to the reading of this document, there were many quarrels between the factors and the Nawab's officers who were exacting taxes from which the factories, except that at Surat, considered themselves free by this and former agreements. These differences led to a deadlock in trade, and in 1682, when the new Governor, Mr. Hedges, came out, he found commerce almost at a stand-still and the English full of complaints against Nawab Shaistah Khan's customs officers. The English resolved to appeal to the Nawab at Dacca, at this time the capital of the lower provinces. The local collector of customs, Parmeshwar Das, did all he could to prevent them, interrupted their boats, and beat their boatmen. So great was his opposition that Hedges was obliged to get away secretly at night, and, following the Hughli and Jalingi rivers into the main stream of the Ganges, ultimately reached Dacca on the 25th October. At the end of a month he obtained a promise of redress, and he returned to Hughli full of hope, only to meet with disappointment and further harassment from the Nawab's officials. In April, 1683, Kasimbazar received a visit from the Governor, whose object was to investigate a charge made against Mr. Naylor, a dyer in the factories. This man was accused of trading in silk with "interlopers," *i.e.*, all not belonging to the Company, as, to the Greeks of old, all the rest of the world were "barbarians." The Company had the greatest hatred of these interlopers and punished severely any dealings with them, so that Naylor could hope for no mercy, especially as letters, fully proving his guilt, were found. The Governor's next duty was to expel a man who was acting as a private servant with Job Charnock. This man, James Harding, had come out to India as a writer in 1671, and had been dismissed from the Company's service. Charnock was rebuked for employing him against what he must have known to be the wishes of the Company. The factors at Kasimbazar appear to have all come in for trouble during this visitation, for many of the silk weavers complained that Richard Barker and John Threder, second and third on the Council, took overweight on all the silk brought into the warehouse, and this they proved by their books. Nothing seems to have been done in this matter, and the two factors remained on at Kasimbazar. The next man in the factory to fall foul of Hedges was one John Watson, and in this quarrel the factors got the better of the Governor, and his bitter opponent, Job Charnock, was no doubt instrumental in obtaining his dismissal, for in 1684 Hedges was recalled and disappears from the Company's service. In October of the same year, Kasimbazar was visited by the new President, Gifford, but his visit did not produce any occurrence of interest. Job Charnock's pay while he was head factor at

* Steward (15), page 303, and Appendix. The figures in brackets refer to the place of the book in the Bibliography.
† 1681, according to Broome (14), Vol. i., p. 9.

Kasimbazar appears to have been about £60 a year, but he must have been engaged in some illegitimate trade, for we find that the merchants in the neighbourhood made a claim against him for Rs. 43,000. When the claim came into Court the decision was in favour of the plaintiffs, and they were supported by the Nawab of Bengal, Shaistah Khan, who ordered Charnock to appear before him at Dacca. Charnock refused to go and made many efforts to get the decision revised. In order to prevent his escape the Nawab's troops were sent to watch the factory. For some time the relations between the English and the Nawab's officials had been strained, the cause of the quarrel being generally connected with customs fees. At Kasimbazar the conduct of the Foujdar was considered very oppressive and ultimately led to a breach, preparations for war being made on both sides. These matters were reported to the Court of Directors in the despatches of 1685, and the Agent in Bengal was censured for having been "too timid and submissive towards the Nawab." Troops were sent from England and from Madras, but such open hostilities as took place were outside this district. In 1696 Charnock managed to evade the surveillance of the Nawab's troops and got away to Hughli, where he was appointed head of affairs. He set to work at once to raise a company of Portuguese infantry and ordered the troops sent from England to come up to Hughli. Seeing the determined attitude of the English, Shaistah Khan thought it better to come to terms and proposed to submit the disputes between his officers and the factors to arbitration. The Company claimed compensation for loss of trade, and restitution of money extorted from their servants by the Foujdars. The claim in all amounted to over 66 lakhs of rupees, and included the following items from the Kasimbazar factory:—"For what Bul Chund forced from Mr. Vincent at Cassumbuzar 14,000; for detaining ye agent with ye silk at Cassumbuzar 40,000."

The Nawab was not prepared to admit such an enormous claim, and, taking the initiative, ordered his troops to seize the English factories and imprison the factors.

In 1689 Shaistah Khan resigned, and shortly afterwards died. He was followed on the *musnud* by Ibrahim Khan II., who released the captured agents. He made peace with the Company and invited Charnock and others, who had fled to Madras, to settle again in Bengal. To this the Emperor of Delhi agreed, for, though he hated the English, he was quick to note that his revenues were less during their absence. A condition of peace and prosperity continued until 1695, when Subah Singh, a rich landholder in Burdwan, assisted by the Pathans residing in Orissa, broke into open rebellion and managed to capture Rajmehal and Maldah. From there, in 1696, he marched on to Muxsudabad and Kasimbazar. The inhabitants of Muxsudabad offered no resistance to Rahim Khan, the Afghan Chief, and leader of the Pathans. Horrible massacres took place, and arriving at the property of one Niamat Khan, who held a *jaghir* just outside the city, the rebels called upon him to join them. This he refused to do, saying that he owed allegiance to the Nawab only. His nephew, Tehuver Khan, an officer of the Nawab's Cavalry, challenged Rahim Khan, or any of his men, to single combat, but the cowards set on him in a body and cut him to pieces. Niamat Khan, though without protection of any kind, mounted a horse, and, with a sword in his hand, threw himself on the enemy, and making straight for Rahim Khan, struck fiercely at his head. The blow fell on the Afghan's helmet and the sword broke in pieces. In his impotent rage Niamat Khan flung the hilt at his foe, with such accurate aim, that it knocked him off his horse. Dismounting, Niamat Khan tried to seize his enemy's dagger to renew the fight, but, although he succeeded in getting the weapon, his stroke could not pierce the strong chain mail which protected the Afghan's throat. Overpowered by numbers, he and his servants were soon slain and his estate was plundered.* Kasimbazar fell into the hands of the insurgents, and by March, 1697, they had seized all the country west of the Ganges. When the Emperor heard that Nawab Ibrahim Khan was unable to cope with the rebels he sent for his grandson, Azim-u-shan, to supersede him. Zuberdast Khan was placed in charge of the Nawab's forces

* Wilson (3) gives as reference Stewart's "Bengal," pp. 207-209; it should be 332-333.

and at once the tide began to turn. This general defeated the Hindu rebels and their allies, recovered Rajmehal and followed his enemies to Muxsudabad, driving them out of the district and on to Burdwan. The subsequent course of this war does not concern us, except in so far as it emboldened the English to press for further grants. Although Azim-u-shan was the nominal ruler of Bengal the actual power was in the hands of the Diwan of Muxsudabad, Murshid Kuli Khan. He was highly thought of by the Emperor, who created him a Nawab in 1704. In 1702 one of the periodical seizures of the European factories had taken place, but the firmness of President Beard, who captured a number of the Emperor's vessels, ended the trouble. In 1703 the first steps towards the union of the old and new East India Companies took place, and trade resumed its normal conditions. The final amalgamation of the Companies was completed 1707-8. In 1704 the water in the Bhagirathi being very low the big boats from Patna loaded with saltpetre could not get past Muxsudabad, and two factors and six soldiers were sent up to transfer the cargoes into smaller boats. To lessen the possibility of interference they took as presents for Murshid Kuli Khan, looking-glasses, sword blades, cups, plates, rose water, broadcloth, velvet, etc.* We now come to a very important year in the history of the district, 1706, during which Muxsudabad was made the capital of Bengal. Murshid Kuli Khan removed the *adalut* (courts) and the mint from Dacca and built a palace at Muxsudabad.† Muxsudabad was in future to be known as Murshidabad. The old name is used by the mass of the people, upon whom even stirring events make little or no impression. Trade in the English factories at Kasimbazar had for some time been of a spasmodic character, owing to the constant dread of attacks from the Nawab's officers. Things became more settled, however, after Murshid Kuli Khan had made himself secure as Nawab *de facto*, and two of the Company's factors, Bugden and Freake, left Calcutta in 1707 to place the trade at Kasimbazar on the old footing. They were encouraged by the fact that Murshid Kuli Khan expressed a desire to meet the merchants and come to terms with them. In the meanwhile, Aurungzebe, after a reign of 47 years, died on the 21st February, 1707. He was succeeded by Bahadur Shah, father of Azim-u-Shan. The latter was re-appointed Nawab of Bengal, with Nawab Murshid Kuli Khan as deputy and Nawab of Orissa. Whether Murshid Kuli Khan was sincere it is impossible to say, but the Company's boats on the Bhagirathi were continually molested by subordinate officers, so much so, that, in February, 1708, the Calcutta Council thought it necessary to strengthen Kasimbazar by sending Mr. Calvert and thirty-five soldiers. They were to be employed to protect the saltpetre boats coming down from Patna and to see them safely past Murshidabad and on their way to Fort William. On the whole, however, life at Kasimbazar seems to have been fairly peaceful. Side by side with the English the Dutch were carrying on their trade, and it is a sign of security that, by request, a chaplain was sent down in 1709 to baptize the child of the Chief o the Dutch factory at Kasimbazar. In this same year, Murshid Kuli Khan was summoned to the Court of the Emperor at Delhi, and during his absence Sher Bulland Khan, who was acting as Diwan, saw an opportunity for a little extortion on his own account. He sent for Mr. Pattle, head of the Kasimbazar factory, and demanded Rs. 45,000, as the price of his protection. After reference to Calcutta, Mr. Pattle paid the amount, getting in return a written promise of protection for all English trade in Bengal, Behar, and Orissa. In 1713 the skill of another of the East India Company's surgeons was rewarded by the Emperor Furokshah. Mr. Hamilton,‡ waiving his personal claims, begged for grants for the English, and a *Firman*§ was issued in 1717, "confirming all former privileges, authorising the Company to

* For details *v.* Wilson (3), p. 226.

† According to Orme (42), Vol. ii., p. 19, it was Mir Jaffer Khan who removed the capital from Dacca to Muxsudabad in 1756. There is no doubt that the transfer was made by Murshid Kuli Khan, as stated by Stewart (15), p. 369, and Hunter (8), p. 173.

‡ Mr. Hamilton died December 10th, 1717, and was buried in St. John's churchyard, Calcutta.

§ This *Firman* is given at length by Broome (14), in Appendix C.

issue *dustucks* exempting any goods specified therein from search or duty, and placing the use of the mint, at Murshidabad, at their disposal." Murshid Kuli Khan regarded these favours with disgust, and it was necessary to conciliate him with presents. Murshid Kuli Khan died in 1725; his son-in-law, Sujah-u-din Khan, succeeded him, and reigned until 1739. His rule was favourable to the English, and trade in the district increased and prospered. The next Nawab of Bengal was Serfiraz Khan, son of Sujah-u-din, and he, too, allowed the English to continue their prosperous course. He did, however, call upon them to contribute towards the expenses of repelling the invasion of India by Nadir Shah. He died fighting at Gherriah, in January, 1741, and the *musnud* was tenanted by his successful rival, Ali Verdi Khan. During his reign, which was a continued struggle with the Mahrattas, he levied war taxes on the English, but did not otherwise disturb them. In 1742 permission was given to strengthen the factory at Kasimbazar, as an attack by the Mahrattas was anticipated. A masonry wall with bastions at the corners was built round the factory. In 1747 Ali Verdi Khan had to purchase peace with the Mahrattas by ceding Cuttack and by payment of an annual subsidy of twelve lakhs. This payment was called *Chouth*, and had originally been granted as a tax which the Mahrattas might levy. Ali Verdi Khan had avoided payment for some years. Already in 1748, the Mahrattas were again interfering with the Company's cargo-boats on the river, and the officer sent to protect them on their journey down the river with goods and treasure, either from Kasimbazar, or Patna. A letter, dated February 19th, from Edward Eyles, one of the Kasimbazar Council, gives us an insight into these raids. He reports that he had sent Ensign McKion, with all the soldiers available, 150 buxerries,* four field-pieces, and ammunition, to Cutwah to secure as much of the goods as possible. He complained that Ensign English had not waited at Plassy to protect the boats, and further, that on the arrival of the Mahrattas that officer allowed himself to be outwitted by them. He did not send for help, and leaving his budgerow,† fell into the power of the enemy. Ensign McKion was directed to relieve English of his command. On February the 21st an inquiry was held at Kasimbazar, and the facts of the disaster at Cutwah ascertained. Besides the cargo and treasure belonging to the Company, no less than Rs. 35,000, the property of a private individual, had been looted. No help could be obtained from the Nawab, because he could not leave Murshidabad, fearing that in his absence the Mahrattas would attack the city. The Kasimbazar merchants felt that they could not for some time send any more goods by river for fear of further loss, not only to themselves, but to the contractors. The native merchants at Kasimbazar were at this period considerably in debt to the factory, and Mr. Eyre reported to the Calcutta Council in March, that he had confined as many of the debtors as he could, hoping thus to prevail on them to discharge their debts. To raise money he had tried to negotiate a bill on Patna, but failed, as the Shroffs‡ had absconded, to escape from the extortions of the Nawab, who wanted all the money he could get to pay his troops, and indeed had much difficulty in getting them to move owing to money being due to them. The Company suffered from other plunderers besides the Mahrattas. In April, one of their boats was stopped at Hajiruhatti and a bale of goods stolen by Raja Anoopanian. The thief fled to Murshidabad and the Company's Agents were instructed to demand restitution. There is no record of the success or failure of this demand, but it is extremely unlikely that the bale was ever recovered. Among the "interlopers" trading in this district the most numerous and successful were the Armenians. They happened about the end of 1748 to have two cargo-boats stopped by order of the Nawab, and this being reported to Calcutta by the local factors, a threat was issued that no Armenian ships would be allowed to pass Fort William. By this means no doubt the Kasimbazar merchants hoped to frighten these active competitors. In the month of January, 1749, the Nawab sent an order from Murshidabad directing his

* The name given to a body of armed police, Broome (14), p. 92.

† A large boat with one part covered with mats to form a sort of cabin.

‡ Bankers, or more literally money-lenders.

Diwan at Dacca to discourage trade in that city. It thus fell to the merchants at Kasimbazar to try to propitiate the Nawab, and a horse was sent to be presented to him on a favourable opportunity in return for which he was expected to allow trade to proceed in Dacca. Among the stray records* for 1748 is one dismissing Mr. Wadham Brooke, chief of Kasimbazar; but no particulars are given as to the events which ed to his punishment. It would seem further, that the order was subsequently cancelled, since in January, 1749, Brooke wrote to Calcutta that it was necessary to keep the Nawab in a good temper. Ali Verdi Khan had heard of a fine Arab horse for sale in Calcutta, and had no doubt thrown out hints that it would be an acceptable present. In August, the Armenians appealed to the Nawab to assist them in their dispute with the merchants at Kasimbazar, and Ali Verdi Khan, seeing an excellent opportunity to extract money from both parties, sent his troops to surround the factory. The English tried to propititate the Nawab through the Seths, or bankers, of Murshidabad. Their demands were extortionate, Rs. 30,000 for themselves, and four lakhs for the Nawab. After many negotiations the Armenians were satisfied, but the English had to pay to the Nawab, through the Seths†, no less than Rs. 12,00,000. In March, 1750, the Nawab had gone with his army as far as Midnapur hoping to check the advance of the Mahrattas. The enemy, however, slipped past him, and twelve thousand of them got within about four or five miles of Murshidabad, where they came into collision with the troops led by Mir Jaffer Khan, the Paymaster-General. The action was not decisive. Mir Jaffer had to retreat to Murshidabad, but he was not followed, the Mahrattas being content to send out small parties to plunder the district. By May, 1751, Ali Verdi Khan was back in his capital. One of his first acts was to demand the surrender of Ram Kissen Seth, who had carried goods through to Calcutta without paying taxes at Murshidabad. The Company's President replied that the Seth's father and grandfather were the Company's *dadni*‡ merchants, and that as Ram Kissen was greatly in debt to the Company he could not be surrendered. By December, 1751, Brooke had either really been dismissed or transferred, since we find Mr. W. Fytche at the head of the Kasimbazar Council. He had unpleasant news for his masters in Calcutta, who learned from him that they might consider the balances due from sundry merchants, from 1744 to 1747, as bad debts. Only Rs. 25,657-2-9 had been collected, and the merchants had either died, or run away, or were too poor to make any payment. Raw silk and silk piece-goods were becoming very dear owing to the raids made by the Mahrattas. The workmen and weavers had many of them been plundered and driven out of their burning homesteads. A Turk, named Haji Salius, having lately died, his estate had been received into the Calcutta Treasury. This came to the ears of Ali Verdi Khan, who at once sent a message to the merchants at Kasimbazar that he demanded the Turk's estate. The man, he argued, was a foreigner and had died intestate in the Nawab's dominions. The demand was accompanied by threats that troops would be sent to the factory unless the money was paid. This was reported to Calcutta, and in reply the merchants there were directed to satisfy the Nawab's claim, the sum amounting to Rs. 5,092-1-9. Ali Verdi Khan next turned his attention to the French, whose factory was at Farashdanga. Having no excuse for molesting the English, he sent his troops to surround the French factory, but finally allowed the merchants to resume business on payment of 50,000 sicca rupees. Money must have been easily made in those times, for there does not seem to be any limit to the bribes and extortions to which the trades had to submit. Like the daughter of the horse leech, the Nawab for the time-being, with a string of satellites, was ever crying "give, give," and if they did not give, the cry was merely changed into "take, take." For the past decade the mass of the population had been in a state of waning prosperity, and at this period their condition was at its worst. The people were taxed to maintain an army to repel the Mahrattas, and they

* Long (13).

† These Seths, of whom Jaggat Seth was the head, were part founders of the rich Jain banker families now so prosperous in Azimganj and Baluchar.

‡ Dadani, money advanced, *i.e.*, merchants taking advances.

could neither reap, nor sow, nor tend their silkworms from daily dread of attacks. Products were scarce and prices high, and the factors were again asked to explain the very high price of raw silk. They gave the same reasons as before. They had for similar reasons been unable to supply the full amount of their contracts, and further, the cotton crop of 1751 had been almost entirely destroyed by storms and heavy rain in the month of April. Towards the end of 1752 the garrison at Kasimbazar was looking to its defences. They found it very difficult to get carpenters as they were all employed by the Nawab, and on this account the officer in command had to write to Calcutta for gun carriages. Iron work, too, was very dear. A young writer, Mr. Hugh Watts, was sent to Kasimbazar as an assistant. He had come out on the "Portfield" and notes that he was well treated, and that his passage had cost Rs. 1,000, arcot.

The Council in Calcutta had long wished to establish a mint of their own, and in 1753 they deputed Mr. Watts, head factor at Kasimbazar, to approach the Nawab on the subject. He was obliged to use the greatest secrecy to prevent the interference of Jaggat Seth, the Murshidabad banker. This man was a large purchaser of bullion and no doubt made a large profit at the Murshidabad mint. He, therefore, opposed the establishment of an independent mint; and as he had considerable influence with the Nawab, Mr. Watts' negotiations were sure to fail if he came to know of them. As a matter of fact they did fail, and Watts recommended that a direct appeal should be made to the Emperor at Delhi.

There is nothing particular to notice until we come to the records for 1755, when we find "writers" here sharing a general reprimand on account of bad writing and carelessly kept books. The season's accounts are recorded as "slovenly to a degree that we are quite ashamed of."

Although the Mahrattas did not further molest this district there were troubles in store for the small body of English at Kasimbazar. Ali Verdi Khan died April 9th, 1756, and was succeeded by his son Suraj-u-Dowlah, a weak, cruel, and vicious youth. His hatred of the English was well known. The English were at this time making preparations for war with the French, and the Nawab forbade any further strengthening of their defences. Finding that, as regards the Fort in Calcutta, his orders had been ignored, he gave up an expedition against the Nawab of Purneah, and sent an army of 3,000 men, under the command of Raja Doulat Ram, to surround the factory at Kasimbazar. The factory was not actually attacked until the young Nawab himself arrived, on the 1st June, 1756, with the rest of his army. The defences of the factory were, as we have seen, far from strong. The factors had a few guns, but they were of small calibre and some of them were honeycombed with rust, and practically useless. The "whole stock of ammunition did not exceed 600 rounds." "The garrison consisted of only one officer, Lt. Elliott, and forty-four regular soldiers, of whom twenty were Portuguese, and several Dutch, together with about 250 matchlock men."* An appeal was made to Calcutta, but they would not send any help; indeed, it is difficult to see how they could have done so. Mr. Watts, the head factor, was summoned by Suraj-u-Dowlah, and under assurances of safety he went out to the Nawab's camp accompanied by Mr. Forth, the Company's surgeon. They were received with abuse and threats, and forced to sign a *Moochulka*, or obligation, promising that within fifteen days the work on the new Fort in Calcutta should be demolished, with other humiliating terms. The Nawab then sent for Mr. Collet and Mr. Batson, the factors next in rank to Mr. Watts, and they too were compelled by threats to put their names to this impossible document. The next act was one of treachery, for in defiance of the safe-conduct given, all four men were imprisoned, and the factory being too weak to withstand such a force, surrendered on June 4th. Lt. Elliott, overcome with shame, shot himself. The factory was plundered and the small garrison taken prisoners. The native matchlock men either bolted, or joined the enemy. With the exception of Mr. Watts, the European prisoners were sent to Murshidabad. The Nawab took Mr. Watts with him, as well as the factory guns, and turned his steps towards Calcutta. Hyde tells us that the Kasimbazar guns were used to bombard

* Broome (14), p. 49.

Fort William. After the seizure and sack of Calcutta, with the terrible tragedy of the Black Hole, Suraj-u-Dowlah ordered Mr. Holwell, and others* to be sent up to Murshidabad in irons, believing that Mr. Holwell could be forced to reveal the position of treasure which the Nawab firmly believed had been hidden by the English. In Murshidabad they found Hastings and Chambers, also prisoners. When Suraj-u-Dowlah returned to Murshidabad he had the prisoners brought before him, but, finding he could get nothing out of them, let them go. They made their way to Chinsurah, where the Dutch showed them hospitality. The brutal nature of Suraj-u-Dowlah was not alone displayed in his treatment of the English. He had taken the *musnud* more or less by force, and certainly without consulting the Emperor, Alumgir II. The people of the city of Murshidabad were in a state of fear, knowing not who would be the first to feel the young tyrant's displeasure. No sooner was he in power than he attacked the palace of his aunt, Gheseeta Begum, on the bank of the Moti Jhil, and succeeded in possessing himself of the treasure amassed by her late husband, Nuazish Mahomed. He next proceeded to turn out various officials, replacing them by his own disreputable satellites. Among others, he dismissed Mir Jaffer Khan, the Paymaster General, and this man, later on, was to be the cause of Suraj-u-Dowlah's ruin, and, indirectly, of his death.

The remnant of the British forces had retired to Fultah, there to await the arrival of Col. Robert Clive, from Madras, with all available troops. As we are not concerned with events outside this district, I shall only give a brief sketch of Clive's career, until history again reaches the neighbourhood of Murshidabad. The enemy's fort, at Budge-Budge, having been successfully besieged, the ships containing Clive's army proceeded up the river to Alighur Fort, where Clive was joined by some native troops. He continued his progress along the high road. Calcutta was re-occupied without much trouble between the 2nd and 4th of January, 1757, a portion of the army was sent to attack Hughli, which place was taken by Captain Coote on the 10th. On the 12th, Bundel fell, and by the 16th the troops were back in Calcutta. In the meanwhile, war had been declared between England and France, and as Clive wished to be free to attack the French possessions, he made overtures through Jaggat Seth and Omichand, to the Nawab. Suraj-u-Dowlah would not listen to any terms, and on the 30th January, crossed the river, north of Hughli, with 43,000 men, 40 guns, and 50 elephants.

Clive had no wish to be embroiled with Suraj-u-Dowlah at a time when Admiral Watson was waiting to co-operate with a land force against Chandernagore. On the other hand, any sign of fear would have encouraged the young Nawab. Clive therefore sent "messengers to solicit peace," and at the same time prepared to fight. To oppose an army of over 40,000 men, Clive had 700 Europeans and 1,200 Sepoys; to this force he added 600 sailors from Admiral Watson's ships. On the morning of the 5th February, the English attacked Suraj-u-Dowlah, routing his troops with a fierce charge. The Nawab then agreed

* With Holwell were Court, Burdett, and Ensign Walcot. They were made over to the Commander-in-Chief, Mir Muddun, to be sent as prisoners to Murshidabad. Placed in a country boat, they suffered the greatest discomfort during a tedious voyage lasting over a fortnight. The prisoners had no shelter to protect them from sun or rain, and their food was of the coarsest. Their allowance of rice had to be washed down with muddy river water, and the effect of such diet on Europeans soon became evident. They suffered from boils, as did many other survivors from the horrors of the "Black Hole." Holwell seems to have been the most vigorous among the prisoners, and to him fell the duty of feeding and tending his "more helpless companions." "On arrival at Murshidabad they were led in chains through the crowded city." It is said that the Nawab, Suraj-u-Dowlah, was not aware of the indignities suffered by these four Europeans. Holwell, continued in such bad health that in February, 1757, he was sent to England in the "Syren." A note in Dr. Busteed's book (5) would suggest that pressure was brought to bear upon the Nawab. A certain Mr. Weston who, like his patron, had forsaken the medical profession for commerce, reported that Suraj-u-Dowlah's forbearance to Holwell, and the latter's release from fetters, was due to the intercession of the Nawab's wives, instigated by certain natives of Calcutta who loved Holwell.

This same Weston evidently had a poor opinion of the prospects of a medical man in India in those times. Holwell left his profession for the East India Company's Civil Service, and Weston followed suit, remarking:—"What could I expect from following the medical profession, when I saw a regular-bred surgeon, and so clever a man as Mr. Holwell, charge no more than 50 rupees for three months' attendance and medicine."

to peace, and a treaty was signed on the 9th. Clive also sought the Nawab's permission to attack the French, but this was not given until Admiral Watson threatened to "raise such a conflagration as would not be extinguished by all the water of the Ganges."* Permission was then given.

Suraj-u-Dowlah had made many enemies in Murshidabad, men of influence whom he had slighted as he had done the Paymaster General, Mir Jaffer. Mir Jaffer, Omichand, one Khoja Wazid, and others, secretly sought Clive's help in order to depose the young tyrant. If they were successful, Mir Jaffer was to be placed on the throne. Clive employed Mr. Watts, of the Kasimbazar factory, as his agent in these negotiations, which were carried on through April and May, 1757. We are told that the conspirators worked so secretly that Suraj-u-Dowlah had no suspicion of any except Mir Jaffer. He sent for the deposed Paymaster General, and forced him to swear on the *Koran* that he was not guilty of any treachery. Clive was inclined to deal with Mir Jaffer only, to the exclusion of the rest.

The pact between Clive and Mir Jaffer, in 1757, becoming known to Omichand, a rich Hindu banker, he threatened to report the matter to Suraj-u-Dowlah unless he received blackmail to the amount of thirty lakhs of rupees. It was then that Clive stooped to deceit, meeting fraud with fraud. An agreement was drawn up to pay to Omichand, not the sum demanded, but twenty lakhs, if the scheme was successful. This document was first drawn up on white paper, and all mention of Omichand's name was omitted. A second bond was drawn up on red paper, in almost the same terms, but with Omichand's name in it. The false red paper was shown to the blackmailer.

This district again becomes the scene of history. When all was ready, Clive accused the Nawab of breaking the treaty made in February, and practically declared war.

Clive, with his army, left for Plassy on the 13th June. On the 16th, he reached Patlee. Major Coote seized Cutwah, and possessed himself of the enormous store of rice in its granaries.

Clive, and many of his officers, were inclined to rest here and entrench themselves against attack, but the bolder counsel of Major Coote prevailed, and the army continued its march to Plassy and encamped there, June 22nd, in a mango grove, only a mile distant from the enemy. At dawn the following day, the 23rd, the Nawab's troops took the initiative. They numbered 40,000 foot and 16,000 horse, with 50 cannon; and were further strengthened by a detachment of artillery, manned by French soldiers and commanded by Mons. St. Frais. Against this vast force Clive could muster only 3,000 infantry, of which only 1,000 were European troops; and eight cannon. He hoped for help from Mir Jaffer, but none came. Our promised ally contented himself with remaining neutral. During the morning the fight consisted mainly in a duel between the opposed artillery. About midday rain fell heavily, and, as the Nawab's gunners had not placed their ammunition under cover, much of it was irrevocably damaged. A lucky shot from one of our field-pieces mortally wounded Mir Muddun, the Nawab's Commander-in-Chief, cutting off one of his legs. Mir Muddun in his terrible plight managed to get away to Munganapara, where he died and is buried. The loss of their general caused a panic, and Suraj-u-Dowlah, whose tent was well out of the way of danger, was advised to retreat. Those in the plot with Mir Jaffer, influenced by motives of personal revenge, represented to the Nawab that his only safety lay in retreat, and, these counsels prevailing, orders were given to draw off the artillery. The retreat began about two o'clock in the afternoon, and as the enemy fled, Clive moved forward, checked however, temporarily, by a false alarm that a force of cavalry was attacking his baggage. It was soon seen that the men were part of Mir Jaffer's army, and the British forces pressed forward again. The gravest resistance we encountered was from the French, who fought bravely, but found no support from the Nawab's troops. Advancing at the charge, Clive's infantry routed this small body, causing them to flee, leaving their guns behind. When once the retreat began victory was certain, as the Nawab's troops bolted without order or discipline, making for

* Marsham (31), p. 49.

Murshidabad. Baggage, tents, cannon, all they possessed, were left behind, and became the spoil of the victors. Clive lost during the fight twenty-two killed and fifty wounded, mostly Sepoys. He reported that all his troops had fought most bravely, giving special praise to the 39th British Regiment,* and their colours still bear the motto won at Plassy, *Primus in Indis.*

As night fell, the pursuit ceased, and the British forces bivouacked at Daudpur. Here Clive received a message from Mir Jaffer, assuring him of his fealty, and during the night, Mir Jaffer's army arrived, and camped close to Clive's victorious force. Suraj-u-Dowlah had fled on a dromedary, and was soon safely hidden in his palace. His next step was to call together his Council; but he found neither comfort nor advice. Giving up all hope of further resistance, Suraj-u-Dowlah retired to the zenana, where he collected his jewels, and prepared to escape. Disguised in old and torn clothes, he took with him only his favourite concubine and confidential eunuch.

Early the next morning there was a cordial meeting between Lord Clive and Mir Jaffer. With their combined forces they set out at once for Murshidabad city. Fearing treachery, Clive, however, let Mir Jaffer precede him, and did not enter the city until the 29th July. Then with a guard of 200 Europeans, and 300 chosen Sepoys, he took up his residence in the Moti Jhil palace. His first duty was to install his ally, Mir Jaffer, and this he did in the main palace before the chief nobles of the Nizamat. Taking Mir Jaffer by the hand, Lord Clive led him to the throne, saluting him as Nawab Nazim, of Bengal, Behar, and Orissa. It then became the duty of the newly appointed Nawab Nazim to carry out his part of the contract.† They repaired to the treasury, but not finding as much money as they had hoped for,‡ Clive suggested that they should resort to the Seths, to make up the amount required. One crore of rupees was to be given to the East India Company as compensation for loss and damage to their Kasimbazar factories; fifty lakhs were to go to those Europeans who had suffered loss during the sack of Calcutta; twenty lakhs to compensate their native servants and friends; and seven lakhs over and above these sums, the troops were to receive as a gratuity. Clive received sixteen lakhs as his share, and large sums were claimed by members of the Council.

Omichand had journeyed to Murshidabad, hoping to receive at once a portion of his reward, but when the chief Hindus of the city were called into the presence of Lord Clive and the Nawab, he found that there was no place assigned to him. As he stood wondering what this studied rudeness might portend, he was addressed by Mr. Sefton, by Clive's order. When Omichand heard that the red paper which he held was a fraud, he fainted, and fell into the arms of the bystanders. He was carried home, where he lay almost insensible for days. He was perhaps a scoundrel from our point of view, but this cruel blow was more than even he deserved, and it shattered his intellect for ever. Even a pilgrimage which he took did him no good, and he died about a year-and-a-half later. We can only pass over in silence an act which stains the honour of one of the greatest men that ever promoted the British rule in India. In addition to the money payment, certain privileges were granted by the Nawab, but they did not refer to this district.

In the meanwhile, Suraj-u-Dowlah had made his way to Bhagwangola, and from there to Rajmehal. Here he approached the hut of a Fakir,§ to get fuel to cook his food. As bad luck would have it, the Fakir had formerly been a victim of Suraj-u-Dowlah's cruelty, and seizing this opportunity to revenge the loss of his ears, he sent word to Suraj-u-Dowlah's enemies. The deposed Nawab was taken back to Murshidabad. Mir Jaffer might have spared him, but he was asleep when the prisoner arrived. His son, Miran, a blood-thirsty youth, had Suraj-u-Dowlah confined in a room near his apartments, and proposed to kill

* 1st Battalion Dorsetshire Regiment.

† See Biography of Mir Jaffer, Part II.

‡ About two crores of rupees, Marsham (31).

§ Religious beggar, or hermit.

him at once. He could not, however, persuade any of his companions to assist him. At last Miran found a willing instrument in one Mahomed Beg who, entering Suraj-u-Dowlah's room, killed him with a sword. The body of the murdered man was then placed on an elephant, and taken out and buried in the Roshnibagh Cemetery.* Clive left Murshidabad, but Major Coote, who had been sent in pursuit of the French, under M. St. Frais and M. Law, returned, after dispersing the enemy, and quartered his troops at Kazimbazar. Mir Jaffer was not permitted to remain in peace, and was threatened by the Nawab of Oude, Sujah-u-Dowlah, who was joined by the Shahzada with an army of 40,000 men, Mahrattas, Afghans, and Rohillas. Mir Jaffer appealed to Warren Hastings, who had been appointed President at the Murshidabad Court. Hastings sent word of the danger to Clive, who entered into a correspondence with the Shahzada, to gain time. When his preparations were made, Clive returned in February, 1759, to Murshidabad, and taking with him Miran and all available troops, he left the city on the 13th March, to attack the Shahzada. In gratitude for the help which left him free from danger, Mir Jaffer conferred upon Lord Clive, an estate, south of Calcutta, worth thirty lakhs of rupees. The letter conveying this gift was written by Warren Hastings, and sent to the Council in Calcutta.

In 1757 the East India Company got its long-coveted mint in Calcutta, but the coins issued bore the head of the Emperor.

We have now traced the progress of British power in Bengal, from small things to great. The East India Company, from the date of the victory of Plassy, became the paramount power. A student of history will recognise, however, that there was another critical period, and one, the evil of which was of the Company's own making. Defeat in any of our contests with Kasim Ali would have thrown the Company back, even if it had not reduced the English again to the position of subjection they occupied before 1757. As regards further historical incidents they will be but briefly alluded to. They will be found in the lives of the Nawab Nazims, in Part II. I shall shortly turn aside, to follow the origin and growth of the administrative machinery from which the various "Codes" and "Procedures" in use at the present time have slowly been evolved.

Mir Jaffer had been nominated by the English to succeed to the *Subah*, as a reward for his support against the late Nawab. He had been a distinguished general under Ali Verdi Khan, whose half-sister he had married. Deposed for disaffection, he was, however, after a time reinstated and appointed *Bakshi*, or Paymaster General. On his dismissal from this office by Suraj-u-Dowlah, he commenced, as we have seen, to plot against him. Difficulties soon arose about the payment of the price of Mir Jaffer's elevation. The treasuries of Murshidabad contained, no doubt, a large amount of coin, but, henceforth, the sources from which they were replenished began to dry up. Individuals still continued to accumulate wealth, but the ordinary administration of the Government and the collection of the revenues had become disorganized.

The following description of the treasuries of Murshidabad is mainly taken from the "Sair-i-Mutakharim." The translator of that work† states that Mr. Walsh, the commissary of the army, informed him that he accompanied Colonel Clive, Mr. Watts the Resident, Mr. Lushington, Ram Chand the writer, and Naba Krishna the munshi, into the vaults of the palace. They found stored up there £176,000 in silver, £230,000 in gold, two chests of gold ingots, four chests of set jewels, and two smaller ones, containing loose stones and gems. It is supposed, however, that this was only the outer treasury, and that the English were deceived by their astute Bengali associates. The custom, says the chronicler, was common even with private men, of keeping the more precious articles, as well as the bulk of the coined money, within the

* In this account I have followed Marsham (31). Macfarlane (19) says that Suraj-u-Dowlah was brought before Mir Jaffer, who intended to spare him.

† "Sair-i-Mutakharim," Vol. I., Part II., p. 773, note.

zenana, or women's apartment. This inner treasury of Suraj-u-Dowlah is asserted to have contained eight million pounds sterling. The whole of this enormous sum is said to have been distributed between Mir Jaffer, Ram Chand, Naba Krishna, and Amin Beg Khan. It is not probable that the new Nawab succeeded in retaining much of his share, but we know enough about the circumstances of the others to render this marvellous story not altogether incredible. Ram Chand, at the time of the battle of Plassy, was a writer on Rs. 60 a month. He died ten years afterwards, worth £720,000 in cash and bills; and he also left 400 large water pots, 80 containing gold, and the rest silver; £180,000 in land; and jewels to the value of £200,000. The wealth of Naba Krishna may be estimated from the fact that he was able to spend £90,000 upon the funeral of his mother. His salary in 1767 as political *banian** to the Company, to which post he was appointed at the personal recommendation of Lord Clive, was only Rs. 200 a month. With reference to the proportion of the spoil that fell to the share of the English, the Committee of the House of Commons, in 1773, disclosed a total of £3,388,575, which represents, it must be remembered, only the sums which were acknowledged to have been received. It was impossible that this vast sum of money should be paid over on one and the same day; but coin to the value of eighty lakhs of rupees was immediately placed on board barges and sent down the river to Calcutta.

Clive left Bengal, in February, 1760,† and no sooner was he gone than the Shahzada‡ made preparations for attacking Murshidabad. Frustrated in a preliminary attempt on Patna, by a force of 300 English, and 1,000 Sepoys, under the command of Col. Calliand and Miran, the son of Mir Jaffer, the Shahzada combined his forces with those of our old enemy, M. Law. He might even then have given up his intention had he not been further strengthened by the Naib of Purneah. The combined forces, by a circuitous march evaded their pursuers, and again appeared before Patna. The Patna garrison was weak, Fullerton, with the few men he could muster, managed to protect the factory, and keep Shah Alum at bay. Captain Knox, from Murshidabad, had only 200 Europeans, 300 native cavalry, one battalion of Sepoys, and five cannon; but with these he utterly routed the allies, leaving the pursuit of the vanquished to Col. Calliand and Miran. What might have been a decisive victory was spoiled by the rebellion of Miran's troops. They insisted on returning to Murshidabad, in order to demand from the Nawab the arrears of pay due to them. Unfortunately, the Nawab's funds were very low. Very much the same condition of things existed in Calcutta, where both English and native troops were clamouring for pay. The Governor, Mr. Vansittart, seeing no other way out of his troubles, since his treasury also was empty, entered into a treaty with Mir Kasim Ali § to overthrow Mir Jaffer. Mir Kasim Ali, the son-in-law of Mir Jaffer, was to be made Nawab, and in return was to give to the East India Company the revenue of the provinces of Burdwan, Midnapur, and Chittagong. In September, the Governor, at the head of a considerable force, arrived in Murshidabad, and Mir Jaffer, powerless to resist, resigned in favour of his treacherous son-in-law. Even his own troops declared against him, and the poor old man to whom the British owed so much, had to beg for life, and a safe escort for his family to Calcutta. The first act performed by the new Nawab was the payment of Miran's rebellious troops; and, to satisfy the claims of the army under Mr. Vansittart, he sent six lakhs of rupees to the Government treasury at Calcutta.

Warren Hastings was so outspoken in reprehension of the course of conduct by which the natives were being oppressed, that he was subjected to the grossest insults from his brother Councillors. He was charged, together with the Governor, in a minute presented by Mr. Batson, with acting the part rather of a retained solicitor of the Nawab, than of a servant of the Company. An altercation ensued.

* Money-lender, or cashier, who looked after the financial affairs of the political department.

† "History of British India," C. Macfarlane (19), 1862.

‡ Eldest son of the Emperor of Delhi, Shah Alum.

§ See Biography, Part II.

BATTLE of PLASSY,

GAINED BY COLONEL CLIVE,

June 23rd, 1757.

A *Position of the British Army at 8 in the Morning.*

B *Four Guns advanced to check the fire of the French Party at the Tank* D.

C *The Nawab's Army.*

D *A Tank from whence the French Party cannonaded till 3 in the Afternoon, when part of the British Army took post there, and the enemy retired within their Entrenched Camp.*

E & E *A Redoubt and Mound taken by Assault at half-past four, and which completed the Victory.*

G *The Nawab's Hunting House. The dotted Line* B E *shows the encroachment of the River since the Battle.*

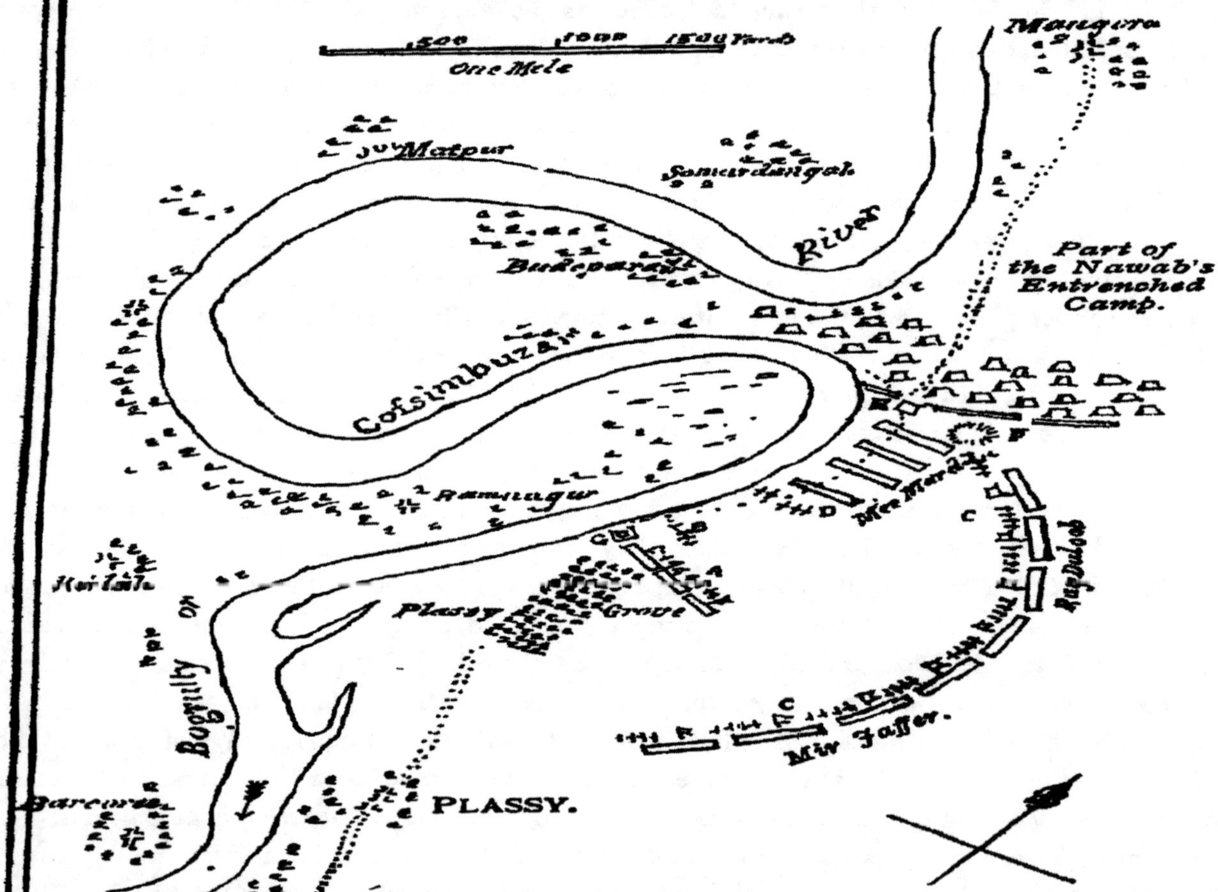

FROM AN OLD MAP IN THE MURSHIDABAD PALACE LIBRARY.

Mr. Batson gave him the lie, and struck him in the presence of the Board. Within less than a month war was declared against the Nawab by the majority of the Council, while both the Governor and Warren Hastings remained neutral. But news of the expulsion of the English from Patna arrived at this time, and Warren Hastings recorded his altered views in the following minute:—"It was my resolution, as soon as war should be declared, to resign the Company's service, being unwilling to join in giving authority to pass measures of which I disapprove. . . . But since our late melancholy advices it is my intention to join my endeavours for the good of the service as long as the war shall last."*

The name of Warren Hastings is so closely connected with the history of this district that a few lines must be devoted to his career.

The Prince Regent said of him, that "he was one of the most deserving and at the same time one of the worst used men in the Empire."†

Born the 6th December, 1732, at Daylesford, he died August 22nd, 1818. He was educated at Daylesford, and Newington, near London, and at ten years of age was sent to Westminster. In 1777 he and other old boys gave a large cup to the school. He was next taught accounts, etc., by Thomas Smith, of Christ's Hospital, but he had no head for figures, and was made a writer to the Honble. East India Company. He embarked for India, reaching Calcutta, 1750, in his eighteenth year. In 1752 he was posted to Kasimbazar to make "bargains" for stuffs with native brokers.

In 1756 he married the widow of Captain Buchanan, of the Company's service, and by this wife he had two children a daughter who lived nineteen days, and a son, sent home for education. Mrs. Hastings died at Kasimbazar soon after the birth of her son, and is buried there in the old English cemetery. Warren Hastings left Kasimbazar for Calcutta, in 1761. In 1756 he was saved from Suraj-u-Dowlah by an ancestor of the Maharajah of Kasimbazar.

In 1772 he became Governor of Bengal, and the Directors exhorted him to economy and the putting down of abuses, and complained that, owing to bad treatment of the natives, silk had risen 50 per cent.

Governor for two years, he was then Governor General of India for eleven years. Warren Hastings married Mrs. Emhoff, in 1775, in Calcutta.

Though he passes out of our particular district history, his influence as Governor of Bengal was felt for good. He was said to be a favourite with natives, and to have given to Bengal peace such as it had never known. He was clever with his pen, so that even Francis acknowledged him as his superior.

More money was soon wanted, and a victim was found in Ram Narain, the Governor of Patna. Ram Narain was seized, and thrown into prison, where he remained for two years, to be at last murdered by Mir Kasim. The native community seeing that the English raised no voice to stay these cruel proceedings, thought that Mir Kasim was powerful enough to resist them, and the Nawab Nazim himself, encouraged by false hopes of support, began to plunder the boats belonging to the Company, as they passed down the Bhagirathi. Reprisals on the part of the English at Patna led to the murder of Mr. Amyatt, the seizure of the Kasimbazar factories, and despatch of all prisoners to Monghyr. The Council in their extremity turned to Mir Jaffer, whom they promised to restore to the *gaddi*,‡ if he would free them from the "Frankenstein" monster they had raised in Mir Kasim. A treaty was therefore drawn up, and signed by both parties, July 10th, 1763.

The proximate cause of hostilities was on this wise. Mir Kasim, after much negotiation, had agreed to a Convention, also accepted by Mr. Vansittart, that a duty of only 9 per cent. should be paid by Englishmen, which was below the rate exacted from other traders. This Convention, however, was repudiated

* Hunter, "Imperial Gazetteer." † Sir C. Lawson (35). ‡ Lit. cushion, throne.

by the Council at Calcutta. The Nawab, in retaliation, resolved to abandon all duties whatever on the transit of goods, and to throw the trade of the country perfectly open. This resolution was still more disagreeable to the Company's servants than the Convention had been. A deputation, consisting of Mr. Hay and Mr. Amyatt, was despatched to Monghyr, where Mir Kasim had fixed his residence. But it was now too late for negotiation. Disputes between the *gomashtas* of the English and the Mahomedan officers were breaking out daily in every District of Bengal. Mr. Ellis, the chief of the Patna factory, threatened to commence hostilities by occupying the city with his Sepoys. The Nawab seized some boats laden with arms for that place, as they were passing up the Ganges. Mr. Ellis surprised and took the city of Patna; and Mr. Amyatt, who was on his way to Calcutta, was attacked by the people of the Nawab, and massacred with all his attendants. The scene of this tragedy, which served only to stir up the English to revenge, was the beautiful reach of the Bhagirathi which lies between Murshidabad and Kasimbazar. The war opened favourably for the Nawab. The English at Patna were attacked while scattered through the town, overpowered, and taken prisoners. The whole of Bengal, as far south as the present district of Nadia, was occupied by the Mahomedans, and the factory of Kasimbazar was for the second time plundered. The English concentrated their forces at Agradwip, near Nadia. After some trifling engagements, they recovered possession of Murshidabad, and encountered the main body of the Nawab's forces at Gherriah, near the source of the Bhagirathi from the Ganges, on July 24th, 1763. In the end, the victory of the English was complete, and, as the result of the battle of Gherriah, Bengal was for the second time conquered. Mir Kasim fled to Monghyr, where he caused the two Seths whom he had dragged with him from Murshidabad, to be thrown from the bastions of the fortress into the river, and ordered the murder of his English prisoners at Patna. The battle of Buxar finally drove him to take refuge among the Rohillas, and he is said to have retired finally to Delhi, where he died in 1777, in great indigence and obscurity.

On the first outbreak of hostilities, the English had resolved to depose Mir Kasim and to place a more complaisant Nawab on the *musnud*. Negotiations were accordingly opened with Mir Jaffer, who was residing, for the sake of safety, at Calcutta. He was willing to consent to every demand made upon him, and was accordingly reinstalled at Murshidabad. The price of this new Revolution amounted to more than £1,700,000; and in addition, the Company's servants gained their main object, the exemption of their own goods from all duties, and the reimposition of the old charges upon all traders but themselves. Mir Jaffer gained but little, except the transmission of the title to his family. He was already broken by age and by disease. His death took place in January, 1765, and is said to have been hastened by the unseemly importunity with which the English at Calcutta pressed upon him their private claims to restitution.

Najim-u-Dowlah, the eldest surviving son of Mir Jaffer, was chosen by the English to succeed his father, and in accordance with the explicit conditions of his advancement, divided £140,000 among the members of Council. This payment is the more noteworthy, as there could be no pretext for saying that it was the reward for any services rendered, or compensation for any loss. The new Nawab was about twenty years of age at this time, and died within three years; but his short rule witnessed one more of the steps by which the Mahomedan power was superseded. In May, 1765, Lord Clive arrived at Calcutta with full power as Commander-in-Chief, President, and Governor in Bengal. Among his sweeping reforms was the settlement of the relations between the Nawab and the Company. Within two months after landing in India he proceeded to Murshidabad. The Nawab was required to resign the management of the revenues and the command of his troops. An annual sum of Rs. 53,86,131, *(sicca)*, was allowed him for the expenses of his Court, and the administration of justice. He was further required to submit to the control of a board of advisers in all his affairs. This board was composed of Raja Dulabh Ram, Jaggat Seth, and Mahomed Reza Khan, and in addition, a servant of the Company was always to reside at Murshidabad, and exercise a general superintendence. The character of the young prince may be conjectured from the joy with which he accepted these proposals. "Thank God," he exclaimed, "I shall now have as many dancing girls as I like." The rent-roll, which he abandoned with a light heart, is estimated in Grant's "Analysis of the Finances of Bengal," at Rs. 2,56,24,223. To this total, which was the revenue of Bengal proper, alone, there must be added sixty-five lakhs proceeding from Behar, and eleven lakhs more as the annual revenue of Midnapur, then the only portion of Orissa which recognised Mahomedan authority. The total income of Bengal, with its dependencies in 1765, was about three crores and thirty-two lakhs of *sicca* rupees. Lord Clive next proceeded to the English camp in the north-west, and there received in person, from the Emperor Shah Alum, the grant of the *Diwanni*, or financial administration of Bengal, Behar, and Orissa. The date of this memorable event was August 12th, 1765. In the following year, Lord Clive took his seat as finance minister, at Moti Jhil palace* near Murshidabad, and in concert with the Nawab, who sat as Nazim, opened the *Punya,* or ceremony of annual collection of revenue. On the 8th May, 1766, a few days after this ceremony, Najim-u-Dowlah died.

Having done his best to check evils among the civilians, Clive next turned his attention to the condition of the army. Discontent was ever rife; pay had often been in arrears, and mutiny frequently on the verge of breaking out. After the battle of Plassy, there had been, as already described, a distribution of extra pay to the troops, the expenditure being borne by Mir Jaffer, who regarded it in the light of a reward for the exertions which had raised him to power and honour. This allowance had been continued, under the name of double *batta*† to European officers, and they now regarded it as their right. Lord Clive issued an order dated January 1st, 1766, abolishing this extra *batta,* except during actual service. We are not particularly concerned with the resistance with which a great number of the British officers opposed this order; it suffices that the seniors among them were court-martialed, and dismissed from the service. Bengal was now at peace, and when Lord Clive again quitted India he said, addressing the Select Committee:—"I leave the country in peace, I leave the Civil and Military departments under discipline and subordination; it is your duty to keep them so."

Saif-u-Dowlah, a brother of Najim-u-Dowlah, a youth of sixteen, succeeded him. By the treaty with the Company, which placed him on the *musnud,* his annual stipend was fixed at *sicca* rupees, 41,86,131. He died of small-pox in 1770.

Mobarak-u-Dowlah, another son of Mir Jaffer, and a minor, was appointed Nawab, and, at first, similar arrangements were made with him as had endured during the lives of his two brothers. On his accession, the Governor and Council of Fort William agreed to pay him an annual "stipend" of *sicca* rupees, 31,81,991 The Court of Directors in England had, however, resolved on a new policy, to which the minority of the Nawab readily lent itself. They had determined to "stand forth as Dewan, and by the agency of the Company's servants to take upon themselves the entire care and management of the revenues." This resolution was formed in 1771, and Warren Hastings, the first Governor General of Bengal, was to carry it into effect. In the same year, they had ordered the annual stipend of the Nawab to be reduced to sixteen lakhs of rupees. This reduction was accordingly effected in January, 1772. In April of the same year, Warren Hastings arrived in Calcutta, and before that month was out another great reform had been effected. Mahomed Reza Khan, the Naib Diwan at Murshidabad, and Raja Shitab Rai, who filled the same office at Patna, were both suddenly apprehended, and brought down as prisoners to Calcutta. Their offices were abolished, and the principal office of revenue was transferred from Murshidabad to Calcutta. The Council, with Hastings at its head, was constituted a Board of Revenue, assisted by a subordinate native functionary. The supreme judicial power in criminal cases was, at the same time, vested in the President and Council. But it was soon found that this additional duty involved too great responsibility

* This palace no longer exists.

† *Batta* (Urdu), perquisites, allowance, wages.

and in October, 1775, the Court of the Nizamat Adalut was moved back to Murshidabad. The name of "Collector," together with many of the functions discharged by that officer, owes its existence to the reform of 1772. There was yet one more step to be taken. Lord Cornwallis, in 1790, announced that he had resolved to accept the superintendence of the administration of criminal justice throughout the provinces. The Nizamat Adalut was a second time transferred from Murshidabad to Calcutta, to consist of the Governor General and members of the Supreme Council, assisted by the head native law officers. In 1793 four Courts of Circuit, each superintended by a covenanted servant of the Company, were established for the trial of cases not punishable by the Magistrates.

The only function of Government that remained to the Mahomedans was thus transferred directly into English hands, and the city of Murshidabad ceased to bear any longer the semblance of a capital; and the Nawab Nazim lost the last shadow of his authority. Mobarak-u-Dowlah died 1796.

In his "Voyages and Travels by the Ganges," Vol. i., pp. 96, 186, Valentia states that the magnificent jewels which the Nawab was wearing at the time of his visit, 1802, had been taken out of pawn for the occasion, and that the creditors were waiting downstairs to watch, and receive them again on his departure. He describes the palanquin of the Nawab as being all of cloth of gold, with panels of glass, and doors of the same material.

In 1768 the East India Company, in consultation with Mahomed Reza Khan, tried to come to some arrangement with the Mahrattas, to whom arrears of *chouth* had been promised by Governor Vansittart, in 1763. Finally, the Mahrattas accepted the revenue of Orissa in place of these arrears.

In 1769 the district was visited by a severe famine, due partly to failure of the crops in 1768. Prices were high, and as Government dues were collected as usual the ryot's stock of ready money was soon exhausted. Though the early part of 1769 looked promising, the "rains" ceased early in September, and the winter rice crop failed as a consequence.

Perhaps 1770 was the most terrible year in the records of the district, for to add to the terrors of scarcity, came disease, cholera, and small-pox. Instead of some relief of taxation, which the people might rightly have expected, they found themselves burdened with an additional 10 *per cent.* land tax. This burden, it is surprising to find, was laid upon them, not by some irresponsible bureaucrat at headquarters, but by a Mussulman, Mahomed Reza Khan.

In February it was necessary to send 40,000 maunds (over 1,400 tons) of rice to feed the troops at Berhampur. The provincial council, sitting in Murshidabad, reported that it was quite impossible for the Nawab to guarantee the usual quantity of silk. The industry suffered from the death of rearers and cultivators of mulberry, and sickness and want sapped the energy of those that remained. Troops of ryots, rendered beggars by the famine, flocked into the towns. To these rice was given, under the sanction of a Committee, to the amount of Rs. 87,000, of which sum the East India Company gave Rs. 40,000 and the Nawab Nazim Rs. 47,000. Even this was not sufficient, and at one time rice was selling at 3 seers for the rupee, that is 6 lbs. for 2s. Rice was (1901) worth 2¼d. a lb., or 1s. 1½d. for 6 lbs. of the best Patna rice. To the credit of the rich, it is recorded that there was no lack of charity, and many starving persons were relieved by private distribution of food. Bad as matters were in this district, they seem to have been worse in the neighbouring districts, and the Murshidabad Council was besieged with petitions for help and remission of taxation, from Rajshaye, Birbhum, and Dinajpur. In July the Resident of Murshidabad reported that in and around the city 500 people died daily of starvation, and that things were worse in the villages out of reach of help.

Driven by want, the small cultivators sold cattle, ploughs, all they possessed. They ate the little store that should have given them seed for the next harvest. They sold even their children, and finally were driven to eat leaves and grass. The overcrowding in Murshidabad bred disease, and small-pox was added to the horrors of famine. It spread with great rapidity, and devastated the homes of the poor and the rich alike. In the palace, the Nawab, Saif-u-Dowlah, died, and the streets were packed with dead quicker than they could be removed. Dogs, jackals, and vultures fed on the corpses as they lay on the ground. Those who could, fled the city, and their houses and lands became ruined and laid waste, so that the once great city lost its greatness for ever. In the district and around the city millions died. With the "rains" came hope, turned to reality when the September harvest was reaped. Still, the effects of want could not be removed by magic. Life was at such a low ebb that thousands died unable to digest the food put before them, and the *autumnal fevers* wrought havoc among the devitalised population. The *aman*, or cold season crop of rice in December, was also very abundant, and plenty reigned where only a few months before starvation and disease killed without check.

PLASSY MONUMENT.

In 1769 Richard Becher had been appointed Agent to the Governor General at Murshidabad, with partial control of the District revenues.

In 1770 he bravely wrestled with this great famine in Murshidabad, but was handicapped by the system which divided the management between Europeans and natives. Becher left some notable letters, which W. W. Hunter says greatly inspired him in 1870 when writing the "Annals of Rural Bengal," and dealing with the events of the year 1770. Becher retired in 1774. Seven years after, in 1781, having lost his money in helping a friend, he was allowed to return to the Company's service as Mint Master in Calcutta. He died in 1782.*

In December, 1770, Mr. Becher reported that the rice sent by the Council in Calcutta had enabled him to keep all who were directly dependent on the English. The Resident received great help from Mahomed Reza Khan. It is sad, though true to human nature, that certain accusations were made against some of the Company's officers of having made a profit out of the people, compelling them to sell even the grain stored for seed.† No names are given, and perhaps it is as well. Tanks and wells dried up, and to add to the trouble many homesteads were destroyed by roving incendiaries.

It is the nature of the Bengali that makes it so difficult to help him. He resents assistance, even when he most needs it, and his resentment becomes fierce antagonism when his domestic privacy is invaded, as seen in many instances during years of plague and famine, and after repeated proof that help will be given without thought of reward; without even expecting gratitude.

Much of the land depopulated in 1770 remained uncultivated even nine years later, and, indeed, the population decreased until 1785. The land became *jungle*, and wild beasts increased notably. Even twenty years after the famine the jails contained many debtors for revenue.

Notwithstanding that the land tax was in no way decreased, but, as stated, rather increased, the full amount was never collected, even with the assistance of troops. During 1771 gang robbery and robbery by professional Thugs increased.

The year of famine and disease was followed by three years of plenty, but the people were gone, and the sunshine and rain fell on a forsaken country; one-third of the population had died or fled: 10,000,000 people! That the help given by the Company had been inadequate was due more to ignorance than hardness of heart.

In 1771 the Murshidabad Council were asked to advance £4,000 to Nadia to provide loans for the ryots to cultivate the soil, to replace cattle, and to obtain seed. They granted £2,500. Crime was rife, and many stole the food required to keep body and soul together.

The *Pachetra* or Customs were collected by the Government officers under the new system.‡

The total receipts in the Murshidabad Treasury for 1771-72 were Rs. 1,57,56,576. Acting on the advice of the Committee of Circuit at Kasimbazar, the Revenue work was removed to Calcutta under the Board of Revenue. Reviewing the loss of life during the famine, from which the province was slowly recovering, Hastings estimates that "at least one-third of the inhabitants" had died, and, this notwithstanding, the revenue for 1771 had exceeded that of 1768. That it did not decrease was due to the severe methods adopted. The *Najay*, or tax on waste lands, was most oppressive, as it fell heaviest on those villages that had lost most from famine or disease. Under the old system, the Nawab Nazim looked to the farmers of the revenue for a fixed sum, and did not care by what means these men collected the money, nor how much over and above they took for themselves. There was no unity of system, and everywhere oppression. The orders of the Court of Directors were to abolish the Naib Diwan and to take the collection of revenue entirely out of the hands of the native officials. Fixed rates and uniform for each district were introduced. The Committee appointed to revise the Revenue System comprised:—The Governor, Messrs. Middleton, Dacres, Lowrell, and Graham. The first step was to give notice that all lands would be let on five years' leases.

The questions to be dealt with were:—1, The original ground rent, called *Asal;* 2, *Abwabs*, a collection of taxes levied, some by the Nawab's Government, some by the Revenue farmers, and some even by the

* "The Thackerays in India." Hunter (33).

† Hunter (17), p. 420-21.

‡ Letter from Hastings to the Home Directors, 3rd November, 1772.

sub-collectors to whom the taxes were further farmed out. One of these was the *Najay*, already mentioned. The first step the Committee took was to abolish such of these miscellaneous taxes as were manifestly oppressive. These included :—(a) Customs charges on necessaries of life carried on the rivers in the district; (b) Fines for petty crimes *(Basu Jama)*; (c) Tax on marriage *(Halderry)*. The consequence of the remission of such burdens was rightly foreseen to be increase in population and increased comfort and, therefore, stability of the family life.

New leases were to be given (*Amulnamas*) in which were clearly stated the payments which the Revenue Collectors could legally claim. The form of deed (*Pottah*) was drawn up by the Committee.

The next step was to study economy in the work of collecting the revenue. The scale of the collecting establishment was to be the same for each District. Zemindars* were to be treated as farmers, and the revenue to be taken directly from them. The lands were farmed to the highest bidder. The Committee arrived at Kasimbazar, in July, 1772, and took in hand the settlement of the income to be paid to the Nawab Nazim, and the appointment of officers to manage the Nizamat affairs. Mr. Middleton was appointed Resident at the Murshidabad Court, and, in addition, was chief factor at Kasimbazar and Collector of Revenue for the Rajshaye district. The local Board of Revenue at Murshidabad was abolished, and the district revenue officers placed under the Board of Revenue in Calcutta. In September, the Committee left for Dacca, Mr. Middleton remaining behind to take up his post at Murshidabad.

In 1780 the Treasury at Murshidabad was called upon by Hastings to provide funds for his war in Madras, which added greatly to our territory in the Carnatic and Mysore, and ended in 1781 in a peace with Scindia, the head of the Mahrattas, for so long our tireless foes. This over, Hastings turned his forces against the French and Tippoo Sahib. We did not free ourselves from the Mahrattas until 1803, when their power in Orissa was finally broken and the province annexed to Bengal.

The 29th March, 1787, marks the date on which the East India Company took over the *entire* administration of the district, substituting its own men in many offices for the Nawab Nazim's officers. The Nawab's power was merely an *umbra*, or shade, and the people, already at a low ebb from taxation for the struggle, the Mahrattas were at the mercy of bands of robbers. Mr. E. O. Ives, Collector of Murshidabad, in 1784 appealed to the Local Government for help, stating clearly that the force at his disposal was quite insufficient to cope with these marauders. In May, 1785, he again urged the necessity for help, as the strength of the robber bands was increasing, and by June had reached the alarming total of 1,000 men. Their refuge and stronghold were in Birbhum, and from there it was an easy step into this district, as they are contiguous along our western boundary. To check these inroads, an officer was sent from Murshidabad in 1786, to assist the local Raja of Birbhum. This officer's name was Foley.

Agriculture was at a stand-still, and many of the Company's factories were abandoned. Foley remained in charge until Lord Cornwallis finally separated Birbhum from Murshidabad, and placed a Collector, Mr. W. Pye, in charge of the newly formed district, thus relieving the Collector of Murshidabad of a heavy responsibility.

1793 was the year in which Sir John Shore became Governor General, and the same year saw the death of Nawab Nazim Mobarak-u-Dowlah, whose eldest son was proclaimed his successor on September 28th. The new Nawab Nazim was the eldest of a family of twenty-five; twelve sons and thirteen daughters. During 1826 *Suttee* was declared illegal.

In 1835, with Lord William Bentinck at the head of affairs, many changes, wise and unwise, took place. The idea that the Government had duties to perform as to the education of the masses passed from theory into practice, and one lakh of rupees was ordered to be set aside for the opening of English schools, and

* Originally revenue collectors, not landholders in the true sense of the word. At the present time the word is used for a landholder.

even more than the amount assigned by the Home Government was actually spent. Hitherto, money had been granted to schools teaching Sanscrit and Arabic. These institutions were warned that monthly stipends allowed to certain scholars would lapse when the recipients passed out of the colleges.

Medical science, too, received a great and lasting impetus in 1835, from the founding of the Calcutta Medical College.

Berhampur has the unenviable notoriety of being one of the first places in Bengal where signs of mutiny appeared among the troops. Fortunately, although it seemed at first that the vigorous measures taken by the European officer in command were only likely to lead to further trouble, wise and conciliatory counsels prevailed, and the revolt was checked before it assumed any serious features, or spread to the city of Murshidabad, where thousands of malcontents were only waiting to see what the Nawab Nazim would do, before taking up arms against the Europeans. It must be remembered that there were no British troops in Berhampur cantonment at that time, and none anywhere nearer than Calcutta, about 120 miles away. The native troops at Berhampur, in February, 1857, were the 19th B.I.; a corps of irregular cavalry, and a battery of artillery with native gunners. Unfortunately, the Government chose at this critical time to send a detachment of the 34th B.I. up country from Barrackpur, a very hotbed of discontent and incipient mutiny, and the place in which the "greased cartridge" story was just then causing considerable excitement. These men were in charge of stud horses, and were to be relieved by a detachment of the 19th B.I. at Berhampur. The first party reached Berhampur on February 18th, and a week later, February 25th, a second detachment of the 34th B.I. arrived, in charge of European sick. These, too, were to be relieved by the 19th B.I., on reaching Berhampur. On arrival in the station they were lodged in the infantry lines, and they soon communicated to their fellow Sepoys the story of the progress of the mutiny, and the rumours as to bone meal in the flour, and cartridges greased with the fat of pigs and cows, and thus insulting to the faith of both Hindus and Mahomedans. It is certain that in the telling they did not soften down any of the dreadful things that, according to rumour, Government was about to do in order to ruin their *caste* and compel them to become Christians. The causes of the mutiny were many and far-reaching, and cannot be discussed in this work, but the lies concerning the bone meal and the greased cartridges were the levers principally used to work upon the minds of the ignorant native soldiers.* These were things they could understand, and which touched them on the tenderest spot, while such matters as the annexation of Oude and interference with the rights of adoption, were above their comprehension.

The 19th B.I. had already heard these rumours, for news travels with incredible speed through the bazars of India; but so far there had been no sign of insubordination among them. They had gone to their commanding officer with their story, and he had suggested that they should examine the grease for themselves, explaining, we may suppose, that linseed oil and wax alone were used in the manufacture of the suspected cartridges. The arrival of the 34th B.I., however, roused again their fears and suspicions, especially as the story they brought with them came from the very headquarters of the Government and the neighbourhood in which the suspected ammunition was being manufactured. The day after the arrival of the second party of the 34th B.I. there was a parade of the 19th B.I. with blank cartridge.† The Sepoys, fearing some design against their *caste*, refused to take the percussion caps served out, because they said the cartridges were defiled, and that the new greased cartridges, said to have been sent from Calcutta, had been mixed with the old ammunition in order to deceive them into using what they abhorred. This suggestion must have come from some agitator, since it was clearly shown that no made-up ammunition had been received

* Fitchett (41)

† Beveridge (12) gives the date of the arrival of this second party as February 24th, and the date of the parade as the 26th, Kaye (11) gives the 25th as the day of arrival, and says the parade took place on the following day. In the margin, however, Kaye gives the 27th as the date, an error for which the printer may be responsible.

from Calcutta ; only powder in barrels and certain regimental stores. The adjutant of the 19th B.I., Lt. McAndrew, reported the action of the regiment to Colonel Mitchell. The Colonel at once went to the lines and called together his native officers in front of the quarter-guard. He addressed them in an angry manner, unwise in the extreme at this juncture, when the lives of many Europeans might depend on the exercise of tact and common sense. He pointed out that the cartridges served out to the men were the same as those they had been using, and that they had been made up by their predecessors a year before. He then threatened that he would have the regiment sent to Burma or China if the men again refused to accept the cartridges. In a petition subsequently submitted by the regiment were found the following words, referring to Colonel Mitchell's address to his native officers :—" He gave this order so angrily that we were convinced that the cartridges were greased, otherwise he would not have spoken so." This habit of blustering to cover deceit so common among themselves gives every excuse for the mistake.

Colonel Mitchell then returned to his house, and issued an order that the cavalry and artillery were to attend the parade next morning. No doubt this order was freely discussed in the infantry lines, and gave rise to surmises and suspicions which caused the Sepoys to work themselves into a state of excitement, resulting in panic, and accompanied by much shouting and beating of drums. Towards ten o'clock at night the uproar in the lines reached such a pitch that it aroused all the residents in cantonments who had gone to bed, and among them the Colonel. He got up at once, dressed hastily, and rode to the house of Captain Alexander, whom he directed to prepare the cavalry for any emergency. A similar order was issued to the gunner officer, and by midnight, Colonel Mitchell, with the European officers, the cavalry, and the artillery, was ready, with his forces drawn up on the parade ground near the native lines. The mutinied infantry were also drawn up in line, their muskets loaded with the very cartridges they had refused in the morning. To obtain these, they had broken open the *bells of arms.* Any unwise act at that moment would, there is no doubt, have been followed by a terrible slaughter, for it is by no means certain that the cavalry and gunners would have remained faithful when once their comrades had committed themselves and were in open revolt. It is, on the other hand, quite certain that the *budmashes** of Murshidabad city would have gladly joined in the carnage. Colonel Mitchell loaded the battery guns and placed the cavalry on either side, covering the mutineers. He then caused the bugler to sound the assembly for the native officers. As they stood round him, the Colonel, on whose side the Goddess of Fortune was ranged that day, again spoke to them in an angry and threatening manner. They seem to have listened patiently, and when he had finished his harangue, the words of which have not been recorded, they begged him to be lenient with the men of the 19th, who, they said, were panic stricken with fear lest their *caste* should be broken and their religion insulted. They asked him to withdraw the cavalry and artillery, assuring him that the mutineers, when they saw that they were not going to be attacked, would quiet down and return to their duty. After much wavering, Colonel Mitchell consented, and, as the cavalry and gunners disappeared, the mutineers went quietly back to their lines. The parade on the following morning was quiet and orderly, and the men showed no signs of the excitement of the previous night ; indeed, it is recorded that they viewed their past conduct with regret. The matter could not, however, be overlooked, and for several days a court of inquiry sat to consider the causes of the outbreak and the course to be pursued with regard to the future. Colonel George Macgregor persuaded the Nawab Nazim to openly declare himself on the side of the English, and by this means the fermenting masses in the city of Murshidabad were quieted down, and order was restored ; though the minds of the people were for some time in a state of very unstable equilibrium. Great blame must be attached to the men of the 34th B.I., whose stories practically provoked the immediate outburst which took place on the 26th February.

These very men were present when General Hearsay addressed the unsettled troops at Barrackpur, and

* Blackguards.

explained to them that the story about the fat of pigs and cows was surely invented by some malicious agitator. The report of the mutiny at Berhampur reached Calcutta on March 4th. The 19th B.I. were at once ordered down to Barrackpur, while the 84th British Regiment,* then at Rangoon, was sent for to garrison Berhampur. On reaching Barrackpur the men laid down their arms "without a murmur" in the presence of the European troops drawn up ready to check any disturbance. The 19th B.I. were paid up to that date, and received also money to cover travelling expenses to their homes, after which ceremony their uniform was stripped from them, and they were disbanded. As the outcome of councils held at Berhampur, steps were taken to protect the residents in case of any further rising or invasion of mutinous troops from elsewhere. The buildings formerly used as a hospital for European soldiers were roughly fortified as a refuge for Europeans, cannon were mounted, and houses and huts in the immediate vicinity pulled down. Among the buildings so destroyed was a large house used as the Berhampur College.

Following on the mutiny came the end of the East India Company and its traditions. The Proclamation of the 1st November, 1858, marked a new era, and a government as part of the British Empire.

Already, before the disgrace of the mutiny of 1857 was forgotten, Berhampur was the theatre of another display of rebellion in 1859. This time it was not our native troops that had revolted, but a section of the British Army. A certain number of regiments lately out from England, and filled with undersized lads, many of them the scum of the London slums, had, from their physical appearance, been christened "Dumpies." For the reason that this fresh mutiny arose among these regiments, it was known as the "Dumpy Mutiny." In May, 1859, one of these regiments, the 5th European Regiment,† stationed at Berhampur, broke into open rebellion, "seized the barracks, and defied their officers." A royal regiment, whose loyalty was above suspicion, was sent down from Barrackpur to quell the mutiny and bring the "Dumpies" to their senses. Fortunately, this show of force was sufficient. A court of inquiry followed, and most of the mutineers were sent home at the public expense, and dismissed from the service.

Perhaps the most notable occurrence during recent years was the severe earthquake in 1897, which made itself felt almost all over Bengal, and which did very serious damage in this district. The facts as they occurred here I know only by report, but, as they seem to have been very similar to those of which I was an eye-witness, I will relate first what occurred in Midnapur, where I was then stationed. About 5 p.m., on the 12th June, I was sitting in the Midnapur club with my wife and the Assistant Magistrate, when I heard a sound as of an express train coming into a station. This it could not be, as there was then no railway open at Midnapur, and it was accompanied by a rumbling in the earth, quickly followed by a rocking motion, which at once convinced me it was an earthquake. We hurried outside, where my wife had to sit down on the ground, as the motion made her feel sick, as if at sea. The Assistant Magistrate, even, was very pale, and several people told me, later, that they had experienced the same feeling of "sea-sickness." The club-house swayed to and fro, and the hanging lamp in the verandah swung from side to side, almost touching the beams. Looking round, we could see the trees swaying violently, but none fell. The houses shook, but the only damage done was to double-storied buildings. The earthquake lasted about five minutes. People in carriages and on horseback were for the most part unaware that anything was happening out of the common, until they saw the trees and houses oscillating. One gentleman was thrown from his bicycle and injured his knee. The huts in the town did not suffer much, and no serious accident occurred. The earthquake was not without its humorous side. The 12th was the great day of the Moburrum, and, perhaps fortunately, the people were crowding the streets, watching the passing of the *tazzias*. A number of natives were sitting on the coping of the culvert which spans the main drainage outflow, and as the earthquake caused the bridge to rock, they were tipped backwards into the muddy,

* The 2nd Battalion York and Lancaster Regiment.

† 1st or 2nd Battalion Northumberland Fusiliers.

black stream. Their struggles caused much amusement to the crowd, and when they emerged, covered from head to foot with mud, they attracted quite as much attention as the procession of *tazzias*. In this district, and generally throughout Bengal, the effects of the earthquake were much more serious. Calcutta and many other towns were wrecked in certain parts, and it must have taken crores of rupees to repair the damage done. The effects of the earthquake were still visible when I came to this district, in June, 1898. The estimate of damage done to Government buildings in Berhampur was Rs. 60,000, while in Murshidabad town, the damage done to the Nizamat buildings alone was put down at three lakhs of rupees. The old palace was much shaken, and the walls cracked in numerous places, but no part of it fell. Many vases and valuable ornaments were overthrown and broken. Pictures were damaged by falling plaster and bricks, and one brick went right through the canvas of a large painting of the burial of Sir John Moore, which hangs in the large dining-hall, causing a very ugly rent. The Nawab Bahadur was sitting in a room on the ground floor of the new palace which faces the river, and was helped out by his servants at the first rumblings of the earthquake. As it was, his escape was only by a few seconds, for as he reached the river bank, the whole of the second storey of that palace fell with a crash. The handsome Nizamat stables, in the town, were greatly damaged, and two bungalows on the top of the stables were destroyed. The repairs to the old palace were completed in August, 1900. The upper storey of the new palace is not to be rebuilt. Taking the reports sent in from various parts of the district, I have selected the following notes :—In the neighbourhood of Goas and the Jalingi, fissures in the earth, with discharges of sand and water, were observed in nine places, chiefly on marshy land. Most of them were small, but one fissure is said to have extended for two miles, varying in width from two feet to half an inch. In the Kandi sub-division some twenty-five fissures were reported, the largest being five hundred feet in length, and from eight feet to half an inch wide. Near Jangipur discharges of water and black mud occurred from the bed of the Bhagirathi river. The height of these discharges was not remarkably great, being generally three to four feet. The direction of the earthquake was the same as noted at Midnapur, namely from N.E. to S.W., the duration was also about five minutes. The Berhampur Church was damaged, but the rest of the single-storey barracks did not suffer much. None of the double-storied buildings, however, escaped serious damage. In the Cantonment no accidents occurred ; but in the town of Berhampur ten lives were lost, those of some beggars and children who were being fed, crushed by the downfall of the house in which they were receiving charity. In Kasimbazar two lives were lost. The destruction in Azimganj was very great, greater even than in Murshidabad. The houses of the Jains were wrecked, and two of their temples collapsed. Hardly a single building escaped without some injury. The cost of putting right the damage was estimated at ten lakhs, but this was probably an exaggeration. With all this damage to property it is remarkable how few lives were lost. In Azimganj eleven people were killed, in Murshidabad six, and in the Jangipur sub-division five. In the Kandi sub-division no one was killed, but one woman was severely injured. It is interesting to note, as showing the delicacy of certain scientific instruments, that this earthquake was recorded on the seismometers at Edinburgh and in the Isle of Wight. The following is a brief record of previous shocks affecting this district :—

1762. Earthquake of a very severe nature felt over the whole of Bengal, but no special mention of damage in this district.

1766. Felt along the banks of the Ganges.

1803. Felt throughout Bengal.

1810. April 1st, Bengal. Felt in Murshidabad ("Asiatic Annual Register," 1811, xii., 10,463).

1811. February 1st, severe and general in Bengal, but no distinct mention of effects in Murshidabad district. ("Asiatic Annual Register," 1811, xii., 10,463.)

1819. Felt in Tirhoot, and probably here, but nothing noted.

1822. General in Bengal. In Berhampur it lasted two minutes, and its course was N.N.W. to S.S.W. ("Asiatic Journal," xiii., 1822.)

1823, '25, '27, '28, '29, Calcutta; '33, Tirhoot; '34, '35, '39, '42, Bengal; '43, '45, '46, '47, '48, '49, '50, '52, '58 (general in Bengal); '61, '65, (Boalia) '66.

From records of the "Geological Survey of India," Vol. xviii., p. 200, containing a report on the Bengal earthquake of July 14th, 1885, by C. S. Middlemiss, B.A., we learn that the shock was felt over 230,400 sq. miles. The curve of greatest intensity was to the east of the Murshidabad district. Its effects were noticed in the Magistrate's *Administration Report*.

In 1869 a shock was felt in Berhampur, 10th January, 5.10 p.m., *circa;* damage slight, old cracks re-opened, but no new ones.*

There are no hot-water or mineral springs in this district. The formation is not suitable. For similar reasons there is no mineral wealth.

The Maharaja of Kasimbazar is the owner of coal-fields in Jerria and Raniganj, but there is no coal in the district.

* "Memoirs of the Geological Survey of India," Vol. xix.

CHANGES IN THE CIVIL AND CRIMINAL ADMINISTRATION.*

THE first attempt to alter native methods was made by Warren Hastings; but, in the main, he retained the laws as followed by the Mahomedan rulers.

The *Foujdari Adaluts*† were first appointed by the President in Council, in 1772, and the Collectors of Revenue added criminal work to their other duties. The *Sudder Adalut*, or Chief Court, was also established in Murshidabad, in 1772, in the Mobarak Munzil Gardens, formerly known as Findal Bagh, some five miles from Berhampur, and four and a half miles from the Nizamat palace. Besides Court buildings, there was a spacious mansion for the Judges. All these are now standing, and when the Court was removed to Calcutta, the houses, obtained by purchase, were used as a country residence by the Nawab Nazim. Nawab Nazim Feradun Jah, father of the present Nawab Bahadur, generally spent six months of the year in this pretty and healthy spot. The first *Sudder Adalut* was under a *Committee of Revenue*, to which the duty of revising the rulings of the lower Courts was entrusted. The *Sudder Adalut* was, in fact, the First Appellate Court. It was in 1770 that two of these Committees were appointed, one at Murshidabad, and the other at Patna. Famine and disease made this year one to be remembered with dread. Up to 1757, the year in which British rule in Bengal really started, the reins of both civil and criminal justice had remained in the hands of the Mahomedans, and their laws were in force. When the change came it was gradual, and the same laws and form of tribunals were continued. In the towns, the sources of administration of the Criminal Law were:—1. The Nawab Nazim of Bengal "in all capital cases." 2. His Deputy in cases of "quarrels, frays, and abusive names." 3. "The Foujdar in all cases not capital; judgment and sentence being passed by the Nawab." 4. "The Mohtesil in all cases of drunkenness, selling spirituous liquors, etc." 5. "The Katwal, a peace officer of the night, dependent on the Foujdari." In the rural districts, both civil and criminal justice were dispensed by the Zemindars, each in his own district.

The English rulers soon saw that many changes were necessary. As already stated, a Revenue Committee was started in 1770, and in 1771 the Directors of the East India Company proclaimed their intention of taking over the management of the revenues, practically absorbed in 1765. The new task was by no means a light one, since it necessitated a remodelling of the existing rights of property in land. All administration was to be under the direct control of the East India Company, and not through the Nawab; though all native agency could not be dispensed with.

The first steps were towards the improvement of land settlement and the collection of revenues. Up to 1769, the authority in such matters rested with Shitab Rai, of Patna; and for the rest of Bengal, including Murshidabad, with the famous Mahomed Reza Khan, Diwan of Murshidabad. The first step towards reform was the institution, in 1769, of Supervisors, selected from among the servants of the East India Company. In Murshidabad, these were directly subordinate to the Agent to the Governor General at the Court of the Nawab Nazim.

1. The Committee of Circuit, composed of the Governor and four Councillors, recommended the opening of Provincial Courts, superintended by the Collectors of Revenue. The Courts dealt with:—

i. *Civil.* Disputes, real or personal; inheritance, marriage, "caste," debts, contracts, and rent suits. Cases of succession were referred to the Governor.

* "Tagore Law Lectures" (34). † Magistrates' Courts.

ii. *Criminal.* Mahomedan law and law officers remained, but on a new system. For each district a *Foujdari Adalut* was appointed. Its officers were:—a Kazi, a Mooftee, with two Moulvies as expounders; and the English *Collector* as Superintendent.

The *Foujdari Adaluts*, as a whole, were subordinate to the *Sudder Court*, or High Court, at Murshidabad. The officers of the High Court were:—(*a*) Darogah (appointed by the Nawab Nazim), a chief Kazi, a chief Mooftee and three Moulvies. It was:—(1) a Revisional Court. (2) In capital cases it prepared a judgment and warrant for the Nawab. As control, an English Committee was appointed. In 1773 or 1774 this ceased to exist, as the High Court was transferred to Calcutta. In 1775 it was moved back to Murshidabad, and there remained for fifteen years, the Nawab retaining supreme control in criminal matters.

A Chief Civil Court (*Sudder Diwanni Adalut*) also existed at Calcutta, under the President and Members of Council, with native assistants, and was an Appellate Court for all civil suits over Rs. 500. The year 1790 saw the Criminal Chief Court again removed to Calcutta, but for three years more the administration of justice was carried on in the name of the Nawab. Gradually the Mahomedan law and administration were replaced by the East India Company's regulations and officers. In 1773 the Supreme Court of Judges was appointed by the Crown, to be independent of the East India Company, the Charter being finally issued in March, 1774.

Then, as now, there was a desire to separate the *judicial* from the *executive*, and frequent conflicts then, as now, arose between the High Court of the Crown and the Council of the East India Company. Into these matters we need not enter, as they are outside local history. It is enough to say that in the beginning the High Court was objected to by the natives, as its methods were quite opposed to their ideas and traditions. In 1772-3 Diwan Mahomed Reza Khan was removed from power in Murshidabad, partly through the animosity of Nanda Kumar.

Warren Hastings was Governor of Bengal when Sir Elijah Impey and three *puisne* Judges arrived to constitute the High Court, and Nanda Kumar, thinking that the enemies of Hastings were too strong for him in the Council, brought an accusation against him of accepting bribes to depose the once powerful Mahomed Reza Khan; and further charged Hastings with selling public offices. This document was sent from Murshidabad to Hastings' chief opponent, Francis, who read it out at a meeting of the Council. Nanda Kumar had asked to be allowed to proceed to Calcutta, there to confront Hastings before the whole Council. Hastings refused to meet him, and, after declaring the meeting closed, left the room. His enemies then voted Col. Clavering to the chair, and called in Nanda Kumar. It was then that Hastings called the Judges to his aid, and Nanda Kumar was at once arrested on charges too well known to need repetition. His trial and fate are also well known, and historians and lawyers still wrangle over the question. Thus passed away a man whose power in Murshidabad had been responsible for many an intrigue.* The cause of the complaints made by the Zemindars was that the High Court had the power to summon them to Calcutta in private suits, seizing their estates if they failed to appear. They were also liable to suffer the great disgrace of being sent to jail, a horrible place in those days, and degrading to persons of high "caste" and rank. The High Court next refused to recognise the power of the Nawab Nazim in criminal suits. Endless stories are told of the tyranny exercised by the Supreme Court, often at the instance of dismissed servants, or spiteful rivals. Criminal justice in 1777 was in a state of chaos. Endless petitions were sent from all districts to the Governor.

In 1775 the Superintendence of Revenue was vested in the Provincial Councils, one of which sat in Murshidabad. European collectors were recalled under the provisions of the *Regulatory Act* of 1772; and native *Amils* took their places. From the Amil there was right of appeal to the Provincial Council.

* The house in which he once lived is still inhabited by his descendants in Kasimbazar.

The majority of the Council favoured the reappointment of Mahomed Reza Khan. It was naturally opposed by Warren Hastings, who had dismissed him. The opposition was in vain, and Mahomed Reza Khan returned as Diwan to Murshidabad, to be ousted again in 1778, when Warren Hastings was supreme in the Council, from which death had removed many of his bitterest enemies.

In 1779 there was open conflict between the Council and the High Court. In 1780 the powers of the Murshidabad, and the other five Courts, were confined to revenue matters, and District Civil Courts were established to deal with claims of succession or inheritance, real property, and personal property.

Cases of Revenue and Rent suits alone went to the Provincial Councils, and Collectors had no control over the new Civil Courts. Ultimate appeal from these Courts was to the Supreme Civil Court. By this means civil justice was separated from revenue collecting, with which the Supreme Court could not interfere. The struggle between the Governor General in Council and the High Court, to which allusion has already been made, led to the framing of the *Act* of 1781, which ratified the above division of labour.

In 1786 Lord Cornwallis reunited Civil and Criminal Courts of Justice with management of revenue under the Collector who had succeeded the Provincial Councils; these bodies having ceased to exist. He removed the Nizamat Adalut to Calcutta (1790), from Murshidabad. In this district the change only now took place. Appeal in civil suits lay from the Collector to the Board of Revenue, and to the Governor General in Council. This was a reversion to the old system, abolished in 1780; and had for its object the institution of a head to each district, to whom all might apply. In 1793, after studying the working of this system, Lord Cornwallis again separated the revenue from the judicial work; Revenue Courts were abolished, and suits formerly tried by them made over to Civil Courts, under separate officers, Judges, subordinate Judges, and Munsiffs; thus doing away with a system under which the Collector was not unfrequently plaintiff as well as judge. The duties of the District Collector were definitely laid down in 1793.

They were as follows :—

1. To collect the amount of the fixed revenue assessed upon the lands of the Zemindars, independent Talookdars, or other actual proprietors of land, with, or on behalf of whom a settlement has been or may be concluded.

2. To collect the stipulated annual revenue from the farmers of estates.

3. To levy the rents and revenues from estates held *Khas* (Government lands).

4. To make the future settlement of *Khas*, or farmed estates, agreeably to the regulations and instructions which they might receive for that purpose.

5. To prosecute for the recovery of the dues of Government from lands, of whatever description, held exempt from the payment of revenue, under illegal or invalid tenures.

6. To pay the pensions and allowances included in the public revenue, and other pensions and compensations.

7. To execute the instructions which might be issued to them by the Court of Wards regarding disqualified landholders and their estates.

8. To superintend the division of landed property paying revenue to Government, which might be ordered to be divided into two, or more, distinct estates.

9. To apportion the public revenue on lands ordered to be disposed of by public sale for the discharge of arrears of revenue.

10. To collect the tax on spirituous liquors and intoxicating drugs, or other articles.

11. To procure lands for native invalid soldiers, who might accept a provision in land.

12. To collect the tax for defraying the expenses of the police.

13. To perform the above and all other duties according to the rules that have been or may be prescribed, by any *Regulation* published in the manner directed in *Regulation* xli., 1793.

14 To transmit such annual, monthly, or other accounts as they now furnish, or may be hereafter required to send by the Board of Revenue, or any officer under that Board empowered to require such accounts.

15. To conform to all special orders that have been, or may be issued to them by the Board of Revenue, or by public officers empowered to issue such orders.

Having thus confined the Collectors to their exclusively *executive* functions, the next step was to re-organize the Courts of Justice and render them efficient and independent. Accordingly, by the next *Regulation*, Government, in the language of its preamble, divested itself "of the power of interfering in the administration of the laws and regulations in the first instance; reserving only, as a Court of Appeal or Review, the decision of certain cases in the last resort."

The Civil Court in Calcutta received all appeals from the District Courts. It consisted in 1801 of three Judges, chosen from among the East India Company's covenanted servants; and in 1811 was altered to a Chief Judge, and as many *puisne* Judges as the Governor thought necessary. Next below this came the Provincial Civil Courts, four in number, for Bengal, Behar, and Orissa, to which appeals lay from lesser Provincial and Town Courts. Later, two more Provincial Courts were added. Again, below the *Zillah*, or District Courts, there were two classes of subordinate Judges:—

1. *Registrars* empowered to try cases for Rs. 200, and under. Their sentences were not valid until revised and approved by the District Judge.

2. *Native Commissioners* who, under *Regulation* xl. of 1793, could try civil suits for sums not exceeding Rs. 50 (sicca). The seniors of this class were called *Sudder Ameens;* the rest *Munsiffs.*

The system thus inaugurated in 1798 lasted, in more or less its original condition, until 1873. By *Regulation* xxiii. of 1814, the District Judge received increased powers, including the right of appointing and removing the subordinate civil native Judges, a right previously in the hands of the Chief Revenue Court. Further changes followed by *Regulation* v. of 1831. Munsiffs received power to try suits for money and property up to Rs. 300; and land suits of similar value, except in the case of rent-free lands. The Judge might make over to his Sudder Ameens, suits to the value of Rs. 1,000; and a class of principal Sudder Ameens was established, with powers to deal with cases in which the amount in dispute did not exceed Rs. 5,000. Registrars' Courts were abolished. In 1833 the Provincial Courts of Appeal were done away with, and their powers vested in the District Judges in suits above Rs. 5,000, with right of appeal from them to the Sudder Diwanni Adalut. Between 1793 and 1831 certain changes took place in the Collector's duties. By *Regulation* viii. of 1794, the Judges received authority to refer to the Collector all cases cognizable by them previous to 1793. The Collector's report was submitted to the Judge, who could approve or alter it at his discretion. The Collector thus resumed his judicial functions. In 1795 the Collector received summary powers in claims for arrears of rent. This order was superseded by *Regulation* vii. of 1799, by which the Civil Courts were directed to give priority to rent and revenue cases, in order to assist the Zemindars to realise their rents, money being required for Government revenue. *Regulation* v. of 1812 gave the *ryot* (peasant) a remedy against the landlord, when the latter distrained for rent; such cases were referred to the Collector in 1824. *Regulation* xiv. gave the Collectors full judicial powers in all rent suits; but the execution of their decrees remained with the Civil Courts. In 1831 Judges were deprived of jurisdiction in suits relating to rent. The Collector's award was final, subject to a civil suit to be laid before the Civil Court. These changes all had for their object, quick realisation of Government Revenue. They did not work without oppression and injustice; but, in 1837, a proposal was laid before the Legislative Council, which became law as *Act* x. of 1857, giving even more power to the Collector, and abolishing the interference of the Civil Courts in the following cases:—

1. All suits for the delivery of *Pottahs* or *Kubooliats*, or for the determination of the rates of rent at which such *Pottahs* or *Kubooliats* are to be delivered.

2. All suits for damages on account of the illegal exaction of rent, or of any unauthorised cess or impost, or on account of the refusal of receipts for rent paid, or on account of the extortion of rent by confinement or other duress.

3. All complaints of excess in demand of rent and all claims to abatement of rent.

4. All suits for arrears of rent due on account of land, either *Kherajee* or *Lakhiraj;* or on account of any rights of pasturage, forest rights, fisheries, or the like.

5. All suits to eject any ryot, or to cancel any lease on account of the non-payment of arrears of rent, or on account of a breach of the conditions of any contract by which a ryot may be liable to ejectment, or a lease may be liable to be cancelled.

6. All suits to recover the occupancy or possession of any land, farm, or tenure, from which a farmer, or tenant, has been illegally ejected by the person entitled to receive rent for the same.

7. All suits arising out of the exercise of the power of distraint conferred on Zemindars and others, by the *Act*,* or out of any acts done under colour of the exercise of the said power as hereinafter particularly provided.

8. All suits by Zemindars and others in receipt of the rent of land against any agents employed by them in the management of land, or collection of rents, or the sureties of such agents for money received, or accounts kept by such agents in the course of such employment, or for papers in their possession.

Many of these cases were referred to Deputy Collectors, with right of appeal from them to the Collector, and from his Court, again, to that of the Divisional Commissioner. In cases below the value of Rs. 100, no further appeal lay from the Collector, except in cases of enhancement and those of title to land. After a trial of this system for ten years, the Bengal Legislative Council, by *Act* viii. of 1869, revised the jurisdiction of the Civil Courts. The *Act* was known as the *Landlord and Tenant Procedure Act*, 1869; and Murshidabad was one of the districts to which it applied. It is not difficult to understand that the judicial arrangements of the district working under so many *Acts*, and portions of *Acts* still unrepealed, could only lead to confusion, as indeed it did, and called forth a remedy which came in the shape of the *Bengal Civil Courts Act* of 1871.

Warren Hastings, averse to radical changes, had incorporated into his scheme, which we have noticed as introduced in 1772, the old Mahomedan criminal law and its officers. He also arranged a system of Police in 1793. This was entirely remodelled in 1813. It was seen that the Criminal Courts under the East India Company's supervision did not give satisfaction. Mahomed Reza Khan † was reappointed as superintendent of all criminal justice, and as his headquarters were in the chief city of this district, the criminal chief Courts returned to their original locality in the Mobarak Munzil Gardens. This method remained in effect, as we have seen, for fifteen years, after which the Sudder Nizamat Adalut went back to Calcutta. During these years Mahomedan criminal law, with the Nawab Nazim at its head, remained in force.

In 1790 Lord Cornwallis decreed that the criminal jurisdiction could no longer be left to "the sole discretions of any native, or indeed of any single person whomsoever." This important decision led to the removal of the Nawab's powers, which for the time were vested in the Governor General in Council; and to a remodelled system of criminal justice. Hitherto, Zemindars had been responsible for "public safety and the maintenance of the public roads." This was ensured by a clause in their agreements. They were to keep the peace, to bring thieves to justice, and to restore stolen property. It was found that this system led to collusion between the thieves and the supposed public guardians. In 1772, therefore, the police work was made over to the *Foujdari Adaluts*, and in 1774 Bengal was divided into four police districts. The head of the police in each of these was the *Thannadar*, whom the Zemindars were bound to assist. "Foujdars were appointed to apprehend all offenders against the public peace." This system, too, was a

* See Sections 112 and 114. † *v.* Forrest (43).

failure, and was altered in 1781. The Foujdars and Thannadars were abolished, and the Civil Court Judges were invested with power to seize all criminals arrested in their districts. They passed them on to the nearest criminal Court. The next step empowered the Civil Judges to fine and inflict corporal punishment in unimportant cases. As a check, reports of all trials and convictions were sent to the Presidency office under the Governor-General, every month, to an officer called the *Remembrancer of the Criminal Courts.* This system was slow and clumsy, and failed to cope with the amount of crime. A law was passed to expedite matters in 1790, instituting *Courts of Circuit,* under English Judges, with native assistants learned in Mahomedan law. In 1793 matters stood as follows:—

The supreme power of the Nawab Nazim in Murshidabad was abolished, and the Governor General and Council were the controlling power over the subordinate District Courts. In 1801 the Governor General, etc., were replaced by a Court, consisting of a Chief Justice and *puisne* Judges, sitting in Calcutta, and from that time both Civil and Criminal High Courts worked independently of the local Government.

Immediately below the Supreme Courts were the four Courts of Circuit. Their duties included Sessions at the various chief stations; the duties being divided among the Judges, the Chief Judge generally remaining at headquarters. These Courts ceased to exist in 1829. Bengal was then divided into twenty divisions, each under a Commissioner, in whom was vested the powers formerly exercised by the Courts of Circuit, plus those of the Board of Revenue, but acting under the Nizamat Adalut in the former, and under the Sudder Board of Revenue in the latter instance. The work thus thrown on the Commissioners was more than they could carry out satisfactorily. Thus in 1831, to relieve them, district Magistrates were authorised to refer criminal cases to the Sudder Ameens for investigation only. The year 1832 first saw the appointment of *Assessors,* who were to assist the newly appointed *District and Sessions Judges.* Their status was not very clearly defined, and they derived their powers from the *Regulations* of the Courts of Circuit and *Act* vii. of 1835. In 1854 Lieutenant Governors were first appointed, and Bengal came under the guidance of Sir F. Halliday. The authority for appointing District and Sessions Judges was never clearly defined, and on this account the *Bengal Sessions Court Act* of 1871 was introduced, providing for their appointment by the local Government, and further authorising the Lieutenant Governor to vary the limits of their jurisdiction. The *Act* confirmed existing appointments, and protected the Judges from the consequences of any act previously committed. This *Act,* when superseded by the *Code of Criminal Procedure,* was repealed in 1872. The appointment of Assistant Magistrates began shortly after the Police changes in 1793. In 1807 Magistrates received increased powers, again added to from time to time. District Superintendents of Police were appointed for the first time in 1808, and in 1816 they were ordered to submit yearly a full report of all matters referring to police work in the district. In 1817 an attempt was made to bring the police department under uniform regulations. The head native officer was the Darogah, with authority over mohurrahs, jemadars, and burkandázis in his *thannah* (circle). The Darogah is now represented by the Inspector and Sub-inspector. The Mohurrir, the term including at present the writer constable, was the Darogah's clerk and responsible for the records and general office work of the thannah. He also acted for the Darogah, when that officer was absent. The third in rank, the Jemadar, checked the attendance of the Burkandázis, and looked after their arms and kit. He was further to see that all prisoners were properly guarded. At the bottom of the scale came that wonderful person the village watchman, or *Chowkidar.* He was the local village policeman, and his post was hereditary, with many quaint privileges, and the power of appointing a deputy when the successor was a woman. He reported, and does to this day, births and deaths, being responsible for the diagnosis in the case of deaths, and being the source of our "vital statistics." In the towns there was a superior native officer, known as the Kotwal. In 1829, when Courts of Circuit were abolished, the Magistrate and the police fell under the authority of the Commissioner, and the Superintendents of Police ceased to exist for a time, but were again appointed in 1837. For the people at large, the police were a terror, dreaded perhaps less by the guilty than the innocent. Oppression of all kinds existed, and corruption was not only found among the rank and file, but extended into the higher ranks. The Magistrates were in many cases idle or inefficient, and the department was not to be tolerated as it stood.* The first step to reform was the reappointment of the Superintendents. In the towns were also appointed honorary Magistrates, European and native, from the non-official class.

Matters, though improved, remained in an unsettled state until 1861. Guided by the report of a Commission, which had examined into the police question during the previous year, *Act* v. of 1861 was passed by the Legislative Council. A new system of police came into force, with an Inspector General dealing directly with the local Government, with Deputy Inspectors General, District Superintendents, and Assistant Superintendents. Certain of these officers were invested with magisterial powers. The venerable institution, the village watchman, was left as before, the post, still often hereditary, and more than once held by infants and girls, whose duties were performed by proxy. These changes bring us up to the present times, when the district Government consists of:—1. District and Sessions Judge, generally remaining, as in Murshidabad, at headquarters; Sub-Judges and Munsiffs at headquarters; and a Munsiffs' Court in the chief town of each Sub-division.

2. A Magistrate at headquarters, but responsible for the whole district, in which he must spend a fixed number of days on tour. A European Assistant, or a Joint Magistrate, and as many Deputy Magistrates and Collectors as the size of the district requires. These latter are generally natives. A Sub-divisional officer is posted in the chief town of each Sub-division. The District Superintendent of Police has his office at the Sudder, but he is supposed to spend a large part of his time in inspection of the various thannahs. The right of appeal lies, except in certain cases, from the lower to the higher District Courts, and from these, on points of law, to the High Court in Calcutta, and even to the Secretary of State, or Privy Council, according to circumstances.

The change from the old Mahomedan and Hindu law was gradual, and may be said to have commenced with the *Indian Law Commission* of 1834. More radical changes occurred when the district passed from the hands of the East India Company, in 1858, to the Crown. The *Civil Procedure Code* and the *Criminal Procedure Code* became the law of the land between 1858 and 1861; and to them was added the *Penal Code*, from January, 1862.

Respect for local customs, of race, and religion preserved many of the Mahomedan and Hindu laws, notably those referring to marriage, religion, and succession to property. By the *Bengal Civil Courts Act* of 1871, the District Judge received authority over the Courts in his district.

The *Bengal Police Act* of 1867 did away with Municipal Chowkidars, and appointed town police, to be paid for by the town.

* "Tagore Law Lectures" (34), p. 197.

TOPOGRAPHY.

In the earliest times of which we can speak with any certainty, this district formed part of Rádha, one of the five divisions of Bengal. A portion to the east was possibly included in *Bagdi*, traces of which remain in *Baguri*, a name often used when speaking of the east of this District. Subsequently, the country formed part of the kingdom of Magadha, to be afterwards included under the rule of the kings of Gaur; a city long in ruins, and now, as Magadha before it, a name in history.

The *Sirkars*, as recorded in Toder Mull's list, 19 in all, were arranged with reference to the rivers Ganges and Bhagirathi. Of these we are only concerned with No. 16 and No. 11. No. 16 of the group "South of the Ganges and West of the Bhagirathi" was called Audamber or Tandap, and covered the greater part of the Murshidabad district and part of Birbhum on its borders. This *Sirkar* contained 52 Mahals, and brought in a revenue of between Rs. 5,97,570 and Rs. 6,01,985. Part of this district was included in the Sirkars in the Ganges delta, and No. 11 was the Sirkar of Sátgáon, which took in the south-western part of Murshidabad. The rent-roll of Toder Mull was superseded in 1658, and in 1722 (?) Murshid Kuli Khan issued a list known as "The Perfect Rent-Roll." In this he divided Bengal into 34 *Sirkars*, with 1,660 Pergunnahs, with an estimated revenue of Rs. 1,42,88,186. Later on this revenue was increased by the inclusion of fees for the renewal of leases, remissions, and levies for feeding the Nawab's elephants, much to the disgust of Zemindars, who had up to that time regarded these fees as a perquisite.* By the time that the East India Company took over the Nawab's *diwanni*, or revenue, the total estimated amount from all sources was, for all Bengal, Rs. 2,56,24,223, which shows that the Zemindars must have had great opportunities for amassing wealth and exercising oppression. One of the main lines of traffic, a road from Patna, entered this district at Suti.† From that town a road passed south to Muxsudabad, as the city was then called, and on to Plassy. From the west communication was along a road passing through Kasimbazar and on to the banks of the Ganges. In this respect there has been little improvement, and the roads in the district are few and bad. One of military importance passes from north to south, on past Plassy and Nadia to Calcutta, through Murshidabad city, Berhampur and Burwa; divided in the north, one branch leading to Bhagwangola on the Ganges, the other passing north-west to Rajmehal. The amount of possible water communication, however, renders this paucity of roads less of a hardship than it would appear. The *Mahal* Kankjol in the north-west of this district is one of the oldest, being mentioned in Toder Mull's list.

I have drawn up a list of the *Sirkars* and *Mahals* as they were at various times, taking first the list given in the "Ain-i-Akbari," and Mr. Beveridge's arrangement, which compares that list with the one given in Hunter's "Gazetteer." At the present time, although some of the names, *e.g.*, Chunakáli, Kankjol, Goás and Patkabari remain, they have no territorial significance.

Mr. Beveridge compares the list in the "Ain-i-Akbari," p. 394-408, with that in Hunter's "Statistical Account of Bengal."

* Blochmann (28); note p. 219. † Blochmann (28); p. 223.

I. *Sarkár Taudah* (North Radh-Bagri (Baguri)).

1. Ashrafbag.
2. Buitáli.
3. Chang Nadiya.
4. Chunákali (Ionaghatti-(Ain)).
5. Daudshahi.
6. Dhawa.
7. Diwanapur.
8. Gaukar (Gaukarah (Ain)).
9. Ibrahimpur.
10. Kankjol.
11. Káshipur.
12. Kátgárh.
13. Kumár Protáp.
14. Mangalpur.
15. Nashipur.
16. Nawa Nagar.
17. Samaskhana.
18. Swarup Singh.
19. Sultan uzial.

II. *Sarkár Sharifabad.* (The South Rarh.)

1. Akbarsháhi.
2. Bárbaksing.
3. Bazar Ibrahimpur.
4. Bhátsála.
5. Bihrol.
6. Fattisingh.
7. Husain uzial.
8. Khargaon.
9. Mahalaudi.
10. Manaharsháhi.

III. *Sarkár Mahmudábád.*

1. Fathipur Nausika.
2. Kulberia.
3. Kutubpur.
4. Pátkabari; Ghiásábád; Barmapur (Berhampur?); Babhangola (Bhagwangola?).

IV. *Sarkár Bárbakabád.*

1. Bárbakpur.
2. Gowas (Kahas (Ain)).
3. Guzarhát.
4. Lashkarpur.

The spelling in the two lists does not always agree, but of the above the following are found in Rennell's Map of 1780.

1. Chunácally.
2. Goass.
3. Patkabarry.
4. Futtasing.
5. Coolberya.
6. Daudpur (Daudshahi?).
7. Bogwangola (Babhangola?).
8. Berhampur (Barmapur?).
9. Dewanserai (Dewanapur?).
10. Luskeerpur (Laskarpur—only a very small portion of this Pargannah is in Murshidabad, the rest is on the east of the Ganges).

The following occur in Sherwill and Gastrell's Map, 1852-55:—

1. Gururhat (Guzarhat) } in Rajshaye.
2. Lushkarpoor } in Rajshaye.
3. Goas } in Rajshaye.

Shumskanee.

4. Koolbureea.
5. Putkabaree.
6. Futtahsingh.
7. Mahlundee.
8. Behroul.
9. Dhawa.
10. Nowanugger.
11. Koour purtap (Kumar Pratap).
12. Gunkur.

Chandpoor (Nashipur).

13. Kankjole (Bhagulpur).

At one period Murshidabad, together with Nadia and Jessore, formed the ancient Kingdom of Vanga, or Banga, whose inhabitants are described as a boat-using people. They grew rice as their staple crop, uprooting the seedlings to transplant them 1,200 or 1,500 years ago as they do at the present day. Vanga was not a kingdom of much importance; its kings are not mentioned nor its capital known.* Much of its glory has departed. In far-gone times it owned the city of Rangamati, now represented by one house and a silk *filature*. The city of Murshidabad was once nearly the size of Delhi, stretching from Baluchar to Amaniganj, a distance of some five miles.

Originally forming part of the Rajshaye Division, it was transferred to the Presidency Division in 1875, and forms the north-western corner of that Division.

A small, but both historically and commercially important district of Bengal, Murshidabad lies between 23° 39′ and 24° 46′ north latitude and 87° 40′ and 88° 45′ east longtitude. In shape it closely resembles an isoceles triangle, with its apex to west of north near Jafraganj. Its northern and eastern boundaries are formed by the main stream of the Ganges, which separates the district from those of Maldah and Rajshaye. The Jalingi river, an effluent of the Ganges, forms the south-eastern limit between Murshidabad and Nadia, while its southern and western boundaries are lines separating it from Nadia and Burdwan on the south, Birbhum and Bhagalpur on the west. The area of the district is 2,143 square miles, lying almost in equal portions on either side of the Bhagirathi river, which runs, roughly speaking, from north to south. The district was somewhat reduced in size when, in December, 1879, the Rampur Hát Sub-division was taken from Murshidabad and added to Birbhum. That part of the district lying to the east of the Bhagirathi is known as *Bàguri*, while the western portion is called the *Rarh*.

The names *Rarh* and *Baguri* carry us back to very ancient times. The *Rarh* was one of the principal divisions of Bengal under the Hindu kings. The first invasion of Mussulmans was in 1203 A.D., when Mahomed Buktyar Khilji descended upon Bengal. One of the first of his conquests was the *Rarh*, then under the rule of Lachman Ray. The Mussulmans settled in the conquered tracts. The fertility of the soil attracted them, and their rulers encouraged the influx. Indeed, during the reign of Sultan Gias-ud-din Khilji, rent-free lands were granted to many Syuds, preachers, and learned men. He further ordered the building of mosques, in which they could read prayers and teach.

The soil of both divisions is in the main alluvial; but while it is entirely so in the *Baguri*, lying between the Bhagirathi and the Ganges, the north-west and western parts are of older formation and raised somewhat higher than the rest of the district. The limit between the alluvium and the higher ground on the west is marked by a bank of stiff clay, gravel, and nodular limestone, and it is thought that this bank marks the western limit of the Ganges in ancient times. This bank disappears as it passes downwards towards Birbhum, where it amalgamates with the general alluvium. In the north-west of the district there are a few isolated clay hillocks and some stony *jungle*. The soil of the eastern and southern parts of the district is naturally the richest, but the west, too, as we shall see later on, is fertile and gives good crops. The *Rarh* is intersected by numerous "bhils"† connected with the rivers, and as the water in these sinks, the principal crop of *Aman*, or winter rice, is sown. The Belun, Sakora, and Palace "bhils" near Khargaon form, according to Hunter, the "Bishnupur Swamp," which was connected with the river, in 1800, at the expense of the Government. Nearly all the "bhils" are connected with the Bhagirathi by streams. There are also in the *Rarh* two very large artificial tanks—one, the "Sagor Dighi," is situated near the station of that name on the railway line from Azimganj to Nalhati; the other is the "Ramna Shaikh Dighi."

The eastern portion of the district is subject, almost yearly, to moderate floods, and the crop chiefly grown

* Pargiter "Jour. Asiatic Soc., Bengal," Part I., 1897, p. 97. Map, p. 133.

† Tanks, pools, or lakes; called also *jhils*.

is the *aus*, or early rice, crop. Thus it will be noticed that each division is the compliment of the other. The *Baguri* also yields excellent cold-weather crops, including mulberry, and vegetables and tobacco after the rains are over. On the *Rarh*, besides rice, are grown :—Sugar-cane, mulberry, tobacco, and various vegetables. The district takes its name from the chief town, called in early times Muxsudabad. The change of name occurred in the time of Nawab Murshid Kuli Khan, when he removed the capital of Bengal from Dacca to this district, as narrated in the chapter on the history of the district.

RIVERS.

For its size the district is traversed by a very large number of rivers. The Ganges can hardly be said to belong to the district; but it forms the northern and eastern boundaries, and its waters go to form the other rivers. It is navigable for large vessels all the year round. The most important river is the Bhagirathi, an effluent of the Ganges given off at Chápgháti, close to the Suti Thannah.* Its course is at first south-easterly, but after reaching Jiaganj it flows almost north and south, leaving the district just to the north of the battlefield of Plassy, and ultimately uniting with the Jalingi to form the Hughli river. On its banks stand all the principal towns of the district, and up and down its waters passes the traffic from these parts to Calcutta. From the 15th of June to the 15th of October, and later in good years, steamers and large boats can pass, and the river forms the shortest route for large trade and passenger steamers running from Calcutta to Patna and other towns on the Ganges. During the other months of the year the Bhagirathi is only navigable for small boats, despite the trouble and money devoted to attempts to keep open a deep channel by *training* the worst parts of the stream. Of these, that part of the river opposite Berhampur is the most troublesome. The silt at the mouth is almost unmanageable, though no end of schemes have been tried and proposed for keeping it down. This river is thought to have been the main channel of the Ganges at one time. In some old maps it is called the Kasimbazar river. Its tributaries are:—the Bansloi and Págla from the west near Jangipur; and the Chora Dekra, a branch of the Dwarka river, also from the west, near Saktipur. During the rains the Bhagirathi and the other rivers overflow, and serious floods are only prevented by numerous and expensive *bunds*.† It is proposed to abandon the chief of these on the left bank at Laltikuri, giving the water more space to the east, and saving the yearly expenditure for repairs to this "bund." The banks are soft, sandy mud, and cut away easily, so that slight changes in the course of the river frequently occur. Much of the original town of Jangipur is in the river bed, and on the right bank many houses have been cut away from Azimganj. The bed of the river is mostly sand mixed with clay, and silt poured in from the Ganges, and cut down from its own banks. The Bhairab and Sialmari rivers are two unimportant and, except for small boats, unnavigable, effluents given off by the Ganges between the Bhagirathi and the Jalingi. The Jalingi river is given off some few miles above the village of Jalingi and, flowing south-west, it forms one of the boundaries of the district. It is an important channel for traffic from the south-eastern part of the district into the Hughli and so to Calcutta. On the west, the only navigable river is the Dwarka, which has two tributaries entering from the south-west, the Mor and the Kina. As a rule, the floods in the west are not excessive, and indeed add to the fertility of the district, the rich soil being planted with rice and other crops as soon as the waters subside.

During the years 1854, 1856, 1857, 1867, 1871, and again in 1881 there were serious floods.

It would seem that whenever the water rises to anything over 28 feet on the gauge, floods may be expected, and the highest record is 29 feet 6½ inches in 1871.

Near Berhampur, the course of the river was altered and shortened in 1813, by the cutting off of a

* Police Station. † Embankments.

loop inward to the east. The old *bund* and the bed of the river lie by the side of the road to Murshidabad, and though full of water during the rains, nearly the whole of it is cultivated when the waters subside. How marked the change was can be seen by referring to old maps. According to the latest available reports, the river-borne traffic during the year is decreasing.

Ganges.—The mother of rivers, sacred to all Hindus during life, and at death the channel by which many of them hope to reach their heaven, it deserves first notice as one of the rivers of the district. Its right bank, from Furuckabad in the north to Jalingi in the south-east, forms the boundary line of the district on the east. The local name for the Ganges, below Suti, is the *Poddah*, and where it touches this district it is at its largest size, a truly noble stream. The volume of its waters is subsequently diminished by its efferents, the Bhagirathi, the Bhairab, and the Jalingi. Its course is at first south-east for about twenty miles; it then gives off the Bhagirathi, continuing in the same direction south-east by east for another sixty miles to the point where it gives off the Jalingi, at the small town of the same name. It leaves the district almost at the south-east corner. The Ganges is navigable for even large steamers throughout its course in connection with this district. It abounds in fish and crocodiles, man-eaters and fish-eaters infest its waters. Another fairly common inhabitant is the Gangetic porpoise *(Platinista)*, a remarkable mammal. The water of the Ganges is preferred above all others by the Hindus for drinking purposes.

Bhagirathi.—The Bhagirathi is given off from the main stream of the Ganges near Suti, and it is the chief river of the district next to its parent stream. Its course is winding, but the general direction is southward to Burwa, where after a run of seventy miles it passes into the Nadia district, to be there joined by the Jalingi to form the beginning of the Hughli. During the "rains," or from June to September, it is in good years navigable for the largest steamers, and forms the shortest route from Calcutta to Patna and the north-west. Nearly a week is saved when this river is open. It is, however, passable only for quite small boats at other times, in spite of the large outlay every year devoted to keeping the channel open. One of the worst parts and most difficult for navigation is just opposite Berhampur, and it is there that the chief *training* works may be seen. By means of long lines of bamboo and mat "fencing," the Public Works Department officer contrives to keep an open and fairly deep channel; but, except in the most favourable years, from December to July, the small local steamer running between Gorabazar and the railway terminus at Azimganj, finds its career gradually checked, and it shortens its course first to Khagra, then to Lalbagh (Murshidabad city). Between Lalbagh and a point a mile or so below Azimganj there is always plenty of water. Opposite the palace and grounds of the Nawab Bahadur the river is in many places fifty feet deep, even in the hot season. No soundings have been taken, but it would be very interesting to know the nature of the river bed in these deep places. The people, always ready with some imaginative or superstitious reason, often say that it is in honour of the Nizamat family, and this explanation is satisfying, and checks curiosity as to the nature of the river bottom. The Bhagirathi is a curious river in several ways.

The *Jalingi* is the second largest efferent of the Ganges in the district. The course of this river is even more tortuous than that of the Bhagirathi, but its general trend is to the south-west, and it forms the south-eastern border of the district for fifty miles from Jalingi to Balli. At the latter place it enters the Nadia district to unite with the Bhagirathi. The traffic on this river, though less than that on the Bhagirathi, is considerable. In some ways the Jalingi is a more satisfactory stream than the Bhagirathi. Its waters never sink so low as those of the Bhagirathi, and boats of under two feet draught can pass along it at even the dryest times of the year. The traffic along this river adds to the revenue of the Nadia Rivers Circle, and the tolls for fisheries bring in about Rs. 2,000, a year.

The *Mor* rises in the hills near Bhagalpur, in north latitude 24° 31′; 87° 1′ 2″ east longitude. Flowing south-east, it passes across the Birbhum border to join the Dwarka at Rungaon, in the Kandi Sub-division of this distict.

From its source to its junction with the Dwarka the Mor is about eighty miles long, rapid, and shallow, except in the "rains," when it is often a swollen torrent, overflowing at times, but, on the whole, doing more good by the deposit of alluvium than harm by its inundation.

The *Dwarka*, or Báblá, the continuation of the Brahminee river, is the most important stream in the *Rarh*, and gives to the Kandi Sub-division the valuable water supply needed for cultivation. The river rises in the Birbhum hills, 23° 57′ north latitude, 88° 10′ east longitude. Its general direction is eastward, and almost parallel with the Mor, which it joins at some eighty miles from its source. The river is called the Báblá more often than Dwarka, previous to its union with the Mor, the combined streams then bearing the name Dwarka. Like all hill streams, it is very rapid, and liable to sudden flood, and that part of the Kandi Sub-division known as the Hijal is annually flooded. As in the case of the Mor, no great harm is done even with high flood such as occurred in 1900.

One hears a great deal about the floods in the Kandi Sub-division, caused by the overflow of the Dwarka and the Mor, which bring down a considerable amount of water from the hilly country on the west of Murshidabad district. The damage done by these floods is generally overrated. It is to show how little real damage is done that I have introduced a note on the floods of the year 1900. The flood was recognised as one of the worst for many years.

A few days before the floods, from the 15th September, a strong east wind was blowing, with showers. On the night of the 18th of September heavy rain began to fall, and rain continued to come down in torrents without any break until the morning of the 21st. The daily rainfall from 8 a.m. to 8 a.m. on the 18th, 19th, and 20th was as follows:—

19th	September	2.34 inches.
20th	"	6.67 "
21st	"	5.22 "
	Total	14.23 inches.*

On the 20th September the volume of water in the river Mor was visibly increasing, and the increase was put down to the heavy rainfall. About midnight there was a sudden rise, showing that the increase was due to supplies from the hill streams in addition to the local rainfall. The river overflowed its banks, and the streets of Kandi were for a time knee-deep with water. The flood began to subside almost at once, and by 5 o'clock on the morning of the 21st, the water had receded four inches. At Bahorah the bank of the Mor gave way. The weak spot was about three miles south-west of Kandi, at the Hararband (Harar Embankment). Through this breach a large volume of water escaped, thus saving the town of Kandi from any serious consequences after the overflow. The flood water found its way eastward, submerging fields and flooding villages, and passing finally into the swampy lowland in the eastern part of the Sub-division known as the Hijal. The Dwarka also overflowed and broke through its banks, damaging crops and mud houses in the interior of the Sub-division. There was a large breach at Gabtolah and some smaller ones at Puranderpur, and also towards the main road leading to Berhampur. Such a flood has certainly not been seen for eighteen years, nearly half the Sub-division was more or less flooded for a short time. The water, in the deepest part of the floods, is reported to have been two feet higher than during any recent flood.

The cold-season rice crop, the ***Aman***, generally grown in the country round Kandi, is not as a rule

* Information supplied by 1st Grade Assistant Surgeon Akhoy Kumar Pain.

sown in the Hijal, which received the brunt of the flood. In ordinary years this part of the Sub-division is more or less submerged. This year, however, the rainfall during the earlier part of the season had been scanty, and the Hijal was generally cultivated, as there seemed little danger of loss from floods. These crops were mostly destroyed. With this exception, the damage done was not great, perhaps a quarter was lost, but a good *rabi* crop compensated for that loss.

A certain number of mud houses were necessarily damaged by the flood water. Such loss, however, can be easily repaired at any time. Naturally, too, the greatest suffering occurred in the villages in and around the Hijal. In the Kandi police thannah the following villages reported damage to houses:—

Puranderpur	Kotaldighi	Chandalparah
Chandraprosadpur	Pyrakole	Gopalnagar
Ghanesampur	Sasparah	Durgapur
Parbatipur	Bhowanipur	Titpur
Khidiqur	Banipur	Gosaidoba
Harinagar	Baglochra	Andutea
Gobindpur	Nutangram	Rusorah
Rajarampur	Shikantopur	

Many of these are only quite small hamlets, and the damage done was slight.

In Bharapur, Gokarna, and Khagram police thannahs slight damage to houses was recorded.

Nearly all the roads in the Sub-division were damaged to some extent. Notwithstanding the heavy downpour and the general dampness no special increase of sickness was reported. The flood water did some good by washing streets and drains. The price of food was not noticeably affected by the floods, which, after all, lasted only a few days.

The length of the Dwarka in this district is about forty-six miles, and, from a point near Talibpur, it turns back into Birbhum. Again it leaves that district and pours its waters into the Bhagirathi at about 23° 43′ north latitude; 88° 10′ east longitude.

Bhairab and Sialmari.—These two unimportant streams are given off by the Ganges between the mouths of the *Bhagirathi* and the *Jalingi.* They flow south and south-west, and finally join the *Jalingi.* These streams are connected with a series of *bhils*, and form a convenient means of communication during the rainy season, for small boats only. This is the more convenient, owing to the almost entire absence of roads.

The *Pagla and Bansloi* rise in the Santal Pergunnahs and flow into this district from the north-west. The Bansloi, the larger of the two, empties itself into the Bhagirathi opposite Jangipur.

SUDDER (Headquarters of the District).

Boundaries.—The Sudder Sub-division is bounded on the north by the Shahanagar and Bhagwangola thannahs, and the river Ganges; on the east by the rivers Jalingi and Ganges, south by the district of Nadia, and on the west by the river Bhagirathi.

Total Population of Sub-division including Municipality.—454,919 (1891).

Population of Chief Town.—Berhampur, 24,397 (1901).

Names of Thannahs in the Sub-division.—Buruah, Jalingi, Goas, Sujaganj, Gorabazar, Daulatabad, Hariherpara, and Nowada.

JANGIPUR.

Boundaries.—The Jangipur Sub-division is bounded on the south by Sagordighi and Bhagwangola thannahs, on the east and north by the river Ganges, and on the west by the district of Birbhum and the Santal pergunnahs.

Total Population of Sub-division including Municipality.—317,179 (1891).

Population of Chief Town.—Raganathganj, 10,921 (1901).

Names of Thannahs in the Sub-division.—Raganathganj, Diwansari, Shamsherganj, Suti, and Mirzapur.

KANDI.

Boundaries.—The Kandi Sub-division is bounded on the east by the river Bhagirathi, on the south by the district of Burdwan, to the west by the district of Birbhum, and on the north by Nabagram and Assanpur thannahs.

Total Population of Sub-division including Population of the Municipality.—297,122 (1891).

Population of Chief Town.—Kandi, 12,037 (1901).

Names of Thannahs in the Sub-division.—Gokarna, Bharutpur, Khargram, Kandi, and Borowan.

LALBAGH.

Boundaries.—The Lalbagh Sub-division is bounded on the south by the Khargram and Gokarna thannahs, and by Sujaganj, on the east by Daulatabad and Goas thannahs, on the north by the Diwansari thannah and the river Ganges, and on the west by the district of Birbhum.

Total Population of Sub-division including Municipality.—181,726 (1891).

Population of Chief Town.—Murshidabad, 15,168 (1901).

Names of Thannahs in the Sub-division.—Assanpur, Manullabazar, Shahanagar, Bhagwangola, Nabagram, and Sagordighi.

NOTES ON THE CHIEF TOWNS IN THE DISTRICT OF MURSHIDABAD.

THE "Sudder," or headquarters, of the district of Murshidabad is Berhampur. Up to 1875 it was the residence of the Commissioner of Rajshaye and in that Division. Hunter suggests that the name Berhampur is derived from *Brampur*, an officer of one of the earlier Nawabs Nazim.

The connection is difficult to see, as Berhampur was a piece of waste land to the south of Kasimbazar until selected as the site of a cantonment in 1757. The barracks were not finally complete until 1767, and led to the ruin of more than one officer who, with the laxity which disgraced that period, saw the possibility of making a fortune out of the Company's contracts. The cost amounted to £302,270, or at 2s. equals Rs. 30,22,700 (thirty lakhs). In 1786 the locality was considered very fine and even healthy.

The barracks then sheltered two European regiments, seven or eight regiments of Sepoys, and some Artillery, with 15 guns.

These barracks were the theatre in which the first overt acts of mutiny were played in 1857. To the north and west lies the town of Kasimbazar. The one and only good road in the district connects Berhampur with Murshidabad and Azimganj, the railway terminus. Berhampur was famous for its dhobies (washermen), and even now they are good, and destroy less than their rivals in other parts.

Passing along the road above mentioned, towards Murshidabad, the following places of interest meet the eye:—Two miles south of Murshidabad, on the right, the Moti Jhil (Lake of Pearls), which holds numbers of crocodiles, sometimes caught by the princes with a hook baited, and attached to a float made of a slice of plaintain tree. The palace, built by Suraj-u-Dowlah, on its banks has long been a ruin. Some of the building materials are said to have been brought from Gaur, the old capital of Bengal. This palace was the home of the Agent to the Governor General until 1785. From there the Agent went to Moydapur, and, later, to Berhampur.

Three miles south of Murshidabad, on the left (from Murshidabad to Berhampur), is a fine avenue of so-called *Deodars*, between two and three miles long. This avenue leads to Moydapur, once the Civil Station, with jail, and asylum for insanes—abandoned in 1878, December 31st. The jail and asylum buildings still exist and are maintained as a possible cholera camp, and for the sake of the timber and fruit trees. North-east of the Moti Jhil is the old *Katra Musjid.*

BERHAMPUR.

Berhampur, which is, as before stated, the headquarters of the district, is a composite town and the successor of Kasimbazar. From north to south it is made up of:—Farashdanga, the site of the town water-works and the spot where the French once had a factory; Nimtollah, marked by the Armenian Church, Calcapur, with the old Dutch Cemetery and site of the Dutch factory; Kasimbazar; Khagra; the Cantonment (Berhampur) and Gorabazar, which, as its name implies, sprang up to meet the wants of the British troops occupying the barracks. By road about 118 miles, and by river about 161 miles from Calcutta, the town stretches along the left bank of the Bhagirathi river in 24° 5′ north latitude; 88° 17′ 2″ east longitude. It only extends inland for a quarter to half a mile. In "Thornton's Gazetteer" it is said to be five miles from Murshidabad. As the distance between the two places is, at the present time, nine miles, it is evident that a very considerable portion of the city of Murshidabad has disappeared, even since 1858. The site on which the town and cantonments stand is flat, damp, and when the river is full, actually below the level of the surface of the stream. Malarial fevers are endemic with almost regular seasonal rise and fall. Cholera, though never very serious, claims a certain number of victims yearly. Dysentery, diarrhœa, and diseases of the chest are common, and enteric fever is not uncommon among Europeans. Natives dread the place, and my own experience is that, even if not actually ill, one is never free from *malaise*. The cold season is a mere mockery and brings little recuperation.

The aspect of the town from the river is pleasing, and the college and the barracks show up well. The Civil Station is well furnished with trees, and, indeed, is one of the prettiest in Bengal. Most of the Europeans live in the old barracks or field officers' quarters. Of the three double-storied barracks on the east side of the picturesque square, the one at the north corner is used as a Municipal Office. The other two hold the Courts of the Magistrate and his Deputy Magistrates and Collectors.

BRIEF HISTORY OF THE BERHAMPUR WATER-WORKS.

The scheme of the Berhampur Water-works was first mooted so far back as April, 1894, during the Collectorship of Mr. Kennedy; and the Maharani Surnamoyi of Kasimbazar expressed her willingness to bear the whole cost of the undertaking. The preliminary arrangements were not, however, completed when, in February, 1896, Mr. Levinge became Collector of Murshidabad. Mr. Levinge expedited matters, and in consultation with Mr. Silk, the Sanitary Engineer to Government, accepted Messrs. Martin & Co.'s tender for Rs. 188,834, the final sanction of Government having been given to the scheme on the 2nd March, 1897. Messrs. Simpson & Co.'s tender for supplying engines for Rs. 51,000 was also accepted. The lamented decease of the Maharani Surnamoyi, however, occurred on 25th August, 1897, before the project took shape; but she had already, with great generosity, undertaken to pay the full amount necessary to complete the works. The final estimate for the work, including subsequent modifications of the original estimate, amounted to Rs. 271,000. Of this amount, a little more than Rs. 162,000 had been paid by the Maharani before her death. The present Maharaja, the successor of the Maharani, generously undertook to carry out the wishes of the late Maharani and to meet the balance of expenditure. The Maharaja has actually paid Rs. 28,000, and has undertaken to pay when required, the balance, still due, of Rs. 72,000. The works have been constructed by Mr. A. Kimber, Engineer to Messrs. Martin & Co., under the supervision of Mr. Silk, Sanitary Engineer to Government, whose services were lent for this purpose, free of cost. The works were to be maintained by the contractors for one year in good working order, before being handed over to the Municipality. The following is a brief description of the water-works, which will exemplify their utility to the public:—The works are designed to give a daily supply of eight gallons per head of the population of Berhampur, equivalent to 200,000 gallons a day. The water is pumped up from the Bhagirathi, through a nine-inch pipe, 760 feet in length, laid in a masonry tunnel from the engine-house to the bed of the river. The water is then pumped at the rate of 200,000 gallons in eight hours into the settling tanks. There are three settling tanks, each having a capacity of 229,000 gallons. There are two filters, into which the water passes from the settling tanks, each of which is capable of filtering the whole daily supply, but both filters will ordinarily be in use. The filtered water passes into the outlet chamber, and from there into the "clear-water" reservoir. From the "clear-water" reservoir the water is pumped, to the town and the elevated reservoir, through a nine-inch pipe. From the elevated reservoir the water flows through the main and distributary pipes, having a total length of twelve and a quarter miles, and the water is drawn for public use from 132 standposts placed in the principal streets of the town.

It will thus be seen how great a boon has been conferred upon the public of Berhampur by the Kasimbazar Raj in defraying the cost of these works and supplying good drinking water. In recognition of the importance of this sanitary undertaking, and of the munificence of the late Maharani and the present Maharaja, Manindra Chandra Nandy, His Honour Sir John Woodburn, at the request of the Maharaja, kindly consented to open the water-works. It was at first hoped that the water-works would have been completed by the 1st April, 1899, but this having been found impossible, it was arranged to have the formal opening on the 31st July, 1899, during His Honour's River Tour.

At the ceremony of opening the Berhampur Water-works the Maharaja made the following speech:—

"Your Honour, Ladies and Gentlemen, on my own behalf, as heir and successor to the late Maharani, as also on behalf of the Berhampur public, to whom she made a gift of these works, I beg, most respectfully to tender you my, as well as their, grateful thanks for the honour you have this day done to her memory; and I only regret that she is not alive to hear how kindly and eloquently her munificent liberality has been spoken of by the head of the local Government, and to thank him for the trouble he has taken in coming here to open the water-works.

"Your Honour will, no doubt, recollect that at one time we had good reason to fear that your other duties and arrangements might prevent you from performing the ceremony which has been just completed; but your gracious presence to-day has happily dispelled those fears and filled our hearts with joy. Indeed, it is graciousness like this which is not only a proof of the interest you take in such works of benevolence, and of your sympathy in the welfare of the people committed to your parental care, but also goes a great way to create that solidarity and good feeling which ought to exist between the rulers and the ruled, and to stimulate others to follow the noble example set by the illustrious dead.

"And although this is neither the time nor the place to dwell upon those noble qualities of head and heart which have so greatly endeared you to our nation, yet I cannot allow this opportunity to pass without offering to you the tribute of my admiration, and the homage of my gratitude for those kind, considerate, and statesman-like measures which you have adopted for dealing with the plague in Calcutta.

"Once more thanking you for the honour you have this day done to the memory of my lamented aunt in such eloquent and feeling terms, I beg to resume my seat, wishing your Honour every success in the office which you now hold in this country and a happy and peaceful life in your own country after you have retired from that office."

Kasimbazar, the northern part of Berhampur, was a prosperous and large town, almost a suburb of Murshidabad, until 1813. Then, principally owing to accidents over which man has little control, its commerce fell away, and disease killed, or frightened away, most of its inhabitants. Now only part of Berhampur, it was at the zenith of its prosperity before Berhampur was even thought of, and was only waste land by the riverside. The ups and downs of the "East India Company's" trade have been recorded. A census taken in 1829 gives Kasimbazar 1,300 houses; 3,538 inhabitants, composed of 1,325 Mussulmans and 2,213 Hindus and others.

Ichabod! Ichabod! for the glory has indeed departed from this once large and wealthy town. To fix its position accurately, it lies in 24° 7′ 40″ north latitude, and 88° 19′ east longitude, on the left bank of the Bhagirathi river, which was frequently in former times called the "Kasimbazar" river. It is so marked in the old sketch map of the battle-field of Plassy. Its condition is not quite so bad as depicted in the

"Imperial Gazetteer," but parts formerly full of commercial life, Farashdanga (French factory), Nimtollah, where the Armenian Colony lived, and where their church still stands, in excellent preservation, thanks to the Armenians in Calcutta, are now deserted.

Calcapur, the site of the Dutch factory and the old Dutch cemetery, is now a *jungly** waste, dotted here and there with the ruins of what must have been handsome dwellings. Even before Murshidabad reached its greatest prosperity, Kasimbazar was the home of trade and commerce in these parts. Portuguese, French, Dutch, and Armenians, all in turn have had their day and disappeared. British trade, amidst many ups and downs and change of hands, remained and prospered. The country between the "Kasimbazar" river, the Ganges, and the Jalingi was known to the end of the eighteenth century as "Kasimbazar Island." Kasimbazar was flourishing before Calcutta was founded; but its early history is vague and unsatisfactory. Many of the changes which took place in the fortunes of the Kasimbazar factories have been noticed as they occurred in the history of the district. The downfall of Kasimbazar, as a town and as a commercial centre, dates from 1813, when, as elsewhere mentioned, the Bhagirathi made a breach at a place called Kátgunga, just above the present water-works at Farashdanga, and cut across the loop within which most of the town stood, leaving it with Berhampur on the east of the channel instead of on the west. The change took the river about three miles from the old course and spoiled the town's facility for river traffic. The old channel, as it dried up, became filled with dirt and rubbish and converted, for a time, into a pestilent swamp. A violent type of "fever" broke out, killing the inhabitants by hundreds and depopulating the chief portion of the town. The local weavers worked on at the commoner kinds of silk and *ghurrah*, a cotton cloth, until their trade was overwhelmed by cheap goods turned out by Manchester machinery.

Berhampur, originally a piece of waste land to the south of Kasimbazar and Khagra, was selected as the site for a cantonment in October, 1757, after the decisive victory of Clive's troops at Plassy. The *Sanad* given by Mir Jaffer granted to the Company 133 acres of land; but the Directors in England declined, at that time, to sanction the works. Later on, sanction being given, the barracks were commenced in 1765, and completed in two years. As the need for a strong garrison disappeared troops were removed, and in 1857 there were no European troops to check the mutinous outbreak, only two guns and a battalion of native infantry, the 19th, and a battalion of irregular native cavalry. The European troops brought from Rangoon to check the mutiny were quartered in the barracks and were not finally withdrawn until 1870. In those days the Civil Court and Treasury buildings were about a mile to the south-east of the barracks. These are now occupied only by the Sessions Judge's Court and record-rooms. The Magistrates' Courts and the Municipal Offices now occupy the three fine double-storied barracks on the eastern side of the Square. The field officers' quarters and the single-storied barracks are used as dwelling-houses by the resident Europeans, both official and non-official; the Magistrate being, indeed, the only official not living in the old cantonment. The present jail was the old Military Hospital, and the old Military Prison forms to-day part of the Lunatic Asylum. A Government College was founded in 1853, and had its home in a large house belonging to an Armenian merchant, Mr. Vardon.† At the time of the mutiny this house was removed, as it was in the way of the present jail, then prepared as a fort and shelter. The College next moved to a large house at Panchanantollah, one and a half miles from the barracks, and from there it was moved into the second row of single barracks on the north side of the Square. The present handsome college buildings were erected and endowed by the Maharani Surnamoyi of Kasimbazar.

* Overgrown with shrubs and wild vegetation.

† Buried in the churchyard of the Armenian Church.

RANGAMATI.*

From the study of the travels of a Buddhist pilgrim, a native of China, Huien Tsiang, Mr. Beveridge concludes, and apparently correctly, that the city of Karna Suvarna mentioned by the traveller was situated on the right bank of the Bhagirathi, at the spot now known as Rangamati, about six miles from Berhampur. In the days of its glory it stood on the river bank, its red cliffs marking the extreme western range of the Ganges. The kingdom, of which Karna Suvarna was no doubt the chief town, is said by M. Julien to have had a circumference of 900 miles—the town itself being four miles round—a fertile and prosperous country, with a population partly, perhaps mainly, Buddhists, and partly Hindus. As is ever the case in Buddhist countries, monasteries abounded. The chief of these was *Lo-to-wei-chi-seng-Kia-lau,* which extraordinary word represents the phonetic rendering by Huien Tsiang of the Sanskrit *Rak taviti Saeighârâma,* or the Monastery of Redlands. I am informed that the word *viti* means a wall, and such a term might with propriety be applied to the red clay cliffs of Rangamati. The monastery no doubt outlasted the town, and in the language of the people was *Rangamati,* which name the site still bears.† In the twelfth century Para Krama Báhv, King of Ceylon, is supposed to have invaded Bengal and destroyed the city Karna Suvarna. Mr. Beveridge thinks the year 1164 is the one in which this event occurred.

The founder, Karna, is he of the Mahabaratta, and not Karna Sen, of whom many fables are related.

In the *Purânas* Rangamati is also called Kusumapuri, but this is an epithet given to many towns, generally by poets.

All that is now left of this ancient and once famous town is a bungalow and a silk *filature* belonging to the Bengal Silk Company. The land from the river bank to Kandi, formerly the property of the Bagdanga Raja in Kandi, was lately purchased by the Nawab Bahadur of Murshidabad. Rangamati is on the west of the Bhagirathi, some six or seven miles below Berhampur.‡ The reddish yellow bluffs, from which the place takes its name, mark it in all probablity the most westerly line of the old Ganges.§ They mark also the true geological division of the district, all to the east being alluvial deposit, pure and simple, and, as things go, comparatively modern. These clay banks of the *Rarh* are the most elevated portion of the district, which is otherwise, in all directions, monotonously flat. In many places near the present bungalow there are signs of the foundations of buildings, and there is no doubt that excavations would be repaid by interesting discoveries. Some years ago, when Mr. Beveridge was District and Sessions Judge of Murshidabad, and Mr. Val. Weston was in charge of the *filature,* "some figures of Buddha were unearthed;" but the landlord would not allow these gentlemen either to continue their work or to remove that which they had found. The figures were subsequently stolen.

The foundations of the supposed palace of the founder of Rangamati, Raja Karna Sen of Gaur, were traced out by Captain Layard, who contributed an interesting note on the subject to the Asiatic Society of Bengal.‖ He thought he could distinctly trace three sides of the palace enclosure, the fourth having been swallowed up by the river. As late as 1845 there stood the ruins of one of the ancient gates. This, too, has long disappeared in the bed of the Bhagirathi. The kingdom of which

* "The site of Karna Suvarna," by H. Beveridge, "Jour. Asiatic Soc., Bengal," Vol. lxii., Part I., No. 4.

† Col. Walford, "Asiatic Researches," Vol. ix., p. 39, and Capt. Layard, "Jour. Asiatic Soc., Bengal," Vol. xxii.

‡ Not fourteen miles, as stated in Hunter's "Imperial Gazetteer."

§ Layard ascribes the name to the gold lavishly poured on the ground by Bibisan in return for a feast provided by a poor Brahmin.—"Imperial Gazetteer," Vol. vii., p. 554.

‖ "Jour. Asiatic Soc., Bengal," 1853.

the original Rangamati was the chief town is thought to have included the country now forming the *Rarh*, Burdwan, and Birbhum. After the Mahomedan conquest (1203), Rangamati was one of the Bengal *Foujdaris* and, as was the custom, it was farmed out to a wealthy Hindu Zemindar, a man of some importance, since it is recorded that he ranked with the Zemindar of Nadia, and at the *Punya* (Rent Audience) held at the Moti Jhil Palace, by Nawab Nazim Saif-u-Dowlah, in 1767, he received a *Khilat* (present of honour) worth Rs. 7,278.

As being a dry and healthy situation on the highest ground in the district, Rangamati was used as a sanitorium for the British troops quartered in the Berhampur Cantonment. The silk *filature* is a very old one, having originally belonged to the East India Company, from whom it was purchased in 1835, by Mr. Lyall, who probably started the Bengal Silk Company, for £2,100. The country round is picturesque, and provides excellent snipe shooting in the autumn and winter months. Both black and grey partridge are also to be found.

The palmy days of Rangamati were during the rule of Maharaja Karna Sen, of whose might and grandeur fabulous stories are told. His palace was at Rangamati, and at Gokarna or Gowkaran, about four miles. away, he kept his cattle, with a majestic dunghill at Gobarhatti, which lies between the two places.

Near Rangamati is Jadupur, with supposed traces of an old moat, that of Jalalluddin. Jalalluddin was the son of Raja Kans, and began to reign 818 (1415-16 A.D.).* When attacked by the Mahomedans, Karna Sen is said to have drowned himself in the Chanti Bhil, leaving behind him a son, Brisha Ketu.

MURSHIDABAD.

The once famous city of Murshidabad lies on the left bank of the Bhagirathi, about nine miles north of Berhampur, and is at present the chief town of the Lalbagh Sub-division. No portion of the old city, called Mahinagar, on the right bank, is now left, except the Khushbagh and Roshnibagh cemeteries; a few ruins there are, but mostly covered with *jungle*.

The Furahbagh Palace, and the great Moradbagh Palace, in which Clive stayed after the battle of Plassy, and in which Warren Hastings lived while resident at Mir Jaffer's Court, are gone. Gone also are the palaces of Gheseeta Begum, and others. Even in the city, on the left bank, many buildings have been ruins for years, and the earthquake of 1897 added to the number. One of the ruined palaces was built by Ali Verdi Khan with material brought from the ruins of Gaur, from which place too was brought the *Kadam* for the Kadam Russul Mosque. This stone was given to the Mosque by one Basant Ali Khan.

A new palace was commenced in 1828, and took ten years to complete, and cost about seventeen lakhs of rupees.

The trees which used to surround it have all gone. Even in 1829 there were 40,118 houses,† of which 14,281 belonged to Mussulmans. The population, 146,176, was composed of 90,086 Hindus, and 56,090 Mussulmans, and included the 5,000 Shiahs, brought together by the fortunes of the ruling Nawabs Nazim.

After the city became the capital of Bengal its trade was very extensive, and the bazars crowded with all kinds of shops. In the opinion of Clive it rivalled Delhi. It was never a healthy place, and want of sanitary improvements only increased its evil repute.

The city is about 124 miles north of Calcutta, in 24° 12′ north latitude; 88° 17′ 2″ east longitude.

* The year that Nur Qutb died (H. Beveridge, "Jour. Asiatic Soc., Bengal," Part I., No. 2, 1892, p. 124).

† Thornton's "Gazetteer" (29), p. 631.

List of Old and Interesting Places in the City of Murshidabad.

1. Mukbera Jafragunj, which belonged to Nawab Mir Jaffer.
2. Tomb of Nawab Zebun Nissa Begum, daughter of Murshid Kuli Khan, and wife of Suja Khan, opposite to the Old Mohimapur Thannah.
3. Tomb and Musjid of Nawab, Masiri Banu Begum, wife of Murshid Kuli Khan, at Juttaputti.
4. The large Imambara.
5. The Palaces.
6. Site of Old Imambara of Nawab Suraj-u-Dowlah.
7. Old Gun, near the Imambara, brought from Dacca.
8. Tirpolia Nowbut Khana, erected by Nawab Suja Khan at the *Chauk* (market place).
9. Chauk Musjid, built by Nawab Mani Begum.
10. Tomb of Serfiraz Khan, at the back of the Nagnia Bagh.
11. Katra Musjid, and Tomb of Nawab Murshid Kuli Khan.
12. The old "Jahan Kusha" Gun.
13. The Kadam Shariff.
14. Old Sudder Diwani Katcheri of the Mobarak Munzil. In this garden there is also the Masnud of the Old Subadars of Bengal, a squat stone table, upon which the *Gaddi*, or Cushion was placed.
15. Moti Jhil Garden, or site of Gheseeta Begum's Palace, used as the English Board of Revenue Office in 1765.
16. Khush Bagh, containing the Tomb of Nawab, Ali Verdi Khan.
17. Roshni Bagh, containing the Tomb of Nawab Suraj-u-Dowlah.
18. Morad Bagh, or site of the Old English Residency.
19. Site of Munsur Ganj Palace.
20. Bhabani Than or Krita-Ishwarit. A very old and sacred Hindu Temple.

The Moradbagh, on the right bank of the Bhagirathi, was the headquarters of the Collector of Rajshaye District in the later years of the eighteenth century. The arrangement was an awkward one, and led to the reduction of Rajshaye, the country south-west of the Ganges, being divided between Nadia, Jessore, and this district in 1793.

Not the least interesting feature of the large Palace is the Armoury, situated on the ground floor in the western wing. There is a very large collection of curious old swords and spears, daggers, cannon, and camel-guns. There is, however, unfortunately, no catalogue, and no means of telling to whom the various weapons belonged, or whence they were obtained. We have, however, some interesting information (communicated by H. Beveridge for Hara Prasad Shastri to the Proc. A. S. B., Jan., 1893, p. 24) concerning one of the cannon in the collection. It is a brass gun, mounted on a carriage, apparently of native manufacture. The gun is three feet in length and probably about a four-pounder. The muzzle is shaped like a demon's head, with pointed ears, a human face, and crocodile's jaws. The gun is decorated with floral designs, and has an inscription on a raised shield about the middle of the upper surface. The inscription was deciphered by Babu Shasi Bhushan Datta, Deputy Magistrate of Berhampur, and runs somewhat as follows :—

Victory to Kali.
Her name is Truth.

The Honourable
Krishna Chandra,
Rai Maharaja,
the respected, the royal.

The Honourable Roop Ram,
Chatto Padhya, the engraver.

Kishore Das Karmaker (blacksmith).

THE "NADIA" CANNON,
MURSHIDABAD PALACE ARMOURY.

SOME OF THE MURSHIDABAD FAMILY JEWELS.
AIGRETTES, ARMLETS, BELT BUCKLES, ETC., OF DIAMONDS, RUBIES, AND EMERALDS.

The gun belonged to Raja Krishna Chandra Rai, of Nadia, and he probably, according to Mr. Beveridge, received it as a present from one of the Governors of Calcutta. The gun, no doubt, found its way into the Nizamat Armoury after the Battle of Plassy.

Jiaganj is on the left bank of the Bhagirathi, opposite to Azimganj. Here, too, dwell many families of Jains, though the main colony is in Azimganj. It contains some large houses, the property of Jain merchants. The town is about three and a half miles from Murshidabad city, and forms part of the Municipality of Azimganj. Though its importance as a trade centre is not what it once was, it is still considerable, and the place is the depôt for much merchandise, which is carried across the river in boats to the railway terminus at Azimganj. Rice, jute, silk, sugar, and a small quantity of cotton find their way here for export. The Jiaganj jute press belongs to Mr. Yule, who also manages the cargo ferry. From Jiaganj, from June to November, a steamer starts twice a week for Dhuliyan, calling at Azimganj, on the opposite side, Gardi, Raganathganj, Jangipur, and other places for goods and passengers. The line is well patronised, paying well, though the season is short.

Jiaganj possesses a police station, post, and telegraph offices, and is one of the London Missionary Society's centres. The pastor, the Rev. A. Joyce, is nobly assisted by his wife, a doctor of medicine, who has built a mission hospital for women, for both out- and in-patients. Lately, Dr. Edith Joyce has been assisted in her work by Miss Alice Hawker, also a graduate in medicine. The hospital was opened in 1899. The southern part of Jiaganj is known as Baluchur, and is the home of many prosperous merchants. Dhunpat Singh, and Chattrapat Singh, two influential members of the Jain community, live there. The revenue returns of 1876-77 quoted in the "Imperial Gazetteer" give the imports into Jiaganj—mainly salt, oil-seeds, tobacco, and ghee. Of these it may be noticed that mustard seed has risen in price to an alarming extent. In 1898 one could purchase a good mixed seed, white and black, giving 12·8 seers of oil per maund, for Rs. 4 as. 8; in 1900 the price was more than once over Rs. 6 per maund, and never below Rs. 4 as. 8.

JUNGIPUR.

This Sub-division is situated to the north and north-west of the district, extending along both banks of the Bhagirathi, between 24° 19′ and 24° 52, north latitude, and 87° 51′ and 88° 24′ east longitude. In area it occupies 576 square miles. It contained, in 1872, 668 towns and villages, or 1·16 to the square mile; and a population of 273,487, or 475 inhabitants to the square mile.

The Sub-division is divided into five *thannahs*, or police circles—Raganathganj, Mirzapur, Pulsa, Suti, and Shamsherganj. The chief town and Municipality is, one might now almost say was, Jangipur, or that part called Raganathganj, on the right bank of the river. The town, with courts and offices, stood originally on the left bank of the river.

Slowly the town disappeared into the river, until it became necessary to remove the courts to the town of Raganathganj, on the right bank, where they now occupy a fine old double-storied house, formerly the property of a very wealthy Armenian, Mr. Masik. The Sub-jail, Hospital, and District Board Bungalow are also close by. Just outside the town, to the north, is the silk factory of Baliaghatta, managed by Mr. Robert Moore, for Mr. M. Ferguson, of Berhampur. In olden times this, with several other factories, belonged to the East India Company, and Jungipur was a very important centre of the silk trade. The population of Jungipur town, in 1872, was 11,361. The "Imperial Gazetteer" gives the municipal revenue for 1876-77 as £957.

Tradition ascribes the founding of the town to the Emperor Jahangir, and much of its importance was, and is still due to its position. Being near the mouth of the Bhagirathi, it forms the chief toll station for boats passing from the main stream of the Ganges, or Poddah, as that part of the river is called, into the Bhagirathi, and thence along the Hughli river to Calcutta, passing through the length of the Murshidabad district. In 1872 the total traffic was 377,508 maunds (about 13,821 tons), which had diminished to 140,318 maunds in 1874. The number of boats registered is about 10,000, and the toll represents about one-third of the entire revenue of what is known as the Nadia rivers circle, which is in charge of the Executive Engineer living at Berhampur.

KANDI.

At the time Hunter's "Imperial Gazetteer" was published Kandi formed part of the Sub-division of Rampur Hát. In 1872 Kandi contained a population of 235,227 persons; 159,273 Hindus, and 74,158 Mahomedans, five Christians, and 1,791 classed as "others"; of this total 111,324 were males, and 123,903 females. The area of the Sub-division is 450 square miles, with 1·14 villages, and 523 people to the square mile. Comparing these figures with the returns of the census of 1881 and 1891, we find an increase:—

	1881.	1891.
Population	294,809	297,122
Males	—	145,117
Females	—	152,005
Population to the square mile	576	580
Villages and towns	—	724

In January, 1873, the old Sub-division of Jumoo Kandi was abolished, and included in the Sub-division of Rampur Hát, then part of the Murshidabad district. The "Imperial Gazetteer" notes that the cost of Sub-divisional administration in 1870 was £2,604 8s. Rampur Hát was separated from the district, and the Kandi Sub-division again formed.

The chief town of the Sub-division is Kandi, or, as it is sometimes called, Jumoo Kandi, about nineteen miles from Berhampur, in a south-westerly direction,* close to the Mor river as it passes into Murshidabad from Birbhum, 23° 58′ north latitude, and 88° 5′ east longitude. The town is a municipal one.

It is a fairly well-built and well-kept town, and most of the land in and about it belongs to the well-known family of the Paikpara Rajas, who owe their aristocratic origin to the gratitude of Warren Hastings. Ganga Govind Sinha, the founder of the family, was born in Kandi. As Hastings' *banian*, he amassed a large fortune, much of which he afterwards devoted to the building of shrines. According to Hunter, quoting tradition, the *Shrad*, or funeral ceremonies, which he performed in memory of his mother, were the most magnificent ever known in Bengal, costing twenty lakhs of rupees. Among other extravagances, "the guests were fed on *Mohaproshad*, or holy rice, brought in relays from the temple of Jagannath, in Puri."

The visitor to this district must first find his way to Nalhati Junction on the East India Railway. From this station, the only railway in the district makes its way to Azimganj, passing through Takipur, Nowada, Bokhara, Sagordighi, and Shahapur, places of no particular importance, beyond the dignity and utility that a railway station confers. This is not a "complaint book"; but the best that can be said of the train service on this short line of twenty-seven and a half miles is that it is bad, and that the East India Railway Company has ever turned a deaf ear to petitions from the people of Murshidabad. It can fairly be said that these petitions do not contain anything unreasonable. The country through which the line passes is

* The "Imperial Gazetteer" gives it as "south-east," probably a printer's error.

flat and ugly, but the view as one approaches the terminus is very picturesque, and the houses and temples of Azimganj, some white, some painted in bright colours, tell no tale of the narrow, dirty, undrained streets which surround them. Just as the traveller enters the town there is a fine rose garden on the left-hand side of the railway. This garden, which is a mass of colour in the cold season, and produces many very beautiful roses, is the property of Rai Dunpat Singh Bahadur. There is a fine artificial tank, from which the garden is irrigated, and the owner has built himself a small but pretty "pleasure-house" by the side of the tank.

This, our only railway, with its terminus at Azimganj, connects us, as noted, with the East India Railway at Nalhati Junction, and passes through :—

	Azimganj	...	27½
6½	Shahapur	...	21
10½	Sagordighi	...	17
19½	Bokhara	...	12½
	Nawada	...	8
23½	Takipur	...	4
27½	Nalhati	...	—

The Murshidabad district extends to Bokhara, where there is a bungalow for travellers and inspecting officers, and a very bad road to Raganathganj (Jangipur). Nalhati Junction is an uncomfortable place, with no refreshment room.

The compiler of Murray's "Guide to Bengal" complains that the Nawab Bahadur does nothing for travellers. Why should he? Nevertheless, a traveller with sufficient courtesy to write to His Highness at Murshidabad will always find a carriage at his disposal, and the best of entertainment at the palace as long as he stays in the district. This same compiler also complains that the train is allowed to stop while officials get down to shoot ducks or deer. I am quite sure that there are no deer, and few ducks. The statement itself is the only "canard" that needs shooting.

The river Bhagirathi presents at all times an animated appearance, with its crowd of country boats bringing merchandise for export by rail, or waiting to take any necessaries up and down the river to both ends of the district. Twice daily the small steamer from Berhampur plies to meet passengers arriving by the mid-day and evening trains. There may also be seen steamers and flats, either ready to make the bi-weekly journey from Azimganj to Dhuliyan and the north, during the "rains," or lying up in the dry season, waiting for an insignificant stream to become a large and important river and water-way for traffic, with a current running six to seven miles an hour. The river, here, at Azimganj, is about one eighth of a mile wide. The distance from the station to the *ghat* (landing stage) is over-stated as a quarter of a mile in Murray's handbook. To a stranger, and at night, it probably seems longer than it really is. Descending a couple of hundred yards to the river bank, the visitor can be ferried over to Jiaganj, where there is a small bungalow belonging to the District Board. Here one may rest, but must be prepared to make his own arrangements for food. The road on to Murshidabad, narrow and winding in the town, soon opens out as a good, wide track running by the river until we reach Baluchar (sand bank), which is included in the Azimganj municipality, and had once many busy looms, and was the home of the ivory carvers. It is of little importance now, and marks the former probable northern limit of the city of old Murshidabad in its palmy days. From Baluchar there are houses and shops on either side of the route as it insensibly passes through Nashipur in the Murshidabad municipality, along the Jutapati road and the Rana Kabza, through one of the old city gates, "Tirpolia," with its *Nowbat Khana*, into the Chauk and present city of Murshidabad, after passing the long wall of the *Kila Nizamat*. Here a road to the right leads to *Dekhan*, or south gate of the Palace grounds, the main gate into the Nawab Bahadur's Palace enclosure. At night, as one passes along the same route, the only noticeable feature is the brilliantly lighted palace of the Raja Bahadur of Nashipur, and further on, and on the same side, the lamps of the Jafferganj cemetery, facing the Jafferganj mosque, which stands out well. The cemetery is a large one and full of neat graves.

No less than seventy-seven priests are employed here in daily readings of the Koran; a complete reading occupies three days. Their pay varies from four to six rupees a month.

If the visitor will make his arrival known to H.H. the Nawab Bahadur of Murshidabad, he is almost certain to receive an invitation to rest and put up in the palace, from which, as a centre, he can make excursions to the various sights of interest. Across the river there are two more cemeteries older than that of Jafferganj. The *Roshni Bagh* (the Garden of Light) lies about a mile from the river bank in a south-westerly direction. It is full of fine trees, which give a welcome shade, and the cemetery is well kept by servants, as in the case of all the cemeteries paid for by the local Government. In this garden of graves, the one of most historical interest is that of Nawab Suraj-u-Dowlah. The original mausoleum had become more or less a ruin when the local Government took these old graveyards into its care, and a new, but smaller and possibly less ornate, structure was built over the grave (circa 1863). The present edifice measures 36 feet by 20 feet, and has three doorways.

The mosque in the north-west corner of the cemetery bears the date of 1156 H.A. (1743 A.D.). Two miles further down the right bank of the river, and still south-west, lies the *Khush Bagh*, or garden of delight. Its walls were built by the order of Lutifunnissa Begum. The main grave with its mausoleum lies to the west, near the mosque. It is 65 feet square, and under its roof lie also the graves of Suraj-u-Dowlah's brother and his father, Ali Verdi Khan. Over each of the flat tombstones is spread an embroidered "chadar" or quilt. There being nothing more of interest on the right bank, except the foundations of the Furahbagh and Moradbagh Palaces, we return to the left. The palace enclosure is about three quarters of a mile long, from the Madrassah (College) to the Dekhan Darwaza (south door), and contains many buildings of interest.

Entering this south gate we have on the right hand a low range of buildings occupied now by the Eurasian Bandmaster, Mr. De Souza, the bandsmen, and Sepoys of the Nawab Bahadur's guard. He has sowars and infantry.

To the left, on the river bank, is a large and roomy house, in which, until quite lately, Darab Ali Khan, an aged eunuch, lived. He was ninety-eight years of age, and had been with the Murshidabad family for over eighty years. He died of blood-poisoning from a wound of the scalp. He fell while in his bathroom, cutting his head severely. This, except for a small mosque, is the only building directly on the river bank, so that there is a clear view of the river and the *jungly* country on the right bank. Along the right side of the enclosure, and next the Sepoys' lines, are the various gateways leading to the *deories* (apartments) belonging to the brothers and the family of H.H. the present Nawab Bahadur. The first belongs to the sons of the late Daud Mirza, H.H.'s eighth brother. Then comes the deorie in which H.H. the Begum Saheba lived formerly, occupied now by the Chotu Saheb, whose only son is being educated at St. Xavier's College, in Park Street, Calcutta. The next gateway leads into the same deorie.

Between this last and the main gateway into the deorie of H.H. and his sons with their families, is what is called the new Palace, built by Mr. Vivian, when P.W.D. officer of the Nadia rivers division. A handsome iron railing encloses a garden space in front, and the main entrance is a fine Norman archway with open-work iron doors. In the earthquake of June 12th, 1897, the whole of the upper storey came down with a crash a few seconds after the present head of the family had been carried out of the building by his attendants. Much of the débris has been cleared away, but piles of bricks and broken pillars as late as the beginning of 1901 bore witness to the damage done. It is being repaired but without the second storey. A few rooms at the north end are used by Prince Munah Saheb, otherwise it is uninhabited. We now come to the entrance gate of the chief deorie, inside which are the houses inhabited by the Nawab Bahadur and his family. Opposite this gate, and midway between it and the river, is a small thatched, one-roomed summer-house, in which the Nawab Bahadur has always spent the daytime since the earthquake. It is surrounded by a pretty garden enclosed within a wooden fence.

Other places to be noticed are :—

Aurungabad, a police thannah in the extreme north of the district in the Jungipur Sub-division, was at one time a town of some importance. It lies on the route from Berhampur to Rajmehal, 24° 27′ north latitude, 88° 2′ east longitude.

Suti is situated 24° 35′ north latitude, 88° 6′ east longitude, forty-two miles north-west of Berhampur and 210 miles from Calcutta by river. The Bhagirathi here comes off from the Ganges. The town is not one of any importance, but deserves to be mentioned and remembered as the field on which a battle was fought July, 1763, between the British forces and those of the Nawab Nazim Mir Kasim Ali. The fight was one of those upon which depended freedom from tyranny, and our troops ended by routing their adversaries and taking the Nawab's cannon and supplies, which amounted to 150 boat-loads of rice. Suti is a police thannah, including 128 villages, 4,816 houses, and a population of 34,662, almost all Mussulmans—28,499 to 6,163 Hindus. Such was the condition of the circle in 1858. The census of 1891 gives us the following figures for comparison :—Total population, 69,532 ; number of houses, 12,957. No distinction of races is made in the 1891 census.

Goas, once a large pergunnah, is represented by a large village and police thannah. It lies 114 miles north of Calcutta, 24° 13′ north latitude, 88° 29′ east longitude.

Bhagwangola is situated on the right bank of the Ganges, about 136 miles north of Calcutta, 24° 20′ north latitude, 88° 20′ east longitude. It was, until late years, a large grain mart, from which rice was sent by boats. It has lost most of its trade and importance. The decadence of Murshidabad city has considerably reduced its trade. It may also be remembered as the resting-place of the ill-fated tyrant, Suraj-u-Dowlah, in his flight towards Rajmehal.

Azimganj is a municipal town on the right bank of the Bhagirathi, facing Jiaganj, which is included in the same municipal area, already noticed. The home of the Jain community, its importance was vastly increased when it became the terminus of the railway from Nalhati Junction. Three trains run daily between these stations, a distance of twenty-seven and a half miles, and a small steamer from Berhampur meets the mid-day and the evening trains. As the river gets shallow, this steamer cannot approach Berhampur, and in bad years runs only from Lalbagh to Azimganj during the cold and hot seasons. The town possesses a hospital presented to the Municipality by Gunpat Singh, but the building is low and dark, and not at all what might be expected from so rich a town. The town contains many handsome Jain temples and well-built houses belonging to the Jain merchants.

There is a village of the same name on the Jalingi river, in the Sudder Sub-division. It is the site of a police station, but otherwise of no importance.

Plassy.—Although Plassy is no longer in this district it was so in past time, and, as one of the most important battle-fields in history, is so closely connected with Murshidabad that this history would be incomplete without some account of the place. The locality takes its name from the large number of *palas** trees which formerly grew there. Its red flowers are very attractive and exhale a pleasant odour. The area of the original Plassy has been much reduced by the destructive action of

* *Butea frondosa*, Roxb.

the Bhagirathi river, and of the famous mango grove in which Clive's troops bivouacked on the eve of the battle, only one tree remains. Jaggat Singh's hunting lodge has long disappeared, and his garden is marked by only one or two large trees (*v.* p. 14). What is left, and the memorial monument erected by the Government of Bengal, lie on the left bank of the river, twenty-two miles south of Berhampur.

The main road from Berhampur to Calcutta passes close to the battle-field.*

* According to the "Imperial Gazetteer," one of Suraj-u-Dowlah's Generals was buried at the foot of the solitary mango tree above mentioned. This is not so, but the villagers believe that one of Mir Muddun's legs is buried there. His tomb is at Munganapara, two miles away.

POPULATION.

IN 1860 the inhabitants numbered 1,100,080 (Gastrell);* by 1872 they had increased to 1,214,104. Before the next census was taken Rampur Hàt, with a population of over 260,000, was cut off from the Murshidabad district. The fact of increase, however, can be shown by adding the above figures to the totals of the censuses of 1881 and 1891:—1,226,790 and 1,250,946. The proportion of Hindus to Mahomedans was about as 1·78 to 1; the census of 1872 gave 555,310 Hindus and 412,822 Mahomedans.

The steady increase of population points to general prosperity and freedom from severe famines or epidemics of disease. The last census, taken in 1901, shows a total population of 1,333,184, again an increase! The figures, however, must, in part at any rate, be accepted as an improvement in census taking. When the census figures are compared with the district medical statistics, the *death-rate* is found to exceed the *birth-rate!* Either the Government methods of registration are still imperfect, or there is some miraculous power which causes *abiogenesis!* The balance between Hindus and Mahomedans is no longer in favour of the Hindu, though the difference is not very great:—Hindus, 644,492 (includes Brahmo, 20, and Jains, 998), Mahomedans, 676,899 (of these some 5,000 or 6,000 are Shiahs, the rest Sunnis). After the Burmese War, 1885-87, one of the captured Princes was sent to Berhampur as a political prisoner. Monotony, and the climate of Berhampur, thinned out the family and its followers, and now the census shows six Buddhists only. The population is spread over an area of 2,143 square miles, in five towns and 3,668 villages. They occupy 283,078 houses: 18,914 in the towns, and 264,164 in the villages; 653,346 are males, 679,838 are females. While the district table of population by religions is careful to include 20 Brahmo-Somaj and six Buddhists, it omits nine *animists* and 318 Christians. These appear to be confined to the towns. Of the total population, 330,672 males and 194,968 females are unmarried; 299,671 males and 309,185 females are married; widows, 175,685; widowers, 23,003. The educated section is small; only 73,476 persons are returned as *literate*, and of this small proportion only 3,838 *are women*. Of the men, a respectable minority is *literate* in more than one language, as the total of the various sub-classes comes to 76,466.

The census records of languages spoken in the district show that the majority of Mahomedans use the *Bengali* language, and 5,367 persons speaking *Urdu* are included under *Bengali*, as are also 134 who speak the *Mal Paharia* dialect. The *Bikaneri* dialect is spoken by ten individuals among the *Marwari* merchants in Azimganj. Taking the figures as they come we have:—*Bengali*, 1,223,665; *Hindi*, 93,926; *Ooriya*, the language of Orissa, 492, here servants (bearers) and palki bearers are, no doubt, largely represented; *Khas (Naipali)*, one male, and one female, man and wife(?) *Assamese*, one solitary female, probably an Ayah; *Marwari*, 46; *Panjabi*, six; *Mahratti*, four—a great contrast to the days of old, when the Mahrattas overran Orissa, and blackmailed the Governors of Bengal; *Gujerati*, 15. This brings us to the end of the *Aryan* languages. The next group contains the dialects of the aborigines:—*Mundari*, 224; *Kora*, 505; *Korwa*, 49; *Santali*, 12,508. The *Dravidian* group includes:—*Oraon*, 1,430; *Telegu*, two (domestic servants?) The *Burmese* group is represented by the six exiles from Mandalay. In the *Iranic* section we find *Persian*, 14, and *Pashtu*, 147. The list ends with languages foreign to India

* Bib. (2).

which are spoken in the district: *English*, 142, and *Arabic*, one. French, also spoken by a number of gentlemen in the silk industry, has not been returned.

The next point of interest is contained in the "tables," which disclose the number of those that are not whole, and free from blemish. The total number of afflicted persons in the district is 3,747: males, 2,304; females, 1,443; 559 are *insane*; 688, *deaf-mutes*; 1,520 are *blind*, the chief causes being *cataract* or *ophthalmia*, mainly from neglected *small-pox*. Of *lepers* there are 997, and it is time that these persons were provided with a proper asylum, or hospital, both for their own sakes and for the good of society. A note to this "table" of troubles tells us that some of these suffer from more than one affliction. In this district, and elsewhere, there is a greater proportion of male than female children. Age is a matter of guess-work with all but the better classes who can afford "*horoscopes*," or with those born in a municipal area where any serious attempt is made at registration. Registration, such as an Englishman regards satisfactory, there is none; and in this district births were not registered at all until 1884-85, as a result of placing the vaccination work in the hands of the Civil Surgeon. Girls are considered to arrive at womanhood at an earlier period than that at which boys attain manhood; thus many girls are classed in "age groups" above that which is accurate.

The following list of inhabitants, according to "castes," is taken from Mr. Risley's book,* with the figures for 1891 added from the Census Report. Similar information for 1901 is not yet available.

	1872.	1881.	1891.
Aguris	249	153	
Agarwals ...	347	408	
Brahmans ...	38,749	33,935	31,541
Buna	2,320	387	5,560
Binds	787	887	
Bhumij	42	152	
Bhuiyás	494	153	
Bhúinmális ...	1	2,426	11,996
Bháts	150	59	
Bhars	0	41	
Beldárs	538	195	
Bauris	6,536	4,512	3,607
Báruis	3,683	3,014	1,960
Báitis	1,584	1,210	
Baidyas	2,258	1,474	1,232
Bágdis	23,929	33,197	39,651
Bábhans	0	160	
Cháins	26,133	20,649	36,686
Chamárs ...	33,366	20,374	34,698
Chandáls ...	21,764	18,854	24,319
Chásátis	0	0	5,173
Chásádhoba ...	6,320	4,812	6,326
Dhánuks ...	4,487	4,802	5,357
Dhobás	5,295	6,900	4,588
Doms	10,400	7,877	6,800
Dosádhs	2,435	1,886	2,721
Gandhabanik ...	11,016	9,874	7,322
Gareris	224	652	
Ghásis	0	14	
Goálás	39,953	35,411	35,516
Gonrhis	7,222	8,302	
Gurkha†	0	0	1,659
Halwais (*v.* Mayaras)	0	614 (*v.* Mayaras)	
Haris	18,954	9,176 (*v.* Bhuinmalis)	
Jáliyás	3,014	2,848	
M. Jolhás ...	766	199	4,175
Jugis	5,855	5,240	4,071
M. Kahars ...	0	0	1,733
H. Kahars ...	3,416	4,769	2,514
Kaibarthas ...	102,517	100,355	91,900
Kalwár (*v.* Sunris)	0	108 (*v.* Sunris)	
Kámárs	7,450 (Lohars)	8,952	5,567
M. Kalus ...	0	0	3,345
Kándhus... ...	2,584	1,112	
Kapális	1,536	100	
Káyasths ...	17,077	15,655	13,566
Kewats	0	341	
Khandáits ...	1,545 (Ghatwals)	1	2,824

* Bib. (4). † Misprint? There are no Gurkhas in this district.

	1872.	1881.	1891.		1872.	1881.	1891.
Kharias	0	4		Pásis	265	56	
Khatiks	0	3		Pátnis	2,529	2,066	1,745
Kharwárs ...	141	188		Pods	86	8,137	13,065
Khatris	9	670	3,319	Rajpoots ...	13,141	8,955	6,695
Kochh	17,646	17,582		Rajwars	0	163	
Koiris	7,171	930	1,973	Rajbansi	0	0	9,159
Korás	606	967		Sadgops	29,321	38,008	36,658
Kotals (*v.* Chandals)	0	1,768	1,435	Sánkharis ...	422	371	
Kumhars ...	11,278	10,487	9,087	Santáls	3,002	1,663	4,879
Kurmis	3,222	4,515	2,061	Sonárs (*v.* Subarnabanik)	0	0	4,128
Laheri	274	81		Subarnabaniks ...	5,342	3,286	3,269
Máls	29,281	8,368	13,637	Sudras	31	6	
Mális	2,483	3,613	1,454	Sunris	16,411	13,039	10,724
Málos	7,386	7,598	5,050	Surahiyás (*v.* others)	0	390	
Mayarás	3,062	5,359	3,539	Sutradhars ...	10,070	12,071	8,023
Muchis (*v.* Chamárs)	0	10,076	(*v.* Chamárs)	Támbulis ...	1,172	732	
Musahars ...	0	1,091	1,594	Tántis	17,409	10,349	10,854
Nágars	0	2,463	2,534	Telis	39,189	20,730	19,823
Nápits	15,057	13,459	13,789	Tiyars	12,033	7,735	15,158
Nunias	0	80		Turis	472	17	
Oráons	6,131	2,499		Vaishnavas ...	21,464	25,034	18,381

The weak point about these figures is that there has been a want of uniformity in returning the population under the same "caste" headings at each census. For instance, *Halwais* are returned with *Mayaras* in 1872 and 1891; but in 1881 a return of 614 *Halwais* is given. Even with this, the number of *Mayaras* in 1881 is greater than in the other two years. Again, *Haris*, returned separately in 1872 and 1881, are massed with *Bhuinmalis* in 1891. The figures cannot therefore be accepted as of more than approximate value. The want of uniformity is reduced to absurdity in the case of the *Khandaits*. In 1872, 1,545 are given separately, and with them are included the *Ghatwáls;* in 1881 one solitary *Khandait* is recorded, while they reappear, to the number of 2,824, in 1891.

The Santals, of whom there are 12,508, live for the most part in the west and north-west, near Sagordighi. They are by nature, hunters and nomadic, but there is no scope for their energies, and they must settle down to agriculture and daily labour. Among many curious customs, "taboo" exists among them. This "taboo" prevents them from mentioning the names of certain relatives, under any circumstances. Bodding* describes the ingenious ways they have of avoiding the name of a relative, when it is the same as that of an outsider, whom they wish to mention. If it is absolutely necessary to use a name which is "taboo," the speaker must be careful to spit before speaking. If a "taboo" name is mentioned by accident, the speaker must spit at once, spitting being an unclean thing. It is thus admitted that a bad thing is going to be, or has been, done.

Another point which needs explanation is that some of the so-called "castes" are "castes" of occupation, and may therefore include Mahomedans. Thus, in the Census Report of 1891 we find Mahomedans returned by occupation :—

M. Jolhas	4,175	M. Kahars ...	1,733	M. Kalus ...	3,345

* "Jour. Asiatic Soc., Bengal," Part III., 1898, p. 2.

These *Jolhas* are mostly Mahomedans, working as weavers; very few Hindus being included, they are returned as *Tantis.* According to Dr. Wise, these *Jolhas* were Hindus, converted to the faith of Islam. This is no doubt true, as there are no "castes" among Mahomedans in the same sense as *caste* is understood among Hindus. In the Census Reports of 1872 and 1881 there is no distinction made between Hindu and Mahomedan *Kahârs.* In the Census Report for 1891 they are given separately. These Mahomedan Palki-bearers are more correctly called Dooli-walas, or Sawari-walas, and their number is said to be diminishing. The true *Kalu* "caste"-men are a "sub-caste" of *Telis,* and are Hindus. From habit, however, the title has been given to Mahomedan oil-pressers and oil-sellers in northern Bengal. The census of 1891 returns the Mahomedans by title:—

Pathans	...	...	...	10,404
Syuds	...	...	...	7,383
Shaikhs	...	...	...	568,048
		Total	...	585,835

This is not a very rational method, as a Pathan may be a Shaikh. The Pathans are, moreover, merely travellers, though some may reside permanently in the city of Murshidabad.

The Hindus of Bengal are not regardad as pure Aryans by their up-country brethren, and the majority are doubtless descended from aborigines. It is recorded that in the tenth century it was felt necessary to send priests of the pure school of Kanouj to rouse up the Hindus of Bengal, who were letting their religion become degenerate. This little handful of men, however, did little to improve the Brahmins, and these held supreme power over the minds of the masses. In the twelfth century, Ballab Sen reported that he could find only nineteen families of *Rarhi* Brahmins who were walking in the way of strict Hinduism. This ruler tried to shame the majority into reform, by reducing many of the backsliders to the lowest grades, as a punishment, and as an example. The order of Kulin Brahmins was established, and their "caste" was ordained the highest and purest. Even such acts as would be sinful in other men could not lower, or degrade them. As might be supposed, the result of such an institution has, in the main, been pernicious, since some of these men have profited by the protection it gave them to set the worst example of profligacy. Below the Brahmins of the *Rarh* there are in Bengal four others:—1, Vaidika; 2, Sapta-Sati; 3, Acharya (Jains); and 4, Agrodanis. The first three claim to be anterior to the reign of Ballab Sen, but the *Vaidika* alone preserve an honourable position, partly due to descent, and partly to merit. They do not give their daughters in marriage (often a mockery) to Kulins of Bikrampur, nor will they act at the various ceremonies for any Brahmin or Sudra, unless tracing origin from Kanouj.*

The Sapta-Sati are few in number, and are being absorbed by the *Srotriya.* As for the Acharya and Agrodanis, they are hardly classed as Brahmins. The Patel Brahmins, once the highest of the order, fell into evil ways, neglecting their duties, marrying into lower "septs," or even "castes." To these men, however, the conversion of many aboriginal tribes was due.

Education has already produced a somewhat levelling effect even among the Brahmins, and many of the sharp distinctions which marked one grade from another are fading away. Men are losing touch with much of the old-time ceremonial, but the Hindu religion still finds a stronghold in the women of the country. When once they give way, the "caste" system will be doomed.

Next to the Brahmins, in Hindu grades, come the *Vaishya* "caste," a small and isolated body, with whom the reformed Ballabi Vaidyas and Kayasthas will not eat. Following we find the Vaidya and Kayasthas, who separate themselves from the Sudras, though it is held by many of the latter that Ballab

* "Jour. Asiatic Soc., Bengal," 1893, Part III., p. 1.

Sen classed them with the *Nova-Sakka.* Their title of descent is not clear. Ballab Sen was himself a *Vaidya*, and the Brahminical thread was worn by a section of the "caste." The *Kayasthas* are a "caste" of great antiquity. Pure *Sudras* do not exist in this district, nor, indeed, in Bengal so far as I know, and are represented by *Varna-Sankaras*, mixed "castes" resulting from intermarriage of different grades.

Gardeners *(Mali)*; blacksmiths* *(Lohar)*; makers of bracelets from shells *(Sankhari)*; weavers *(Tanti, Jolha)*; potters *(Kumár)*; and braziers *(Kansari)*, claim descent from Visrakarma, the Architect of Heaven, and, as a class, the artizans *(Karus)* worship him as a deity. According to the legend, the *Sutrahara* "caste" refused to supply the Brahmins with wood for the sacrifices, and for this they were degraded. The *Chitrakara* brought a similar punishment on their own heads, through the exceeding badness of their work; while the *Sonars* or *Suvarnakara* were caught stealing gold given for the making of an idol. One quaint tradition tells that the *Sonars* sprang from bits of the trunk of Gonesha; another that Shiva made the first potter out of an old *Kulsi* (earthen water-pot).

A Sudra Brahmin will officiate at the ceremonies of the following castes :—

Sankhari	Kumár	Gop-Goala
Tanti	Malákár	Madhu-Napit
Kàmár	Nápit	Baroi

Outside this circle are :—Gandhabanik, Teli, Tambuli, Kansari.

Local custom sometimes varies the order of "caste," the most useful being placed above those of less value to the priestly class. These mixed *Sudra* "castes" have five servants, who attend all family ceremonies :—*Brahman, Máldkár, Dhoba, Napit*, and *Nata.* These five will also serve other "castes" except the very lowest :—*Bhuinmali, Chamàr, Patni*, and *Sunri.* Even here there are curious distinctions, for while the *Nàpit* will shave a *Sáhá*, he will not cut and trim his nails. As in all human communities, time brings changes and schisms. Thus, from the *Chandals* have sprung no less than eight "sub-castes," the same Brahmins acting for all; only the *Kaibarthas* must maintain a priest of their own. There is a border-land between the *Sudras* and the lowest "castes," called *Nicha.* Such are :—

Basti	Kandhu	Lohait Kori
Baqqal	Kapáli	Nar
Bhat	Karni	Parasara Das
Berna	Kanal	Pátial
Halwah Das	Kawnli	Sutar

Most of these are only local varieties, and many of them, though enumerated by the late Dr. Wise, are unknown in this district. Of these *Nicha* "castes" there are two sub-divisions :—

1. Antya-ja—Inferior.	*Nata*—Mimic, Actor.	*Bhilla*— ————
Dhoba—Washerman.	*Manjhi*—Fisherman, Boatman.	*Meda*—Midwife.
Chamar—Currier.	*Varnda*—Cane-splitter.	

2. Antyarasayim—Dwellers outside the town, out-castes :—

Mehter Dom Dosadh Pan Hari	Sweepers, buriers of the dead, etc.

* "Karnakars" are brass or silversmiths, or workers in any metal.

Certain "castes" have their degradation marked by exclusion from the temple of Jagannath at Puri. Such are :—

Sunri	Kahar	Tiyar
Nama-Sudra	Rajbansi	Bhuinmali
Dhoba	Chamár	Hari
Jogi	Dom	

Change of residence may affect "caste." Thus, the *Kahars*, *Ahirs*, and *Kandhus*, resident in Bengal, are repudiated by their up-country "caste"-fellows. They marry into other grades, and become thereby *Khonta*, or debased. The laws of "caste" are in many cases very intricate, and without meaning to a European. Two of the lowest "castes" despised by all are the *Chamárs* and *Rishis*. Yet there are strict differences between them, though it would seem impossible for such to exist. A trade practised in one district may bring disgrace if followed, by the same man, elsewhere. One of the strangest sects of the Hindus is the *Panch Piriya*, concerning which I have not been able to gather any reliable information.

TABLE OF DATES OF FEASTS AND PUJAS DURING THE YEAR 1900.

Dates.	January.	February.	March.	April.	May.	June.	July.	August.	September.	October.	November.	December.
1st										Durga Puja (28)	Jagadhatri Puja (34)	
2nd					Akhaytratia (8)				Radha Astami (23)	Ditto		
3rd						Jamai Sasti (13)				Ditto		
4th		Sripanchami Sarashati Puja (2)								Bejaya (29)		
5th					Janavi Saptami (9)						Rash Jatra (35)	
6th				Basanti and Anana Puja (5)								
7th				Ditto		Ganga Puja (14)	Ulta Rath (17)	Julan (18)				
8th				Ditto	Sita Nabami (10)			Ditto	Ananta Brota (24)	Lukshmi Puja (30)		
9th				Sriramnabami (6)				Ditto				
10th								Ditto				
11th								Rakhi Purnima (19)				
12th				Chaitra Sankaranti (7)								
13th	Uttaravan Sankaranti (1)					Snan Jatra (15)						
14th					Full Dol (11)							
15th											Kartic Puja (36)	
16th			Dol Jatra (Hooli) (4)					Manasa Puja (20)	Jetastami (25)			
17th								Jamastomi (21)	Bodhan Nabami (26)			
18th								NandaUtsab (22)				
19th												
20th												
21st												
22nd										Kali Puja (31)		
23rd									Mahalaya (27)			
24th												
25th										Vhratriditia (32)		
26th												
27th		Shivaratri (3)			Sabitribrata (12)							
28th												
29th						Rath Jatra (16)						
30th												
31st										Gosta Astami (33)		

(1) *Uttarayan Sankaranti.* The day from which the sun's progress to the north of the Equator begins. The beginning of the Summer Solstice. The last day of the month of Pous.

(2) *Sripanchami Sarashati Puja.* The fifth day of the moon's increase, on which the goddess Saraswati, the goddess of learning, is worshipped.

(3) *Shivaratri.* The fourteenth night of moon, on which Shiva is worshipped.

(4) *Dol Jatra (Hooli).* Festival during which Krishna is placed in a swinging cot, and is worshipped with red powder. This festival followed the killing of Metrashur (monster with form of a ship).

(5) *Basanti Puja.* The worship of Durga in the Spring.

(6) *Sriramnabami.* The birthday of Ram, one of the incarnations of Vishnu.

(7) *Chaitra Sankaranti.* The last day of the Bengali year, in the month of Choitra. Shiva is worshipped; water and *pindas* are also dedicated to deceased ancestors.

(8) *Akhaytratia.* The third day of the moon's increase. The beginning of the golden age (Satya Juga). Offerings of rice, water, and other things; men gain eternal virtue.

(9) *Janavi Saptami.* The seventh day of the moon's increase in the month of Baisakh, Ganga is worshipped.

(10) *Sita Nabami.* The birthday of Sita, the wife of Ram.

(11) *Full Dol.* Full moon of Baisakh. The god Krishna is worshipped.

(12) *Sabitribrata.* A religious observance, in memory of Sabitri, the model lady of ancient India, whose devotion to her husband saved his life from the hands of Jam (the god of death). On this day husbands are worshipped by their wives.

(13) *Jamai Sasti.* The day of the moon's increase, in the month of Jaista, on which sons-in-law are honoured.

(14) *Ganga Puja.* The worship of Ganga (rivers Bhagirathi and Ganges).

(15) *Snan Jatra.* The bathing festival of Jagannath, a manifestation of Vishnu, or Krishna.

(16) *Rath Jatra.* The car festival of Jagannath, during which Jagannath goes in a car from his temple to a garden house.

(17) *Ulta Rath.* Jagannath returns by car to his temple.

(18) *Julan.* A festival in the month of Shraban, from the eleventh day of the moon's increase to full moon. On these days Krishna is worshipped.

(19) *Rakhi Purnima.* The last day of Julan on the full-moon day, on which a twist of thread, with a small packet containing a few carminative seeds is bound round the wrist, for blessings throughout the year.

(20) *Manasa Puja.* The worship of Manasa, the goddess of the serpent race.

(21) *Jamastomi.* The birthday of Krishna.

(22) *Nanda Utsab.* The birthday festival of Krishna, which took place in the house of Nanda, the foster-father of Krishna.

(23) *Radha Astami.* The birthday of Radha, beloved companion of Krishna.

(24) *Ananta Brota.* A religious observance in which Indra is worshipped.

(25) *Jetastami.* The eighth day of the moon, in the month of Aswin. King Jemut Bahan, son of King Sali Bahan the Great, is worshipped by women, for the blessing of good fortune and sons.

(26) *Bodhan Nabami.* The ninth day of the moon, in the month of Aswin, on which Durga is invoked.

(27) *Mahalaya.* The day of new moon, in the month of Aswin, on which cakes (Pindas) are offered to ancestors.

(28) *Durga Puja.* The goddess Durga, wife of Shiva, representing the universal energy, and the mother of the universe is worshipped. She was also worshipped in Spring as Basanti, but this Puja is observed, as Ram Chandra worshipped her in Autumn for killing his enemy Ravana.

(29) *Bejaya.* The day on which Ram Chandra gained a victory by killing Ravana.

(30) *Lukshmi Puja.* Lukshmi, the goddess of wealth, is worshipped.

(31) *Kali Puja.* One of the manifestations of Durga is worshipped. The day after this "Puja" (*lit.* praying, religious festival) children receive presents, generally small clay figures. In this district the figures are but poorly fashioned. In Nadia the Bhashans (sculptors, modellers) turn out very high-class work. The second day of the new moon is the day on which sisters show their love for their brothers. The girls paint their brothers on the forehead, and in return for this cheap attention expect presents of money or clothing. The night of the Kali Puja is known in some localities as "the green-insect-killing night"—insects which usher in cooler weather.

(32) *Bhatriditia.* The second day of the moon's increase, on which brothers are honoured by their sisters.

(33) *Gosta Astami.* The eighth day of the moon's increase, in the month of Kartic, on which Krishna became cowherd, before which he was a calf-herd. Cows are worshipped on that day.

(34) *Jagadhatri.* Durga, or the mother of the universe, is worshipped. Jagadhatri is Durga in another shape.

(35) *Rash Jatra.* A festival in memory of Krishna's dance with the milkmaids.

(36) *Kartic Puja.* On the last day of the month of Kartic, the god Kartic, the son of Durga, and Commander-in-Chief of the gods, is worshipped.

JAINS.

The Jains of the district are a fairly large community, and, according to the latest census, live mainly in Jiaganj and Azimganj, where they carry on a lucrative trade as grain and produce merchants, with which they combine money-lending. They are a dissenting sect of Hindus, having, however, the same distinctions of "caste." Although the "castes" do not intermingle, a high "caste" man may marry a woman of pure stock even if she be of a lower "caste." Plurality of wives is allowed; *suttee* is forbidden, and the widows of *Sudras* may marry again. Jains, or Arhatas, as they were originally called, regard life as sacred, and will not, knowingly, kill any living thing. They sweep the place on which they are going to sit, and sometimes even the ground on which they walk. They prefer to eat by daylight, lest eating at night they should swallow an insect. The Azimganj Jains lease the fishing of the Bhagirathi opposite the town to prevent destruction of the fish. No Jain may touch animal food, or drink alcohol in any form. Like Hindus generally, they burn their dead, and acknowledge the members of the Hindu Pantheon. Jains give, however, the highest respect and worship not to these gods, but to holy men, or saints, who have in their belief been raised above the gods. In this they somewhat resemble the *Sangatas*, followers of Buddha, but they deny Buddha, and do not consider themselves in any way connected with Buddhism. Differing thus from Hindus, they diverge further by denying the authority of the *Vedas* and many of the *Puranas*. Their chief authority is the *Yoga*,

Their gods, "the spirits of perfect men," are called *Jineswara, Arhat, or Sidd'ha,* but apart from these collective titles, each has a proper name.

Their beliefs include the eternity of matter, and transmigration of the soul. As a rule, the Jains are peaceful and industrious, taking kindly to education. The founder of the Jain community in the district was Jaggat Seth.*

There are four orders of priests, as with Hindus:—

1. Brahmachári—student.
2. Grihasti'ha—householder.
3. Vanaparasta—hermit.
4. Bhiashuce—mendicant.

They strain water through a cloth before drinking. They believe only what is evident to the senses.

MAHOMEDANS.

The Mahomedans form about 45 *per cent.* of the population of the district. Slavery was part of the Mahomedan rule, and existed through all the years they were in possession of Bengal. To it the Hindus submitted, even though it meant banishment for slaves, and sometimes eunuchs were sent to the Delhi Court from Bengal.

Murshid Kuli Khan, when Nawab Nazim, is said to have enacted a law which provided that any Amal or Zemindar failing to pay revenue should, with his wife and family, become Mahomedans. Acceptance of the faith also protected Hindus against punishment for murder or adultery (Bernier, vol. i., p. 144). With the advent of English rule these tyrannies disappeared, but a great number of Hindus accepted the faith of Islam for its own attractions, and thus it comes about that a very large number of the Mahomedans of Bengal are the descendants of converted Hindus.† There can be little doubt that this is the case with the tradesmen and shopkeepers, since a well-bred Mahomedan will not engage in trade unless obliged. Even the author of "The Mussulmans of Bengal," who objects strongly to the "conversion" theory, remarks concerning the "lower orders":—"These classes, speaking roughly, consist of two bands of men; those descended from foreign ancestors, and those descended from indigenous races and tribes who have embraced Islam. Among the crafts tailoring is distinctly a favourite with Mussulmans." Again the same writer, p. 109, says:—"Mussulman traders and shopkeepers found in any part of Hindustan are mostly descended from Hindu ancestors belonging to the trading classes who, even after their conversion to the Mahomedan faith, have adhered to their ancestral profession, and also have bred up their children in the same profession."

Until the beginning of the nineteenth century the only great divisions of Mahomedans were those of *Sunni* and *Shiah.* The latter included the rulers of Murshidabad, but they have decreased in power and numbers, while the *Sunnis* have, on the whole, increased. At present there may be said to be the following sects of Sunni Mahomedans:—

1. *Sabiqi-Sunnis* of the lower orders, holding a debased and Hinduised form of religion. This is the oldest and, in some parts, most numerous sect.

2. *Ferazi,* found mostly in the Jangipur Sub-division. A most uncompromising and stern sect of Sunnis, who refuse to pray standing behind a *Sabiqi* or a *Táaiyani,* and will not eat or drink with them. The sect was founded by Sharia'tullah and Dudhu Miyan, his son, and they consider themselves to be the only followers of the *Fraz,* or divine command. Their numbers are not very great.

* Those who wish to go further into the question of Jain beliefs may refer to "The Asiatic Researches," Vol. lx. pp. 214-232.

† Compare this with the argument in "The Mussulmans of Bengal," by Khondkar Fuzli Rubbee, Bib. (40).

3. *Táaiyani*:—Followers of the Patna School of Mulavi Karamat, cultivators, thatchers, and hide merchants.

4. *Rafi-yadain*:—So called from the custom of touching the ears with the hands each time that the words "*Allah Akbar*" are pronounced. They fold the arms over the chest while praying, not over the navel as is the custom with other sects. A large sect, almost equal in numbers to the Sabiqi.

The Mahomedan religion has lost much of its purity in India, and is debased by the introduction of rites belonging to the conquered races among whom the Mussulmans settled. We have noticed the intolerance of Nawab Murshid Kuli Khan, but, on the whole, other religions were treated with great forbearance.

Sunnis in Bengal, moreover, fast, and carry out the ceremonies for mourning the so-called martyrdom of Hassan and Husain,* although the rites belong to the Shiahs and are forbidden by learned Sunnis. All vie with one another in the manufacture of *tazzias*. The Id-ul-fitr, at the end of Ramzan, and the Id-ul Qurban, or Baqr-id, are religiously observed by Shiahs and Sunnis alike. One feature of the Id-ul-fitr, at the palace of the Nawab Bahadur, is the sacrifice of a camel. Portions of the flesh are always sent to the friends of His Highness. I have eaten the meat one or twice, and consider it coarse and inferior to second-rate beef. Another religious festival, the *Barah-Wafat*, the anniversary of the death of Mahomed, is observed by the Sunnis on the 12th day of *Rabia-ul-awal*. At one time, in Akbar's Court, the day was observed as the "Moulid" or birthday of the Prophet. This, however, is only a matter of choice, since Mahomed was born and died on the same date. The Bengali Mahomedan shows a respect for *Pirs*, saints or holy men, not found anywhere outside India, and his offerings are not infrequently made on a tree, side by side with those to the resident Hindu deity. As a rule, however, each saint has his *Durgah*, or shrine, one of the most venerated by Murshidabad Mahomedans is that of Fakir Shah Farud Shukr Gunge, at Munganapara, about two miles from the battle-field of Plassy, and in the enclosure of this Durgah lies the body of Suraj-ud-Dowlah's Commander-in-Chief, Mir Muddun. Another revered spot is the Shrine of the "Apostles of Islam."

In the *Musnad-i-auliya* or shrine of the "Apostles of Islam," at Chunakhali, there is an inscription in the *Tughra* character, which is of historical value, as it fixes the extent of the reign of the Emperor Saifu'd-din Abu'l-muzaffer Firuz Shah (II.). The parts of the inscription which may be usefully quoted are:—"This mosque was erected in the reign of Saifu'd dunyau'd-din Abu'l-muzaffer Firuz Shah . . . by his grand vizier. . . . This engraving was done on the 2nd Mohurram, 896, Hijra?" (Sunday, November 15th, 1490, A.D.O.S.)†

Three kinds of *Pirs* are venerated:—

1. Pir tariqat *(fashion)*.
2. Pir haqiqat *(time)*.
3. Pir marifat *(learned)*.

whose virtues differ somewhat. Outside the worship of *Pirs*, who may have been holy men, there has now crept into the Mahomedan religion the worship of certain, apparently, quite legendary beings.

Of these, Khwajah Khizr, in whose honour the annual *Berà* festival is held, is a very mysterious

* In these parts two biers are carried in the procession, in the belief that Hassan and Husain died the same day. In Persia, and parts of Northern India, only one bier is carried, and this is as it should be, for Husain, who was killed at Karbulláh, 10th of Mohurram, in A.H. 61 (A.D. 680). Hassan had then been dead ten years. He was poisoned at Medina, 28th Cafar (A.D. 670).

† Beveridge, "Proc. Asiatic Soc., Bengal," Feb., 1893, p. 55.

person, who has been identified as Elijah, and Kaikobad, or Alexander the Great. At the present time the Pir is supposed to dwell in the rivers and seas, protecting people against drowning and shipwreck.

In times of sickness and in times of joy and success, vows and offerings are made to Kwajah Khizr; but his great day is that of the *Berá*. This festival is held on the night of the last Thursday of the Hindu month, Bhadar (August and September), which is supposed to mark the end of the "rains"—Hindus join in the festival, and every one who can raise even a few *pice* purchases a little paper boat to float down the Bhagirathi river on a raft of plantain stems bearing a small oil lamp. Although with less splendour than in the days of his ancestors, the Nawab Bahadur of Murshidabad keeps up the festival, generally making it an occasion for inviting his European friends to dinner. The raft is about forty feet in length. Entirely of plantain stems, it is made to look something like a *house-boat*, and is one mass of little, twinkling lights. As the raft passes the Murshidabad palace there is a grand display of fireworks. The display over, the men on the raft get away in boats, leaving the half-lighted and smoking skeleton to fade away into the darkness among its less ambitious sisters. Dr. James Wise states (22, p. 390) that the festival was first kept at Murshidabad by Suraj-u-Dowlah.

Zindah Ghazi, *Ghazi Miyan* or *Sat Pir*, is supposed to protect travellers and wood-cutters from tigers and crocodiles. Before entering a jungle, or narrow stream, Mahomedans, and Hindus, pile up little mounds of earth, and lay rice, plantains, and sweetmeats on them. This done, they go fearlessly on their way.

Pir Badr is, no doubt, Badruddin or Badr-i-Alam, who died at Chittagong, A.H. 844 (A.D. 1440?). He lightens the labours of Kwajah Khizr by protecting sailors and fishermen who pray to him when starting on a journey, or when overtaken by bad weather. Whether Ghazi Miyan is a separate person, or the same as Zindah Ghazi, it is impossible to say, but anyway, his "shadi" is not kept in this district, though here and there a shrine in his name may be found.

Panch Pir, worshipped and invoked whenever danger threatens, and by Mahomedan boatmen when setting sail. The collection of five saints is equally revered and worshipped by some Hindus. Indeed, the Panch Piriya sect of Hindus is divided into two sections, that neither eat together, nor intermarry (*v.* Wise, 22). The invocation of the Panch Pir is always accompanied with the sacrifice of a cock. Who these five saints were is not known.

The next Pir in Dr. Wise's list shows an extraordinary catholicity of choice, and it is difficult to understand the position of Sheikh Sadu, or *Miran Ji*, unless we regard him as the "horrid example." He is reported to have led a life of continual debauch, assisted by the genii of a magic lamp. He was finally destroyed by these servants of wickedness. He is worshipped by prostitutes, and by Hindus and Mahomedans who wish to see into the future. Thursday, generally regarded as unlucky by Hindus, is the day set apart for the worship of Miran Ji.

Earnest Mahomedans, seeing that their religion was degenerating, made strenuous efforts to improve the people. This movement of reform began with the nineteenth century. The earliest of the reformers was one Haji Sharia'tullah, a man of humble origin, born in the Faridpur Zillah. At the age of eighteen he made a pilgrimage to Mecca, where he remained for about twenty years as a disciple of the Wahabi teachers. In 1820 he returned to India, and, passing from village to village, preached the new doctrine. He taught that Friday prayer, observance of the Ids, and the Mohurram were opposed to the true Faith of the Prophet. Strange to say, these sweeping reforms did not excite much opposition, but when he taught that it was a sin, and one learned from the Hindus, to allow the midwife to cut the umbilical cord when it was the duty of the father, his views caused the greatest excitement, and many of his followers forsook him. Nothing daunted, Sharia'tullah continued his teaching with marked success, especially among the lower orders, by whom he was regarded with veneration. He was a man of blameless life, and very careful in avoiding strife. The influence obtained by the son, Mahomed Mushin or Dudhu Miyan, was even greater than that of the father. After a pilgrimage to Mecca, Dudhu Miyan devoted himself to carrying on the work begun by Sharia'tullah, but he was of a fierce and stern nature and a typical socialist. He preached the equality of mankind; earning thereby many enemies among the landlord class. He formed the people into a society, appointing Khalifahs to the various circles in Bengal. When he could not convert by persuasion he resorted to force and torture, and soon became hated and feared by the Hindus. It is related that, failing to convert certain ryots he tied their beards together and forced them to use chilli powder as snuff. Still, among cultivators and artizans he had a large following! Not content with opposing illegal cesses levied by landlords, he taught that the earth belonged to God alone, and that no one had any right to levy taxes on it. Many excesses and lawless acts were committed by Dudhu Miyan and his followers, and in 1838 he was charged with plundering houses. In 1841 he was tried on a charge of murder, but acquitted. In 1844 he was again tried, this time for trespass and illegal assembly; in 1846, for abduction and plunder, when, together with a large band of followers, he attacked a factory at Faridpur, belonging to Mr. Dunlop. Convicted by the Sessions Judge, he got off on appeal to the Sudder Adalut. Dudhu Miyan would no doubt have been a great instigator of lawlessness and rebellion during the mutiny, had he not been confined in jail. After a stormy life, Dudhu Miyan died in 1860, leaving behind him the sect known as the Ferazis. So far as Murshidabad is concerned, this sect is mainly confined to the Jangipur Sub-division. Their opposition to vaccination was overcome with difficulty. This district, as a whole, was hardly affected by the new doctrines of Sharia'tullah or Dudhu Miyan and subsequent reformers. This is no doubt partly due to the presence and influence of the Shiah Nawabs.

The classification of Mahomedans, given above, requires some modification, as it is not recognised in this district. Dr. Wise, however, was a careful inquirer and observer, but he may have been referring mainly to the people living near Dacca. It appears that the chief sects among the Sunnis in Murshidabad are the Hanafis. The number of Ferazis in the district is not very great. There are some in the neighbourhood of Jangipur, and some dwell in the *Baguri*, on the east bank of the Bhagirathi. Ferazis, Hadaitis, Ali Hadis, Rafiyadainis, and Wahabis are in the main merely different names for the same thing. There is no important distinction to mark any of them as a sect apart from the rest. The Shiahs who, as I have said, live in the city of Murshidabad are neither increasing nor decreasing in numbers.* A Mahomedan gentleman gives the chief sects of the Sunnis as:—

1. Hanafis.
2. Shafais.
3. Maliki.
4. Hambali.†

The four names mentioned as taken from Dr. Wise's essay:—Sabiqi, Farazi, Táaiyani, and Rafiyadain—are considered to be merely offshoots of the Wahábis that first of all arose out of the Hambali sect of the Sunnis. These offshoots have many other names besides the four mentioned:—Ismailia, Gair Mukalledin, etc. In this district the Ferazis are generally cultivators. The Rafiyadainis are spreading, but their number is small. Their chief leader is Moulvi Ibrahim. The Ferazis are said to be peaceful and intensely religious men. The Táaiyani and Rafiyadainis, on the other hand, are more pushing and, at times, inclined to be turbulent. The Sabiqi belong to

* Private letter from Khondkar Fuzli Rubbee Khan Bahadur.

† Moulvi A. Burr, in a private letter.

the Mahomedan stock of the early conquerors. It is evident therefore that there are many local differences as to the naming and position of the various sects of Mahomedans.

Leaving out, then, the numerous minor sects, the two main divisions among Mussulmans are Shiahs and Sunnis. The Shiahs are probably more in evidence in this district than in any other part of Bengal, since the Nawab, his relations and followers belong to that sect. About 5,000 would represent the total of Shiahs in the district, and nearly all of them live in the city of Murshidabad. The Shiahs are followers of Ali, cousin of Mahomed, and son-in-law, through marriage with Fatima. They maintain that Ali was the true Khalifah, or successor of the Prophet. By the Sunnis they are called "Rafezi" or "forsakers of the truth," while the Shiahs as strongly insist on their orthodoxy and call themselves *Al-Numinun*, or "true believers" (as do also the Sunnis).* This division into Shiahs and Sunnis existed even before the Prophet's death—after his death, the Shiahs claimed Ali as next of kin and divine successor, quoting in support of their argument the 118th verse of the 2nd chapter of the Koran.†

MAHOMEDAN FASTS AND FESTIVALS.

Ramzan, the ninth month of the Moslim year, is a month of fasting, observed by all, from sunrise to sunset. Abstinence is supposed to purge the soul of sin and, further, to all, who in life have strictly observed the fast, all sins will be forgiven. The sick and all travellers may be exempted, but they are ordered in the Koran to set aside the same number of days for fasting at some other period. The fast begins on the day after the new moon becomes visible; but if the sky is cloudy the fast must begin on the day which would have been thirty days from the first of the previous month. Besides the sick and travellers, the aged, the infirm, and pregnant women may be exempted from fasting; also a woman still suckling her child. Children below the age of puberty need not fast. Kept to the letter, this fast is a great tax on the strength, since to be complete not even a drop of water must be taken. This is the greatest of hardships when the Ramzan (a movable fast) falls in the hottest season. In addition to fasting, the true believer must increase the number of his prayers, twenty forms following the usual night prayer. This extra religious office is called the Tarawah or "rests," since the worshippers may sit and rest after every four forms. Many of the strictest Mahomedans go into retreat during the Ramzan, which closely corresponds with the Lent of Christian churches. The most important night of the Ramzan is the night of power, Lailatu'l-Qadr. This is generally held to be the 27th of the month, but differences of opinion allow a choice between the 21st, 23rd, 25th, 27th, and 29th. After sunset the fast ceases, and eating, drinking, and amusements may be indulged in until sunrise. Only those who have kept this fast can enter the door of Paradise called *Raiyan* and particularly reserved for those who keep the Ramzan. There is a hard condition attached to the Ramzan, which must spoil the chances of many who thus seek forgiveness for sin; if any man tells lies during the Ramzan, its efficacy is not for him and, as Mahomed is reported to have said, he gains nothing, by fasting, but thirst.

Shub-i-Barat, the night of the 15th day of Shaban (3rd December, 1900) is marked by increased prayers, for then God is supposed to balance each man's accounts according to his works during the year. The day following is ordered as a fast; but, more often, is a day of feasting, with displays of fireworks.

The *Idu'l-azha or Id-i-zuha* is a festival kept on the 10th of Jelhizza (11th April, 1900). It is the "feast of sacrifice," and is very commonly and, perhaps in these parts, best known as the Baqra-id

* An excellent example of the witty definition:—"Orthodoxy is my doxy; heterodoxy is your doxy."

† Hughes (18).

or "cow festival." It takes its origin from the Jewish day of atonement, on which the Prophet instituted a fast in honour of Moses, changed into a feast, with the sacrifice of animals. Although not distinctly stated in the Koran, Mahomedans generally believe that this sacrifice typifies the sacrifice of Ishmael* by Abraham, in which the angel Gabriel stayed the father's hand and substituted a ram for the human victim. The animals to be offered were goats, cows, or camels.† The animal must be healthy and without blemish, neither blind nor lame. Further, to distinguish this feast from the Idu'l-Fitr, it is also called the Idu'l-Kabir, or great festival. The flesh of the animals, killed as sacrifice, is to be divided into three portions; one for the family, a second for relatives and friends, and a third for the poor.

Idu'l-Fitr.—Following immediately on the Ramzan comes the Idu'l-Fitr or Idu'l Saghir (minor festival). This feast, on the 1st of Showal (2nd February, 1900), marks the end of the long month of fasting, and is a day of rejoicing and alms-giving. On the morning of the last day of the Ramzan all Mahomedans must give alms according to their powers. On the Idu'l-Fitr they must attend the common meeting for prayer in spotless clothing, which is generally new for the occasion. Friends embrace and greet one another, and servants generally receive a small present, of money or clothes, from their masters. The day is marked by excessive eating and drinking, visits are paid to the tombs of ancestors; even the women, in their enforced seclusion, display all their best dresses and jewels, and when possible visit their friends.

The *Mohurram*, (1st May, 1900,) is the first month of the Mahomedan year, and the first ten days of the month are devoted to ceremonies in remembrance of the martyrdom of Husain, second son of Ali and Fatima. In this district the death of Hassan is also mourned at the same time, although it occurred ten years earlier. The festival of the Mohurram is naturally more respected by the Shiahs than by the Sunnis, and, while the former keep the whole period of ten days mourning, the Sunnis regard the tenth day only as sacred, and that only as the anniversary of the creation of the world. Disbelieving in Ali as the first Kalifah, the Sunnis would not be likely to mourn the death of his son. Some days before the Mohurram small bamboo and mat huts are erected by the wayside and near the entrance of the palace gates in Murshidabad. In these are placed jars filled with water, that none may suffer from thirst as did the martyr Husain. Many of the Shiah mosques are draped with black, and *tazzias* are carried in procession through the streets. This mourning gives rise to great excitement and strong feeling among its votaries, and has, unfortunately, led to race quarrels and bloodshed. The mourners, as they go along, wail and cry for the dead martyrs and curse their persecutors. The tenth day is called the "Roz-i-Qatl," and on this day the *tazzias* are carried in procession, with deafening noise of voices and instruments, to a mosque at Amaniganj, about two miles from Murshidabad city. Elephants and horses, all in their finest trappings, accompany the procession. At the Amaniganj mosque prayers are read and the *tazzias* are then thrown into the river.

Akhir-i-Chahar-i-Shambah, the last Wednesday in the month Safar (Wednesday, June 27th, 1900), is the anniversary of the day on which Mahomed's last illness abated somewhat, so that he was able to bathe. On this day those who observe it write on paper seven verses of the Koran which contain the word *Salám*, peace. The ink is then washed off and the inky water swallowed. This same ceremony is also observed in times of sickness and as a charm against evil. This day is not observed as a fast by the Ferazis and sterner sects of Islam.

Ashura, or the tenth day of the month Mohurram, is observed by Sunnis as a fast, being the day on which God created "Adam and Eve, heaven and hell," "the tablet of decree," and "the pen of life and death

* As the story is told it was Ishmael and not Isaac who was to be sacrificed.

† Camels are sacrificed only by rich people.

Nau Roz, New Year's day, is observed as a festival, more especially by Shiahs. The day itself and the following days of the first week of the Mohurram are, as stated, days of mourning with Shiahs. The date is fixed as the first day after the vernal Equinox.

The anniversary of the birth of the Prophet, or *Maulid u'n-Nabi*, is kept on the 12th day of *Rabi'u l-Awwal* (10th July, 1900), but its observance is not universal. *Zikers*, prayers, are recited, and alms given to the poor.

Lailatu'z-raghail is a festival kept on the first Friday in the month Rajab (26th October, 1900). It is the "night of supererogatory devotions." It is not observed by the Sunnis, who deny that it was founded by the Prophet. By far the greater number of Mussulmans in this district are Sunnis, who differ from the Shiahs, as we have seen, on the question of the Kalifah, holding that Abu Bakr and not Ali was the real successor of Mahomed.

CUSTOMS.

Circumcision.—This is so marked and integral a rite among Mussulmans that one would expect to find it laid down as a sacrament in the Koran. This is, however, not the case, and circumcision rests on tradition and the order of the Prophet, taking Abraham as his example. In the beginning, the operation was delayed until full growth was attained, and, as an adult was ashamed to uncover before others he was supposed to circumcise himself. The circumcision of women is not practised in this part of the world, though it is said to take place among certain Arabs. The Jewish rite is performed on the 7th day after the child's birth, but though this is the lawful time among Mussulmans, many postpone the operation until the boy is seven or even twelve years old. Circumcision of adults is rare, except in the case of converts, who may be exempted if they wish, though such avoidance of the rite is regarded with great disfavour. The operation is generally performed by the barber, though it is not at all uncommon in these days to find children sent to a hospital or dispensary for circumcision. The operation, as performed by the barber, has long passed from what we may call the "Sharp Stone Age." The skin is grasped in a primitive forceps of bamboo, and held obliquely while the redundant skin is swept off with one stroke of a razor. Bleeding is arrested with burnt rags. Though a simple operation, the wound often takes a long time to heal, from want of cleanliness in "dressing." There is a belief among certain Mahomedans that Mahomed and seventeen of the Kalifahs were born already circumcised, a belief we cannot unfortunately accept, though, were it true, it would go far to settle the question of "hereditary transmission of acquired physical characteristics."

Food.—Although "caste," as found among the Hindus, does not exist among Mussulmans, the tenets of Islam follow the Jewish law as to clean and unclean animals, and also as to the method of killing animals destined for food. A "true believer" may not eat the pig, which is, above all, an abomination to a follower of Mahomed, and all who know the scavenging habits of the pig in the east are in no way surprised that this should be so. All birds and beasts of prey are unclean and may not be eaten; and also all things living in the water, except true fish. Curiously enough, the elephant and the pelican are included among the unclean, and all insects, including spiders and many crawling things outside the true "Insecta." Though the bee is unclean, honey may be eaten. Certain animals are *mubah*, or indifferent. The hare is one of these. It is forbidden to eat anything dying from disease or killed in any other way than by *Zabah*, or cutting the throat so that blood may escape. The killer, or butcher, may be a Jew or even a Christian, man or a woman; but not a Hindu, idolater or polytheist. To include the sportman's "bag" Sunnis recognise two forms *zabah*:—(1), *Iktiyari*, or that which is made *hálál*, or lawful by deliberate choice, and (2), *Istirari*, as when the animal has been shot by a bullet or arrow. In true *hálál*, or lawful food, the throat is cut and the prayer "God is most great" recited. In *Istirari* the prayer alone may be sufficient, but a Mahomedan will also cut the animal's throat if life is not quite extinct. It is further requisite in theory to divide the windpipe, gullet, and the jugular veins and carotid arteries. To the Shiah there is only one *zabah*, the true hálál. From among the *insects* the locust was excepted and made lawful.

TEMPLES, MOSQUES, CHURCHES, AND MISSIONS.

THE Berhampur branch of the London Missionary Society was founded in 1824, when Mr. Micaiah Hill was sent from Calcutta. Mr. and Mrs. Hill opened seven schools for Hindus, and two for Mahomedan boys. One was started by Mrs. Hill for girls. After three years' work six boys' schools remained, with 280 pupils, and Mrs. Hill opened, in 1827, a second girls' school, the two having forty pupils. Mr. Hill had opened three native chapels and three preaching stations. For some part of 1827 Mr. and Mrs. Hill were assisted by Mr. Gogerly. January 7th, 1829, saw a large new chapel completed. In 1832 Mr. T. Paterson was sent to help, and with an assistant, Thomas Cussons, worked in Murshidabad. In 1837 Mr. Hill reports on his early difficulties:—

(a) No missionary could leave Calcutta without a Government licence.

(b) The natives were unfriendly, and made reports to the civil and military officers.

He complained also of want of sympathy among the Europeans. Their land had to be fought for in the Courts, and numerous Petitions, even to the Governor-General, were presented against him. His services and preachings were frequently interfered with by hooting and cries of "Hari bol," and he was even threatened with assault. By 1837 his position had so much improved that he was able to report progress and sympathy. Hill founded an Asylum for orphans upon ground given by David Dale, C.S.; Pringle, Dale's successor, and other Europeans, subscribed.

To provide funds for a church, in 1838, Mr. Hill planted mulberry extensively, and kept silkworms, which were tended by the orphans. In 1838 Mr. Hill left, and Mr. Lessel took his place. Hill returned in 1842, and the two worked together until 1847, when Hill was transferred to Calcutta. In 1849 James Bradbury came to Berhampur; in 1853 S. J. Hill, a son of Micaiah, came to the scene of his father's labours. Nothing of note occurred until 1880, when a mission-boat was built, enabling the missionaries to travel over a great part of the district. Preaching, teaching, the distribution of tracts, and the sale of the Scriptures, were carried on zealously. From 1879 to 1883 the orphanage was managed by Mrs. Phillips, who made some efforts to visit zenanas. Miss Bloomfield arrived in 1883, and the work among women was further developed. She was shortly after joined by Miss Robinson. The schools have prospered, and the congregation, though small, remains steady. Between 1890 and 1895 the Mission in Murshidabad district was much strengthened by the addition to the staff of the Revs. A. Sims and T. A. Joyce, Miss Tuck, Miss Cockerton, and Miss Nicholas, M.D. There were also three native pastors: K. P. Mukerji, of Berhampur; Paul Biswas, at Jiaganj; and S. C. Ghose at Murshidabad. In 1896 the Berhampur orphanage was a thing of the past. A Christian community of sixteen households live on the "magazine" land, low, damp, and with bad drinking water; nearly all the children have large spleens; the numbers are decreasing.

The Austin Friars are said to have worked in Kasimbazar for a time in 1690.

Early in the nineteenth century Dr. Carey, from Serampur, had established a branch of the Baptist Mission in Murshidabad city, and they worked there and in Berhampur until 1822, when they were withdrawn, owing, probably, to want of encouragement.

L. M. S. Ministers in the District.

1824.	March 8th, Rev. M. and Mrs. Hill transferred to Calcutta		1847.	
1826.	Rev. G. Gogerly " "		1827.	
1832.	Rev. J. Paterson " "		1850.	
1834.	Rev. M. (T. ?) Cussons "	Mirzapur	1838.	
1838.	Rev. T. Lessel "	Calcutta	1852.	
1840.	Rev. W. Glen, M.R.C.S., transferred to Mirzapur	... ...	1841.	
1849.	Rev. J. Bradbury, retired	... ...	1870.	
1853.	Rev. S. J. Hill, transferred to Calcutta ...	... ...	1858.	
1861.	Rev. G. Shrewsbury, left	... ...	1865.	
1864.	Rev. S. J. Hill, died	... ...	1891.	
1868.	Rev. N. L. Das, transferred to Calcutta ...	... ...	1881.	
1875.	Rev. W. B. Phillips " " ...	... ...	1891.	Died, 1896.
1881.	Rev. C. N. Banerji, B.A., retired	... ...	1890.	
1883.	Miss Bloomfield			
1884.	Rev. A. P. Begg, B.A., transferred to Calcutta	... ...	1885.	
"	Rev. S. C. Ghose " "	... ...	1889.	
1887.	Miss Robinson			
1891.	Rev. W. G. Brockway, B.A., and Mrs. Brockway			
"	Miss Tuck			
1892.	Rev. A. Sims, transferred to Calcutta ...	... ...	1899.	
"	Rev. J. H. Joyce (Jiaganj)	... ...	1899.	
1893.	Rev. S. C. Ghose			
1894.	Miss Nicholas, M.D. (afterwards Mrs. Joyce)			
"	Miss Cockerton, sick leave	... ...	1899.	
1897.	Rev. Otto Stûrsberg			
"	February 17th, Rev. Joyce and Miss Nicholas, M.D., were married.			

The idea that natives were paid to become Christians, in some parts of India, is a legend perhaps with some foundation; any way, I find the following, among other items, in the "Diary of an Exile," published in the "L. M. S. Report" for 1897:—

March 2nd.—"Two interesting inquirers to-day, young Brahmins desiring to become Christians. . . . As they went away they asked how much a month they would get if they became Christians, which spoiled it all."

October 2nd.—"Famine over. Lord Radstock's fund, and maize from America for the Mission. The famine left twenty-two orphans on the hands of the Mission, and the Directors L. M. S. sent £144."

Jianganj Mission House and Hospital commenced; a year of famines, earthquakes, riots, and cyclones.

1898.—The Lieutenant-Governor visited Berhampur, February 4th. In his honour the Maharaja of Kasimbazar gave a dinner, to which all Europeans were invited. On April 28th there was a slight shock of earthquake.

July 3rd.—Parupekar Day School teacher dismissed for speaking against Christianity, and stealing school funds!

August 6th.—The Rev. O. Stûrsberg robbed of his cash box, containing partly Mission funds. The case was reported to the police.

Mrs. Joyce started medical work among the women of Jiaganj. At first she found them very shy in coming for treatment, very ignorant, and often prevented by the men. Patients are visited at home, and fees go to the Mission "Medicine Fund." The women rarely come early in an illness, or until village *baids*, and domestic medicines, have failed them. Bengali doctors' fees are small, from Rs. 4, charged by assistant-surgeons, to Rs. 2 by quacks and compounders. A Medical *Act* is urgently required, like that of 1858 in England. Jiaganj Hospital is well built and well furnished. Mrs. Joyce hopes for work among the Jain ladies.

1899.—New church to replace the old "Magazine" church. Subscriptions wanted. Two new stations opened, one at Jungipur and another at Beldanga.

The Rev. T. Brown, B.A., B.D., took Mr. Sims' place. The district is divided for Mission work into three parts: South-eastern half, Rev. O. Strûsberg; western, Rev. Brown; and north, from Murshidabad city, Rev. Joyce.

The annual report grieves over the apostacy of one Ain-nish-din Shaikh, a convert of three years. His relapse was due partly to debts, and want of sympathy on the part of Christian neighbours, but mainly to his wife, described, no doubt with bias, as a "stubborn little woman." The Mission boat "Jessie," after good service became unseaworthy, but an anonymous friend came to the rescue with £150 to build the "Maidie." The year 1899 was the most unhealthy year they have known, and this is borne out by the reports of the Civil Surgeon.

The Khagra School had 289 boy pupils in 1899. Of these twenty-one were Christians; thirteen out of sixteen passed their Calcutta Entrance Examination.

"Caste" prejudice is diminishing. *A Total Abstinence Society* is in existence. There is a great deal of drinking in the district, but the students are temperate. Many pledges have been taken, making the total on the rolls 1,431. The Society found some helpers among the pleader class. The Christian boys' Boarding School contains twenty boys, under Miss Robinson.

The Rev. K. P. Banerji reports that the restoration of the L. M. S. church, near the Racket Court, cost Rs. 2,000.

As regards Sunday Schools, there are sixteen, with thirty-one teachers and three hundred and ninety-seven scholars. The Rev. S. C. Ghose works at Beldanga, and travels in a bullock cart drawn by two bullocks, named *Mark* and *Barnabas*. The Rev. Paul Biswas reports that open-air preaching is generally listened to, but he suffered interruption in Murshidabad from a drunken Fakir and a mad quack. He put up with this for two months, then threatened them with the police, thus putting them to flight.

Mrs. Joyce's Hospital has at times been used as a church. The school in Jiaganj has 150 boys; those of Bokhara and Bhagwangola 112 boys. Three thousand portions of Scripture were sold in six or seven languages at bookshops in Jiaganj and Jangipur, and also by colporteurs.

Hindus and Mahomedans have their "good" and "bad" days, settled by astrologers and printed in their almanacks. Mahomedans fix theirs by the moon; Hindus by moon, stars, and sun. No one but Christians will touch the "sweeper" caste, as it is pollution to touch them. In the Nawab's band there are four Christians who live in Murshidabad.

The old Roman Catholic Church belonging to the cantonment stood opposite the north-east corner of the *bara lal dighi*, or large red tank. It became a ruin after the British troops were removed in 1870, and was finally demolished.

Of the Anglican Church, the earliest available records commence with May 25th, 1841. The Rev.

H. Barry Hyde, formerly vicar of St. John's, Calcutta, and subsequently chaplain to the Bishop of Madras, tells us* that Berhampur became a separate parish in 1788.

The first entry in the Church Register is a note, by the Rev. W. Winchester, of the arrival of the book itself by Messrs. Holmes & Co.'s boat. If the chaplain was ill or absent, one of the missionaries was asked to conduct the services for the troops, and if no missionary was available a layman was to read the prayers and a printed sermon approved by the Bishop. The alms collected were to be distributed among the poor by the chaplain, who submitted his accounts to the Bishop.

From eight a.m. to twelve were the hours fixed for weddings by licence. Those by "banns" were not so restricted. It was the chaplain's duty to visit the hospital twice a week, holding a service during his visit. The regimental schools were visited once a week. A note from the Bishop of Calcutta warns the chaplain that "races, cards, and theatres" are inconsistent with his "calling." Differences of opinion between the chaplain and the commanding officer were to be referred to the Bishop at once. Inscriptions for gravestones had to be approved by the chaplain.

On February 5th, 1842, we find an entry to the effect that:—"The Queen directs that the words 'Prince Albert' be used after 'Adelaide, the Queen Dowager,' in all prayers, etc., for the Royal Family."

A list of church plate, books, linen, and salaries paid to church servants is given—March, 1842:—

> One silver flagon; one silver chalice; two silver pattens; one large prayer-book; one bible; one surplice; two linen cloths for the altar; one red damask cloth for same; and two linen napkins.
>
> *Salaries.*—Clerk, Rs. 14 a month; church servant, Rs. 13 a month; for bread and wine, Rs. 3 a month; dusters and washing, Rs. 2 a month.

There were to be services morning and evening, with Holy Communion three times in each month.

On July 2nd, 1842, the total number of Christians residing in Berhampur and the district, including planters, was 1,024—of these, 738 belonged to the depôts of H.M. troops, the 26th, 49th, and 55th Regts., of whom 279 were Roman Catholics. Of the remainder—286—111 were native converts of the London Mission; 60 were Portuguese Roman Catholics; and 115 were of various persuasions, chiefly Established Church. In August, prayers for rain were ordered by the Bishop, as famine was feared in the Upper Provinces.

1843—April 23rd.—The Chaplain of Berhampur was ordered to visit Rampur Boalia and Birbhum once a year, and Bhagalpur when required. In October, a new order required four visits to Rampur Boalia in the year.

On March 20th, 1844, a bible and two new prayer-books were sent from the store of the Court of Directors for the Berhampur Church. August 29th.—the chaplain was to visit Darjeeling for a week in April, May, and June of each year, and again during September, October, and November, unless a chaplain on sick leave in Darjeeling could do the duty.

1845—December.—The Court of Directors requested the chaplain to be careful with their Burial Registers. 1846.—The Rev. W. Winchester left Berhampur, in August, for four months' sick leave, returning in December. 1847.—The visits to Birbhum increased to four each year. 1848.—Visits to Darjeeling increased to eight. 1852.—The chaplain to visit Murshidabad once a month. He took a month's leave on the 25th May, and during his absence prayers were read by D. Money and F. G. Lock, C.S., alternately. The next note of interest announces the visit of the Lieutenant-Governor, July 30th, 1854, with whom came the Rev. I. M. Bellew.

* Hyde (6).

Thursday, October 5th, of the same year, was marked by a visit from Bishop Bloomfield, whc went on to Murshidabad the next day. During 1855 the services were very irregular and the station had no chaplain. On July 29th the Rev. M. R. Burge, chaplain of Monghyr, being in Berhampur, took the church services. It was much the same in 1856, the services being conducted by soldiers and civilians. In the Register we find the names of Captain Birch, Captain Manning, Lieutenant Ingilby, Mr. Graves and John Fry. Evening service was a rare event. There was a change, however, on July 7th, when the Rev. Robert Bland reported his arrival, but his numerous visits to out-stations left him little time to devote to Berhampur.

On June 21st, 1857, the chaplain records "a panic in the station." The troops in Berhampur and Murshidabad were disarmed, August 1st and 2nd, and British troops re-called to the station. These dates cannot refer to the original "panic," which occurred in February (*v.* p. 22).

In December, the chaplain, the Rev. W. Sturrock notes that:—"The troops are now marched to church at eleven o'clock" on Sunday. 1858.—The hour for parade service was six a.m. from April to December, and eleven a.m. during the cooler months. 1859.—March 20th, parade service seven a.m.; June, six a.m.

During this year a census of religions was taken, and is recorded in the Church Register:—

Europeans, Civilians and Officers	112	Armenians	60
British Soldiers	300		
East Indians (*sic*)	38		
L. M. S.		Soldiers (R. C.)	200
Europeans	20	East Indians	55
Natives	160	Others	8

There was no church parade service on June 19th, 1859, on account of the "Dumpy" mutiny (p. 24). In August of that year the chaplain was informed that he must buy his own surplices, as no more would be supplied by the Government. The Bishop of Calcutta visited Berhampur in September, 1859. By 1860 matters were running in the old groove. Mr. Sturrock was chaplain and the parade services were held as usual, March to May, seven a.m.; May to December, six a.m.; and then at eleven a.m. Nothing of interest occurs until we come to 1861. There was a famine in the North-West Provinces at that time, and we find that a church collection for the Famine Fund amounted to Rs. 67. On March 31st, of this year, a detachment of H.M. 38th Regiment arrived in the station to relieve the wing of the 73rd, going home. January 27th, 1862, the Rev. W. Sturrock made over charge to the Rev. W. B. Bainbridge, LL.B. (Caius Col., Camb.), from Gonda. There had been a revision of the church pay list, which is entered as:—

	Rs.
One Clerk	14
One Bearer	5
One Chowkedar (watchman)	4
Two Chowkedars for the Cemetery ...	8
One Sweeper (meater)	1
One Water Carrier (bhistie)	1
	Rs. 33

The list of church property was as in 1841.

From this time on to the present day there have been periods with a chaplain and times when there was none, and the services have been conducted by laymen or by ministers of the L. M. S.

The Armenian Church in Kasimbazar is now no longer used. It is, however, cared for by the Armenians of Calcutta. A man is paid as caretaker. All the furniture was removed some years ago, only the altar and fine reredos, or painted altar-piece, remaining. Under the protection of the East India Company, the Armenian merchants in the district erected their place of worship in January, 1758. In an agreement, dated June 22nd, 1688, it is recorded that:—"Whenever forty or more of the Armenian nation shall become inhabitants of any garrison cities, or towns belonging to the Company in the East Indies . . . there shall be allotted to them a parcel of ground to erect a church." The Company also gave a grant, to cease at the end of seven years, towards church expenses. There was a small, but prosperous, colony of Armenian merchants in Kasimbazar (Saidabad), founded in 1665, under a *firman* from the Emperor Aurungzebe. With the waning of commerce, the merchants left, gradually, for more prosperous localities.

I shall make no attempt to enumerate all the Hindu temples or the Mahomedan mosques in the district. The Hindus do not possess any universally important temples (such as that of Jagannath at Puri), nor, outside the city of Murshidabad, are there any Mahomedan shrines requiring detailed description. The Maharaja of Kasimbazar, the Raja Bahadur of Nashipur, Raja A. N. Roy, and other rich Hindus have handsome *Thakur baris* (shrines of the gods) attached to their dwellings.

The Jain families of Azimganj have adorned the town with many fine temples. The temple of Shiva at Baranaggur contains twelve idols. It was built in 1755, by the Rani of Nattore, for Rs. 12,00,000. The Priesthood is hereditary.

On the right bank of the Bhagirathi there are two Mahomedan cemeteries of great historical interest. With many other ancient buildings, they are preserved by the Bengal Government. The Khushbagh lies about two miles south of the town of Murshidabad, and contains the tomb of Ali Verdi Khan and other members of the royal family. The Roshnibagh, or "Garden of Light," lies nearly opposite the Nawab's palace. It contains the tomb of Sujah-u-Din, who died in the year 1739 A.D., and probably that of Suraj-u-Dowlah. There are other tombs within the enclosure, and a Musjid, said to have been erected by Ali Verdi Khan. The Katra Musjid, now a picturesque ruin, was built under the orders of Murshid Kuli Khan. It was to serve, not only as a shrine, but as a dwelling-place for the Nawab, and a mausoleum for his body when the spirit of life should leave it. There is little hope of any renovation of the "Katra," as the outlay would be considerably more than either the Government or the Nawab Bahadur probably feels inclined to spend. Murshidabad has lost many links connecting it with the glories of the past, and the Katra Musjid should be kept from total decay, in memory of the man who made the city the capital of Bengal and the home of a line of historically interesting Nawabs Nazim. This Musjid is said to have been copied from one at Mecca.

Before passing on to describe the Imambara, attached to the palace of the Nawab, a mosque and two ruins, in the Jangipur Sub-division, require short notice.

The mosque, still in use, is situated in the Baliaghatta suburb of Jangipur (Raganathganj). It was built about 1560 A.D., when Muxsudabad was a small and unimportant village. The descendants of the original founders still maintain the mosque.

One of the ruins of note is that of a fine mosque at Kharior.

To the second ruin, at Ekánna Chandpara, is attached a legend, or true story maybe. Syud Sharif Makki, with his father and brother, originally settled in Chandpara. Though one day to be rich and powerful, the proud Syud was poor when he first arrived. He entered the service of a rich Brahmin, whom he afterwards rewarded by the free gift of Ekánna* Chandpara. At the same time the Syud is said to have built the mosque to mark his first home in the district. Hosain Shah Badshah, his subsequent title, ruled Bengal from 1498 to 1521 A.D., and died a natural death at the close of a peaceful and prosperous reign.

THE IMAMBARA.

The old Imambara was erected by Nawab Suraj-u-Dowlah. It was on the north of the present main palace. To build the Imambara only Mahomedan architects and workmen were employed; Hindus were excluded from taking part in the work. On the first day of the erection, Suraj-u-Dowlah brought bricks and mortar with his own hands, and laid the foundation of the building himself. In the middle of the Imambara, the "Medina" was situated. The plot of land on which this "Medina" was built had been dug out to the depth of six feet, and had been re-filled with the sacred earth.—*i.e.* earth from Mecca. On the east, the hall or chamber facing west has been fixed as the place for Majlis.

On the west, in the chambers facing east, were placed various representations of the tombs of the Imans, made of gold, silver, glass, and wood, and hundreds of "alums" (sacred flags or standards). During the Mohurram, it is in this part of the building that verses of the Koran are read day and night, without the least interval; at other times the reading is only at fixed periods.

The chambers on the north and south were set apart as storehouses and workshops, where hundreds of men were employed for the management of the lights during the Mohurram. The rooms of the second storey were surrounded with screens of mica, on which were painted various designs of flowers, beasts, and men, etc., with thousands of cressets behind them. When these cressets were lighted at night, they presented a very imposing display. Various kinds of cut-glass chandeliers, wall lamps, and *girandoles*, adorned these various chambers, and, during the Mohurram, the building was magnificently illuminated. In the north and south chambers there were images, two in each, of Borac, representing him as having the face of man and body of peacock. The tails of these Boracs were made so high as almost to reach the ceiling. Instead of adorning the tails with feathers, they were bedecked with beautifully painted shields, china and silver saucers, and hundreds of polished swords and daggers. Hundreds of candles were lighted near these shields at night, to make them more conspicuous. In the north and south of the enclosure were two courtyards, where, during the Mohurram, shopkeepers kept their stalls.

In the year 1842 A.D., this Imambara caught fire and was partly burnt down, and again on 23rd December, 1846 A.D., at midnight it caught fire from the fireworks let off on the occasion of a party given to the Europeans, and was completely burnt down, with all in it. Not a single thing was saved except the "Medina."

The present Imambara was built in 1848, under the management of Syud Sadik Ali Khan, the then Diwan Nizamat.† Its site is slightly to the north of the old building. The old "Medina," which had been saved from the fire, was left in its place; and a new one was erected in the new Imambara. The new Imambara is a large rectangular building, with a central enclosure, and is furnished in the same way as the old one. There are two additional courtyards, one on the west and another on the east. To the west, on the bank of the river, there was a Hindu temple. This was razed to the ground,

* "One anna," merely a nominal rental.

† During the time the present Imambara was being erected the Mohurram ceremonies were held in the Murshidabad High School.

and another was built in place of it at Ichaganj. On the site of this temple, on the bank of the river, a two-storied Musjid was erected. This Musjid commands a very beautiful view. H.H. the Nawab Nazim Munsur Ali sometimes performed his *Id Namaz* in this Musjid.

The following is a translation of the inscription on the Imambara. It was composed by Mullah Mahomed Sharif Shirwain, a man of great learning:—

(1) Inventors of the tide of destiny, with the pen of Divine decree have written this building on the first tablet.

(2) The courage and firmness of Feradun Jah, for honour and greatness, have taken upon themselves the servitude of the son of Zohora.

(3) As Nowbut Khana, Musjid and Imambara are built in one and the same ground, he has therefore established a plan of both worlds.

(4) The management and labour of Sadik Ali, of high origin, have tried hard to complete this heart-pleasing edifice.

(5) His power and ingenuity have laid the foundation in this world, of heaven and a place of sorrow combined together.

(6) Messenger of God placed on thy Jesus-like palm this epigrammatic verse:—

"Behold another *Karbala* is erected in India."

At the time of the erection of this Imambara, H.H. the Nawab, with his chief officers, was present at the ceremony. His Highness laid the foundation stone himself, and also lowered with it another stone, on which he wrote some charms, supposed to be effectual in preserving the building for ever. Mullah Mahomed Ali Fazil Khorasain and Haji Mullah Mahomed Izudi conducted the ceremony. Sadik Ali Khan completed this grand edifice within six or seven months. The builders, in addition to their wages, which were much higher than usual, got food from His Highness's establishment. Owing to this, two days' work was finished in one. Thus Sadik Ali made his name.

It cost more than six lakhs of rupees; and, when the building was completed, all the workmen, from the highest to the lowest, were rewarded with shawls; at that time masons in shawls were to be seen all over the town.

DISPOSAL OF THE DEAD, CEMETERIES, AND BURNING GHATS.

AMONG Christian communities of whatever sect, the custom is to bury the dead, in consecrated ground if available. The ceremony is conducted by the ordained clergy, or by a civil or military officer, with the usual services according to the faith of the departed. Although cremation has made some progress among Christians in England and Europe generally, it has not yet been introduced into India. From a sanitary point of view, it is to be recommended, and especially in large towns where ground is not available for cemeteries, and where the proximity of a collection of decomposing bodies might possibly lead to contamination of the drinking water, or cause the spread of infectious diseases, such as small-pox, plague, or anthrax. The objections to cremation are mainly sentimental, for there is nothing contained in any of our sources of religious teaching forbidding the practice, indeed, there are many who regard the dictum "ashes to ashes" as a reference favourable to cremation. That the adoption of the practice would provide extra facilities for taking life by means of poison is an argument to be counteracted by strict rules concerning registration of certificates as to the cause of death.

For the use of the Christian community there is now one cemetery at the headquarters of the district. It is situated about half a mile from the Civil Station, on the right hand side of the main road from Berhampur to Murshidabad. It is fairly well kept, but, unfortunately, many of the epitaphs have entirely disappeared. We look in vain for the graves of the notorious George Thomas, and—greatest of contrasts—for that of Little Henry, hero of Mrs. Sherwood's well-known story:—"Little Henry and his Bearer." Little Henry was Creighton, the explorer and antiquary of Gaur. There is good evidence that these two interesting beings were buried at Berhampur. A little nearer to the Civil Station, and on the left hand side of the main road, is a lane leading to the "Magazine" Cemetery, the property of the London Missionary Society, and used by the native Christians. The history of the church which stood near this cemetery and was destroyed by the earthquake of 1897 is given elsewhere.

Another cemetery, now closed, but formerly used by the British troops stationed here, lies at the extreme south-east limit of the station, on the way to the rifle butts.

There are two unused cemeteries in Kasimbazar, one of which belonged to the early English residents, the other to the Dutch. They were both at one time allowed to sink into a shameful state of untidiness and dilapidation, and, the matter having been laid before the Local Government by the Bishop of Calcutta, they were restored in 1863, and *malis* (gardeners) were appointed to keep them neat and clean. Many of the monuments had disappeared, and the memorial tablets are missing from many of such as remained to be restored. The tomb of Mr. Lionel Pragel, diamond merchant and Inspector of Indigo and Drugs to the East India Company, is no longer to be ound in the old English Cemetery. He died May 12th, 1793.

The following is a list of the names at present decipherable:—

Captain Anstruther, died 1735.
" Clark " 1783, a descendant still lives in Berhampur.
" Hartle " 1782.

OLD ENGLISH CEMETERY, KASIMBAZAR.
(MRS. HASTINGS' TOMB IS OPPOSITE THE GATE.)

The wife of Col. John Muttock, died 1777, grand-daughter of the famous John Hampden.*

Joseph Bourdieu, died 1790, a merchant of the East India Company.

The infant of Captain John, and Rose Grant, died 1775.

Ch. Crommelin, died 1788.

G. D. Campbell, died 1784, of Rangamati factory. One of his descendants, Sir George Campbell, was Lieutenant Governor of Bengal.

John Peach, died 1790, senior merchant, East India Company.

A. Downie, died 1781.

Mrs. Hastings, died 1759.

This lady, the first wife of Warren Hastings, was the widow of Captain John Buchanan,† one of the defenders of Fort William in 1756. He perished in the "Black Hole." It is related that, being left in very poor circumstances by her first husband, Mrs. Buchanan appealed to Hastings for help, which he gave by marrying her. The marriage probably took place at Fultah. Their married life was not of long duration. Married in 1756, Mrs. Hastings died in 1759, while Hastings was Resident at Murshidabad, to which post he was appointed by Clive in 1758. Mrs. Hastings gave birth to two children, a boy who subsequently died at school in England, and a girl who lived nineteen days only.‡

The monument over Mrs. Hastings' grave is built like a small verandah, with sloping roof, against the south wall of the cemetery. At the east end of this structure is a marble tablet, bearing the following inscription :—

IN MEMORY OF
MRS. MARY HASTINGS,
and her daughter
ELIZABETH,
Who died 11th July, 1759,
In the 2§ year of her age.

This monument was erected
by her husband,
WARREN HASTINGS, ESQUIRE,
In due regard
of her memory.
Restored by [the] Government
of Bengal, 1863.

The total number of graves in preservation in the old English cemetery is eighteen. About half a mile to westward, at Calcapur, is the old Dutch cemetery, also now under the care of the Public

* Probably great grand-daughter, as Hampden died in 1643, having then been married 24 years.

† The statement made by all historians, that the first Mrs. Hastings was the widow of Captain Dugald Campbell, was disproved by the Rev. H. B. Hyde in a paper read at a meeting of the Asiatic Society of Bengal. See "Proc. Asiatic Soc., Bengal," July, 1899.

‡ "The Private Life of Warren Hastings," by Sir Charles Lawson, 1895 (35.)

§ A figure has been left out and it is not quite certain what the correct age should be. We are told that the daughter lived only nineteen days, so the age cannot refer to her, as is taken for granted by the compiler of "Murray's Handbook for Bengal," who puts *nd* after the 2. The inscription was carelessly copied by a native, who has also left out the word *the* in the last line but one.

Works Department. It contains twenty-two tombs in a good state of preservation, but only a few of these bear any inscription. Beginning with the earliest date, we have:—

Daniel Van der Muyl, died 1721.

Gregorius Herklots, died 1739, of the Dutch East India Company.

M. A. Brahe, died 1772.

Tamerus Cantes Vischer, died 1778, Head Merchant, Dutch East India Company.

Johann Gantvoort, died 1792, Surgeon to the Company.

Some of the monuments are of very massive structure, one being forty feet high, and another forty-two feet high.

It will not be necessary to describe the simple ceremonies attending the burial of Christians of whatever sect, and we can now pass on to the Hindu and Mahomedan methods of disposal of the dead. Hindus, as a rule, burn their dead on a funeral pyre and, where possible, commit a portion of the ashes to the waters of one of the sacred rivers, the Ganges being preferred above all others. Children of tender age, and persons dying from cholera, leprosy, and snake-bite* are generally buried; so too are the bodies of Hindus too poor to bear the expenses of cremation. The last mentioned, however, not infrequently throw their dead into the nearest river if they can do so without detection, since such pollution of rivers is now forbidden. Hindu Bairagies (followers of Vishnu) always bury their dead.

Suicides used to be buried, but are now generally burnt. In the case of a child of two years and under, the little finger of one hand is incised or cut off before the body is buried.†

Every Hindu desires a son, and generally adopts one if none is born. The son is chief mourner and puts the fire to his father's funeral pyre. The chief mourner shaves head and face at the time of cremation. Other near relatives shave later. The Jains on the third day shave off the beard only, and pare their nails. Brahmins shave on the tenth day after the death; Kshatrias on the twelfth; Vaidyas on the fifteenth; and Sudras on the thirtieth day, or even later. Some Brahmins put sugar and curds into the mouth of the corpse before it is burnt; food is also placed on the chest of the corpse, and water by the side of the pyre. On the evening of the cremation the favourite food of the deceased is placed on the site of the pyre and cakes called *Pindas*. For two or three days after the death, milk, water, and ghee are placed to the left of the door of the house; on the third day, rice, sugar, and milk, together with a stick for cleaning the teeth, are placed on the site of the funeral pile. In these matters there are certain local differences, but the custom is mostly as described. According to Grierson, those who bury their dead among the Hindus place the body in a sitting posture, facing the north, and with funeral cakes in its hand.

Mahomedans always bury their dead. The deceased is washed with water in which the leaves of the *Bair* tree *(Zizyphus jujuba)* have been boiled. This is done to preserve the body from decay, but is of no value in that respect. A hole is then torn in the centre of a clean sheet and the head of the corpse passed through it, so that half the sheet lies over the back and half over the front of the body. If the deceased is a *Sunni* the relatives prepare the body for burial, but among the *Shiahs* there is a particular class of men who perform these ceremonies. The body is carried to the grave and laid in it with the head to the north. All the members of the

* The bodies of those dying from snake-bite are sometimes placed on a raft of plantain stems and floated down the nearest river, in the hope that some *Ojah* (sorcerer) may meet them and cure them. This practice is dying out.

† There is a belief that the spirit of the same child returns to the mother's womb to be born again when dying very young. To prevent this, one little finger is cut off.

funeral procession help to roof over the grave with bamboos and thatching grass, and to fill it with earth. Before leaving the cemetery the mourners give alms to beggars and pay the grave-digger's fee. In Murshidabad there is a large and well-kept cemetery for the members of the Nizamat family.

The following are the arrangements made in various municipalities for the disposal of the dead. In the rural areas there are rarely any fixed places either for cremation or burial, and it is greatly to be desired that each village should be obliged to set apart places for these purposes.

Mahomedans, Christians, all Bairagies, and most paupers are buried. Hindus, as a rule, burn their dead, either in special burning *ghats*, such as are found in most municipal towns, or in waste places near a village. The banks of a river are the site of the funeral pyre when possible, and any stream connected with the Ganges, the mother of rivers, is greatly favoured. Such a holy stream is the Bhagirathi river, flowing through the district of Murshidabad. This river was probably at one time the main stream of the Ganges. Hindu males shave the head during the *shradh* or funeral ceremonies on the death of father or mother. They shave also when performing *Prayaschitya*, or atonement, and when on a pilgrimage to the sacred city of Allahabad. Again during the "Chura Karan," or ceremony of investiture with the sacred thread of the Brahmins, the head is shaved. Mahomedans shave their infants on the fifth day. Shaving among the Mahomedans is practised more for cleanliness and class distinction than on account of religious custom.

During the *shradh*, or funeral ceremonies above mentioned, *pindas*, funeral cakes, are offered. In the month of Bhodra (September) water is offered to the dead, and this rite is called *Tarpan* by the Hindus.

The Mahomedans place food and water where the poor can get it, as an act of charity for the benefit of the dead.

Among the Hindus, children of tender age are not always cremated. Brahmins shave on the tenth day of *shradh*, other "castes" on the twenty-ninth day after the death. There are distinctions also with regard to the offerings of food to the dead. By Brahmins this act is performed on the fourth day, by other "castes" on the thirtieth day. Persons dying of small-pox, cholera, and leprosy are more frequently buried than burnt, even among the Hindus, as is also the case, already alluded to, with children under twenty-seven months. Those dying of snake-bite are often buried.

Among some of the lower "castes" the body of the deceased child is placed on a raft made of plantain stems and floated on a river, as they think that the death of one so young may be unnatural and that as the raft travels on its way it may be met by an *ojha* (a sorcerer) who will restore the body to life.

Among the Jains, the beard only is shaved, and the nails are pared on the third day. As regards the offerings of food to the dead by Hindus, flour and sugar cakes are sometimes placed in the right hand or on the chest of the corpse. For two days after the death has occurred, milk and water and *ghee** are placed on the left side of the door of the dead person's house. On the third day, rice sugar, milk, and a tooth-stick† are put on the site of the funeral pile.

Mahomedans, as stated, invariably bury their dead, and the near relatives shave the head, face, and arm-pits. Mahomedans do not offer food to the dead.

The Bairagies, a sect of religious mendicant Hindus, bury members of their own community. The followers of Vishnu generally bury their dead, as do members of the *Dandis* and *Paramhansas* sects of

* Clarified butter.

† Most natives of India use a twig frayed at one end to clean the teeth. The idea of always using one tooth-brush is not in favour; twigs are, according to custom, offered by Hindus, and, besides, twigs are cheap.

the Hindus. In addition to the diseases already mentioned, death from phthisis is generally followed by burial.

Suicides used to be buried, but they are now generally burnt in this district. Shaving the head is mentioned by all, both during the *shradh* and at times of atonement for any grievous crime, such as the killing of a cow. Most Hindus shave the moustache and beard, as well as the head when a parent or very near relative dies. When offering food to the dead a Hindu is generally careful to choose the things the deceased liked when alive.

FOLK-LORE AND SUPERSTITIONS.

THE following information was given with regard to the village treatment of snake-bite. Charms are used in nearly all cases; a bandage is applied above the wound and the poison sucked, or squeezed out. This answer was given by an educated Mahomedan, and applies generally to the more intelligent classes. Among the rest the bandage is either neglected, or so applied as to be useless. No food is given to the person bitten, and the juice of certain plants is rubbed into the bitten part. *Mantras* are said over the victim, and he is made to drink oil or melted ghee. Some "snake-doctors" apply a ligature and then burn the bitten part; water is poured over the head of the patient.

Much virtue is said to reside in the *Johar Mohura stones*, stones said, by one of my informants, to be found in the necks of peacocks! This stone is first soaked in milk and then applied over the bitten part. Being porous (the stone is probably lava), it sucks out the poison. To add to the efficacy, both of the *mantras* and the stone, the goddess Manasa should be worshipped. As a rule, in most villages, if anyone is bitten by a snake a *baid* is sent for. These men, often quite ignorant, or possibly having some knowledge of the Hindu system of medicine, rub the limb from above downwards, repeating *mantras* the while. They breathe hard on the limb and on the victim's head to remove the poison. A stone, probably the *Johar* above mentioned, is charmed and placed on the bitten part; cold water is poured on the head and sometimes medicine is given, but this is not essential. The patient is not allowed to sleep or drink "till he is cured, or dead!" The *ojha*, or village sorcerer, is often called in. The victim must be kept awake. It is recorded that one, Nitai Charan Mukerji, of the village of Tenya, in the Kandi Sub-division, is a noted *ojha*, able to cure cases of poisoning. He cuts a jute plant on an auspicious day, and makes string from its fibres. When a patient is taken to him this string is tied round a finger, if the victim has been bitten above the loins; round a toe, if bitten below the loins. *Mantras* are repeated, and the poison accumulates in the tip of the finger or toe, which turns black (very naturally!) The finger, or toe is then cut and the poison comes out like coal tar. These are the "quintessence" of faith cures! After recovery offerings are made to *Manasa Devi*. When a snake appears in a house, milk and rice are offered to the god *Nag*. Some *ojhas* strike the bitten part with a branch of the *Nim* tree, reciting *mantras* the while. Eighty or ninety grains of black pepper are ground up with apamarga root (*Achyranthes aspera*, Linn.) and administered. The root of *manasasij*, dug up on the last day of *Jaistha*, is sometimes given with pepper and *Nim* leaves. The stalk and root of the water-lily are applied to the bitten part. When a person is bitten by a *Bora*, the *ojha* gets on the roof of the hut with six water-pots and, reciting *mantras*, pours the water slowly on to the ground; as the water falls the patient recovers. A mali noted for his skill in these matters lives in Murshidabad. He slaps the face of the messenger who comes to call him, and recites *mantras*, and the patient is vicariously cured! Another method used by *ojhas* is the following:—The man places his hand on the ground, repeating *mantras* as usual. If the hand moves towards the bitten part there is poison. If the hand does not move in that direction, the patient has not been bitten.

The village sorcerer *(ojha)* is a well-known person. He is sometimes appointed after having shown skill in some difficult case. In some villages the office is hereditary. The sorcerer is called in by people who are annoyed by ghosts, or other supernatural powers. The *ojha* is more feared than loved, as the ignorant think that he can transfer disease and do other harm if offended. They receive fees in money or kind, according to the circumstances of the patient. In past times great power was attributed to sorcery, and stories were circulated concerning the powers of certain well-known sorcerers. To-day there are fewer *ojhas.* They may be either Hindus or Mahomedans. They are called upon to treat diseases of children, cattle, women with hysteria, cases of snake-bite, and hydrophobia.* The sorcerers are nearly always men of low caste. The village sorcerer is liable to be replaced by a more successful rival. While these notes were being collected the following paragraph appeared in the *Statesman* newspaper, July 31, 1900:—

"Rival Doms.—The doms in the service of the Patna Municipality complained to their official superior that unless they were protected from the magical spells practised by the Backergunj Ojha-dom they would all strike. Their case is that this *ojha* threatens to kill their children and other near relations if they do not give him money. And several children have actually died owing to his witchcraft. He has succeeded in extorting money from many of them, and they cannot stand it any longer. The District Magistrate has taken cognizance of the case under Section 190 clause *(c)*, and the trial is proceeding before Babu R. A. Narain Sing, Senior Deputy Magistrate, under charges of extortion, cheating, and robbery. The accused is defended.—B.H."

As it is a common practice to hang a stuffed goat-skin at the entrance to a village or house to ward off, or check disease, inquiries were made as to the origin and meaning of the custom. The goat was, and is even now, sometimes used to transfer disease to an enemy. A ring is put in the goat's ear, and the animal is turned loose. If the goat bleats near the enemy's house the design will be successful. Those suffering from chronic and long illness often set a goat at liberty to roam, hoping that it will carry away the disease. Disease may also be transferred to a goat, which is then offered to the goddess Kali.

There lingers a belief in witches among most of the ignorant villagers; and, as I gathered from other sources, many persons of some education are not free from similar superstitions. A witch is believed to have no shadow. One of the ways to detect a witch is to throw salt on her; she becomes at once benumbed. To guard children against witches and witchcraft, the mother spits over their heads. The white sap of the Babul tree (*Acacia Arabica*) has the same protective power. Very often, when a visit from a witch is feared, the women of the house place a ladder near the door, as it is thought that no witch can cross a ladder. The reason of the mother's fear is the belief that witches have more power over infants than over adults. *Mantras* are among the safeguards against the evil power of witches. Supposed witches are submitted to the "ladder test" by the *ojha* who may be called upon to defeat witchcraft. If the suspected person cannot get over the ladder she is guilty. Among many methods of protecting children one of my informants gives the following:—The application of a little cow-dung to the forehead; the juice of the Najdana plant (*Artemisia vulgaris*, Linn.; *A. Indica*, Willd.); saliva rubbed on the child's breast; biting the nail of the left little finger. There are certain "charms" which, worn round the neck, protect the wearer from witches. If a person is bewitched, a piece of the root of the water yam is placed in each ear. This causes the witch to cry out, promising to leave the victim. A chilli may be burnt near the nose of the afflicted person; the pungent smoke will drive out the evil spirit of witchcraft. Turmeric is burnt near the nose of the victim. If he, or she, can tolerate the smoke, he, or she, is certainly bewitched; if the patient cannot bear the reek of the turmeric, the evil is probably due not to a witch but to a ghost *(Bhút)*. Witches are said to leave their homes on Tuesday and Saturday, "to visit some lovely spot to ride on wolves, their favourite animals." If a man is rubbed with oil only he is liable to be attacked by a witch; so, if a witch is about, a little water is rubbed on the head and chest before the man goes to bathe. Further protection is obtained by rubbing the juice of the *Najdana* on the ears and nostrils of

* The Kasauli Pasteur Institute for the scientific treatment of hydrophobia according to Pasteur's method was opened in August, 1900, and is doing good work.

children. Small cakes made of *Kalai* (one of the lentils) are waved round the head seven times, and then given to the dogs to avert evil. The village sorcerer is supposed to be able to detect a witch by means of salt. Without her knowledge he places a little salt on the woman's head: if she cries out she is surely a witch. The effect of the "evil-eye" is classed with witchcraft, and it is a common belief that certain persons, men and women, bring disease and evil to men and animals by "overlooking" them. The methods used to avert evil from such a source are the same as those employed against witchcraft.

It is believed that witches can steal or poison food sent as a present from one person to another. It is the custom, therefore, among those holding this belief, to sprinkle a little salt or ashes on the basket or vessel containing the food. A piece of charcoal placed on the top of the food affords a similar protection.

That disease is an entity, a thing to be dreaded and dealt with as one deals with concrete evil, is set forth as a belief by the majority of the people of the East. As good things come from a source which is called a god, so evil comes from a god and must be propitiated and rewarded, not only in the present, but for favours to come. The goddess of small-pox in Bengal is Shitálá. She is described, in the ideal, as "a golden-complexioned woman, clothed in scarlet, sitting on a lotus or riding an ass." In the spring of the year the Hindus used to inoculate their children, those, at least, who had reached the age of two years. The spring was chosen as the crest of the wave of life, when the virus would most affect the blood, and also because small-pox is undoubtedly more virulent in that season.* The disease is called in Bengali *Basanta rog*, or "spring sickness." The operation was performed by Brahmins, and offerings were made to Shitálá. If the operation was successful, more offerings were made in gratitude. The flowers offered to the goddess were placed on the child's head, to act as a charm. When a person is suffering from small-pox daily offerings are made to Shitálá. The patient drinks water that has been offered to the goddess; sometimes he is bathed in it. It is not uncommon for mendicants to make profit during an epidemic of small-pox in a village, by carrying about a gilded stone or rough image to represent Shitálá. They sing her praises, and demand offerings and presents from the victims of the epidemic, that the wrath of the goddess may be removed and the scourge cease. As Shitálá is supposed to send the small-pox, so also is she believed to be able to take it away. The goddess of small-pox has other names,† and under one guise or another is worshipped by all aborigines, also by Hindus, Mahomedans,‡ and Jains. She is sometimes represented as a naked woman riding an ass, and holding a broom in one hand and a water-pot in the other. On her head she bears a winnowing fan.§

The *mali* (gardener) "caste" are constant worshippers of Shitálá. When any member of a family is attacked with small-pox, the house is cleaned, and none of the family use oil for their bodies. Fish and flesh are forbidden as diet at such times; so also is turmeric. No *pan*‖ is chewed, a penance indeed, as the native of India is extremely fond of this stimulant. A water-pot, with a branch of mango in it, is placed in the sick person's room. The dung of the ass is burnt every evening in the room. When the pustules are drying the patient is made to stand in the court-yard, and water is thrown over him or her seven times, through a brass colander, if the family is rich enough to possess such a thing. Nim¶ leaves, turmeric, and certain grasses are ground to a pulp with water, and rubbed over the body. Among the Jains the dried

* The mortality statistics of this district for each month during ten years, 1890-1899, give the following monthly grand totals:—January, 61 deaths; February, 52; March, 78; April, 117; May, 128; June ("rains" begin), 76; July, 62; August, 43; September, 15; October, 21; November, 60; December, 57.—Ed.

† *Thakurani.*

‡ Only by degenerate classes who have descended from Hindu converts.

§ A small flat tray made of split cane or bamboo, used by women when winnowing rice or other grain.

‖ *Pan* chewing is as common with all races and classes in India as smoking is in England. In a pan leaf are rolled a piece of betel palm nut, a little lime, catechu, tobacco, and the whole is slowly chewed. The composition and quality varies with the circumstances of the user, and there are cheap and expensive kinds of *pan*. The saliva becomes a deep red.

¶ Nim, *Melia Azadirachta*, Linn; *Azadirachta Indica*, Juss.

milk of a tigress is considered very efficacious ; but is rarely available.* The water-pot and mango branch are removed as the patient recovers, and Nim, plantains, melons, and yellow cloth are offered to the goddess of small-pox. On the day on which these ceremonies take place no food may be cooked and no fire lighted : cold food from the previous day is eaten. As a rule, only old women are permitted to attend the sufferer, since it is believed that a young woman capable of bearing children may suffer from looking at a small-pox patient. Shitálá is sometimes a horrible image, painted with vermilion, with large black eyes. A figure of the goddess is made when occasion arises, but in many villages there is a permanent shrine for Shitálá. Often, when there is no image, the goddess is supposed to dwell beneath some sacred tree. *Sankirtan*, or parties gathered together to sing the praises of the goddess, go about the afflicted village. Sankirtan is also practised in the names of *Rudra Devi* and *Kali*, to avert or stay other diseases. The aborigines, in the main nature-worshippers, dread their "Thakurani," or goddess of small-pox. When the disease appears in a house the door is shut, and the inmates will not come out until the disease has gone, or killed them. Mahomedans hang up a goat during a small-pox epidemic, and rich men may parade the *Alum* (sacred flag) to stay the disease.

As with small-pox, so with other diseases: the evil is supposed to be due to the wrath of a god or goddess, or to malice on the part of spirits and goblins. Offerings to the offended deity, *mantras* (exorcisms), charms, and amulets, are used by all classes. Again, the *ojha*, or the *baid*, or *hakim* (Hindu and Mahomedan medical practitioners), is called upon to show his skill. While exorcising a disease with *mantras*, the "medicine man" may pass his hands over the affected part, or rub oil into the skin. Sometimes water, or dust, sanctified by incantations, takes the place of oil ; charms are worn round the neck, the waist, or the arms, generally above the elbow. The amulet may be contained in a little bag of cloth, or incased in metal, copper, silver, or gold. Inside these receptacles are placed *mantras*, written on paper, seeds, pieces of medicinal roots, or, in the case of Mahomedans, verses of the Koran.†

Exorcism is especially necessary in nervous diseases, epilepsy, and the convulsions of children. "Fits" are produced by devils or evil spirits, which, as in the days of the Gadarene swine, must be cast out. Hysteria and delirium are regarded as the work of evil spirits or ghosts. Certain persons have power to drive these away. In the case of hysteria, the possessed or haunted woman sits on a wooden stool in front of the exorcist. Dust or mustard seed is thrown over her when she screams ; she is beaten with a twisted cloth, or with a shoe, and the devil is called upon to quit. In another ceremony for a similar purpose the woman is made to try to lift a pot full of water with her teeth, without spilling any. During this effort *mantras* are repeated and continued until the evil spirit departs. When a child is ill, a person supposed to possess hypnotic powers may be called in : he passes his hands over the patient, reciting *mantras*, or he may pass a bundle of twigs over the body of the child. *Mantras* are repeated over water which is to be drunk by the child. Adults suffering pain from any cause call in similar *ojhas*, or doctors. The man passes his fingers over the painful part. Evil spirits are believed to seek out children and pregnant women to annoy them. To prevent this, charms are tied round the neck or waist—a "cowrie" is commonly used in such cases, as also when men suffer from inflammation or sprains. A ring, thread, or rag, over which special *mantras* have been repeated ; flowers that have been offered to certain deities ; medicinal roots : all these are used as charms to cure or avert disease or injury. In cases of elephantiasis, or injury to the leg, a cowrie is tied round the limb with strands of hair. For hydrocele the tooth of a horse or a crocodile is used as a charm ; for chronic sores medicinal roots are tied up in pieces of rag, and placed over the ulcerated part. When an attack of illness is thought to be due to the wrath of some deity, an image of the

* I find no mention of this in *The Materia Medica of the Hindus* (32).

† The wearing of charms was common in England in the fifteenth century, and many amulets were sold and worn during the "Great Plague" in London, 1665.

offended one is placed on a small platform, and fresh bamboo leaves prepared with *mantras* are offered to appease the god. Some of the lower "castes" take live birds, fowls, or pigeons, and having offered them to the god or goddess to be propitiated, let them fly away, hoping that they will bear away the disease with them. Charms are used against "fever," muscular pains, hysteria, and diseases of children. Sometimes the exorcist drives out disease by blowing on the body of the patient. There are special *mantras* for special diseases, and these are kept secret by the *ojhas*.

Some *mantras* are common property. Thus, "fever" is supposed to be cured by recitations from the epic *Chaha bharit*, which represents Sri Krishna as fighting the worst forms of "fever." Narain and Jarasur are also prayed to in cases of "fever." Jarasur has six hands, three faces, and a fair complexion. He wears a tiger skin. The four upper hands hold a "conch," a "discus," a club, and a lotus. The fifth hand holds a piece of rope, while with the sixth he proclaims protection. His worship takes place in the open air, generally three times daily.

The connection of dancing with folk-lore and religious customs was shown to be common. A dance called *Gajan* forms part of the rites in the worship of Shiva in Magh (January-February), and Choit (March and April), but is indulged in only by the lower "castes" among Hindus. Dancing may form part of the ceremonies of exorcising the evil spirits of hysteria. In other diseases the *ojha* sometimes dances and waves his hands. *Ojhas* use a dance called *Jhonk*, and perform it round persons possessed by evil spirits, chanting *mantras* to the beating of drums. This custom is, however, almost confined to "low-caste" people, such as *Bagdis*, *Mehters*, *Dôms*, etc. Some *ojhas* when dancing hold a piece of burning turmeric in one hand. This the *ojha* repeatedly thrusts under the nose of the patient, as evil spirits are believed to dislike the smell. Other dances are purely of a religious nature. The dancing *ojhas* are said to be mostly found in the *Rarh*, or western part of the district.

One of the questions to which I sought answers, from the illiterate and from nine educated persons varying in "caste" and creed, was—"In what respect are animals connected with religion and folk-lore?"

Many of the written replies were very full and interesting, and from the *précis*, made from the individual notes and occasional records of my own, I give the following account:—

Mahomedans, generally speaking, have no particular respect for animals as connected with religion. As they believe in one God, animals have not that close relationship found in the Hindu polytheism, in which nearly every god or goddess has some favourite animal. The Mahomedans, however, consider the camel sacred, and the rich kill a camel at the *Baqr-Id* (p. 63). The spider and the pigeon are regarded with extreme favour by the followers of the Prophet; the latter because of the help given on one occasion when Mahomed was in hiding. The spider is in favour because it saved Hassan and Husain when pursued by their enemies. The two had taken refuge in a well, over the mouth of which a spider rapidly stretched a web. When the pursuers arrived they concluded that their desired quarry could not be hiding in the well, as the web was intact. The young men were, however, nearly betrayed by a lizard, which rushed out when accidently disturbed by them. On this account, the lizard is despised and hated by Mahomedans. Almost every god and goddess of the Hindu Pantheon is supposed to have a favourite animal, and is represented as riding upon his or her favourite. Such animals are thus known as the "vehicles" of the gods. Shitálá, as we have seen, rides on the ass, a creature generally despised and rarely used by any except the washerman (Dhoba) "caste." Durga is seated upon a tiger (some say a lion), while Shiva rides on a bull; the great god Indra upon the greatest of animals, the elephant; Shasthi on a cat; Gonesha, he of the elephant trunk, upon a rat; Saraswati upon a swan; Ganga upon a crocodile. The squirrel is regarded as under the special care of Ram Chandra. The horse draws the sun's chariot. Bhairub is carried by a dog, and dogs benefit accordingly, being fed each evening by the Jains. Other "vehicles" are:—for Lakhsmi, the pigeon; the peacock for Kartic; the goose for Brahma (this is merely another form of Indra); for Jam, the god of death, the buffalo; and as the *vahán*, or carrier of the moon, there is the antelope. To some deities more than one animal is attached. Thus, the owl is another attendant on Lakhsmi, and of good omen; the *Nilkanta* (blue jay) is sacred to Durga, sharing her favour with *Shankar*, the white-headed kite (fish hawk). The cow, of course, is entirely sacred to all Hindus, and enters into many religious ceremonies. There is nothing surprising in this, as there is no other animal upon which a Hindu's general welfare depends to compare with the cow. Peacocks, monkeys, parrots, doves, and *nilghai* (an antelope) are also sacred beasts, which it is sinful to kill; but the amount of respect that they receive individually varies with the locality.

It is a lesson in long-suffering to see the patient respect that Hindus pay to the monkey, representing the god Hunuman, since there is possibly not one single native who would give the monkey a good character. This brute destroys crops, steals from the shops with impudence only rivalled by the crow, pulls tiles or thatch off the houses to get at some edible that it, or some other monkey, has hidden. In spite of all this, a Hindu when driving monkeys out of a fruit-tree will address them with all respect, as "Ji," "Sri," "Maharaj." No cow is put to the plough in this district. At the feast of the *Diwali*, the new moon of Kartic, the cow receives special honour. The Jains do not regard the cow as wholly sacred. The antelope when met on the right hand is a good omen. As Shasthi is the goddess who watches over children, every child is taught that it is a sin to kill a cat; so also when a fish-bone sticks in a child's throat it bows to the cat, thus hoping to receive help from *Shasthi*. The possession of the caul of a black cat that kittened on a Saturday is supposed to bring luck in lawsuits. The jackal, generally despised, is considered by certain low "castes" to be the wisest of animals. It is a good omen when met on the left-hand side. The monkey god was not the only helper when Rama tried to bridge the waters which divided India from Ceylon (Lănká), since the place of honour given to the squirrel was fully earned by the little loads of sand which it carried on its wet body.

If a butterfly settles on a child's head it is supposed to convey luck and an early marriage. Tame pigeons must not be killed, as they are the companions of the god of fortune. The tiger is worshipped by the Santals, and the whiskers are supposed to have magic power. The crow may bring evil, so it is fed after a funeral ceremony. The crow is wise, and originally obtained its wisdom by eating a piece of the tongue of Khina, wife of Mihir, a great astrologer. Mihir cut out his wife's tongue, because she was more learned than he (or said she was). He fastened the tongue to the ceiling of his room, from which place a crow stole it. The crow is by some regarded as a herald of death. Women worship the fish at the *Sripanchami*, and Narain is said to have appeared as a fish to destroy the wicked by a flood. Small balls of dough, painted red, are thrown into the river to feed the fishes, and this act is expected to bring good fortune to the house. A frog is sometimes placed over an abscess in the arm-pit as a cure. The bear is regarded as a friend of *Ram*, and its hair worn in an amulet is a charm against "fever."

To the question as to ceremonies and beliefs connected with specific diseases only a few answers were submitted.

When cholera appears in a town or village both Hindus and Mahomedans worship *Kalu Pir*. The worship is generally carried out by men only. Bread and goat's flesh are eaten: the goat-skin is then stuffed and hung on a pole at the entrance to the village. It is during epidemics of this disease that the *Alum* is paraded by Mahomedans. Worship of other deities is recorded, either to avert or stay cholera, and *Kali* and *Ola Bibi* are mentioned. Sankirtan parties singing the praises of *Hari* may parade the streets during an epidemic. As regards *Kali*, one informant says:—"The special worship is performed at 12 p.m. by Brahmins, with the music of drums, etc.: no animal is sacrificed." Jains worship *Santenath*, and sprinkle water, sanctified by being offered to the god, about the house to avert an attack of cholera. *Ola Devi* is propitiated with offerings of flowers and fruits. She has four hands, and wears a necklace of skulls, and is smeared with vermilion.

To protect animals numerous ceremonies are believed in : cowherds and milkmen pay special attention to *Bangsana*, but the village gods are expected to protect the village herds. To ensure fine weather for the farmer, an only child is made to place a *peerah* upside down in the courtyard, or it buries a brass cup in the earth. The villagers believe there will be no rain until the cup is dug up. When rain is wanted the images of the village are dipped in water several times a day. To keep crows from the newly sown seed and beasts of prey from the fold, fires are lighted at night. One account from the west of the district is very full, and I give it as it stands, with one or two slight additions from the oral replies obtained in the same neighbourhood :—

"The following rites are believed to be valuable in protecting cattle :—(1) The worship of *Goraknath ;* (2) The worship of *Krishna* and *Satya Naraian*, during which sacred water is sprinkled over the cattle sheds ; some believe in suspending, in the shed, a piece of paper bearing the name of *Arjun*. Other methods which may keep away evil are :—placing a beehive, or the shell of a tortoise, in the cattle shed. In some places, where bullocks are shod, some of the nails have the value of charms after certain *mantras* have been said over them by an *ojha*. To protect crops, cultivators put the following magic square in the field :—

1	8	9	14
11	12	3	6
7	2	15	8
13	10	5	4

"Whichever way these figures are read the total is thirty-two.

"In the case of oil-seed crops, the earthen pot from which the seed has been taken is preserved. If insects attack the crop, some of the offenders are caught and put into this pot. The pot is heated until the insects die, and this sacrifice of the few is supposed to kill, or frighten away, the rest. A stem of maize, painted red, is planted in the middle of a field as a protection against insects. Certain roots, dug up at the rising of a lucky star, and placed in a field, will prevent birds and insects destroying the crops. A *handi* (round earthen pot, red in colour, after baking), painted black and white is set on a pole as a scarecrow.* The cultivators, who grow mostly vegetables, perform certain rites to protect their crops. It is held by them unlucky to walk among certain crops with shoes on. No woman in a certain state of health, or in dirty clothes, may go near, or tread, in a field of melons or *patal* (or "palwal," *Tricosanthes dioica*, Roxb.). Failure of crops is often attributed to such unlucky happenings. Ceremonies of purification are then necessary. Holy water is sprinkled over the field and incense is burned. In some localities the shell of a crab, killed on a Saturday or Tuesday, is made into a lamp, which is lighted and placed in the middle of the field, on the top of a *handi* painted black. To ward off hailstorms, a sorcerer is sometimes called in. He takes a trident and a rosary and, stripping himself naked, tears his *dhoti* (large loin cloth) to pieces to propitiate the storm god. A stolen article is hidden in the earth to protect crops. To stop heavy rain, a naked woman places a wooden stool in the courtyard : the god of rain will sit upon it, and the downpour will cease. It is lucky if there is an only daughter who can stop rain by burying a metal cup : no more rain will fall until the cup is dug up."

* These charms are seldom trusted to work alone ; men or boys act as caretakers, and watchmen, by day and night. Where, as in Bengal, there are no hedges, or walls, dividing the fields, antelope, deer, pig, an occasional elephant, cattle, and monkeys may do great damage. Thieves, too, are not unknown. Often a watchman is paid to guard a number of fields. That he may be safe at night, and have a good view at all times, he builds a roofed *machan*, or hut, raised well above the crops.

Another informant writes:—"A pig is used to protect cattle from harm. The pig is let loose among cows or buffaloes: they attack the pig, and may trample it to death. The body is then burnt. When rain is needed many villagers pour water over the body of the image of Shiva, or other village gods. Sometimes the images are dipped in a well, or in water in which sugar has been dissolved. For fair weather Indra is worshipped. Mahomedans *pray* for rain."

From another part of the district comes the following:—"To ensure sunshine and favourable weather, *Indra,* the god of the skies, is worshipped during the month of Bhadrak, on the twelfth day. His image, made of mud, and painted red, is first worshipped and then thrown into the river. He may also be invoked when rain is required. *Manasa* is worshipped to keep away snakes—a branch of a tree, or a pan of water may be used to represent the goddess. A ceremony for the benefit and protection of cattle from evil and disease is observed in the month of Kartic. It is called the *Bhagabati jatra*, and *Mahadev* and *Goberdhan* are worshipped."

Among the ignorant classes there is a belief that disease can be got rid of or transferred to persons and things by performing certain ceremonies. A knife, some rice, or *dal* (peas, lentils), and turmeric are placed under the head of the sick person at night. The next day these articles are given to a beggar or stranger, who will carry away the disease. In the north of the district rice, betel-nut, and some vermilion are tied in a rag smeared with turmeric, and the little parcel is thrown down where three roads meet. Whoever treads on the parcel is supposed to catch the disease and relieve the sufferer. A patient suffering from "fever" will wrap himself in a black blanket. If a person passing asks, "Who are you?" the sick man replies, "Take my disease." Another charm is worked by placing seven nails, seven pieces of charcoal, one plantain, one sugar cake, one pan leaf, one betel-nut, and a lamp with oil and wick in a new earthen saucer painted red. This is passed seven times over the head of the patient, then taken to where three roads meet, and thrown down.

Turmeric, coloured rags, mustard seed, and the worship of Shiva may cause the transfer of disease. To get rid of *ague* the patient smells, during the day, at a packet of turmeric, seeds, etc. in a rag. At night he throws this out into the street, and whoever treads upon it will get his disease. On Sunday, Tuesday, or Saturday, the *ojha* is called in to repeat *mantras* over a piece of bone with three red patches on it. The patient or his friends throw the bone where three roads meet, and, as in other cases, anyone treading on it catches the disease. The jawbone of an ox is a favourite in this charm, which is known as *Thikun.* There is a method by which one may escape injury from treading on these "transfer packets." If the passer-by notices that he has trodden on such a packet, to avert ill results, he must turn round and tread on it again.

If no suitable image of a deity is to hand, a stone will do. Smeared with vermilion and with a few flowers before it, the stone becomes the home of a god, or goddess. In cases of "palpitation of the heart," a stone called "Eshab" is worn over the affected region. Another stone called "Hijrul Eahud," is thought to contain a fetish or spell which will cure gonorrhœa. Under many peepul (*Ficus religiosa*) and banian trees (*F. Indica,* Roxb.) single stones, or little heaps of stones, are frequently seen. Every stone bears its little dab of vermilion, and has most probably been anointed with oil. A ceremony connected with the worship of Shasthi takes place in the month of Jaistha (June). At this it is common to see women of all classes—Hindus, Mahomedans, Jains, and Aborigines—concerned for the safety of their children, worshipping the goddess, and placing flowers before the stone in which she is supposed to reside. In Bengal the spirit of a Pir, or Mahomedan saint, may inhabit a stone. The stone which has the power of drawing out snake venom has been mentioned elsewhere; and another stone, *Chumbuk Patha,* or lode-stone, is said to possess similar powers. The "Lingam" stone is mentioned as the abode of the creative principle: it is, however, much less commonly seen in this district than farther north.

Rags are tied to trees as offerings to *Petnis* (female evil spirits), supposed to be fond of rags. They are believed to inhabit trees,* or stones. Certain infantile diseases, insanity, and mental disease in women with certain symptoms are often ascribed to the power of *Petnis.* A woman desiring children will hang a piece of stone to a banian or peepul tree. This signifies that she wishes for a weight in her body. There is a famous peepul near Bishnupur, on which a number of stones hang. Near Beldanga there is a tank in which barren women bathe, as the special deity residing there can make them fruitful. Rags and coins are generally offered by the childless to the spirits in certain sacred trees; women whose children have died also tie rags to such trees. If the rags have disappeared when they return after a certain time they feel that the next child will be spared. Travellers may tie rags to trees, or make some small offering to the resident deity, believing that such offerings ensure them safety on their journey. When a tank or well is completed, gold coins, or cowries, are sometimes thrown in to make the water sacred. Cowries are often thrown into the Ganges by bathers, as offerings to *Ganga.* Rags are fastened to banian, tamarind (*T. Indicus,* Linn.), peepul, and some other trees, to propitiate the saint inhabiting them in spirit. *Taina Pir,* or *Gudri Pir,* are thus recognised. Stones are placed at the foot of trees supposed to be inhabited by *Dhelai Chandi.* In a village, called Marhgaondhana, there is a famous *Haritaki*† tree to which barren Mahomedan women of the lower classes are said to resort. They bathe, then stand beneath the tree in their wet clothes and appeal to the resident saint. They hold out their *chadar* (long cloth used as a skirt and cloak), and if any fruit falls into it the omen is good. A belief exists that life may be prolonged by taking the fruit according to the following rule:—"One fruit to be taken every morning, with salt, in the rainy season; with sugar in autumn; with ginger in the first half of the cold season; with long pepper in the second half; with honey in the spring; and with treacle in the two hot months." Rags are tied to trees as offerings by persons suffering from chronic wasting diseases. At Anduliah, near Kandi, there is a tree known as the Shitálá tree, inhabited by the small-pox goddess. About four miles from Kandi, to the west, there is a *banian* tree, worshipped when cholera is about. Rags, coloured with turmeric, are tied to the Sheorah (Siora *Trophis aspera* (Retz. ?) tree, to scare away disease and evil spirits. Little statuettes of horses, made of clay, are offered by Mahomedans at the graves of *Pirs.* Rags and coins are also frequently coloured red when used as offerings.

The Hindu girl is married long before the age of puberty, and to remain unmarried at that age is considered, by some "castes," to be a disgrace. At the first signs of puberty the girl is put away in a separate room for three days, and not allowed to see any male. She must live on coarse food, and give up all luxuries. This treatment is sometimes repeated for three days in succeeding months. On the sixteenth day the husband, with the family priest, having bathed, worships the sun. Then both husband and wife make offerings to the gods, feasting, and feeding beggars. Hair on the upper lip is considered the first sign of puberty in boys. This is called *Neaj* and *Shelka Kunda.* Among Mahomedans, girls go through a ceremony known as *Godibharai.* Fruits, etc., are tied round her waist, and she puts on a red *sari* (long cloth used as skirt and cloak). In the case of the Hindu girl a second part of the marriage ceremony takes place. When boys and girls attain puberty *Surya* is worshipped, and, in some parts, the marriage ceremony above noted takes place. Among Brahmins the boys perform a ceremony called *Upanayan.* A Mahomedan girl is often rubbed over with turmeric, after which she bathes. Among Shiah Mahomedans the attainment of puberty is one of rejoicing for both boys and girls. *Masi Bhini* is a ceremony then performed. Among Sunnis there are no special rites.

* Like Dryads.

† *Terminalia Chebula,* Retz. The fruit of this tree is noted in Hindu systems of medicine for its tonic qualities. For the story of the supposed origin of this tree readers are referred to "The Materia Medica of the Hindus," Bib. (32).

CLIMATE AND METEOROLOGICAL TABLE.

As in the rest of Bengal, the year is divided into three ,fairly well-marked, seasons :—March, April, May, and one half of June, the "hot season"; June, July, August, and September, "the rains"; and October, November, December, January, and February, the "cold season." The *Rarh*, or west of the district, was and is more healthy than the east, or *Baguri*. The people, even the Mussulmans, are of poor physique. Nothing shows this as does a consideration of the average of height and weight.

Measured in the District Jail.		Height.		Weight.
500 males	...	5 ft. 2¾ in.	...	106⅓ lbs.
100 females	...	4 ft. 10⅓ in.	...	90½ lbs.

The "hot season" is the most healthy, next comes the "rains," then the "cold season," as shown by the mortality "tables." As the river sinks the numerous "jhils" (tanks, lakes, ponds) drain off, and, where the land is not cultivated, it becomes swampy and a common cause of febrile complaints among the people. Kasimbazar lake is part of the old river-bed, and from malaria and intestinal fevers the people in its neighbourhood are sallow, and many suffer from enlarged spleen.

Many parts of Kasimbazar were depopulated and destroyed by disease after the change of the channel of the Bhagirathi in 1813. Mirzapur, too, once a thriving town, and the home of the indigenous silk weaving, of which some few looms remain, was ruined by "fever" about 1862, and quite half the inhabitants died within a few months. With treatment the results might have been less disastrous; but in those days little medical help was available, and quinine was not to be purchased at the post offices, as it can be now-a-days. The epidemic was checked in course of time, but left a population poisoned with malaria, and anæmic. Murshidabad and many other towns and villages suffer from "filth fevers," owing to dirty holes and tanks, black with foulness of all kinds. Cholera is endemic.

As regards malaria, we can check its ravages by careful drainage, by cultivation of swampy soil, and by the filling in of pools, etc., where mosquitoes might breed. The idea that complete destruction of the malaria-carrying species (*Anopheles*) by kerosene oil, etc., is possible is, I fear, Utopian. Further, I cannot agree with those who believe the mosquito to be the only vehicle for malaria. The poison can be conveyed and absorbed from infected water, and possibly from the air.

The bacterial, or "filth fevers" are much more to be dreaded than malaria, and are distinctly preventible. A grave responsibility rests on our Government and on the educated classes of this district and its towns. It may be said that they have no sanitation. It is true that in the towns latrines and cesspools are emptied in a perfunctory manner. The streets are swept without previous watering, and material, quiescent and harmless, is driven about by the sweeper's broom, to breed disease and death. Berhampur has a filtered water supply, but no drainage. Tanks of unspeakable filthiness are to be found in the heart of the town; and should the tank be nearer than the stand-pipe, anyone, with even a slight knowledge of a native servant, can predict the source of the household's water-supply. It is in vain to sweep the streets if the "sweepings" are not taken outside the town, or burnt. These "sweepings" are thrown down anywhere, even into the drainage outflow channel; *e.g.*, north-east of the hospital in our chief town! It is vain also to set up stand-pipes if the waste water from them forms new puddles and local swamps, in which mosquitoes can breed, and filth collect; vain also to talk of progress so long as a single tank is used for washing the clothes, etc., of persons dying of contagious diseases, and as a source for drinking water. Of all our municipalities only one can offer pure water; not one has either proper drainage or "conservancy."

Trenching nightsoil is all very well if cultivation follows, and the soil is not allowed to get sour. A good and cheap substitute is to hand in the *closed tanks* in which anærobic microbes do the work of disintegration.* Tanks should be filled up and deep wells dug, also artesian wells, or those with bucket or pump. Troughs for cattle can easily be made, and masonry tanks, connected with drains, and easily filled from the wells, should be provided for washing linen. If the condition of the towns is so bad from a sanitary point of view, after the working of the municipal system for so many years, what can one hope for in the villages? How many villages seek clean water and, not finding it, boil the dirty water!

Years ago, the late Mr. Ernest Hart exhorted us to teach the people to boil their drinking water! Have any signs of such progress appeared? Local taxation for complete sanitary improvements is impossible, so from the Government funds must come nearly all that is needed, and that need would be small if the people were compelled to do their own sanitary work. Give a certain number of villages good wells with a pump, and, under the present want of control, in a few weeks the pumps will be broken and the wells defiled by filth thrown or blown in, and by dirty pots lowered for water. This was an actual experience in the chief town of a neighbouring district. Until the people change their ideas, no progress can be expected. Let the educated young Bengalis, instead of spreading treason and ingratitude, go out and teach; let them institute extension lectures, with Government help, and go among the villages lecturing on health and the comfort it brings. Thus only can the masses be reached. When the landlord and the rich merchant give up extravagance at weddings and *nautches*—exhibitions which no intelligent man can see without pain, disgust, and sorrow—the money now thus wasted may go to improve the condition of their villages. Let them bring home sanitary truths by precept and example; then, and then only, shall we see any change for the better. The State must take back and bear much of the burden thrown on local bodies. Municipalities, District Boards, and such-like bodies, have neither sufficient knowledge nor sufficient funds to carry out the required improvements. Reform must begin at the top, not at the bottom. Away with the annual farce which, in the guise of an administration or other report, congratulates this or that town on progress which is no progress; or this or that zemindar on a liberality which may bring him a title but does no good to anyone else. Let us cease to live on the hope that at some time something will be done.

Whatever may have been its former repute, the town and neighbourhood of Berhampur has been extremely unhealthy since 1813. We have noted the change in the course of the Bhagirathi in that year, and the formation of a pestilent swamp, breeding *malaria* and "*filth*-fevers," which did so much to depopulate and ruin Kasimbazar. The place is, and has been for many years past, regarded as unhealthy. Its low level makes it extremely damp except for a short period during the "hot season," which is the healthiest. Its neighbourhood abounds in tanks and ditches, from which a damp, chilly mist floats at night, with an odour of decaying vegetation. Many of these tanks are of very large area, and have never been cleaned out. Add to this that low jungle abounds in the vicinity, and we have all the elements which combine with insufficient drainage to complete its unhealthy conditions.

The Civil Station has an evil repute for enteric fever; the Cantonment drains are old, and in many places covered up, so that they cannot be, and are not, cleaned, except for such flushing as they get during

* "A Sewage Disposal Experiment in Calcutta." By A. E. Silk, Sanitary Engineer, Bengal.

the "rains." As a variation to the seasonal changes, the district is subject to cyclonic storms, and especially at the vernal and autumnal equinoxes.

The main feature of all these cyclonic storms is torrential rain—ten to thirty inches of rain *per diem* often during two to four days. Major Cunningham's experiments at Roorkee showed that the sun evaporates not more than "one tenth of an inch of water per diem from the surface of slowly moving water." The effect of these storms is to markedly, and suddenly, reduce the temperature. This is pleasant, but such rapid variation is liable to cause intestinal congestion.* I will conclude this section with a quotation, which does not flatter our climate :—

"January 23rd, 1817.—At daybreak we crossed the Jellinghy. Travelling part of the way in carriages and part in palankeens, we arrived at Berhampur about half-past six, where we dined and slept at Mr. Ahmuty's. It was lucky that he has quarters in that splendid Cantonment, for we had had journey enough, and should have found it tiresome to proceed to Murshidabad, in the Appeal Court of which he is an officiating judge. The extraordinary unhealthiness of Murshidabad, which seems to have been becoming worse year after year, has forced most of the European functionaries to seek residences at some distance, and only to repair to the city for the discharge of their duties. These continued maladies, which had reduced the formerly great population of Murshidabad to a third of its original number, have been discussed in Council, and Government has ordered, as a public act, a correction of the evil, which no representation or persuasion could prevail on the inhabitants to apply. The city is full of thick copses of bamboo, which prevent a circulation of air ; and in the midst of these masses there are multitudes of little stagnant pools. We have directed the bamboos to be extirpated, and compensation, formed on a fair valuation, to be made to each owner ; and we have ordered the pools to be either filled up or enlarged into tanks, which may contain a serviceable supply for the people, while the quantity of the water will prevent its growing putrid. So incorrectly do large bodies of men judge of attentions to their welfare, that *it is probable this operation will be looked upon rather as an oppression than as an act of kindness.*"†

* J. Eliot, "Journal Asiatic Society of Bengal," Part II., No. 1, 1884.

† "The Private Journal of the Marquis of Hastings," Vol. ii., p. 163.

MEAN NORMAL METEOROLOGICAL ELEMENTS FOR EACH MONTH OF YEARS FOR WHICH RECORDS OF THE MURSHIDABAD DISTRICT ARE AVAILABLE.*

MONTHS.	ABSTRACT OF OBSERVATIONS TAKEN AT THE STATION OF BERHAMPUR.							RAINFALL (in inches).		Prevailing directions of wind, as determined by observations of 29 years.	Vapour tension, as determined by observations of 21-22 years.
	AIR PRESSURE	WIND.	TEMPERATURE.			HYGROMETRY	CLOUD.				
	Mean pressure reduced to sea-level and to constant gravity 45° lat. as determined by observations of 16 years.	Mean velocity in miles daily, as determined by observations of 24-27 years.	Mean daily maximum temperature.	Mean daily minimum temperature.	Mean daily temperature.	Mean humidity, 10 A.M., as determined by observations of 27-29 years.	Mean cloud amount, 10 A.M., as determined by observations of 27-28 years.	Mean of the station.	Mean of district.		
			As determined by observations of 16 years.					As determined by observations of 22-26 years.			
1	2	3	4	5	6	7	8	9	10	11	12
January ...	1.041	42	76.8	53.3	65.0	9	2.0	.52	.45	N 46° W	.394
February	.979	56	81.9	55.9	68.9	63	2.0	1.04	.88	N 76° W	.397
March ...	.868	84	92.8	66.0	79.4	56	2.8	1.05	1.06	S 71° W	.499
April	.758	122	100.2	74.4	87.3	58	3.1	1.50	1.66	S 30° W	.634
May	.683	129	95.7	76.0	85.8	71	5.2	5.36	5.37	S 33° E	.811
June	.556	127	92.6	78.5	85.5	82	8.0	9.38	9.60	S 37° E	.936
July	.544	117	89.4	78.7	84.0	87	8.7	10.71	11.11	S 40° E	.963
August	.604	99	88.5	78.5	83.5	87	8.7	11.77	10.11	S 41° E	.954
September ...	.707	88	88.8	78.4	83.6	85	7.9	10.13	9.02	S 38° E	.935
October	.867	52	87.7	74.5	81.1	78	4.4	3.83	3.68	N 35° W	.785
November ...	.981	39	81.8	64.1	72.9	73	2.4	.56	.68	N 20° W	.565
December	1.047	37	76.5	55.3	65.9	71	1.8	.12	.10	N 27° W	.427
Total of the year	9.635	992	1052.7	833.6	942.9	820	57.0	55.97	53.72	—	8.300
Mean of the year	.803	83	87.7	69.5	78.6	73	4.8	4.66	4.47	—	.692

* These records are not all for the same periods. This is unavoidable. As it is, however, not for their own sake that the statistics have been collected, but for the purpose of deducting general considerations, this want of uniformity does not matter.

INDUSTRIES.

Little need be said of agriculture; the methods and crops are those of Bengal in general. One curious feature of the district is that the areas east and west of the Bhagirathi, the "Baguri," and the "Rarh," are compensatory. In the east are grown the early rice crops—"aus"—while the "aman," or winter rice-harvest, is found principally in the *Rarh.* Little corn or grain is grown, rice being the main food-grain of the Bengali. Of the "pulses" a certain amount is grown in the district, but not sufficient for the total supply, and "dal" of various kinds, "Arhur," "Mung," and "Kalai," is imported. The mulberry culture receives notice in the section dealing with the silk industry. Other crops are: sugar-cane, tobacco, jute, turmeric, oil-seeds, and vegetables of various kinds, including those from imported seed (English vegetables). The sugar crop, though not large, is satisfactory, and a paying one. The crushing is done generally with the Bihia mills, invented and sold by Messrs. Thomson and Mylne. It is customary in many villages to hire both the mills, and the large iron pans used for boiling the juice. The figures given in the table showing the number of acres sown with various crops, were prepared in 1900, and they represent the agricultural arrangement of the Murshidabad district for a number of years. Slight variations and changes, of course, occur, but the facts are approximately correct.

MURSHIDABAD DISTRICT.

ACREAGE UNDER CROPS.

English, or Vernacular, Names.

CEREALS AND PULSES.

	Acres.
Rice	521,700
Wheat	144,500
Barley	64,300
Cholum jowar (millet)	—
Cumba or bajra (millet)	—
Ragi or mandua	—
Maize...	300
Gram (pulses)	98,000
Other food grains, including other pulses ...	100,100

OIL SEEDS.

Linseed	30,100
Til or ginjelly	7,800
Others (mostly mustard)	43,100

	Acres.
CONDIMENTS, SUGAR.	
Condiments and spices (turmeric, chilli, etc.) ...	3,000
Sugar-cane	17,000
FIBRES.	
Jute	19,600
Others (hemp, Rhea?)	700
DYES.	
Indigo	22,200
NARCOTICS.	
Opium	—
Coffee	—
Tea	—
Tobacco	800
Cinchona	—
Indian hemp	—
MISCELLANEOUS CROPS.	
Fodder crops (grass, millet)	—
Orchard and garden produce (mangoes, leechees, papaya, plantains, plums)	20,000
Food crops (vegetables)	11,600
Non-food crops (mainly mulberry)	75,000
Total ...	1,179,800
Deduct area cropped more than once	227,100
Net area cropped during the year	952,700

The oil seeds include mustard, black and yellow, linseed, til (*Sesamum Indicum*, Linn.) or "ginjelly," and "others." The table of acreage gives for "others" 43,100 acres, and most of this is, no doubt, mustard seed. The amount grown in the district does not, however, supply the demand. Many villagers of the "Teli," or oilman "caste," crush the seeds with old-fashioned wooden mills turned by a bullock. These wooden mills are wasteful, but the people prefer the oil from them. Similar mills are used in the District Jail for punishment labour, and in the Lunatic Asylum, where they provide that hard and healthy exercise which relieves mental symptoms and induces sleep. Such exercise, however, can be used only for picked cases, and the out-turn is necessarily variable, and often small. In both cases the oil is sold at a price always above the market-rate outside.

The largest output of mustard oil comes from a steam factory in Berhampur (Dyanagur). In 1892 a limited company was formed by certain well-to-do native gentlemen; capital about Rs. 50,000. The company was called "The Berhampur Sambhu Mill Company, Limited." The directors carried on the oil-mill until 1896, when the concern became bankrupt. After a meeting of the shareholders an application was made to the District Judge to appoint a liquidator. This was done August 15th,

1896. The mill was then sold by auction at the Judge's Court, and purchased by Mr. M. Ferguson* for Rs. 19,000. The defunct company paid its shareholders about 8 per cent. on each share of Rs. 100. The present owner seems to be able to make his mill pay, and sells only wholesale. The possible out-turn is 150 to 180 maunds of oil a day, but the mills are never worked to the full; indeed, they are sometimes idle for weeks when the stock of oil is large, or seed cannot be obtained. Mr. Ferguson uses a very ingenious machine for cleaning the seed. The annual output comes to about 8,000 maunds of oil and 16,000 maunds of oil-cake. The latter is principally used for feeding cattle. If carefully used in small quantities, the cake is a capital manure, especially for rose-trees. Mustard belongs to the natural order *Cruciferæ*, and the varieties used are *Sinapis nigra*, *S. alba*, and a hybrid seed. The white seed generally gives most oil, and fetches the highest price. It is generally the custom to mix the seeds. Commercial mustard oil is not free from adulteration with oils from cheaper seeds. The amount of oil produced from the other seeds grown in the district does not call for notice.

Tobacco is grown mainly for home consumption, and principally by the middle and lower classes. The pipe, *chilum*, and the *pan* (*pan*-leaf, *betel-nut* with tobacco, lime, and catechu) are the solace and luxury to the inhabitant of the East that the pipe and glass of beer are to the Western brother. There is very little drinking among the respectable classes and "castes," but the low "castes" consume a great deal of raw spirit. They drink quietly, and often alone, to get drunk, and for no other reason.

From old records we learn that in the prosperous days of Murshidabad there was a considerable trade in hand-made paper at Chunakhali. To-day, only one family is engaged in this work. The hand-workers could not compete with the paper-mills near Calcutta and other cities. The brass utensils of Berhampur are of excellent design and quality, and at one time were famous in Bengal.

ACREAGE SOWN WITH TOBACCO IN THE MURSHIDABAD DISTRICT DURING FIVE YEARS.†

Years.	Acres sown.	Out-turn in Annas out of 16 Annas.‡	Out-turn per cent., taking 100 to represent the normal out-turn.
1895-96	1000	13 Annas	—
1896-97	800	11 Annas	—
1897-98	800	14 Annas	—
1898-99	800	—	84
1899-1900	800	—	84

* To whom I am indebted for these details.

† The magistrate in this case, as in several others, has been most kind in giving me any available information.

‡ "16 annas" represent 100 per cent., or a full crop.

STATEMENT SHOWING THE AMOUNT, NATURE, AND VARIETIES OF ALCOHOL, GANJA, BHANG, AND OPIUM, CONSUMED IN THE DISTRICT OF MURSHIDABAD DURING TWENTY YEARS.

Years.	CONSUMPTION OF EXCISABLE ARTICLES.											NO. OF LICENCES IN FORCE.						
	Country Spirit.		Imported Liquor in gallons.	Ganja.					Bhang.	Opium.	Charas.	Ganja.	Bhang.	Charas.	Country Spirit.	Imported Liquor.	Opium.	Druggists' Permit.
	In London proof gallons.	In gross gallons.		Choor.	Round.	F. L. T.	Flat small Turis.	Total in Maunds.										
				m. s. ch.				m. s. ch.		m. s. ch.	m. s. ch.							
1880-81	5265	8088	—	2 0 12	14 34 9	73 16 6	—	90 11 11	—	64 15 0	—	57	—	—	87	9	96	—
1881-82	—	—	—	5 32 14	23 27 9	65 23 5	—	95 3 12	—	63 25 0	—	57	—	—	82	7	87	—
1882-83	—	—	—	23 19 2	19 15 11	29 18 4	—	72 13 1	—	62 34 0	—	55	1	—	55	5	77	—
1883-84	—	—	—	3 23 0	48 16 7	20 32 4	—	72 31 11	—	63 31 0	—	60	—	—	79	5	84	—
1884-85	—	—	—	0 9 3	60 21 14	13 8 0	—	73 39 1	—	60 21 0	—	61	—	—	81	5	68	—
1885-86	4536	7160	—	0 10 0	37 2 11	30 8 2	—	67 20 13	—	53 30 0	—	60	—	—	78	5	70	—
1886-87	4707	7431	—	4 37 3	29 32 11	48 37 11	—	78 29 9	0 5 0	55 33 0	—	57	1	—	72	5	72	—
1887-88	4022	5720	—	0 0 9	23 3 6	69 31 14	—	92 35 13	2 20 0	61 15 0	0 3 0	58	2	1	67	5	74	5
1888-89	4896	6450	—	14 6 6	20 4 6	60 16 7	—	94 27 3	3 6 14	56 38 0	0 8 4	57	2	1	66	6	73	4
1889-90	4023	5365	—	13 31 7	10 16 3	72 12 4	—	96 19 10	4 23 0	57 12 0	0 10 3	51	2	1	56	6	77	15
1890-91	4229	6661	—	12 1 14	16 13 12	51 20 8	—	99 36 2	4 16 0	53 15 0	0 16 9	43	1	1	41	2	49	12
1891-92	4428	6136	—	6 23 9	8 25 0	56 35 15	—	72 4 8	6 18 0	51 21 0	0 33 0	41	5	3	34	1	50	15
1892-93	3808	5081	—	26 5 11	5 13 1	26 22 1	—	58 0 13	7 11 10	51 5 0	1 2 0	42	4	5	34	1	49	16
1893-94	3935	5833	—	24 13 8	3 26 11	23 38 11	—	51 38 14	7 39 8	47 23 0	0 38 0	42	5	6	31	1	53	115
1894-95	3844	5301	—	26 11 5	—	23 28 14	2 17 3	52 17 6	8 12 9	46 5 0	1 26 0	42	5	3	30	7	52	112
1895-96	3740	4994	—	31 9 2	—	16 3 3	3 11 11	50 24 0	9 27 12	45 14 0	1 17 0	42	4	2	31	6	51	89
1896-97	2529	3254	—	36 6 0	—	3 14 6	0 35 4	40 15 10	8 34 3	42 4 0	0 32 0	43	4	2	31	7	36	57
1897-98	2442	3148	—	34 7 1	0 0 13	5 36 7	0 17 0	40 21 5	10 5 0	39 36 0	0 15 0	42	4	2	31	6	36	33
1898-99	3303	4278	914	39 12 7	0 0 2	7 15 2	1 10 10	47 38 5	10 21 14	42 16 0	0 13 0	41	4	2	31	6	36	95
1899-1900	3552	4585	741	26 34 6	—	23 24 13	3 1 6	53 20 9	11 25 11	44 1 0	0 20 0	41	5	2	31	6	36	66

EXCISE CASES.

Year.	Number of persons brought to trial in connection with cases.								Total.
	Country Spirit.	Imported Liquor.	Other Articles.	Tari.	Breach of Condition of Licence.	Pachwai.	Ganja. Bhang. Charas.	Opium.	
1880-81	—	—	—	—	—	—	—	—	127
1881-82	—	—	—	—	—	—	—	—	66
1882-83	—	—	—	—	—	—	—	—	188
1883-84	—	—	—	—	—	—	—	—	168
1884-85	—	—	—	—	—	—	—	—	197
1885-86	—	—	—	—	—	—	—	—	204
1886-87	—	—	—	—	—	—	—	—	211
1887-88	—	—	—	—	—	—	—	—	200
1888-89	—	—	—	—	—	—	—	—	176
1889-90	—	—	—	—	—	—	—	—	162
1890-91	—	—	—	—	—	—	—	—	186
1891-92	12	—	8	60	3	34	10	17	144
1892-93	5	—	10	53	3	43	3	15	132
1893-94	5	—	57	36	7	74	6	2	187
1894-95	10	—	—	46	4	49	—	31	140
1895-96	17	—	—	50	2	72	6	22	169
1896-97	3	1	—	36	3	35	3	20	101
1897-98	9	—	—	44	3	41	9	13	119
1898-99	13	—	—	25	4	21	8	12	83
1899-1900	2	—	—	14	1	18	7	9	51

LIST OF EXCISE SHOPS WITHIN THE SEVERAL MUNICIPALITIES IN THE DISTRICT OF MURSHIDABAD AS REPORTED IN 1900-1901.

BERHAMPUR.

Khagra—Imported liquor, distillery, ganja, opium, siddhi, majum, and charas shops.

Berhampur—Tari shop.

Kunjaghata and *Hatar Sanko*—Tari shops.

Gorabazar—Imported liquor, distillery liquor, ganja, opium, and tari shops.

MURSHIDABAD.

Panchraha—Imported liquor, distillery liquor, and ganja shops.

Chauk—Country spirit, ganja, opium, siddhi, and imported liquor.

Ichaganj—One tari shop.

AZIMGANJ.

Azimganj—Distillery, ganja, opium, and tari shops.

KANDI.

Kandi—Distillery, ganja, opium, imported liquor, siddhi, charas, and pachwai.

JANGIPUR.

Jangipur—Imported liquor, ganja, opium, and tari shops.

Raganathganj—Distillery, ganja, opium, and tari shops.

THE SILK INDUSTRY.*

THE silk trade was one of the earliest of all the industries which occupied the servants of the East India Company in this district. Their efforts were stimulated by competition with the French, Dutch, and Armenians.

Of the three rivals the Armenians, though few in number, lasted the longest. After the battle of Plassy, Dutch and French *filatures* disappeared, or came into the hands of the English. It is impossible to discover the date at which the silk industry commenced in Bengal, but it must be of great age. Silkworms are indigenous, and for some species we need not seek for any foreign origin. According to the *Commercial Resident* at Jangipur, at the end of the eighteenth century, there was a time when the silkworm was introduced from further east, probably China, since its first home was in the Brahmaputra valley. From Persia, too, India may have received some "seed," as there was a time—fifteenth century—when the silks of Persia were very highly esteemed. In 1619 this silk was being sold in the London market for £1 6s. 10d. the pound; and Mr. Geoghegan† gives the export as 2,000 to 3,000 bales. The first distinct allusion to Bengal silk in the old records is an order to the Company's agents, in 1621, forbidding further purchases. This, it is suggested, was partly due to a hope that the Shah of Persia would grant concessions to an English Company. The negotiations were not successful, and merchants then began to give serious attention to the possibility of extending the industry in Bengal. Factories were established, one of the earliest being at Kasimbazar. A second and larger one followed. The Company's chief factor, from Madras, visited Bengal in 1679, and reported favourably on the prospects. The oldest species of "foreign" worm known to Murshidabad was the *Bombyx textor*, called from its size *bará palu* (big worm). This was re-introduced in 1710, from China. It was being reared in a village near Jangipur, introduced by an elephant dealer from "Tipperah, or Sylhet." By 1796 it had deteriorated in its new home, and the yield was not "much more than one half the quantity of silk that they, in their youth, remember" (Atkinson). The progress of the industry had various ups and downs, factories being at times closed, owing, as we have seen in the historical chapter, to the tyranny of one or other of the Bengal Nawabs. Marked progress commenced about 1750, and the centres of the industry were practically those of the present day. In addition to the yellow silk of the *Bombyx*, "*tusser*" was brought from the jungles of Chybassa and Midnapur. Geoghegan is of opinion that the winding of *tusser*‡ had been going on "for ages."

Four classes of persons benefit by the silk industry:—(1) Cultivators of mulberry; (2) Rearers

* N. G. Mukerji (24).

† J. Geoghegan (25).

‡ The forest districts from which the tusser cocoons can now be obtained in the Central Provinces are:—Chanda, Belaspur, Sambalpur, and to a less degree, Balaghat, Seoni, and Bhandara. In those parts the people interested in the industry are called Dhimars, and the Saj (*Terminalia tomentosa*) leaves are generally used as food for the tusser worms. As an encouragement, the Forest Department of the Central Provinces suggested, in 1892, that *baris*, or farms, for tusser rearing should be granted rent free to the Dhimars, if they were willing to settle in the Forest areas, and work for Government at the usual wages, when not employed in tusser rearing.

of silkworms; (3) Winders, working either in the large factories or in their own homes; and (4) Weavers, especially of the coarser kinds of silk, and *mutka.*

At the period of which we are treating, three species of silkworm were reared:—(1) *Bombyx textor* ("bara palu," annual); (2) *Bombyx fortunatus* ("deshi palu," indigenous?); and (3) *Bombyx cræsi* ("nistari," origin doubtful), three varieties. All these worms feed on the mulberry (*Morus Indica*).

The native methods of winding were very rough-and-ready, and broken threads spoiled much of the silk. The threads were also very uneven in the same reeling, "part single, part double, treble, and in many instances quadruple." When the position of the East India Company was placed on a firm basis, after the battle of Plassy, steps were taken to instruct the people in the improved methods used in the *filatures* under European management. The Kasimbazar factory agent recorded as the reason for dearness of silk in 1757, that the ryots could not attend to their work in peace, owing to Mahratta inroads.

The gentleman chosen as agent by the directors was Mr. Wilder, who devoted his time to improvements in winding off the silk. He worked for the East India Company from the end of 1757 to 1761, when he died in harness at Kasimbazar. He was succeeded by Mr. Joseph Porichon. In 1765, when the East India Company took over the entire management of the Nawab's revenues, further efforts were made to improve and extend the silk industry, not only by the *suaviter in modo,* but by the *fortiter in re.* The directors found it necessary to point out that they did not wish commerce to be increased by means savouring of oppression. In 1772 the Company made it known that certain waste lands would be given rent free, for two years, to those ryots who would cultivate the mulberry. The rent for the third year was to be at half the ordinary rates in the district. The amount of silk increased markedly, but improvement in quality did not accompany the increase in quantity. The Company sought to model its winding methods on those employed in Italy, and the directors sent out Messrs. Wiss, Robinson, and Aubert, with artizan reelers from Italy and France. It is sad to relate that of this *trio* only two reached India. Mr. Aubert died on the voyage. Wiss and Robinson arrived in 1770, and introduced new methods into the Kasimbazar factories and elsewhere. The result was eminently successful, though the means employed were very simple. The Company had imported a quantity of "seed," as the eggs of the silkworm are technically called, from China, in 1771, hoping to improve the Bengal species. One of the factors, Mr. Speed, reported that the results did not come up to their expectation. Change of locality, or bad management, was followed by degeneration of the new importations. Nothing daunted, however, Mr. Frushard and Captain Kyd were deputed to bring further supplies, which did well and started the China species now flourishing in Bengal. A stock of young mulberry plants was brought from China; but apparently these became ornamental trees in the Governor's garden. As ever, progress found checks from the racial inertia so painfully evident in the majority of Bengal ryots. The people had always fed their worms on young leaves, and could not be brought to see the advantage of older leaves. In 1773 the home directors sent over another batch of skilled factors, Messrs. Platell, Baumgartner, Frushard, and Brigante. Improvements went on steadily, and by 1775 a really satisfactory method of reeling was almost universal. An estimate of the amount of new silk exported between 1772 and 1775 gives an average of 187,494 "small pounds" for each year. 1775 to 1785 showed a wonderful increase, the annual average reaching 500,000 "small pounds"; and Bengal silk soon had no rival of any importance, except in China.

1781 was an unfortunate year, as the money which, under peaceful conditions, would have been spent on the purchase of silk, was wanted for the army. The East India Company tried a species of free trade in 1783, leasing certain factories to outsiders known as "adventurers." This system did not succeed; indeed, it is curious that the result was not foreseen. The "adventurer" had no interest in the *filature* beyond a money profit. The Company soon recognised that the new venture was destined to fail, and the trade was again placed in the hands of their own officers in 1785. The contractors were to supply 540,000 "small pounds" per annum; but for many reasons, and not least among them the dreadful blow given to all trade by the famine of 1769-70, they were at first unable to fulfil their undertakings. Things, however, were coming round, and ryots were already returning to land, waste for many years. With 1793 came brighter prospects, and the contract was exceeded by 137,000 pounds. In addition, the Company stored 91,885 pounds belonging to private individuals.

Geoghegan gives a table showing the "ups and downs" of the trade from 1793 till 1808. The satisfactory figures of 1793 were never reached again, and in 1797 the total from all sources was 88,219 lbs. There were no private ventures that year. Again the industry improved and showed a total of 645,421 lbs. in 1799, sinking again and producing, in the worst year of all for the Company—1802—78,950 lbs. In that year private enterprise secured 35,794 lbs., making a grand total of 114,744 lbs. The wars with Napoleon prevented the English silk weavers from obtaining silk from Italy, and gladly as they would have welcomed Bengal silk, they could not get it.

Mulberry cultivation paid the ryot, who could obtain Rs. 8 per *bigah** for his crop. Deducting Rs. 2 for rent, or less, Rs. 1. in some parts of the "Rarh," a very satisfactory return of Rs. 6 or Rs. 7 remained for his labour. Troubles undoubtedly arose from several causes, of which Mr. Atkinson, of Jangipur, instanced the following:—(1) Unsuitable food, poor mulberry leaves; (2) ignorance in the rearing of the worms, and insanitary surroundings of the huts in which they were kept; and (3) a commercial drawback due to cheating on the part of the rearers, who presented good samples, upon which the price of cocoons was fixed, subsequently supplying cocoons from insufficiently fed worms, increasing the quantity at the expense of the quality.

Italian eggs had proved unsatisfactory, and recourse was had to China for further importations of "seed" to improve the stock. Though prizes were offered for improvements, and several "reels" and other appliances were tried, and fresh supplies of Italian "seed" imported, nothing occurred worth recording. With a return to the old methods the trade became more prosperous, and the imports into England rose from the low point at which they stood in 1812. Notwithstanding fluctuations, due to fraud, idleness, or climatic causes, the rise was steady, and the most marked increase was noticeable in consignments from private investors—a sure sign of general prosperity and confidence in the Government. In 1820 the total from all sources was 1,071,447 lbs.; in 1828, 1,387,754 lbs. This high level was kept up until the year 1832, when the imports from Bengal fell, showing in 1835 727,535 lbs. In 1832 the two chief factories in this district were at Kasimbazar and Jangipur, each with its Commercial Resident. Advances were made to cultivators; and, in addition, those who held contracts under the Company enjoyed certain privileges, and protection by the Company. These contractors were exempted from suits in the Civil Courts, except in respect to their dealings with the Company itself. Prices were fixed by the Residents for their own districts. In 1833 the seer† of silk was worth:—

	Rs.	As.
(*a*) March "bund" large	8	8
(*b*) " " small	7	0
(*c*) April " "	7	0
(*d*) "Rains" " "	6	2
(*e*) (*f*) October and November	7	2

* The *bigah* varies, but the Government bigah in Bengal is 1,600 square yards. 3¼ bigahs = 1 acre.

† About 2 lbs.

Filatures were classed by "basins," and in 1831-2 there were 12,039 Company's basins and 3,684 hired ones; total, 15,723. I cannot say how many of them were in Murshidabad, but a fair proportion of them no doubt. Although all *filature* silk was exported raw, some weaving was done at the Kasimbazar factories with *putney* silk, and there were many native weavers.

To return to the kinds of silkworms reared, we find that at this period, in addition to the species already mentioned, there was a China worm, *Bombyx sinensis,* reared in the district. It crossed with the *deshi* species in Kasimbazar. The commonest kind, however, in that part of the district, was the *bara palu, Bombyx textor,* which furnished the major part of the "March bund," considered good silk. This worm also flourished in the Jangipur circle, but, as before stated, the Commercial Resident thought it had somewhat degenerated.

Bombyx fortunatus furnished no less than five crops, viz.:—March, April, June, July, October, and November. They were not of equal value; those of April, June, and July were the worst, and that of March was often precarious. In rank, as a silk producer, *Bombyx fortunatus* was considered next to *Bombyx textor. Bombyx sinensis* came next, and was plentiful in the Jangipur circle, yielding cocoons from January to May, and if well fed and cared for, every month from November to June. This district did not, indeed, could not, entirely depend on its own resources, and imported very largely from other parts, especially from Maldah, where *Bombyx cræsi* gave no less than six harvests, the best of which were in April, June, July, and September. As regards individual yield of silk, the following figures were given by Mr. W. Prinsep in 1832:—"Annual worm—one maund, of eighty 'sicca' to the seer, yields about three seers of good silk (= 7.5 per cent.); small 'deshi' worm, one maund will yield two and a quarter seers of good silk (8.625 per cent.)."

The worms reared in the Murshidabad district generally fed on the indigenous mulberry (*tut*). In addition to this, foreign mulberry was grown. According to Mr. De Verinne, the worm preferred the leaves of *Morus alba*—small leaves of dark colour. He speaks of *Morus alba* and *Morus rubra* as trees twenty feet high. *Morus Indica* was, however, cultivated on the Bengal plan as small saplings one to two feet high, cut four times a year, and stripped of its leaves during the "rains," when cutting would be injurious and cause the plants to rot.

The cultivation on the raised fields in the *Rarh* on the west of the Bhagirathi was, and is still, of this type. The ground having been ploughed, "cuttings," five to six inches long, are planted three or four together, about six inches apart, in rows. Between the rows enough space is left for hoeing, or ploughing. The mulberry does not require irrigation in this district, and will yield at least four harvests a year. If the ground is kept clean and manured, the plants will last ten years or more. Fresh earth should be put on the fields every year, and manure every two or three years. These results are given in good soil; in poor soil four or five years is the longest the plants will last. The plant, when required, is cut three or four inches from the ground. After the "rains" the plant is cut down and the ground ploughed. The tree mulberry is not used in this district, and, indeed, it is less profitable; the "annual worm," however, prefers its leaves. The *deshi* and *nistari* worms prefer the leaves of the small plant. The best month for planting is *Kartic* (October). There is a belief that the first crop of leaves is poisonous. The plant may be cut every two months. As this district is remarkably flat, the mulberry lands have to be artificially raised.

The rearing-houses are generally about 24 feet long, 15 feet wide, and 9 feet high, with a raised floor, mud walls, and a thatched roof, with the ridge about 14 feet from the ground. The door should be on the south side, and light admitted through windows. Two would be sufficient for a house of the above dimensions. A rearing-house thus built would hold 256,000 worms (200 *kahans**). It would

* Mr. Speed, quoted by Geoghegan.

be fitted with five *ghurrahs* or *machans*, each with sixteen shelves (dàlás) measuring 5½ feet by 4½ feet, with a raised rim two to three inches high. These are "leeped" (plastered) with cow-dung. Each shelf will accommodate 3,200 worms (2½ *kahans*). The shelves are supported by bamboos resting on earthen saucers, kept full of water, to protect the worms against ants or other insects. Each house is provided with ten spinning mats (chundrukies or "phungs"), 3½ feet by 4 feet, with "raised work" partitions three inches high. The doorway should be protected by a bamboo "chick" (mat), and one of these should be placed in each window. Other properties required by the rearer are:—baskets for mulberry leaves; a knife (byturnee) for cutting the plant, and a few "gunnies." This establishment cost fifty to sixty-five rupees in the days when Mr. Speed's account was written. We shall see presently what changes have been made since that time.

While the worms are young the mulberry leaves are cut up quite fine, larger pieces being given as the worm grows, until, in the third and fourth stages, the leaves may be placed on the shelves on the stick as they are cut. Silkworms require cleanliness, and should be fed twice a day at least. All dirt and stale leaves are to be cleared away at each feeding time. If the worms require it, they may, with advantage, be fed oftener. As they grow, the worms, with each change of skin, show slight changes of colour. When ready to spin they change from "a greenish cream to a mellow light orange colour." At this stage they are placed on the spinning mats in the open air, facing the sun. When under cover at night, a lamp should be kept burning in the shed, as the worms tend to slacken off when in the dark, and spinning is thus delayed. The average time taken for cocoon spinning is fifty-six hours. During the "rains" and winter *bunds* the cocoon will be ready for reeling about the third day, but at other times after four or five days. The grub is killed by exposure to the sun or by baking in special ovens. The heat of the ovens was formerly tested by the hand, and experience produced very accurate judges of temperature. Nowadays, nearly every oven is fitted with a thermometer, and thus the right temperature is easily kept up. While the baking is going on the oven doors are luted with clay.

Mr. W. Shakespear* gives some interesting notes on the "practices" and "prejudices" of Hindu silkworm rearers. The worm is often held sacred, and prayers are offered, and penances undergone, to ensure its welfare. During sickness, or during critical periods of the silkworm's growth, the rearer abstains from carnal pleasures; and women, parturient or menstruating, are forbidden to approach the sheds. At such times rearers will often neither wash nor be shaved; and certain articles of diet, such as "fish, turmeric, garlic, and onions," are avoided; snuff and tobacco were also forbidden. As a charm against evil, an old shoe containing a bunch of thorns was often hung on the *chick*, in the doorway of the rearing-house.

The method of reeling among the natives in the early part of the nineteenth century, of which we are treating, was somewhat as follows†:—"A small reel (*laya*), eight inches in diameter, was fastened to a spindle and turned by hand, or a large wheel *(gayi)* was also used and turned by a winch. A small furnace, fed with cow-dung fuel, furnished the means of heating the water, in which the cocoons were soaked, to loosen the threads. In the East India Company's *filatures* reeling was done on European models; but the appliances were simple, and the winders are worked now, as then, by hand. While one man or boy separates the threads and maintains the water at a proper temperature, another 'hand,' generally a boy, turns the reel. Spinners and winders vary in skill but they soon acquire the 'temperature sense,' which tells them when to add cold water to the bowl in front of them."

The water in the bowls for holding the cocoons is, in nearly all *filatures*, heated by steam from a central engine-house. At the present time none of the silk companies weave any of their silk; but before 832 the East India Company did a certain amount of weaving, turning out *Korah* and *bandanas*.

* Geoghegan (25). † Dr. Buchanan.

At the present time there are still some native weavers in this district, and in many cases their work is excellent. Nothing could be better value for the money than the large silk pocket-handkerchiefs costing about one rupee each. Good *mutka* is also always procurable for hot-weather suits, and many prefer it to any of the Assam silks sold for that purpose. The coloured silks are really beautiful; these and white silk suitable for ladies' dresses can be purchased at very reasonable rates from the silk merchants in Berhampur. If the industry were advertised and pushed as it should be, the weavers of Murshidabad would have no reason to complain. The hindrance to increase in the silk trade here lies in the people themselves, and their characteristic *inertia*, the ruin not only of this, but of other industries for which this district was once famous. Dr. Buchanan estimated (1807-14) that the value of silk goods sent into Murshidabad and Calcutta by the weavers of this district and Maldah, was ten lakhs annually. He mentions six kinds of silk cloth produced by the looms of Bengal: (1) *Dhuti*, (2) *Nihe*, (3) *Mekla*, (4) *Chelang*, (5) *Jhardar*, and (6) *Mosaris*.*

The *tusser* cocoons formerly existed in all the forests, from "Ramgurh to Midnapur," and are still plentiful in Chybassa and parts of Lohardugger, Orissa, Midnapur, and the Sunderbans, whence they are imported. The cocoons are about the size of a walnut, smooth, blackish brown in colour, and so hard that they are simply thrown together into sacks and carted to the *filatures*. The silk itself is coarse, very strong, and reddish brown in colour. The early history of the *tusser* trade is scanty, but, in addition to the wild crops, it was cultivated in some parts of Bengal, the worm most fancied being *Attacus Ricini*, which feeds on the leaves of the castor-oil plant. In 1834 Mr. Hugon reported that Berhampur imported large quantities of *tusser* thread from Assam; but much of it was not true *tusser*, being lighter and of a fawn colour. About 1832 the East India Company began to give up the silk industry as a Government venture, and it passed into the hands of private firms. The oldest of these firms in this district was the Bengal Silk Company. The East India Company sold their Kasimbazar factories and the Residency to a Dr. McPherson, who carried on the work for some years.† He built for himself a fine house at Banjetti, some two miles from Berhampur, on the left-hand side of the main road leading from the Civil Station to Murshidabad. Little is known as to the history of the other factories in the district. Some passed from the Company into the hands of Armenian merchants; others were built by private enterprise. Dr. McPherson sold his property to Mr. James Lyall, and this gentleman founded the Bengal Silk Company somewhere about 1880. The new company worked the Kasimbazar factory for a time, but pulled down the Resident's house, and with the materials built the house in Berhampur known as the "magistrate's house." This building passed from the Company, probably by sale, to the estate of Raja Asutosh Nath Roy. The house at Banjetti came into the hands of the ancestors of the present Maharaja of Kasimbazar. This gentleman now uses it as a guest-house. In course of time the Bengal Silk Company abandoned the factory at Kasimbazar and started others—Gonatea, Babulbuna, etc. The old factory was long ago pulled down, and the site is used as a garden by the Maharaja of Kasimbazar. Mr. T. Rice, the manager for the Bengal Silk Company at Babulbuna (Berhampur), has kindly given me the following information :—"The Company has thirteen *filatures* in the Murshidabad district, employing, when all are in full work, 2,039 spinners."

Messrs. L. Payen & Co., a prosperous firm under the management of Mr. P. E. Gourju, have *filatures* in twelve villages, employing, when in full work, 3,768 spinners, turners, etc. This firm is very successful in dealing with *tusser* silk at their *filatures* in Bazarpara and Naraianpur. Mr. M. Ferguson carries on a firm under his own name with considerable success.

* Quoted by Geoghegan (25).

† For information concerning this transition period I am indebted to Mr. M. Ferguson, owner of Zemindari and silk *filatures*, who has lived many years in Berhampur and came out as a young man to work under the Bengal Silk Company. Seeing better prospects, he started on his own account.

In 1866 Japanese "seed" was imported into this district, but the worms did not give any better yield than the local kinds. The silk was, however, of good quality, and sold for Rs. 27 a seer.

In 1870-71 reports were called for from the various silk districts, and from this district they were, on the whole, satisfactory. Mr. Perrin, of Berhampur, stated that the mulberry cultivation was flourishing and skilfully carried out by the *chàsás* (cultivators), and Mr. Marshall, one of the founders of the Bengal Silk Company, suggested the offering of prizes for the best cocoons and the distribution of tracts in Bengal setting forth the best methods of breeding and rearing silkworms. On the other hand, complaints were made that the native rearers did not feed their worms sufficiently, and Mr. Malcolm, of Ramnagger, stated that in the Kandi sub-division the silkworms were degenerating from rapid and unduly forced reproduction, and that whereas "twenty or twenty-five years ago" there were but four "bunds" in the year, there were at that time six to eight. There had, however, in earlier times, been five, and sometimes more, "bunds," though perhaps not in the parts known to Mr. Malcolm.

As regards native weavers, their "Korahs" are still well known, especially those of Baluchar and Murshidabad.

Although there would not seem to be much difference between them, all mulberry-plants are not equally useful. To take first *Morus nigra*. While most species of silkworm can be reared on it, *Bombyx fortunatus* (*Chota palu*) will suffer from *flacherie* if fed on this alone, and even the rest yield inferior silk if fed entirely on the leaves of *M. nigra*. Generally speaking, *M. multicaulis** provides the best leaves for feeding silkworms, whether grown as a tree, or in sapling crops, as in this district. The leaves are large and tender, and therefore easy for the young worms to bite.

As this work is not intended to convey practical information, which is given in the "Handbook on Sericulture," I pass over the various species of mulberry, their value as food and their geographical distribution.

Fortunately there are other food stuffs which supplement the mulberry and might even with some worms take its place in case of any failure in the crop. Among these food stuffs are :—"the osage orange, the lettuce, and the tender leaves of the peepul" (*Ficus religiosa*), common by every roadside. The cocoons from worms fed without any mulberry are poor, and many worms do not spin at all if so fed, so that these substitutes would be of value only in eking out the supply of mulberry during the earlier stages. "Young worms may be reared on tender peepul leaves for fifteen to twenty days, and the mulberry allowed to grow uninterruptedly. A difference of fifteen or twenty days in the spring makes a great difference to the growth of the mulberry."

There seems to be some difference of opinion as to the value of the Bengal method of mulberry cultivation. It gives a better yield in proportion to the space occupied by large trees, and that alone would ensure its permanence wherever it has become customary. The leaves are always fresh, and the crop could be rapidly changed if a better species of mulberry were found for any given locality. Trees cannot be changed or renewed in the same economical manner, and soil exhausted after long mulberry cultivation can be restored while growing other crops, such as tobacco or vegetables. It is the waiting which probably prevents its adoption. The trees need take up no good ground, as they can be planted as boundaries to fields. On the whole, the argument would seem to be entirely in favour of the Bengal system, for Bengal, at any rate, whatever may be the case in Kashmir or other places where the mulberry grows well as a large tree.

The details of the Bengal system have already been noticed, but a few words must be added here as to the "cuttings." Mature stalks of mulberry, not thicker than a man's thumb, should be held in bundles of ten or twelve in the left hand and cut with a sharp bill-hook into ten or twelve pieces about nine inches

* One of the varieties of *M. alba*.

long. These pieces are planted at once. "Cuttings" not wanted immediately will live for some time if kept moist and in a shady and cool place. The "cuttings" will not grow "if planted upside down." Care must therefore be taken that the buds look upwards. They may be entirely buried in the soil, or placed in a slanting direction, with an inch or so of the wood above the ground. "Cuttings" thrive best in a loose soil. The first growth of leaves is called *naicha*, and should *not* be given to mature worms, as it produces *grasserie*. If not wanted for young worms, these leaves are readily eaten by cattle. Good manures are *seeti* (or indigo refuse), saltpetre, the sweepings from the shelves of the rearing-houses, and well-ripened dung and vegetable mould. The only warning necessary concerning the use of saltpetre is to keep it away from the leaves, as it causes them to wither. It is best applied in August and September, after the plants have been cut down. The cultivators in these parts have a poor opinion of the June harvest, and strip the leaves if required in June and July, instead of cutting the plant for reasons already given. In the "Handbook of Sericulture" a statement as to the cost of mulberry cultivation is given (p. 11). Including two years' rent, and exclusive, apparently, of manure, the cost of cultivation amounts to Rs. 47 as. 1 per bigah. Against this we have, excluding the crop of *naicha* leaves, six harvests, bringing in Rs. 83, a profit, making all allowance for sundries, of Rs. 30. In round numbers, 100 maunds, an average annual yield per bigah, will rear 200 worms. The price of cocoons is, in favourable years, one rupee for two seers. For "seed," the best cocoons range up to Rs. 2, a seer. This gives Rs. 100, to Rs. 400, as the value of cocoons reared from one bigah of mulberry. When necessary, mulberry can be grown from seed, supplies of which can be obtained from the missionaries at Kalimpong. They gather seed from the indigenous varieties of mulberry which thrive in the Himalayas. The mulberry also grows well in Chota Nagpur, Behar, and best of all in the Punjab and Kashmir. The fruit, white (*M. alba*), black (*M. nigra*), and green (*M. serrata*), is wholesome and pleasant to the taste, while the wood of large trees is considered valuable for making furniture. Cattle eat the leaves with avidity and, *faut de mieux*, the leaves, when boiled, make a palatable vegetable for man.

I have recorded the names of the silkworms reared in the first half of the century. Now turning to the most modern work on sericulture we find five kinds of mulberry silkworms reared in Bengal at the present time. All are reared in this district, but some are favoured more than others :—(1) *Chota palu*, or *deshi palu* ; (2) *Nistari*, called also *Chakra ;* and *Madrasi Palu ;* (3) *Chuna palu*, the China worm ; (4) *Bara palu*. Numbers 3 and 4 are not extensively reared in this district, the *Bara palu* being much more common than the other two. This must be due more to local conditions than to preference, since the *Bara palu* was very much fancied, especially round Jangipur, previous to 1832. Its cocoons are white and large and the silk of extremely good quality. At present the *Bara palu* gives rarely more than one harvest in the year. The eggs are laid in March and hatched in the following January; and this long wait of ten months is no doubt the chief reason why rearers neglect this worm. The "seed" houses are called *Grainage*, and rearers soon learn their value as depôts for reliable eggs. Selection has been made possible since the introduction of choice by means of the microscope, and selected "seed" is called "cellular seed." From this are reared worms giving what is known as "industrial seed," sold to the rearers, having first, as a precaution, been dipped in a solution of sulphate of copper.* The improvements which have helped silkworm rearers to obtain "cellular" and "industrial seed," and to prevent or defeat the diseases to which the worms are liable, we owe in the main to the efforts of the local Government, through their agent, Babu N. G. Mukerji, M.A., author of the English and Bengali Handbooks of Sericulture. Full instructions for cleansing and disinfecting are given in the above-mentioned works. The old rearing-rooms have been described, and they differed little from those now considered most suitable. Rearing-houses are now made with mud walls, or double mat walls filled in with straw, and it is thought better to have two rooms instead

* One part of sulphate of copper (*tutia*) to 100 parts of water, which should be sterilized.

of one. Either or both are often also used as dwelling-rooms by the rearers. "Chicks," as before, keep out parasitic flies, and it is wise to cover the shelves with a fine net, as is done in Burma.* Shallow plates, containing water and kerosene oil, placed outside the windows, act as traps. in which many flies are drowned. Trays should be large, and spare ones always ready, for, as the worms grow, changing their skin four times in thirty days, they take up more room—three times the amount for each moult. In this district the following is regarded as a satisfactory return from ordinary unselected "seed":—"500 layings of *Nistari* eggs, or 800 layings of *Chota palu,*" should produce "1½ maunds of cocoons." From selected "seed" much more is expected. To guard against damage by rats, the rearer fits earthen, or tin, cones, apex downwards, on the bamboos which support the framework for the shelves. These cones are placed about nine inches from the ground, and effectually check the rat as it attempts to climb up to the shelves. Cones are also attached to the tops of the supports, the truncated apex pointing upwards. White arsenic (sankha), mixed with cooked rice, is placed on the cones. If ants are not defeated by placing the supports in bowls of water, as was the old custom, a mixture of sál gum and colza oil, boiled, with a little admixture of the sticky white juice of *Colotropis* (A'kanda), must be smeared on the posts between the ground and the cones. This only requires very occasional renewal. Among the instructions for feeding it is important to note that "wet, fermented, muddy, or dusty leaf" should be rejected. Immediately before spinning, the silkworms, of course, become somewhat torpid, and eat little. Bundles of dry twigs tied with string to the frames of the shelves have been used by the worms when spinning, but the *chundruki* is superior to the other devices.

The old method of hatching out the worms by the natural heat of the breeder's body still exists. We find the Bengali rearer with the eggs of the *Bara palu* and those of the imported European silkworms "in little calico bags" "suspended by strings" from his neck. He carries them inside his clothes day and night during the period of incubation, thus ensuring a "temperature almost uniform."

For other eggs, such as those of the *Chota palu*, *Nistari*, and *Chuna*, the climate of this part of Bengal is very suitable—neither too hot nor too cold. There have been years, however, in which the heat in April and May has been so intense that the eggs have perished. Eggs should not be exposed to the direct rays of the sun, "nor will these indigenous eggs survive extreme cold," which is easier to deal with, as a fire or a lamp can be used. As the young worms appear they are placed on the shelves, and chopped mulberry leaves spread lightly over them. Fresh supplies of leaf are required about every four hours. Feeding is done four times daily after this stage—in the early morning, at midday, and at nine o'clock at night. The cleaning should be effected before the midday feed. A dirty rearer will never prosper; for silkworms under artificial conditions are delicate creatures, and require great care and attention. While silkworms are moulting no food should be given; indeed, none is required; and one of the signs that a change of skin is approaching is a tendency to sluggishness and a disinclination to eat. To ensure safety at these times, the *moulting* worms should be placed together on shelves apart from the rest. The period of larval life is, in the hot weather, twenty to twenty-four days, or even less. The cleaning of the shelves has been alluded to, but a word of warning is required as to the cleaning of the rearing-house. Never raise any dust; indeed, brushes are not at all necessary, and should be forbidden. Pick up rubbish and "leep"† the floor and lower part of the walls with a solution of sulphate of copper. If cow-dung is used—and it frequently is used—sulphate of copper solution, or lime, should be mixed with it. Where these precautions are not observed, many worms are lost from the disease known as *flacherie.* Dirt, excrement, and old leaves should be thrown into a manure pit, with liquid manure from the cow-shed. There is, however, a further reason for keeping the dirt from the rearing-house moist. If dry and thrown down anywhere, it may be carried by winds back into the shed, and with it the germs of disease. When a silkworm dies

* These nets, two for each shelf, have the further value that they enable the *debris* to be easily removed.

† Smearing with a mixture of cow-dung and water or, better, sulphate of copper solution.

on one of the shelves, the body should be removed at once, and that part of the shelf on which it lay well sprinkled with lime. Besides the change of colour noted as the time draws near for spinning its cocoon the worm then becomes more translucent. At this time such worms are to be removed to the spinning-trays. To prevent the cocoons being soiled and spoiled by excrement, the worms are turned towards the ground. When ready, the cocoons are removed from the *chundrukies* and spread out on the shelves. Those required for "seed" having been selected and put aside, the rest are exposed to the direct heat of the sun for about four hours for as many days. The object of this proceeding is to prevent the moth cutting its way out and spoiling the cocoon. The cocoons that have been selected for "seed" are strung together by means of a needle and thread, in such a way as to avoid injury to the pupa. These "strings" of cocoons are suspended over an earthen bowl, into which any parasite grubs will fall, into water, as they bore out of the cocoon. These grubs are then readily destroyed, and further mischief prevented so far as they are concerned. Grubs should also be sought for among the cocoons spread out on the shelves, and when found, destroyed. In the hot months the pupa passes rapidly into the imago, eight or nine days being sufficient to complete the metamorphosis. Cold retards this change, and the silkworm may be fifteen or twenty days before it is ready to emerge as a moth. As the peasants of Bengal call all birds *Chiriya*, so moths, male and female, of any species are *Chakra-Chokri*. The moth cuts its way out quickly when ready, and, commencing in the early morning, will have made its way out by noon.

The females are larger, fatter, and not so active as the males, and the sexes should be separated two or three hours after their emergence. As females make their way out less rapidly than the males, a large proportion of females may be the last to appear, and it will therefore be necessary to leave a few males of those that cut their way out on the previous day.

Disease has played a prominent part in the downfall of the silk industry, for when a rearer may lose—and often does lose—two out of his four yearly breedings, or sees 60 per cent. of his worms die just when the time approaches for the promised reward of labour—a harvest of golden yellow cocoons—he loses heart. These cocoons mean money which, despite all proverbs, is the only way to happiness if a man use it wisely. For this reason many rearers have taken to ordinary agriculture, which may be more reliable, if less lucrative. Further, if labour cannot provide sufficient cocoons, capital, represented by the European factor, must close the *filature*, losing money and depriving the employés of their only means of subsistence. In this district it is possible to point to *filatures* that have been closed since the beginning of the century, and to few new ones to supply their places.

It is only of late years that science has come forward to help the rearer to meet these losses by precautions against, and remedies for, the ills that silkworm flesh is heir to. In Europe, confidence in the power of science makes the silk rearers of France and Italy certain of a good return for their labours, and if the masses of Bengal had the same faith and intelligence, the silk industry would again be on the upward grade. It may be fairly asked why silkworms were more hardy and free from disease in former times than they are now. The disease known as *pebrine* seems to be quite modern, and it is said to have been unknown twenty-five years ago. The silkworms did, even in their best days, suffer from disease, but none, then known, worked such havoc as does *pebrine* (Katá). *Pebrine* first appeared in an epidemic form in France, in 1849. The disease was investigated by Pasteur, and it was found that the black patches on the skin which characterise the malady contained a *micrococcus*, of oval shape and 3 micromillimetres long by 2 *mm.* wide. These are frequently arranged in pairs, or masses. At times rods are seen among them 2.5 *mm.* wide and 5 *mm.* long. The germ received several names:—*Nosema bombycis*, *Micrococcus ovatus*, *Corpuscles du ver-a-soie;* but the one generally adopted in scientific works is *Panhistophyton ovatum* (Lebért).* The coccus multiplies by sub-division, and has been experimentally

* "Bacteriology," Crookshank, 4th. ed. 1896, p. 472.

proved to be the cause of the disease known by such names as *pebrine*, and *Flecksucht*. Not only do these germs affect the worm; they are found also in the eggs, pupæ, and moths.

Metchnikoff, differing from most observers, classes these germs not among the *bacteria*, but among the *psorosperms*. Almost ruining the silk industry in Europe, the disease had spread to Spain, Italy, through Turkey to Asia Minor, on to Kashmir, and even to China and Japan. Fresh "seed" had to be imported into Europe; but it was not until 1866 that any headway was made against the disease. In that year Pasteur discovered a remedy for *pebrine*, and slowly the silk trade in Europe recovered its stability and prosperity. Other diseases from which silkworms must be protected are:—(1) *Muscardine*, called by the rearers, *Chund-Kété* or *Chhit*. In Bengal this disease comes next to *pebrine* in its power for evil, whereas the next to be mentioned, *flacherie*, is placed next to *pebrine* by European silk-workers.

The moulds giving rise to Muscardine are: (1) *Botrytis Bassiana* and *B. Tenella*. (2) *Grasserie* or *Rasá*. Concerning this disease Mukerji quotes a French proverb—"Pas de gras, pas de cocons." The disease is not a serious one, apparently, in Europe, but it has been known to do great damage in the Murshidabad district. In 1892, after a very heavy rainfall, *Grasserie* appeared as an epidemic in the neighbourhood of Gouripur, and in almost every village the rearers lost all their worms. (3) *Flacherie* is known in Bengal as *Kálshirá* or *Shalfa*. As above noted, silkworm rearers in Bengal do not fear *flacherie* as much as do the rearers of Europe, the explanation of the difference being due to the absence of causes leading to fermentation and rotting of "seed" in Bengal.

In addition to the diseases briefly enumerated, the silkworm rearer has to contend with other enemies. His stock may be attacked by the silkworm fly, *Tricolyga Bombycis*. In the open jungle, birds, and ants keep down this pest, but in the rearing-sheds it may do much damage, and the fly is very common in this district. The *Tricolyga* thrives best in the hot and moist seasons, being more rarely found in the cold months. The larva and imago of *Dermestes* also destroy large numbers of worms, as was the case around Beldanga, in this district, in 1896. The local name for the beetle is *Kankutur*, and the larva is known as the *sore-poka*. Not only must the rearer protect his worms from disease and destructive enemies, but he must guard their food, the mulberry, from insect pests.

The cost of cultivation of mulberry, per bigah, is about Rs. 30, to Rs. 40, for the first year, and Rs. 20, for the following ones, each bigah annually producing a considerable number of maunds of mulberry leaves, each maund averaging one rupee in value.* The majority of mulberry growers are also rearers, and return themselves as such. Besides these, there are a large number who combine the cultivation of the mulberry with other agricultural pursuits. The mulberry flourishes best in a light, rich, elevated soil, and requires abundant moisture. It is particularly common in the thanahs of Burwa, Barwan, Goas, and Raganathganj.

The total amount of cocoons produced, on a conjectural estimate, cannot be less than 72,000 maunds.

Large quantities are imported from Rajshaye and Maldah. The average price of a maund of cocoons is about Rs. 30, the cost of mulberry and labour amounting to Rs. 20, or so.

The latest Census Report for the district puts down the number of silkworm rearers and cocoon gatherers at 31,688, about half being males and half females.

The rearers are chiefly lower-class Hindus and Mahomedans. Among the former may be mentioned Chasa, Dhoba, and Kaibartha, "castes." As a class, rearers are a peaceful and quiet people, and litigation is almost unknown amongst them.

The *Chota palu*, *B. fortunatus*, *B. crœsi*, and *Nistari* cocoons are the kinds chiefly reared in this district. *B. textor*, once plentiful, is now reared only in small quantities.

The three great seasons, locally termed *bunds*, for hatching eggs and gathering the cocoons, are those of November, March, and July. The silk of the November and March *bunds* is the best and fetches the highest price.

* Report submitted from the Magistrate's office.

Rearers travel sixty or eighty miles from their homes to obtain worms of a good breed, or from localities noted for early breeding.

Worms attacked by the ichneumon fly spin as usual, perhaps somewhat earlier, and the change to chrysalis is effected about the time that the fly's grub comes to life. It then feeds on the chrysalis, and eventually eating its way through the cocoon, destroys its value.

Rearers near Berhampur are less skilled and careful than "Punras" (hereditary weavers), who are wealthy, and spare neither time nor money for their work.

The "Bengal Silk Association" was constituted in August, 1898. A committee was to meet at Berhampur every month, its object being to combat diseases in the cocoon by promoting the use of Pasteur's system of prevention. Annual subscriptions to the amount of Rs. 6,800 have been guaranteed.

At a meeting a letter from Government was read, in which an annual subsidy of Rs. 3,000 was promised so long as the guaranteed subscriptions continued.

The "District Administration Report" for 1898 records that there were forty-eight *filatures* in the district, which turned out some 484,397 lbs. of silk, valued at Rs. 28,80,955. Of these some twenty-six are the property of European firms; the rest belong to natives. Generally speaking, the out-turn of the European is greater than that of the native *filatures*. They employ over 5,000 persons, when in full work. At certain seasons of the year, generally speaking, from January to March, April to September, and during December, the average daily number of persons temporarily employed is more than three times as great.

The Census Report of 1891 puts down the number of silk-carders and spinners in the district at 12,052 (including women). Children are very largely employed on this work. This number includes those who work in their own homes.

Winders earn three or four, and spinners five or six, rupees a month. Those who work at winding Khamra silk can, according to Mukerji, earn higher wages, but they work longer hours.

The Bengal Silk Company, and Messrs. Louis Payen & Co., are the largest *filature* owners in the district. The largest European *filatures* are those of Gardi, with an out-turn of 34,045 lbs.; Faridpur, with an out-turn of 21,334 lbs.; and Choa, with an out-turn, in 1897, of 19,393 lbs.

As distinguished from ordinary *filature* and *Khamra* silk, may be mentioned two other kinds which are produced in the district. Firstly, there is that used for making what is known as *Mutka* cloth. This is made out of pierced cocoons, *i.e.*, those which have been used for "seed" and have been spoilt by the moth, the continuity of their threads being broken. This kind of thread is usually spun by old women, who can earn a rupee a month or so. It fetches from Rs. 3, to Rs. 6, per seer.

Secondly, there is the *tusser* silk. The reeling of this is more difficult than that of the ordinary silk. *Tusser* silk is turned out at several *filatures*, but the cocoons are not raised in the district.

Filature-wound silk is scarcely at all used for weaving purposes in this district. The export trade is almost entirely in the raw material, which is shipped to England, France, and Italy. *Khamra* silk is used for the native looms. There is no doubt that the industry is declining in the district. No statistics are published, but from what I have been able to learn I think that the annual value probably does not exceed Rs. 2,50,000.

According to the latest Census Report, the number of weavers in the district, including a few dealers, amounts to 11,399. Of these about half are males and half females. It is difficult to say precisely how many looms these figures represent, but the number is, at any rate, rather over than under 2,500.

The *Tanti* "caste" is the weaving "caste" proper, and still contributes the majority of those engaged in this industry. There are also a large number of *Jugis*. There are no Brahmins, but people of many other "castes" take part in the industry.

One weaver stated that he could earn about six annas a day, and his boy about four; but there are times when he can get no work. Another said that his profits on a piece of work, which took him a day and a half to finish, amounted to six annas.

Estimates put down a male adult weaver's earnings, per month, as averaging from Rs. 8, to Rs. 15; and a woman's, or a child's at about Rs. 4; these last often getting food in addition. Their condition is not prosperous, and they are often deeply involved in debt. They do not, as a rule, work for themselves but for dealers, who advance them material, and pay them so much for their labour.

The thannahs of Sujaganj, Doulatabazar, Bhagwangola, Goas, Manullabazar, Assanpur, and Mirzapur all contain a large number of weavers. The town of Mirzapur is the centre of the most skilled work in the district, and though at one time its industry fell into decay, it has lately undergone a comparative revival.

The looms for making the figured silks of Baluchar are of a special kind They are extremely complicated in construction, and Dubraj (an old man of about eighty) is the only person who understands how they are made and set. In the "Naksha" loom (the kind used for weaving figured silks) two men have to work together, one of them devoting his attention solely to bringing up the proper threads of the warp. The cost of an ordinary loom is from four to ten rupees only, while that of the more complicated pattern sometimes amounts to as much as thirty rupees.

The colour of raw Bengal silk is usually yellow, and even where it is white the process of bleaching has to take place before that of dyeing. The bleaching is effected by means of crude carbonate of soda and hot water, or of the ashes of plantain leaves and hot water, or a combination of the two. In the process, the silk loses a quarter of its weight. The cost of bleaching one seer amounts to three annas. After this the silk, as a rule, requires to be dipped in a "mordant" of alum before a dye can be permanently fixed in it. The cost for dyeing a seer of silk is two annas. There are probably not more than a hundred bleachers in the district. They earn about six or eight annas a day and are fairly prosperous, although the demand is somewhat fluctuating, and they cannot get work the whole year round.

There are probably between twenty and thirty dyeing factories in the district, dyers' wages amounting to about four annas a day. Baluchar, Khagra, Mirzapur, and Islampur may be regarded as the chief centres of the industry. Dyeing is done either in the thread or in the piece. Of course, where different colours are intermingled the former method must be pursued.

Deep blue is produced by repeated dippings in a vat of indigo. To make the colour permanent there must be added lime and ashes, obtained by burning indigo refuse (seeti) and seed of the chákandâ, *Cassia*. One dipping is sufficient to produce grey. Lac and "lodh" (*Symplocos*) dust with *saji* and tamarind water, and finally alum, are used for red and pink. Yellow is produced by sawdust of jack wood (*Artocarpus*) and "bakash" leaves. The best orange dye is "kamala" dust, combined with other materials; in Murshidabad these generally consist of "saji," and "lodh." The use of "bakam" (*Cæsalpinia*) wood in conjunction with "kamala" dust, in order to get a deeper colour, is also fairly common in this district. Anatto and Saji are, however, still more usually employed. It is cheaper to use them, and the colour they give is brighter, but not so lasting. The art of producing a fast green is unknown in this district. The green in vogue is produced by "bakash" leaf and jack wood sawdust, followed by the immersion of the silk in an indigo vat which has been already used for dyeing silk blue. To produce purple the silk is first dyed light red by means of "lac," and then put in the indigo vat. Chocolate is black with a shade of red. To obtain this colour the silk is first dyed deep red in the "lac" liquor and is then dipped once in the indigo vat.

Aniline dyes, imported from Europe, are used in this district to some extent, but, though more convenient to use, and more brilliant in colour, they are less permanent than the native dyes.

Handkerchiefs, thin "chadars" stamped with religious texts, and ordinary thin shawls are printed with wooden blocks with the dyes already described.

The dyes used for printing are made stronger, and a quantity of cotton wool is mixed up with each dye for convenience of taking it up on the block. The stamping is done on "mordanted" pieces of silk spread out on tables.

A piece of *mutka* cloth large enough to make a suit for an European can be bought for, from two or three, to twelve rupees. A large amount is locally consumed, and there is a considerable export to all parts of India, and, *via* Bombay, into other countries, Arabia and Persia.

The final verdict on this industry must be that it has come upon evil days. Murshidabad silk is of excellent quality, and with the help of the "Silk Association" the rearers may be brought to see the value of scientific methods. The woven silk, if put on the market with agents in the large towns, should find a ready sale.

Silk Filatures in 1852.

Jangipur	Kawulkuwar
Rajarampur	Rangamati
Katlamari	Rampara
Kartikpara	Baydanga
Dabeepur	Mirzapur
Kasimbazar	Narkelbari
Sunkurpur	Durgachurun's Fy.

While many of these have gone, others have sprung up :—

Baliaghatta—(Indigo formerly?)	Bubalbuna
Choa	Banjetti.

INDIGO.*

THE Indigo industry in the district of Murshidabad has fallen off considerably during the past century, and a number of *Concerns* and factories have been closed.

Space does not permit any general survey of the origin and ancient history of indigo,† its growth and manufacture. That it is a dye of very ancient origin is undoubted, and its main supply came from India after the discovery of the sea route by the Cape of Good Hope. Bengal produced the greater part of the dye sold, and there were many noted "marks" in this district, such as *Cantacobra*, etc. Marco Polo describes the manufacture of indigo, and in Egypt mummies have been found wrapped in cloth dyed with this blue. In India the soil best suited to the growth of indigo lies between 88° and 90° east longitude and 22¾° to 24° north latitude. A light soil is the best, and a favourite spot for sowing indigo is the rich land left available by the partial drying up of many of the large rivers—of course these crops are liable to be lost by the action of sudden floods and cyclonic storms. The number of acres sown with indigo in 1899-1900 was 22,200. The indigo industry in this district connected with the Boalia *Concern* at Muricha (Akriganj) was abandoned in 1899.

The "Bara Jangipur" *Concern* (started by the late H. Masik) consisted of twenty-five working factories in the beginning of 1800, but about fifty years later it was split up into two divisions. These two divisions had gradually to close some of their factories, till the number now in existence is about ten. Out of these the "Bara (big) Jangipur" (or Lurtepur *Concern*, to use the present denomination) possesses five, and the "Chota (little) Jangipur" *Concern* five.

The whole *Concern*, some seventy or eighty years ago, used to turn out from 4,000 to 5,000 maunds (a maund equals 82 lbs.) of indigo, now the two divisions hardly reach 1,200 maunds even in good seasons.

The gradual falling off in production is due to the prices of food grains having risen, and to the fact that the cultivators find it more remunerative to sow their lands with cereals than with indigo. Labour, too, has become very scarce. Whereas in former years *all* the work for the manufacturing of dye was done by manual labour, machinery has now in a great measure to be substituted. Competition with artificial indigo has caused something like a panic among indigo planters, and no doubt the discovery will reduce the output and value of indigo. The natural dye, however, is still preferred by many, and the danger is less than it appeared at first sight.

The system of indigo cultivation and manufacture carried on in most *Concerns* in this district is as

* My thanks are due to Mr. W. Rice for certain information concerning the indigo industry; also to Messrs. E. B. Hills, G. W. A. Coxon, A. Keogh, and Babu Bhagabutty Charan Roy.

† The name itself comes from Indicus, Indian; but indigo was grown in the West Indies, Mexico, and Brazil, as well as in the East Indies. The European plant, *Isatis tinctoria*, yielded indigo or *woad*, as it was called. When commerce with the Indies was opened up the dye from *Indigofera tinctoria* and *I. cærulea*, to a less extent, displaced *woad* from the market. *I. tinctoria* is a plant belonging to the *Leguminaceæ*; "herbaceous or shrubby, with pinnate leaves and small blue, purple, or white, pea-shaped flowers, in axillary racemes."

follows:—Lands are sown with indigo by the ryots (peasant labourers). The ryot gets an advance of from one to two rupees a bigah, for the number of bigahs he has to sow with indigo. The seed is supplied to him *gratis*, and he weeds the land and does anything else that may be necessary for the production of a good crop, instructed by the manager, or an assistant of the *Concern*. When the plant is ready to be cut, the Factory has to find the labour, and bring the crop into the factory, stack it in the vats, and pay for such labour. The first cutting takes place in July, the second about two months later. The plant when brought to the factory is in small bundles. These bundles are tested with a chain, six feet long, and as many bundles as go to this measurement are considered *a standard bundle*. The cultivator is paid at the rate of one rupee for ten bundles.

Another system is that of cultivation of the land by the Factory. The seed is sown at the proprietor's expense.

When the plant is brought to the factory it is stacked in brick vats measuring 20 ft. by 22 ft. by 4½ ft., and pressed down with beams to keep it from floating. Water is allowed to run into the vats until the whole of the plant is submerged. The plant is then allowed to ferment in these vats, for, from ten to fourteen hours, and the process is accompanied by free escape of bubbles of gas and the formation of a reddish brown scum. According to the state of the weather, and the time when the fermentation is complete, the *liquor* is run off into a lower vat, stirred, and vigorously beaten up, either by manual labour or by machinery, till oxidation is complete and the grain or *fæcula* (about 0.05 per cent.) is formed. The colour of the *liquor* changes from green to pale yellow, and much carbonic acid gas is liberated. After this the liquor is allowed to stand till the grain has settled at the bottom of the vats, and the superfluous water is slowly drained off. The *fæcula* is next lifted into a "copper" and heated till it boils. It is then run off on to a large table covered with a cotton sheet, where it is allowed to settle, and the remaining water is filtered off. The indigo at this stage is of the consistency of a jelly, or thick paste. This paste is lifted into boxes, and submitted to a strong pressure, to force out any water there may still be in it. When this is done, the slab of indigo, of the consistency of bar-soap, is placed in the cutting frame and cut into cakes, measuring three inches each way. These cakes, or cubes, are then placed on shelves, and allowed to dry for three or four months. They are next packed in chests and despatched to the market for sale. The above process separates the pure indigo blue from indigo *gluten*, indigo *yellow*, indigo *red*, and other matter, and the "cakes" vary in colour from light blue to blackish blue.

Mr. Henry Masik may be looked upon as the pioneer of the indigo industry in the north-west of the district. He was, I believe, of Dutch extraction. He came out to this country at the latter end of the eighteenth century, started a small factory at Jangipur, and in a few years had built and worked twenty-five factories. He retired some time after the beginning of 1800, with a fortune of about twenty-five lakhs of rupees, leaving some descendants, very well provided for. The bulk of his fortune he took with him. Of these descendants only four are alive, three boys and one girl. They are scattered over the country, and very little is known about them. They have lost nearly all the fortune that was left to them.

During the years 1889-99 the area sown with indigo under the "Chota Jangipur" *Concern* (Ankura Factory) was about 2,500 bigahs; the lowest figures were 1,835 bigahs (1893-94); the highest 3,252 bigahs (1898-99). One year with another, 3,000 to 8,000 persons were employed on the work connected with this factory. Under the Baniagram factory the average area sown during the same period was 1,200 bigahs, and the work found employment for a large number of persons. The yearly out-turn under Ankura varied from 50 maunds only, in 1890-91, to 140 maunds in 1894-95. The Baniagram factory produced in the worst year, 1895-96, only 20 maunds; in the best year, 1897-98, 92 maunds. The value of this indigo is not given, but the *Concern* is still working. The seed is sown by the ryots on their own land, and the crop purchased by the proprietor of the *Concern*, Babu Bhagabutty Charan Roy.

The Baromassia *Concern* ceased to produce indigo after the season 1898, but its working in the previous five years is shown in the following table, kindly furnished by Mr. G. W. A. Coxon.

BAROMASSIA *CONCERN.*

Seasons.	Baromassia Factory.			Jageerpara Factory.			Khamarpara Factory.			Katlamari Factory.		
	Area.	Out-turn.	Coolies Employed.	Area.	Out-turn.	Coolies Employed.	Area.	Out-turn.	Coolies Employed.	Area.	Out-turn.	Coolies Employed.
	bgs.	m. s. ch.		bgs.	m. s. ch.		bgs.	m. s. ch.		bgs.	m. s. ch.	
1893-94	3,000	48 20 0	23,725	1,633	32 0 0	14,600	2,324	70 0 0	14,600	4,759	207 22 0	58,400
1894-95	2,940	139 30 0	22,995	2,010	121 0 0	14,600	2,411	147 10 0	15,330	4,808	257 20 12	36,500
1895-96	2,935	46 34 4	21,900	2,272	38 8 4	14,600	2,402	34 20 0	14,600	5,000	67 31 12	47,450
1896-97	3,013	50 28 0	21,170	2,303	29 9 0	12,775	2,027	57 21 0	16,425	5,500	108 9 0	65,700
1897-98	3,214	79 23 8	30,660	2,303	61 20 0	29,200	2,429	50 0 0	27,375	5,503	124 30 0	40,150

Katlamari,
21st December, 1900.

The table from Patkabari shows one factory closed in 1898 and a reduction in the area of land under indigo.

CHANDPUR Co., LTD.

NAME OF FACTORY.	1889-90.						1890-91.						1891-92.						1892-93.						1893-94.					
	Number of persons employed.	Amount of land growing indigo.	How many people holding rent-free land.	Amount of such land.	Amount of indigo produced.	When abandoned, if not making indigo now.	Number of persons employed.	Amount of land growing indigo.	How many people holding rent-free land.	Amount of such land.	Amount of indigo produced.	When abandoned, if not making indigo now.	Number of persons employed.	Amount of land growing indigo.	How many people holding rent-free land.	Amount of such land.	Amount of indigo produced.	When abandoned, if not making indigo now.	Number of persons employed.	Amount of land growing indigo.	How many people holding rent-free land.	Amount of such land.	Amount of indigo produced.	When abandoned, if not making indigo now.	Number of persons employed.	Amount of land growing indigo.	How many people holding rent-free land.	Amount of such land.	Amount of indigo produced.	When abandoned, if not making indigo now.
		bgs.			m.			bgs.			m.			bgs.			m.			bgs.			m.			bgs.			m.	
PATKABARI ...	1100	6200	—	—	183	—	1300	6084	—	—	354	—	900	6072	—	—	91	—	1100	5746	—	—	142	—	1200	5551	—	—	265	—
BALLY	600	2567	—	—	86	—	900	2876	—	—	216	—	500	2838	—	—	69	—	560	2857	—	—	77	—	700	2044	—	—	137	—
MADUPUR ...	600	3038	—	—	94	—	1100	1100	—	—	215	—	600	2727	—	—	65	—	700	2945	—	—	100	—	500	2777	—	—	36	—
SONATICKRI	700	3306	—	—	109	—	900	980	—	—	247	—	500	3323	—	—	79	—	450	3365	—	—	42	—	600	3284	—	—	133	—

NAME OF FACTORY.	1894-95.						1895-96.						1896-97.						1897-98.						1898-99.					
	Number of persons employed.	Amount of land growing indigo.	How many people holding rent-free land.	Amount of such land.	Amount of indigo produced.	When abandoned, if not making indigo now.	Number of persons employed.	Amount of land growing indigo.	How many people holding rent-free land.	Amount of such land.	Amount of indigo produced.	When abandoned, if not making indigo now	Number of persons employed.	Amount of land growing indigo.	How many people holding rent-free land.	Amount of such land.	Amount of indigo produced.	When abandoned, if not making indigo now.	Number of persons employed.	Amount of land growing indigo.	How many people holding rent-free land.	Amount of such land.	Amount of indigo produced.	When abandoned now, if not making indigo.	Number of persons employed.	Amount of land growing indigo.	How many people holding rent-free land.	Amount of such land.	Amount of indigo produced.	When abandoned, if not making indigo now.
		bgs.			m.			bgs.			m.			b gs.			m.			bgs.			m.			bgs.			m.	
PATKABARI ...	1300	5708	—	—	337	—	900	5585	—	—	47	—	800	8433	—	—	87	—	800	5598	—	—	65	—	1100	4627	—	—	186	—
BALLY	900	2559	—	—	195	—	400	2664	—	—	17	—	700	2424	—	—	109	—	412	2664	—	—	36	—	600	2028	—	—	100	—
MADUPUR ...	1100	2659	—	—	211	—	600	2577	—	—	71	—	500	2982	—	—	126	—	600	2500	—	—	28	—	closed	closed	—	—	closed	—
SONATICKRI	700	3446	—	—	206	—	500	3847	—	—	78	—	500	3586	—	—	83	—	400	3608	—	—	47	—	700	2954	—	—	126	—

This table of work done at the Nurpur Factory shows no falling off in the production, but prices are lower than formerly :—

NAME OF *CONCERN.*	District.	Year.	Average number of persons employed all the year round.	Amount of land growing indigo.	Number of persons holding rent-free land on condition that they plant indigo.	Amount of rent-free land.	Amount of indigo produced.	When abandoned.	Remarks.
1	2	3	4	5	6	7	8	9	10
			men.	bgs.			m. s.		
		1890	65	3532			123 0		
		1891	72	4215			178 0		
		1892	59	3879			118 0		
		1893	45	3884			46 0		
NURPUR FACTORY.	Murshidabad.	1894	62	3008	None	None	127 0	Still Working	
		1895	58	3009			141 0		
		1896	60	2954			106 0		
		1897	40	3084			154 0		
		1898	50	2704			115 0		
		1899	70	3973			154 0		

* Those employed in cultivation are not included.

Nurpur,
7th December, 1900.

Another estate still producing indigo belongs to the firm of L. Payen and Co., whose chief interest is, however, in the silk trade. The name of the *Concern* is "Sujapur," with one out-factory at "Kamnaggar," in the district of Murshidabad. The total number of persons employed in indigo work is about 500 or 600, paid in cash for the work they do, and with no rent-free land.

The amount of land sown with indigo now is about 2,000 bigahs, producing from 50 to 100 maunds, dependent on weather and season.

Here again is an industry that is on the downward road and in a worse condition than the silk industry. We must not, however, lose sight of the fact that giving up indigo does not necessarily mean ruin, as in many cases landowners find that their property yields a better return when let out and sown with cereals, or other crops.

Indigo Factories in 1852.

Kishanpur } Rajshaye, east of Ganges.
Bhugwanpur }
Dogachi
Choukah
Urmari
Dubreebunni
Kaliganj
Monghurpur
Kadamsar
Balagachi
Gysabad

Nurpur
Khandurpaekura
Bampura
Khurbunna
Chandpur
Torapur
Noncha
Katlamari
Rajapur
Furidpur
Sahebrampur
Subdulpur
Dadpur
Akriganj (sunk in the river, factory moved back to Muricha).

JUTE.*

THIS textile fibre is produced from a plant, *Corchorus Capsularis*, belonging to the order *Tiliaceæ*. Its flowers are like those of the lime-tree. Jute is an *annual*, and grows to a height of from twelve to fourteen feet.

The industry itself goes back many years, how long we cannot say, but it is fairly certain that the origin of the present trade with Scotland, etc., does not date farther back than 1830. A Government "Report" issued September 20th, 1900, puts the cultivation of jute in this district at 24,200 acres.† The average out-turn is put down at three bales an acre. In a bale there are usually three and a half maunds, giving 254,000 maunds in all. The land is prepared in much the same way as for cereals, and the seed is scattered, after favourable showers, at the end of March, or April. With seasonable rain and weather, the crop is ready for reaping toward the end of August. After reaping, it is tied up in bundles and put into stagnant water to soak for fifteen or twenty days. The dirtier the water, the quicker the fermentation. After being well soaked, the stalks are taken, as many as a man can well hold in his two hands, and beaten on a pole placed in the water. After it has been thrashed in this way the bark slips off, is shaken out, washed, cleaned, and put into the sun to dry. It is then made into small "morahs" or "hanks," and made up into a "bhoja" (load ?), weighing about ten, fifteen, or twenty seers, and brought into the market for sale. The jute is sold to Calcutta buyers, who pack it in bales, each weighing three and a half maunds, or put it up, in native fashion, in round drums of about one maund each. The buyers send their bales to the Calcutta market, or direct to the jute mills, of which there are many in and around Calcutta.

It is impossible to give the actual amount exported from this district; but it would be quite safe to say that, keeping back some ten or fifteen thousand maunds for local consumption for string and rope, the balance, about 240,000 maunds, goes to Calcutta. The prices ruling at Jiaganj during the four months of the season, viz., from the 15th of September to the 15th of January, in 1890 and 1891, were, per maund, Rs. 4-10; in 1892-93, Rs. 4-4-6; in 1893-94, Rs. 5-7-6; in 1894-95, Rs. 3-6-3; in 1895-96, Rs. 4; and in 1897-98, Rs. 4-2.

The year 1893-94 was a year of scarcity, hence prices rose. Then followed a year of plenty, when prices fell to Rs. 3-6-3 a maund. The average for the past three seasons has been about Rs. 4-2 a maund.

In Jiaganj, which is the principal jute market of the district, there are about twenty to thirty merchants who speculate in jute, and there are about a dozen brokers. There is no record of the number of jute growers in the district. Mr. Yule has a jute press and warehouse at Jiaganj.

Jute is principally used in making jute cloth for "packing," for linoleum, and for carpets. It is also mixed with wool and worsteds; a large quantity is also made into sacks. The Calcutta trade is entirely in "Hessian" cloth and sacks (gunnies) of all descriptions. The finer qualities of cloth are made in Europe and in Great Britain. Dundee is probably the centre of the jute trade in the British Isles. The

* I am indebted for much of this information to Mr. Yule, of Jiaganj.

† The table showing distribution of crops on p. 97 gives 19,600 for the previous season, showing therefore an increased area of jute cultivation in 1900 by 4,600 acres; but the crop in 1899 was heavier, by 360,000 lbs., than that of 1900.

industry is an increasing one, and there is a great future before it. This is a pleasant record after the depressing conclusions concerning silk and indigo. The causes that chiefly affect the rise and fall of the jute market are the failure of crops consequent either on a very dry season and failure of seed, or on heavy floods submerging the crop when young. A high range of prices for rice one year will affect sowings of jute the following year, the soil being equally adapted for growing both crops. On the other hand, if the jute crop has been a small one, and prices have ranged high, the sowings of rice will in all likelihood be curtailed and jute planted instead.

According to an official return published on August 15th, 1900, the licences granted the previous year for jute presses and warehouses in the suburbs of Calcutta yielded an income of Rs. 13,392; while Rs. 13,990 were paid to the Commissioner of Police for services rendered by the Fire Brigade.

There is no record obtainable to show the value of the amount of jute grown annually in this district. The estimated out-turn of jute for the years 1895 to 1899 is given in the following table:—

Year.			Out-turn in bales of 400 lbs.
1895	...	...	41,900
1896	...	...	39,800
1897	...	...	38,200
1898	...	...	41,300
1899	...	...	51,700

MUSSEL-PEARL FISHERIES.

THE pearl fishery has no separate existence as an estate, but forms part of several estates, of which Bhandardaha is the most important and substantial.

The estate of Bhandardaha in the Hariherpara *Tauzi* (revenue section) has a revenue of Rs. 3,450-14-9, only a small portion of which results from its pearl fisheries. It is the property of the Bhagirathipur Babus, viz:—Nilkishta, Chaudhuri, and others. The other estates need not be described, as they are of less importance. The fisheries are found in a series of *jhils* (lakes) which mark the line of an old river, which is only a continuous stream during the heavy "rains"—July to October. The line of those under notice stretches in an irregular manner over an area of about thirty-eight miles in length from the north; again irregularly southward, bearing east. These *jhils*, with others of minor importance, are situated in the Bhagwangola, Daulatabad, Shahanagar, Hariherpara, Gorabazar (striking a nullah, or channel, which flows into the Bhagirathi), Baruah and Nowada thannahs (Police circles), stretching from the Gobera Nullah to Rukunpur. The principal owners of property along this line are:—The Bhagirathi Babus,* Mr. Hills, of Patkabari, and Babu Kedernath Mukerji.

No rent is charged by the *zemindars* for the fishing; but the pearl-divers are prohibited from selling to any one except the proprietor. The fishers gather together in gangs of fifteen to twenty-five, and work, in batches of eight to ten, at intervals along the line, selected generally with regard to their own convenience. By diving they collect the mussels, and at once pile them in heaps on the bank. There the mussels lie until they die, and the bivalve shells open. The pearl-bearing mussels are picked out, and after the pearls have been collected the shells (not always) are thrown back into the water with other débris. The crops of pearls and mother-of-pearl are sold by *jokas* (baskets holding four to five seers), and the price is always fixed beforehand. Of the profit, the *zemindar* retains 40 to 50 *per cent.* The rest is divided among the workers. The pearl-fishers make very little out of their actual labour, earning only one and a half annas (about twopence) a day. What attracts them is the possible profit on the pearls, etc., in which the *zemindar* does not share. These pearls† are sold in the *bazar* at Khagra (Berhampur), Baluchar (Murshidabad), and Azimganj. The proceeds are divided among the divers and pickers. A great number of mussel shells are sold for the manufacture of shell lime, but the shell contains too much animal matter to be very useful for this purpose.

No means are adopted to feed or protect the mussels. Large branches are sometimes placed in the *jhils*, to which the mollusc can attach itself. Re-stocking is left to nature and the currents from the rivers during the flood season. During the "rains" most of these *jhils* are connected with each other and with the rivers east, west, and south-east; indeed, at that time, in a good year, it is possible to get from the Bhagirathi at Berhampur to the Jalingi river by means of *jhils* and *nullahs*. Occasionally valuable pearls are procured, fetching even Rs. 200 each. Such a find is, however, very rare, and when there is no careful

* Used here in the sense of gentlemen landowners, squires—Babu = Mr., and Sir, as a form of address.

† The majority are "seed" pearls; but I have seen several the size of a pea, and purchased one the size of the largest of peas. Most of them have a somewhat golden tint, but this one was greyish, and almost black in one spot. They look very well when mounted.

re-stocking and preservation, the size and number must necessarily decrease. The largest pearls found of late years rarely exceed £1 to £2 in value. Certain "castes" eat mussels, and no doubt rob the fisheries. Another enemy is the water rat, which destroys a considerable number. The pearl-fishery season is during March, April, and May, when the water is low and almost stagnant. The total annual value of the industry is said to be about Rs. 3,000, but correct figures are not easily obtained, and I fear this estimate is much above the mark. During the season the various branches of the industry find employment for about three hundred men and women.* One hears of pearls that were taken from the Moti Jhil and Soulah Jhil in days gone by. The mussel is a *Unio*, and probably a variety of the pearl-bearing *U. Margaratifera.* This mussel is found in fresh water only, and about the middle of the nineteenth century was a source of profit to the dwellers along the banks of many Scotch streams, especially in Perthshire.

* Here is another source of income which will cease in a few years, unless some of the proprietors bestir themselves and use a few simple means to protect the mussels. Means such as those employed near Rochelle (France) might be adopted, with the necessary local modifications.

IVORY CARVING.

"NEARLY a hundred years ago, the man who started the first firm of ivory-carvers was Tulsi Mistry, of Enatuli Bagh (then part of Murshidabad city), Jiaganj, under whom some twenty "hands" worked daily. After his death his son, Ram Kishore Mistry, became the proprietor. During his time seventeen men worked under him. Then his son, Lal Behari Mistry, succeeded him; and I have succeeded my father." These are the words of the only master ivory-carver now left, Nilmani Bhasker.

There is an ivory-carver in Berhampur, but he is not very skilled. Nowadays, Nilmani Bhasker is the only workman worth naming in the city of Murshidabad, and he turns out excellent work. In bygone days, even up to 1860, there were many good ivory-carvers in and around Murshidabad. As the town became less rich and less important, the sale of ivory-carving diminished. Another reason, indirectly dependent on supply and demand, as noted, was the higher price of ivory. Many firms died out, the proprietor having no son, or relative, or fellow "caste"-man to take on the work. Nilmani Mistry, or Bhasker, employs sixteen men, but few of these are really expert carvers. The quantity of tusks indented for from Calcutta yearly by the above firm is two maunds on an average, but thirty years ago they used to require six or seven maunds. Figures of every description, of animals, Hindu gods and goddesses, processions of the *Rath Jatra*,* the worship of Kali, boats, ships, walking-stick handles, and the like, can be obtained. It seems as if the industry must die out unless some effort is made to advertise it and bring it to the notice it really deserves.

SALTPETRE.

UNTIL nearly twenty years ago most of the saltpetre used was obtained from India. Owing to the rise of the American trade, that of India has diminished. The produce in this district was never very great, but, from competition and want of encouragement, it has now almost disappeared. It lingers still in a few villages; but there is no export, and the amount made is very small. The nitrate of potassium, *Surah*, can be bought in any bazar, and is used for curing meat (salt beef, "Hunter's" beef), and as a diuretic medicine. As a medicine it is safe and reliable for horses and cattle in doses of three drachms to one ounce. Saltpetre is also a reliable manure, as shown by experiments at the Dumraon farm, where the *increase per acre*, after treatment with saltpetre, was, in different years (1885-86 to 1889-90), from thirteen down to four maunds of grain and forty-five to eight maunds of straw. It would seem from these experiments that saltpetre gives the best results for the first two or three years in poor or exhausted soil, and is of less value on the same land in subsequent years.†

* The procession of the cars of Jagannath, Boleram, and Shubadra from the temple to the garden-house; best seen in Puri, where the great temple of Jagannath is.

† "Agricultural Ledger," 1893, No. 10.

BIBLIOGRAPHY.

1. "History of the French in India from the Founding of Pondicherry, 1674, to the Capture of that Place in 1761." By Major G. B. Malleson, B.S.C., 1868.

2. "Statistical and Geographical Report of the Murshidabad District." By Captain J. E. Gastrell, 13th Regiment, N.I., Revenue Surveyor, 1860.

3. "The Early Annals of the English in Bengal, being the Bengal Public Consultations for the First Half of the Eighteenth Century." By C. R. Wilson, M.A. Vol. i. 1895.

4. "The Tribes and Castes of Bengal." By H. H. Risley. 2 vols. 1891.

5. "Echoes from Old Calcutta." By H. E. Busteed C.I.E. 1897. (3rd Edition.)

6. "The Parish of Bengal, 1678 to 1788." By H. B. Hyde, M.A. 1899.

7. "Bihar Peasant Life." By G. A. Grierson, B.C.S. 1885.

8. "A Statistical Account of Bengal." By W. W. Hunter. Vol. ix. 1876.

9. "Berhampur Church Records"; from 1841.

10. "Reports of The London Missionary Society"; from 1824 to 1899.

11. "A History of the Sepoy War in India, 1857-1858." By John William Kaye, F.R.S. 3 vols. 1880.

12. "A Comprehensive History of India from the First Landing of the English to the Suppression of the Sepoy Revolt." By Henry Beveridge. 3 vols. 1862.

13. "Selections from Unpublished Records of Government for the Years 1748 to 1767." By The Rev. J. Long. Vol. i. 1869.

14. "History of the Rise and Progress of the Bengal Army." By Captain Arthur Broome. Vol. i. 1850.

15. "The History of Bengal from the First Mahomedan Invasion until the Conquest of that Country by the English, A.D. 1757." By Charles Stewart, M.A.S. 1813.

16. "Hindus of Eastern Bengal." By Dr. James Wise. *Journal of the Asiatic Society of Bengal.* Part III. 1893.

17. "The Annals of Rural Bengal." By W. W. Hunter, K.C.I.E., LL.D. Vol. i.

18. "Hughes' Dictionary of Islam." By T. P. Hughes, B.D., M.R.A.S. Dedicated to Dr. French, the First Bishop of Lahore. 1855. Allen & Co., London.

19. "History of British India." By Charles Macfarlane. 1862.

20. "Memoirs of the Geological Survey of India." Vol. xix. Oldham. Catalogue of Indian Earthquakes from the Earliest Times to the End of A.D. 1869.

21. "Considerations on Indian Affairs, etc." By William Bolts, Merchant and Alderman, or Judge of the Hon. The Mayor's Court of Calcutta. 2 vols. (2nd Edition.) The First Volume was issued in 1772. Vol. ii., really an Appendix, was issued in 1775.

22. "The Mahomedans of Bengal." By Dr. James Wise. *Journal of the Asiatic Society of Bengal.* Part III. 1894. Page 28, *et seq.*

23. "A Note on the Parganas of Murshidabad." By H. Beveridge. *Proceedings of the Asiatic Society of Bengal.* June and July, 1892.

24. "Handbook of Sericulture." By N. G. Mukerji, M.A. Bengal Secretariat Press, Calcutta. 1899. (May be had in English and Bengali.)

25. "Silk in India." By J. Geoghegan. Government Printing Office, Calcutta. 1880.

26. "Vaccination Reports." Bengal. From 1869 to 1900. By Various Superintendents and Sanitary Commissioners.

27. "Murray's Handbook for Bengal, North-Western Provinces, and Burmah."

28. "Geography and History of Bengal." Blochmann. *Asiatic Society's Journal*, 1873. Part I., page 211.

29. "Thornton's Gazetteer." 1858.

30. "Small Game Shooting in Bengal." By "Raoul" (Dubus). Newman & Co., Calcutta. 1899.

31. "A Guide to Bengal," being a Close Translation of Ishwar Chandra Sharma's Bengali Version of that Portion of Marsham's History of Bengal which comprises the Rise and Progress of the British Dominion; with Notes and Observations by Major G. T. Marshall, Secretary and Examiner to the College of Fort William.

32. "The Materia Medica of the Hindus." By Udoy Chand Dutt. 1877.

33. "The Thackerays in India." By Sir W. W. Hunter. 1897.

34. "The Tagore Law Lectures." By H. Cowell. 1872.

35. "The Private Life of Warren Hastings." By Sir Charles Lawson. 1895.

36. "Storms and Sunshine of a Soldier's Life. Lieutenant-General Colin Mackenzie, C.B. 1825-1881." By his Wife. David Douglas, Edinburgh.

37. "A Familiar History of British India from the Earliest Period to the Present Time." 1859. By J. H. Stocqueler. Tenth Thousand. Revised and brought down to 1865 by James H. Siddons.

38. "Early Records of British India, etc." By J. Talboys Wheeler. 1878.

39. "Memorandum of the Material Condition of the Lower Orders in Bengal from 1881-82 to 1891-92." By F. H. B. Skrine, Bengal Secretariat Press. 1892.

40. "The Origin of the Musalmans of Bengal," being a Translation of "Haqiqate Musalman-i-Bengalah." By Khondkar Fuzli Rubbee, Diwan to H.H. The Nawab Bahadur of Murshidabad, G.C.I.E.

41. "The Tale of the Great Mutiny." By W. H. Fitchett.

42. "Military Transactions in Industan." 3 vols. Orme.

43. "Selections from State Papers," 1772 to 1785. Vol. i. G. W. Forrest, B.A.

PART II.

BIOGRAPHIES.

Nawab Nazim Murshid Kuli Khan.

PART II.

BIOGRAPHIES.

I.

MURSHID KULI KHAN.

NAWAB NAZIM MUTAMAN-UL-MULK, ALA-U-DOWLAH, JAFFER KHAN NUSAIRI, NASIR JANG.

1704-1725 A.D.

THIS remarkable man had no pedigree to boast of. He was the son of a poor Brahmin, and was purchased by Mahomed Shafi of Ispahan, who brought him up as his own son, and gave him the name of Mahomed Hadi. Manumitted by the heirs of Shafi, Murshid Kuli Khan came to the Deccan, and, by force of personal ability, rose in favour with Aurungzebe, and was soon appointed to the office of Diwan of Hyderabad and Berar. While serving in this capacity he applied to the Emperor for the Diwanni of Bengal, with a promise that, if appointed, he would make many improvements and augment the revenue of the province. His personal merit and past services in the Deccan, both in "Cabinet and Field," induced the Emperor to grant his request. He accordingly nominated him to the post, and dignified him with the title of "Kar Talab Khan."

At that time the offices of Nazim (Governor) and Diwan (the Revenue Officer) were kept perfectly distinct. The business of the Nazim was to defend and protect the country from foreign insult, or domestic insurrection, and to ensure strict obedience to the laws; the work of the Diwan was to collect the revenues, and to disburse all the requisite expenses. The Diwan was, in a certain degree, subject to the Nazim, being obliged to comply with all written orders for money, from that officer, for the service of Government; but the Nazim was responsible to the Imperial Exchequer for any improper use of that power. He received his regular salary from the Diwan, and was not entitled to any further emolument.

Mahomed Hadi, Kar Talab Khan, on receiving the appointment, proceeded to Dacca, and entered with alacrity upon the business of his office. He appointed experienced revenue collectors in different districts, prepared the assessment papers, and drew up rent-rolls, copies of which he sent to the Emperor, together with the full account of the Jaghirs; recommended the transfer of all Jaghirs of officers to Orissa, with the exception of the Nizamat stipends. This was sanctioned by the Emperor, and the income of Bengal, thus unburdened, and increased, showed a large surplus over the expenditure. This, again, was the means of placing the whole of the zemindars under the control of the Diwan, who, by his authority, enforced a very considerable rise in their rents, and thereby augmented the revenue of the State.

The Diwan soon found it inadvisable to remain in the same place with the Nazim, whose haughty temper could ill brook the constant interference of the Diwan in all pecuniary transactions, or frequent opposition to his Royal Highness' commands. He resolved, after consultation with his friends, to fix his residence at Muxsudabad, the name of which he afterwards changed to Murshidabad, when he himself received the title of "Murshid Kuli Khan."

In 1704 he left Dacca, without taking leave of the Viceroy, Prince Azim; carrying with him all the public officers attached to the Diwanni.

Kar Talab Khan having fixed his residence at Muxsudabad, assembled there all the public officers of his department; and at the end of the year, having made up his accounts, in which were clearly exhibited the great additions he had made to the revenue of the provinces, prepared to set out for the Court of Delhi, in order to lay them personally before the Emperor. On presenting the papers, however, to the two Kánongoes, whose signatures were requisite to sanction their being audited in the Imperial Exchequer, one of them, named Darp Narain, refused his signature, unless bribed by a present of three lakhs of rupees. The Diwan made a promise to pay one lakh after his return from Delhi. Darp Narain still refused. The Diwan, conscious of the accuracy of his statement, then refused his demand of a bribe, and, having obtained the signature of the other Kánongo, proceeded to the imperial camp in the Deccan; and, having first presented the Emperor and his Ministers with a very large sum of money, and a number of curiosities brought from Bengal, he then submitted his accounts to the Imperial Exchequer. They were immediately audited by the Vizier, with much credit to him. He was, in consequence, dignified by the Emperor with a dress of honour, standards, and kettle-drums, and re-appointed to Bengal as Diwan of the three provinces of Bengal, Behar, and Orissa, in his own right, and as Deputy Nazim to the Prince in the provinces of Bengal and Orissa on the part of the Prince, with the lofty title of "Nawab Murshid Kuli Mutaman-ul-Mulk, Ala-u-Dowlah, Jaffer Khan Nusairi, Nasir Jang."

On his return to Bengal he changed the name of Muxsudabad to Murshidabad, established a mint there, and finished the erection of a palace and public offices, to render the city the capital of the province.

The departure of Prince Azim-u-Shan from Behar threw the whole of the authority into the hands of the Deputy Nawab, and gave him the united powers of Nazim and Diwan, and an unlimited control over the three provinces. For, although the Prince appointed his son, Farrukshah, to be his representative in Bengal, it does not appear that he was authorized to do so by the Emperor; and the Diwan paid little attention to his nomination.

The offices of Nazim and Diwan, hitherto separated, being now, in the absence of the Prince, united in his person, Murshid Kuli Khan appointed Syud Ikram Khan to be his deputy Diwan over the province of Bengal; and his son-in-law, Sujah-u-Din Mahomed Khan, to be his deputy Diwan in Orissa. At the same time he appointed Bhooput Roy and Kaisar Roy, two Brahmins, whom he had brought with him, to confidential posts; the former as Secretary to the Treasury, and the latter as his private secretary. He also annexed the district of Midnapur to Bengal, although it had always before constituted a part of Orissa. He put defaulting zemindars in confinement, and appointed experienced and expert revenue collectors from among the Bengalis, who received the assessments direct from farmers and paid the amount of the revenue into the public treasury. The Nawab next ordered the whole of the lands to be re-measured, and having ascertained the quantity of fallow, and waste ground, belonging to every village, he caused a considerable proportion of it to be brought into cultivation, for which purpose he authorized the collectors to make advances of money to the lower orders of husbandmen to purchase stock, and to reimburse themselves by a certain portion of the produce. Thus the zemindars were entirely dispossessed of all interference in the collection of revenue or expenditure, while the assessments increased and the land improved.

No charges for militia for collection of revenue were admitted. With only two thousand cavalry and four thousand infantry, headed by Nazir Ahmad, who was originally a head peon (messenger), he governed the country, and enforced the collection of revenues; for, so severe were his regulations, and such the dread of his power, that his commands were implicitly obeyed, and it was sufficient for him to send a single messenger to sequester a zemindar, or to seize on a culprit, even at a distance.

Such were the respect and dignity kept up at his Court, that in his presence no one was allowed to salute or speak to another, nor were any of his officers or Rajas allowed to sit before him. Whoever deviated in the smallest degree from his general regulations, was certain to experience the effects of his resentment.

In the affairs of government he showed favour to no one, and always rewarded merit wherever he found it; but he placed confidence in nobody. He examined the accounts himself every day and signed them, and at the end of the month enforced the full amount due to be paid. In case of default he would confine the zemindars, collectors, and clerks in the "hall of forty pillars," and set over them resolute *dunners*, with orders not to allow them to leave the hall till the full amount of the instalments was paid up.

The collections and the accounts for the year were finished in the month of *Choit*, the last month of the year; and in the month of *Baisakh*, the beginning of the year, having finished the ceremony of the *Punya* (rent-day collection), the Nawab generally despatched to Delhi the revenue, amounting to one crore thirty lakhs, chiefly in specie, in bags, and laden upon two hundred carts, escorted by a guard of three hundred cavalry and five hundred infantry, and accompanied by one of the sub-treasurers. The Nawab, attended by his principal officers, would accompany the convoy up to Jhapaida; and, in order to remove any further responsibility from himself, he had the event recorded, in addition to his own despatch to the Vizier, in the Royal Gazettes, by which all the Governors on the route were apprized of the circumstance, and were obliged, by the regulations, to have carts and escort ready to forward the treasure to the capital. Along with the revenue he sent, as presents to the Emperor and Ministers, a number of elephants, hill horses, antelopes, hawks, shields of rhinoceros hide, sword-blades, Sylhet mats, filigree work of gold and silver, wrought ivory, Dacca muslins, Kasimbazar silk, the "Gangajali" of Sylhet, over which a snake cannot pass; also a number of European articles procured at the port of Hughli, or presented by foreign merchants.

By such conduct, Murshid Kuli Khan conciliated the Emperor and his Ministers. His star was in the ascendant, and he rose in dignity and honour, being made commander of seven thousand horse. His influence at the Imperial Court was such that the appointments in Bengal were made chiefly at his recommendation. If any man procured a nomination through any other interest he met with trouble, and his situation was made unpleasant.

After the death of Ikram Khan, the Nawab appointed Reza Khan deputy Diwan of Bengal. Reza Khan was the husband of Nafissa, the grand-daughter of Murshid Kuli Khan.

After paying the Imperial revenue of one crore thirty lakhs of rupees, and defraying the expenses of the Nizamat, the surplus was buried.

In 1707 Aurungzebe died, and his eldest son, Bahadur Shah, ascended the throne in Delhi. The Nawab sent the usual congratulatory presents, and received a robe of honour and a *sanad* of confirmation to the Nizamat.

Prince Azim-u-Shan went to Delhi, leaving Serfiraz Khan to act as his deputy at Patna. Prince Farrukshah, who was at Dacca, proceeded to Murshidabad and took up his residence at Lalbagh, in that city, where he lived on terms of cordiality with Murshid Kuli Khan, who defrayed the expenses of the Prince's household. When Bahadur Shah died, in 1712 A.D., and his eldest son, Mahomed Shah Badshah, ascended the throne, the usual presents and revenue were sent, and the Nawab confirmed in his post.

Sultan Farrukshah, after the death of his father in battle, had determined to contest the throne, and with this view he applied for assistance to Murshid Kuli Khan, who refused him help, declaring that nothing could make him deviate from his duty to the reigning king at Delhi, and that as his uncle was now on the throne the revenue was his, and could not be given to any other.

Having received this reply from the Nawab, the Prince did not press the point further, but went to Patna. On his way, the adherents of his family joined him, and many indigent men flocked to his standard, with a view to future benefits. Having borrowed considerable sums of money from the bankers of Patna and Benares for the outfit of his army, the Prince entered Patna with pomp, and with the help of the two brothers, Syud Abdullah and Syud Hassan Ali, Nazims of Oudh and Allahabad, who were under great obligations to his father, and who had reasons for dissatisfaction with the Emperor, Farrukshah was proclaimed king, and letters written to all parts of the country, inviting all officers and soldiers to join his standard.

The two brothers made all military preparations, and seized upon the treasure of the year's collection of Bengal, amounting to one crore ten lakhs of rupees, which had arrived at that time at Allahabad, under the charge of Sujah-u-Din Khan, the son-in-law of the Nawab of Bengal. This was a most fortunate event for the brothers, as it enabled them to recruit for their army and to collect the materials of war.

Thus relieved from anxiety as to funds and partisans, Farrukshah appointed Syud Hassan Ali as Vizier, and considered himself Emperor in earnest. He gladly accepted the proposal of Rashid to appoint him Subahdar of Bengal. In 1713 A.D., Rashid, instead of accompanying his master, took the route to Murshidabad, intending to surprise the Nawab and to get possession of the province without difficulty, as it was known that Murshid Kuli Khan kept no more troops than those actually employed in the collection of the revenue. Rashid had already entered the passes of Teriagarhi and Sikligali before the Nawab was aware of his intentions, but he ordered his corps of two thousand cavalry to encamp outside the city, and having joined to them as many of his infantry as he could collect, with a few guns, awaited the approach of the enemy. When the troops of Rashid had arrived within three miles of Murshidabad, the Nawab gave the chief command to two officers, named Mir Bengali and Syud Anwar, and ordered them to oppose the enemy—himself remaining engaged in transcribing the Koran. An engagement ensued, in which Syud Anwar was killed and Mir Bengali compelled to retreat. The Nawab was, however, not at all dismayed by these events, and kept on writing. Hearing the news of Mir Bengali's retreat, he only made a sign to Mahomed Jan and the Foujdar of Murshidabad, who were standing before him, to go to his assistance, and himself, after finishing the task of writing fixed for the day, rose, and collecting the palace guards and a few other troops, slaves, and the zemindars of Karimabad, proceeded on his elephant to the assistance of his retreating troops. His presence gave courage to the troops; they returned to the attack, and an arrow from the bow of Mir Bengali having pierced Rashid Khan, he fell from his horse, and his army was subsequently totally routed, and many prisoners were taken. A large quantity of plunder thus obtained was ordered to be distributed among the troops, and a pyramid of heads was ordered to be erected on the road to Delhi, that it might remain a monument of this victory and serve as a warning to others.

Sultan Farrukshah, who had not yet finished his work with his uncle, the Emperor, received with sorrow and grief the news of the death of Rashid, while yet on his way to Delhi. Ever after this victory of Murshid Kuli Khan, no officers cast a longing eye on Bengal, nor did anyone dare to speak against its ruler.

As soon as Farrukshah was firmly established on the throne, in 1713 A.D., Murshid Kuli Khan prepared the usual presents and sent them to the Court, with the amount of the year's collections, with the same punctuality as he had hitherto done, and the new Emperor conferred on him the united offices of Nazim and Diwan; the former of which he had hitherto held only as a deputy, and, as with his predecessors, the recommendation of Murshid Kuli Khan was equally accepted by Farrukshah also, and it was on his recommendation that the nephew of Manick Chand was appointed to be Imperial Treasurer, with the title of "Jaggat Seth."

As a further proof of his influence at the Court of Delhi, it is stated that Syud Hassan Ali Khan, Paymaster-General, brother of Kutb-ul-Mulk Syud Abdullah, the vizier, wished for the title of "Nasir Jang," which had been formerly conferred on the Governor of Bengal. As one title cannot be given to two men at the same time, an Imperial Mandate was issued in the name of Murshid Kuli Khan to exchange it for another equally honourable, but the Nawab wrote that in his old age he was not desirous of new titles, and that he would never sell the title given him by the Emperor Aurungzebe.

On the death of Syud Reza Khan, the deputy Diwan of the province, the Nawab procured that appointment for his grandson, Mirza Asadullah, son of Sujah-u-Din Mahomed Khan, the deputy Nazim of Orissa, with the splendid title of "Serfiraz Khan."

In same year the office of Deputy Nazim of Dacca was conferred on Mirza Lutfullah, the husband of his grand-daughter, the daughter of Sujah-u-Din—and for him was procured his own title, "Murshid Kuli Khan II."

In 1719 A.D., corresponding to 1133 A.H., the unfortunate Farrukshah was put to death by the very men who had raised him to the throne, and Prince Rafi-ul-Kadr was crowned. But Bengal had nothing to fear from these changes of kings, or other outside disturbances. Murshid Kuli Khan went on doing the work of administration with extreme freedom, and without fear of anybody. He was indefatigable in the extirpation of robbers and thieves. The public roads were safe during his administration, and the inhabitants of the towns and villages could sleep securely in their houses.

Excepting Shaistah Khan, there has not appeared in Bengal, nor, indeed, in any part of Hindustan, a ruler that can be compared with Nawab Murshid Kuli Khan for zeal in the propagation of the faith; for wisdom in the establishment of laws and regulations; for munificence and liberality in the encouragement and support given to men of family and eminence; for rigid and impartial justice in redressing wrongs and punishing offenders; "in short, whose whole administration so much tended to the benefit of mankind and the glory of the Creator."

His judicial decisions were so rational and just, that they were as much respected and obeyed as the decrees of those monarchs whose names are most renowned for equity and justice. He slept but little, and carefully observed the stated times for prayer. From breakfast till noon he employed himself in copying the Koran, and in administering justice; and every year he sent Korans of his own writing, with valuable offerings, to Mecca, Medina, Najaf, and other holy places.

He maintained five hundred Koran readers, beadsmen, and chanters, who were constantly employed in reciting the Koran and in other acts of devotion. During the first twelve days of Rabi-ul-Awwal, which include the day of the birth and death of the holy Prophet, he feasted people of all conditions; and on those nights the road from Mahinagar to Lalbagh, which is a distance of three miles, was illuminated with lamps, so arranged as to represent verses of the Koran, mosques, trees, and other figures, which could be clearly distinguished and read from the other side of the river. Nearly a hundred thousand men were employed on these occasions; and on firing a gun, the whole route was illuminated at once, exhibiting, in an instant, such a sheet of light as astonished the beholders.

He also used to perform the festival of the prophet Khizr—called the "Bera" (*v.* p. 64). In the month of Bhádar, the time of the rising of the river, a large raft, 125 cubits wide, of plantain trees and bamboos, built on inverted earthen jars, ornamented with flags, lamps of talc and coloured paper, and fireworks of various kinds and quality, is launched at Mahinagar, a mile or so above the palace of the Nazim, and floats down with majestic pomp.

How he always provided against famine and severely prohibited all monopolies of grain, is noted in the Historical portion of this work. He took no delight in hunting; he never indulged in wine nor in any intoxicating drugs; neither did he amuse himself with singers or dancers. He always kept constant to one lawful wife, and, out of excess of delicacy, would not suffer any strange woman, or even eunuchs, to enter the apartments of his seraglio—so much so, that any slave girl once out of the harem would not be allowed to re-enter it.

He possessed very extensive learning, and paid great respect to men who were eminent for their piety or erudition. He wrote with great elegance, and was a remarkably fine penman; his skill in arithmetic enabled him to scrutinize all accounts himself. He was a brave soldier, a liberal benefactor, upright and just in his dealings, and a steady protector of the weak; so that the meanest peasant was secure, during his administration, from injustice and oppression. He despised all the refinements of luxury, particularly in dress: no highly seasoned dishes were served on his table, neither frozen sherbet nor cream, but only plain ice! During the winter his household steward used to collect in the mountains of Rajmehal a sufficient stock of ice for the rest of the year. The whole was done at the expense of the zemindars of that district. He liked fruit, and in the mango season an overseer was stationed at Rajmehal to keep a regular account of the choicest mango trees in Maldah, Cutwah, and Hussainpur, and guards were put over them to see that no one purloined the fruit, and that the whole crop was regularly sent to Murshidabad. The zemindars dare not cut down a mango tree nor touch any of the fruit that the overseer had appropriated for the Nawab's table.

He made no retrenchments in any royal grant, nor in those of any former Subahdar, for charitable purposes; on the contrary, he increased them. No zemindars or rent collectors could, with impunity, oppress anyone: vakeels of zemindars were constantly in search of complainants, and whenever they met with anyone who had reason to be dissatisfied, they used every endeavour to pacify him; but if it happened that a well-founded complaint reached the ears of Murshid Kuli Khan, the offender was sure to suffer severely. If the officers of justice, out of partiality or respect to rank, neglected to redress the wrongs of the meanest person, upon a representation thereof from the party aggrieved, the Nawab tried the cause himself, and in his decisions showed neither favour nor affection to anyone, the rich and the poor being of equal value in his sight. His sentences were in conformity to the commandments of the Koran, according to the findings of Kazi Mahomed Sharaf, a very learned and religious expounder of Mahomedan law.

In the beginning of his administration, the Katwal (Senior Police Officer of the town) of Hughli forcibly took away a young girl from the house of her father, a *Moghul*, and Ahsanullah, the Foujdar of that place, suffering the offence to pass unnoticed, the father carried his complaint before the Nawab, who commanded that the offender should be stoned to death, conformably to the ordinance of the Koran; and notwithstanding all the entreaties of Ahsanullah, who was a great favourite, the sentence was actually carried out.

It is said that a Mahomedan beggar having asked charity of one Brindaban, a Hindu landholder of Chunakhali, he was displeased at his manner and turned him out of the house. The fakir collected a number of bricks, with which he erected a wall on Brindaban's road, and gave it the name of a mosque, and from it called the people to prayer. Whenever Brindaban passed that way he vociferated the summons to prayer, and so vexed him, that in rage he threw down, unfortunately for him, some of the bricks, abused the fakir, and drove him away. The fakir complained to Murshid Kuli Khan, and Kazi Mahomed Sharaf, in an assembly of men learned in the Mahomedan law, sentenced Brindaban to be put to death. The Nawab was not willing to take away his life, and asked the Kazi whether there was not any way of evading the strict letter of the law, to save the poor Hindu. The Kazi answered, "There may be so much delay as to allow time for his intercessor to be put to death first; but after that he must absolutely be executed." All the endeavours of the Nawab in his behalf were ineffectual; and although Brindaban was recommended to the Emperor's mercy by the Prince Azim-u-Shan, yet it was of no avail; for the Kazi killed him with an arrow from his own hand. After the execution, the Prince complained to Aurungzebe that Kazi Mahomed Sharaf had killed Brindaban in a fit of insanity, but the Emperor wrote, with his own hand, on the Prince's letter, "Kazi Sharaf Khuda ki taraf," that is, "Kazi Sharaf is on the side of God." After the death of Aurungzebe, Kazi Sharaf applied for leave to resign; and all the entreaties of the Nawab could not prevail upon him to continue in office.

The Nawab being now far advanced in years, and finding his health decline very fast, ordered his tomb to be built with a mosque, and Katra. On the east of the city of Murshidabad, a large mosque with shops round it, high turrets, a reservoir of water, and a market (the duties collected from which would keep the whole in repair), was built in the course of a year, and underneath the flight of stairs a tomb was constructed to receive the remains of the Nawab after his death. This ostentatious building is yet standing in a dilapidated state, well known as the "Katra Musjid." It was built in 1137 A.H., 1723 A.D.

As Murshid Kuli Khan had no male issue, he appointed his grandson, Serfiraz Khan, his public and private successor, and sole executor of his last testament; and having delivered to him the keys of his treasures and valuable effects, he admonished him to behave with justice and humanity to all those who were placed under his authority. He died, in 1139 A.H., corresponding to 1725 A.D.* He ruled twenty-four years, and the revenue of Bengal, exclusive of the Jaghir of the Nazims and other officers, and other duties, was Rs. 1,40,88,000. The income of the Jaghir of the Nazim from Bengal was 5,82,08,500 dáms, and from Orissa 2,38,25,300 dáms, aggregating 8,20,33,800 dáms, which, at forty dáms to a rupee, would amount to Rs. 20,50,845.

Serfiraz Khan deposited the remains of his grandfather, conformably to instructions, in the tomb underneath the long and high flight of stairs of the mosque, and having given every assurance to the officers and employés of the Nizamat that he would retain them in their respective posts, he took up the work of administration on the same principles as his grandsire. He removed all the effects of the deceased, with the exception of the public treasure, to his own house, and sent the intelligence of the event of the Nawab's death to Delhi, as well as to his father in Orissa.†

* Wheeler (38) gives 1724 as the year of the Nazim's death; Marsham (31), and Fuzli Rubbee (40), 1725 A.D.

† Taking this biography as No. 1 of those to be given of the Nawabs Nazim, the notes have mainly been taken from Persian writers, and translated, or copied, for this work by the direction of the present Nawab Bahadur of Murshidabad. Facts and opinions from other historians have been added by the Editor. Nos. 5, 15, and 16, have been drawn up by the Editor from the various works given in the Bibliography and from Records in the Nizamat Palace Library.

II.

SUJAH-U-DIN MAHOMED.

MUTAMAN-UL-MULK, SUJAH-U-DOWLAH NAWAB SUJAH-U-DIN MAHOMED KHAN BAHADUR ASAD JANG.

1725-1739.

SUJAH-U-DIN MAHOMED KHAN, out of ambition, considered the death of Murshid Kuli Khan in 1725 A.D. (1139 A.H.), as a stroke of good luck for him. He immediately sent his application, with presents, to Mahomed Shah, through his agents, and, leaving Mahomed Taki Khan, his son, to represent him in Orissa, started for Bengal attended by his confidential officers and a select corps of cavalry. On his way he received the *firman* constituting him Nazim of Bengal and Orissa, at a place near Midnapur, which he named on this account "Mobarak Manzil," or propitious place, and in commemoration of this event, he ordered a market and *Serai* (rest-house for travellers) to be built there.

When the news of Sujah-u-Dowlah's arrival reached Serfiraz Khan, his first impulse was to oppose him, and he made preparations accordingly; but on the advice of his mother and grandmother, for whom he entertained the utmost affection and respect, he desisted from such unfilial conduct, and gladly advanced to receive his father, and conducted him to Murshidabad. After resigning the palace to Sujah-u-Dowlah, Serfiraz Khan retired to his own house at Naktakhali, and from that time he never failed to pay his respects to his father personally every morning. He followed the example of his grandfather in devotion, and retained the Koran readers appointed by Murshid Kuli Khan, as his companions. Urged, however, by unfortunate impulses, he neglected business and dissipated much of his time with the women in the seraglio, and was much addicted to amusements and luxury.

Sujah-u-Dowlah, though advanced in age, was brave, and generous to his troops; but he also was inclined to luxury and dissipation. He was by descent an Afshar of the tribe of Turkomans of Khorassan, the same from which Nadir Shah, the King of Persia, sprung. His father held a high post under the Emperor at Berhampur in the Deccan, and one of his forefathers, named Ali Yar Sultan, was the Governor of Furah, a province of Khorassan, when Tahmasp was King of Persia.

Sujah-u-Dowlah, immediately after his succession to the throne of Bengal, despatched forty lakhs of rupees in specie, being part of the private fortune of his predecessor, to the Court of Delhi, with the usual presents to the Emperor and his Ministers, consisting of elephants, horses, clothes, etc., and in return he received a confirmation of his appointment, and the additional titles of "Mutaman-ul-Mulk, Sujah-u-Dowlah, Sujah-u-Din Mahomed Khan, Bahadur Asad Jang," with a commission of command of seven thousand horse, a palanquin with fringes, a robe of honour of six cloths, a jewelled sword, a horse, and an elephant, with the insignia of "Fish and Bells."

He soon after this gradually took up the ways and manners of kings, and surpassed all his predecessors in splendour and munificence. The palace and buildings of Murshid Kuli Khan were considered too confined and insufficient for him. They were pulled down, and a new palace, *Mahal serai*, *Tirpolia*, private hall, mango house, hall of forty pillars, Ruh Afza, Jelaw Khana, public office, audience hall, arsenal, and other buildings, more suitable to his idea of grandeur, were erected. The new year's day, Mahomed's birthday, and the two Ids* were celebrated with royal splendour, and on these occasions the Nawab was dressed in brocade set with valuable jewels, adorned with strings of pearls round his neck, and a *surpech* or turban with "jigha" on his head; sitting in a "palki" with fringes, or on an elephant with golden howdah

* *Vide* pp. 66, 68.

NAWAB NAZIM SUJAH-U-DIN MAHOMED.

and brocade canopy. He was followed by "Jhapank" and "Nalki," field-officers, risaldars, tumandars, omrahs, and grandees, slaves from Africa, Turkistan, Kurdistan, with flags of many colours; eunuchs, punkah pullers, "fistas" wavers, sword and shield bearers, Asaburdars, Sontaburdars, yasawals, jelodars, chaushans, tarrakoo goyans, horses of Arabia, Irrakia, with harness of gold, gold-worked saddles; elephants, beautiful and majestic, with golden letters on embroidered coverings, silken ropes, and golden rods to drive them; drum beaters, Kurnachians, Sarnachians, jalajul strikers, tury singers, flags, and other insignia; flag bearers, with gold and silver standards. Then came nowbat-nawazans, ramishgarans, singers, and kurtal, surnal, sherpanja, ektara, and brass cannons, every piece in its proper place both right and left, front and back, moving in measured paces, was the train that on festival days accompanied him. The Subahdar distributed alms like showers of rain to the poor that flocked to him on all sides, unchecked. He answered the *salams* (bows) of the people with both hands. Surveyors with silken ropes measured the way, and at every mile shouted out the distance. All this was a sight of which the solemnity and grandeur can hardly be conceived, or described. A corps of twenty-five thousand cavalry, and as many infantry, constantly moved with him wherever he went, and if a detachment of this force was deputed to any necessary duty, it had to return and take its place as soon as the work was over. Rewards and favours were constantly distributed among the followers and their hearts gained; the troops were kept happy, and the officers and commanders constantly shared the bounties of the Nawab's plentiful table. His servants and dependants always received the benefit of his generosity, so much so that even the sweepers, fan bearers, and standard bearers received elephants as rewards. Of money, the lowest gift to the lowest menial would often amount to not less than five hundred rupees. To the learned and virtuous he was a warm friend, to the religious and godly he was respectful and generous. In justice he was impartial; to reward merit and punish the wicked he was ever ready. Morad and Nazir Ahmad were two men, the creatures of Murshid Kuli Khan, notorious for oppression and cruelty. Sujah-u-Dowlah ordered their conduct to be closely investigated, and finding them guilty, condemned them to death, and confiscated their property.

Nazir Ahmad had begun to build a mosque and garden, in the village of Dehparah, on the bank of the river Bhagirathi. After his execution the Nazim finished the musjid in a superb style and the garden with great beauty and elegance, with a large reservoir of water, running canals, flower beds, fruit trees, and artificial springs, and named it *Farah bágh* or "Pleasant Garden"; and in the summer season retired thither with his family, and passed his time in the enjoyment of every luxury.

A yearly feast was given to the officers, secretaries, clerks, and other servants of the Nizamat. The work of the administration was altogether left to Haji Ahmad, brother of Ali Verdi Khan; Roy Alum Chand, the Diwan, and Futteh Chand, Jaggat Seth, the Imperial Banker; while the Nawab lived in luxury and pleasure.

In the year 1739, corresponding with 1151 A.H., during the reign of Mahomed Shah, Emperor of Delhi, on Farrukshah being removed from office, the governorship of Patna was again annexed to Bengal, and Sujah-u-Dowlah was required to fill it. Sujah-u-Dowlah was unwilling to leave Bengal to fill the post himself *personally*, and wished to depute one of his own children; but his wife, Zinat-u-Nafissa, daughter of Murshid Kuli Khan, refused to part with her son, Serfiraz Khan, or to confer the post on the other son by another wife, and the difficulty could only be solved by giving the appointment to Ali Verdi Khan, who was therefore invested with the robes of honour and sent to Patna. The mother of Serfiraz Khan, who was of the same opinion as her husband on this point, sent for him to the gate of her apartment, and gave him a robe of honour on her own part; after which, Ali Verdi Khan proceeded to receive the insignia of office from Sujah-u-Dowlah, consisting of sword, dagger, turban, and "jigha" (head ornament of gold set with jewels), an elephant, and other gifts. After a few days he started for Patna.

In 1732 (1144 A.H.), during the great perturbation caused by the approach of Nadir Shah, Sujah-u-Dowlah fell ill, and feeling the near approach of death, sent Durdana Begum and her son to Orissa. He then appointed his son Serfiraz Khan his heir and successor, and enjoined him to regard Haji Ahmad, Roy Royán, and Jaggat Seth, as his steadfast counsellors. He was to follow their advice in all affairs of moment. Although Serfiraz Khan bore no cordiality towards these men, yet, for fear of offending his dying father, he promised to obey his commands. Sujah-u-Dowlah gave him all his treasures, recommended the servants of the Nizamat to his care, and died in A.D. 1739 (1151 A.H.).

During the administration of Nawab Sujah-u-Dowlah, the income from the revenue of the three Subahs was Rs. 4,44,24,223; this accords with that collected by Nawab Murshid Kuli Khan; but there was an increase of Rs 2,17,295, on account of duties, in 1738. This was exclusive of the stipends of the Nazim and other officers. The income of the stipends, that is jaghirs, of the Omrahs was thus made up:—

From Bengal	...		Dáms 5,82,08,500
„ Orissa	...	...	2,38,25,300
„ Behar	...	...	4,45,90,020
„ Fulwari of Rohtas		...	4,00,000
			12,70,23,820

Or Rs. 31,75,596, taking 40 dáms to the rupee.

Sujah-u-Dowlah daily fed at his own table all his acquaintances and friends, and fixed, yearly allowances were given to the widows of Berhampur, his birthplace, according to rank and merit. Any man, from whatever quarter, coming to him, would receive a daily allowance and suitable employment, particularly a man of learning. He was buried in the mausoleum he had built a year previous to his death, on the right bank of the Bhagirathi, opposite to the Palace of Murshidabad. The cemetery is called Roshnibagh (the garden of light).

III.

SERFIRAZ KHAN.

MUTAMAN-UL-MULK, ALA-U-DOWLAH NAWAB SERFIRAZ KHAN BAHADUR, HYDER JANG.

1739-1740.

SERFIRAZ KHAN deposited the remains of his father in the tomb prepared during his lifetime; but, apprehensive of the intrigues of his enemies, did not venture out of the Fort to attend the funeral obsequies.

He took up the administration of the country in place of his father, and, in obedience to his dying commands, entrusted the management of affairs to Haji Ahmad, Roy Royan, and Jaggat Seth; and confirmed them in their respective appointments, following their advice to the letter.

Haji Ahmad and his brother for years past, notwithstanding the numerous benefits conferred on them, had been constantly plotting to render themselves independent of Serfiraz Khan, and were always seeking how to get rid of him. Now, taking up the unfounded accusation of favouring new men, and overlooking the dues of old servants, the Haji, in intrigue with Roy Royan and Jaggat Seth, schemed

NAWAB NAZIM SERFIRAZ KHAN.

to recall Ali Verdi Khan to Bengal. Serfiraz Khan was to be put in confinement for life. They deceived the Nawab by their attention, and prevailed on him, by way of retrenching expenses, to disband a considerable part of his army. The disbanded soldiers repaired to Patna and were enlisted by Ali Verdi Khan.

Serfiraz Khan at last received intelligence of the conspiracy, and at first contemplated recalling Ali Verdi Khan from Behar, and displacing every member of that family from their official situations; but, in an evil hour, he listened to the cajolery of the Haji and his colleagues, and their protestations of attachment to his family, and granted their request to postpone the new arrangements for three months, or to the end of the year—the time for realization of all revenues still due.

During this respite, Ali Verdi Khan made his preparations, and having enlisted the interest of the officers of the army by promises, marched towards Bengal. Ata-ullah Khan having, at the instigation of Ali Verdi, intercepted all correspondence between Patna and Murshidabad, and having stopped all travellers on the road, actually prevented the news of these movements of the conspirators reaching Serfiraz Khan, till Ali Verdi Khan, by rapid and long marches, had moved through the passes of Satgarigali and Teliagurhi.

Surprised and confounded, Serfiraz Khan summoned the Haji to his presence and demanded an explanation of all this. The Haji, with his usual coolness, assurred the Nawab that Ali Verdi was only coming to pay his respects. Serfiraz Khan, however, detained the Haji in prison, and having sent Gous Khan and Mir Sharaf-u-Din at the head of the vanguard, left his own son, Hafizullah Khan, *alias* Mirza Amani, with Yeasin Khan, in charge of the fort and seraglio. He then started, accompanied by his two sons-in-law, Gazanfar Husain Khan (son of Mahomed Taki) and Hassan Mahomed, all his favourite officers and Rajas, with a large body of troops and artillery, on the 22nd Mohurram, 1152 A.H. (1740 A.D.), and reached Bahmania on the first day of March, Diwan Serai on the second; and on the third day encamped at Kumra. On taking the muster, it was discovered that Shahriar Khan, in charge of the ordnance, had treacherously neglected to take into camp any ammunition for the guns; nay, more, it was found on examination, that bricks were packed in place of balls, and in place of powder, sand and mustard seed. He was immediately dismissed, and a Portuguese named Panchu, son of one Anthony, was appointed in his place.

On the fourth day, in the morning, advised by the astrologers, Serfiraz Khan joined the camp and his men displayed such marks of valour and willingness to meet the enemy, that the party of Ali Verdi took fright, and was on the point of turning back. They could then have been, by a single volley, put to flight; but Roy Royan, seeing the situation, advised the Nawab to desist from attacking the enemy till next morning. The astrologers were urging the attack, but Serfiraz Khan, following the advice of Roy Royan, kept his men back.

At this time a letter of apology was received from Ali Verdi Khan, and Serfiraz Khan was so taken in by the tricks played upon him, that he released Haji Ahmad, the root of all the evil, and sent him to bring Ali Verdi Khan to the Nawab's presence. Sujah Kuli Khan and Khwaja Basant went with him in order that they might observe the situation of the enemy and spy out the strength of the army.

Ali Verdi Khan considered the release of his brother as a good omen, for it was his safety that he was afraid of, and that alone kept him back from commencing hostilities. He swore on the Koran that he would come in the morning to pay his respects, and to ask pardon for all his past faults. He then set before the Khwaja two hundred gold mohurs,* as a present. The Khwaja, out of

* Gold pieces worth sixteen rupees.

simplicity, believed all that Ali Verdi said, and assured Serfiraz Khan, on his return, of the sincerity of the cunning rogue. The Nawab, thus deceived, ordered an elegant entertainment to be prepared for the occasion. The troops, also, thinking that matters were to be amicably settled, were totally off their guard. Ali Verdi, with the advice of his brother, prevailed on the troops, with promise of reward of two months' pay, and prospects of large booty, to rise against their lawful master, and made them ready for a night attack, distributing arms and ammunition among them. Gous Khan and Mir Sharaf-u-Din, two faithful officers of the "advance guard," received intelligence of Ali Verdi's preparations, and at midnight came to Serfiraz Khan, and after acquainting him with what was passing at Ali Verdi's camp, proposed to take their master to their own camp for safety; but Serfiraz Khan spurned their good advice, and charged them with creating unnecessary quarrels with friends. In the meantime, the men of Ali Verdi's troops were passing, one by one, over to the camp of the sleeping Nawab, as though going to see their old acquaintances, until the camp of Serfiraz Khan was surrounded by them. Near midnight, Ali Verdi Khan, having divided his troops into three columns, and having left one column, commanded by Nand Lal, to deal with the "advance guard," marched with the other two to the outskirts of the Nawab's camp, unperceived. He opened a cannonade, and one of the first balls passing through Serfiraz Khan's tent, aroused him from sleep and almost awakened him to a sense of his danger and the perfidy of his enemy! Even then he thought that Ali Verdi was coming to pay his respects, and inquired whether the entertainment was ready. A second ball arrived, and all doubts were set aside! In a most undaunted manner the Nawab rushed towards Ali Verdi. Panic-stricken, his troops were flying, with the exception of a body of Afghans, under Gous Khan. These and a few slaves were all that remained with him.

The Nawab's elephant driver, seeing his master's danger, proposed to carry him to Birbhum, to stay with Badiuzzaman till his friends could join him there. Serfiraz Khan disdained the idea of fleeing from "those perfidious dogs," and continued to advance till all his adherents, one by one, fell, and a bullet struck him, and laid him low. The Afghans fell to plundering his tent, and the conspirators, looking on from a distance, rode off immediately they saw their master fall. Mir Hyder Shah and Khwaja Basant, leaving the body of Serfiraz Khan at the mercy of the enemy, hastened to the city of Murshidabad.

There Gous Khan and Mir Sharaf, supposing the ensign, Nand Lal, to be Ali Verdi, attacked him in the dark with their "advance guard," and killed the whole column of troops left there. They took a large quantity of booty, camels, horses, and arms, then hastened to the assistance of their ruler, and rushed with undaunted courage on the enemy. Ali Verdi Khan, who, notwithstanding the victory, was yet staying in the field, was astonished at their defiance of danger, and their bravery. Gous Khan, with both his sons fell, victims to the cannon of Chedi Hazari, and Mir Sharaf-u-Din let fly his arrows at the very breast of Ali Verdi Khan. Though checked by his shield, an arrow pierced the side of Ali Verdi. Mir Sharaf-u-Din had already another arrow in his bow, when Shaikh Janbaz, and Mahomed Zulfikar, old friends of Ali Verdi Khan, came to his rescue, and said to the Mir:—"Your master is killed, why, then, do you continue the war?" The Mir answered:—"For the sake of the honour of the family." They promised to honour the harem, and the Mir then halted, and with the remnant of his men took the road to Birbhum. The Portuguese, Panchu, the new superintendent of the ordnance, who, though deserted, was working the guns alone with effect, was now surrounded on all sides, after the departure of Mir Sharaf, and the magazine was set on fire. He died, poor man, but died bravely. Yet the work was not finished. Ali Verdi had yet another formidable antagonist to encounter. This was the faithful Bijoy Singh, who, with the natural intrepidity of a Rajput, seeing his master fall, rushed forward and, reaching Ali Verdi, was on the point of sending him out of the world with

NAWAB NAZIM ALI VERDI KHAN

a thrust of his spear, when Ali Verdi shouted for help, and Dawar Kuli Khan, coming up in time, saved his friend, and killed the Rajput with his matchlock. Zalim Singh, a boy of only nine years of age, came up with drawn sword to defend the body of his father. Some of Ali Verdi Khan's cowards rushed on the boy, but, pleased by the boy's courage, Ali Verdi ordered them back, and left the remains of the father to the son's care.

Gazanfar Hussain Khan and Hassan Mahomed Khan, sons-in-law of Serfiraz Khan, and other officers and fugitives reached the city the next day. Roy Royan received a bullet in his right hand, and, unable to bear the pain, killed himself by swallowing powdered diamond.

During the plundering of the camp, the elephant driver, unperceived by the enemy, conveyed the corpse of his master, the late Nawab, to Murshidabad, and at midnight his son, Mirza Amani, and Yeasin Khan, the *Foujdar*, caused it to be buried.

Mirza Amani and Gazanfar Hussain Khan made preparations to defend the city, but the troops were unable to support them. They were thus obliged to submit to the conqueror. The inhabitants, as well as the troops, were in consternation when Haji Ahmad entered the city, and assured the people, in the name of his brother, of his protection and favour. Yeasin Khan, under the orders of Haji Ahmad, held the treasures and Mahal Serai of Serfiraz Khan in confiscation, and strong guards were stationed to protect the family.

The following names of the sons of Serfiraz Khan are found in the old records:—(1) Shukrullah Khan, the eldest son; (2) Hafizullah Khan; (3) Mirza Mogul; (4) Mirza Amani (?); (5) Mirza Bhúran; and (6) Aká Mirza. There were five daughters, who were confined as prisoners at Dacca by Ali Verdi Khan.

IV.

ALI VERDI KHAN.

SUJAH-UL-MULK, HISAM-U-DOWLAH NAWAB ALI VERDI KHAN BAHADUR MAHABAT JANG.

1740-1756.

ALI VERDI KHAN'S grandfather was by descent an Afsar of the tribe of Turkomans, and a foster-brother of Alumgir, Emperor of Delhi. His father, Mirza Mahomed, was a servant on the household establishment of Mahomed Azim Shah. Mirza Mahomed had two sons, Mirza Ahmad and Mirza Mahomed Ali, better known as Ali Verdi Khan. Ahmad was the superintendent of the *Abdar Khana* (pantry steward) of Azim Shah; and Ali Verdi Khan, pipe bearer, superintendent of embroidery, and later, of the elephant stables. During the war between the princes, after the death of Alumgir, Ali Verdi stood by Prince Azim, though himself wounded by arrows. On the death of that Prince, both the brothers retired, and, pressed by privation, Ali Verdi proceeded to Orissa, in answer to the call of his father, who was then serving there under Nawab Sujah-u-Din. He arrived with his family in Murshidabad in the first year of Mahomed Shah's (Badshah) reign. Sujah-u-Din did not show him any favour, but is said to have borne him malice. The wife of the Nawab, however, in consideration of the relationship existing between him and Sujah-u-Din, warned Ali Verdi of her husband's intention to harm him, and advised him to go to Persia to her son-in-law. Ali Verdi, however, remained, and summoned his brother, addressed as "Haji," since his return from Mecca. Haji Ahmad arrived with his three sons, Mahomed Reza, Mahomed Syud, and

Mahomed Hashim. They all received suitable appointments under the Governor. How Ali Verdi tricked and deposed Serfiraz Khan has been described.

Ali Verdi Khan was sensible that if he entered the city immediately after his victory over Serfiraz, it would be impossible to prevent the Afghans and Rohillas from plundering the palaces of Serfiraz Khan. He therefore halted outside the city, near Gobera Nullah, for three days, and on the morning of the third day in the month of *Safar*, 1153 A.H. (1740-1 A.D.), entered the city in great state. Thus in his sixtieth year, Ali Verdi Khan sat on the *Musnud* (throne) of Bengal, and assumed the title of "Sujah-ul-Mulk, Hisam-u-Dowlah Mahomed Ali Verdi Khan Bahadur Mahabat Jang." He took possession of the effects and treasures of Serfiraz Khan, and those of his father and grandfather, which, by savings, had amounted to Rs. 70,00,000 in cash, and to Rs. 5,00,00,000 worth of jewels, furniture, etc.

As Ali Verdi Khan did not care to have more than one wife, the seraglio of Serfiraz Khan, including five hundred beautiful women, was taken possession of by his relatives, while the principal wife, with two sons, was sent by the Nawab to Dacca, with a scanty allowance for their support, from the revenue of the *Khas Mahal* (private estate) of Serfiraz Khan. His sister, Nafissa Khanum, condescended to the post of waiting-maid in the seraglio of Nuazish Mahomed Khan, and thus contrived to save the son of her brother Aka Baba, whom she had adopted.

It is said that when the news of the death of Serfiraz Khan and Ali Verdi's victory reached Delhi Mahomed Shah wept and said: "Nearly all the countries of my Empire have gone, and now a place from which I could expect a morsel of food has gone also." Bengal was practically independent and paid little respect to the Emperor.

Ali Verdi Khan, through the agency of Farid Khan, one of the friends of Vizier Kamr-u-Din Khan, petitioned the Emperor, promising that if he was confirmed as governor he would send the whole of Serfiraz Khan's effects to the Imperial Treasury. The helpless Emperor had to accept the proposal, and Farid Khan, according to orders, came to receive the treasures. He reached Behar, when the usurper, considering it unadvisable to let him see Bengal, wrote to him not to take the trouble of coming to Murshidabad, as he would meet him at Sikrigali with presents and the treasure. The Nawab accordingly started in the month of *Rajab*, 1153 A.H., and delivered to Farid Khan seven lakhs of rupees in specie, and seventy lakhs in jewels and other valuables. This done, Ali Verdi returned to Murshidabad.

He obtained the *Sanad* of confirmation as Nawab Nazim of the three provinces, and titles of honour also for himself, his three sons-in-law and other relatives, friends, and adherents. To Nuazish Mahomed, husband of Gheseeta Begum, the eldest sister of Ali Verdi Khan, was given the Diwanship of Bengal, with the deputy governorship of Dacca, to which were attached the districts of Chittagong, (Islamabad), Tipperah (Roshanabad), and Sylhet. He received the title of "Nasir-ul-Mulk, Ihtisham-u-Dowlah, Nuazish Ahmad Khan Bahadur Shahamut Jang." To Syud Ahmad Khan, the second son of the astute Haji, and husband of the second daughter of Ali Verdi Khan, was given the title of "Sowlat Jang." To Zainuldin, husband of Amina Begum, the youngest daughter of Ali Verdi Khan, was given the title of "Showkat Jang," and the deputy Nazimship of Patna. Mir Mahomed Jaffer Khan, husband of Shah Khanum, half-sister of Ali Verdi Khan, was made Paymaster-General and Commander in-Chief; Jiban Roy, Clerk of the *Jághirs*, a trustworthy and faithful servant, received the title of "Roy Royan."

In the commencement of the insurrection of Ali Verdi Khan, Serfiraz Khan had asked help from the deputy governor of Orissa, who, now hearing the sad news of Serfiraz Khan's fate, began to arrange means of defence against Ali Verdi Khan. He also despatched his friend, Mukhlis Ali Khan, the son-in-law of the Haji, to arrange peace with the Nawab. Haji Ahmad and Ali Verdi, naturally fertile in stratagem and deceit, wrote him a most conciliatory letter, and at the same time secretly set this very envoy to the task of alienating his troops from him.

In the month of *Showal*, 1153 A.H., Ali Verdi Khan set out for Orissa with 12,000 well-equipped troops and many guns. Murshid Kuli (II.), on the news of his approach, strengthened the fort of Barapati and sent his family and treasure there. Then taking with him both of his sons-in-law, Mirza Bakir Khan, a Prince of Persia, and Ala-u-Din Mahomed Khan, he reached Balasore at the head of a strong army. Having strengthened the trenches at Phulwar from Teliagurhi to the bank of the river, he awaited the arrival of Ali Verdi, unconscious of the cunning duplicity of Mukhlis Ali.

Ali Verdi, by long and rapid marches, reached Midnapur, and having conciliated the zemindars there by promises, advanced to Balasore and camped on the other side of the Subarun Rekha river. Raja Jagadhar Roy, having refused to assist him, or allow him to pass through his territory, Ali Verdi Khan set his artillery against Rajghat and opened fire. The Raja and his men, unable to withstand the fire, fled into the forest, and the victor passed on unchecked. He next fixed his camp at Ram Chandanpur, at a distance of eight or ten miles from the entrenchments of the deputy governor of Orissa. Envoys were passing to and fro with proposals for peace. This interchange took up a month. Mirza Bakir Khan, with youthful courage and inexperience, imprudently came out of the entrenchments and fell on Ali Verdi, driving his troops back for nearly two miles. At this stage Mukhlis Khan, the traitor envoy, and other Afghan officers, now openly estranged from the deputy, left him and went over to Ali Verdi Khan. On the other hand, Manick Chand, Peshkar of the Raja of Burdwan, who had accompanied Ali Verdi Khan, now deserted him for Murshid Kuli Khan (II.), and was passing, with that intention, towards the deputy's camp, when Bakir Khan, who was following the retreat of Ali Verdi, stopped him, and though friendly signs were made, Bakir Khan thought them fraudulent, and attacked him. Bakir Khan was defeated. The tide turned, for Ali Verdi, seeing this unexpected help, turned about and, encouraging his men, advanced again to battle. Bloody was the engagement, which ended in favour of Ali Verdi Khan; for as soon as Abdul Aziz, the Orissa paymaster, was killed, Murshid Kuli (II.) made good his retreat to Balasore and thence to the Deccan.

Ali Verdi Khan followed him up towards Balasore, but, unable to overtake him, gave orders to Mirza Khairullah Beg and Nurullah Beg to proceed at once to Cuttack* in order to capture Bijoy Singh, and secure the family and treasure of Murshid Kuli Khan (II.), while he himself followed them more leisurely.

On receiving intelligence of the defeat and departure of Murshid Kuli Khan (II.), Murad Khan, paymaster of Raja Parsutam, who had been left in charge, sent the family to the Deccan. The treasure, etc., was being loaded on elephants and camels, when the arrival of Ali Verdi Khan put the whole town in consternation. The people fled in all directions, while the conquerors entered the fort without hindrance, and distributed the treasure and jewels among themselves. These events occurred in 1741, A.D. Ali Verdi made a proclamation of safety and protection, and after a month returned to Murshidabad, leaving his son-in-law, Syud Ahmad Khan Sowlat Jang, as deputy-governor, with an army of three thousand cavalry and four thousand infantry, commanded by Gujjar Khan.

In the same year, "Sowlat Jang" employed, to command the troops, some of the Jemadars (lieutenants) and other officers of the late chief; among others: Salim Khan, Durveth Khan, Niamat Khan, and Mir Azizullah. He then sent back Gujjar Khan to Murshidabad. These men were seeking an opportunity of revenging their late chief, and now gave signs of refractory conduct. "Sowlat Jang" sent Kasim Beg, the Superintendent of the Arsenal, and Shaikh Hidayatullah, the Foujdar of Cuttack, to remonstrate with them and bring them to a sense of their duty. The malcontents finding these messengers unprotected, assaulted them. Kasim was killed, and the Foujdar wounded. The army, in conjunction with the people, rose up in a general insurrection, suddenly surrounded and plundered the palace, and took "Sowlat Jang" prisoner. They then invited Bakir Khan from Sitakul, and placed him on the *musnud* of Orissa and the country up to Midnapur and Hijli.

* The capital of Orissa, and now a large civil station, and the headquarters of the Commissioner of Orissa.

Ali Verdi, hearing the news, lost no time in preparing to remedy the disaster, and supposing that Bakir Khan must have been aided by Nizamat Mulk of the Deccan, collected an army of twenty thousand horse and eighteen thousand foot. He halted on the confines of Midnapur. The troops of Bakir Khan were alarmed, and that part of the army sent towards Bengal returned defeated. Ali Verdi Khan then entered Balasore, and sent Mustafa Khan, Sirdar Khan, Omer Khan, Sarandaz Khan, Balras Khan, commanded by Mir Jaffer Khan, to capture Bakir Khan.

Mir Bakir was meditating flight. He stationed troops on the Jobraghat, at the ferry of the river Mahanadi, which flows past Cuttack, to dispute the passage, and placed the prisoners on the other side of the river, on the route to the Deccan. On receiving intelligence that Ali Verdi Khan had followed him up to a distance of ten miles, he placed "Sowlat Jang" in a cart, accompanied by Haji Ahmad, brother of Murshid Kuli Khan (II.), and two mounted men, with orders to thrust their spears into the litter when the enemy came in sight. It so happened that when they arrived at Balasore "Sowlat Jang," unable to bear the heat, changed places with Haji Ahmad. When the two spearmen thrust their spears into the litter, according to orders, they half killed the Haji, who shouted for help. In the meanwhile Mir Jaffer and Mahomed Amin, with a number of men, fell upon the fugitives, and called loudly for "Sowlat Jang." He was afraid to answer their call, not being sure of the voices, but Mahomed Amin coming near, recognised, and at once released him from the litter, and sent him to Ali Verdi Khan. They then continued the pursuit of Bakir Khan. Murad Khan, paymaster of Raja Parsutam, who had come to the assistance of Bakir, caught hold of his horse's rein, drew him away and helped him to escape. Ali Verdi Khan, considering the recovery of "Sowlat Jang" in itself a great gain, desisted from further pursuit, and having rested some days near the river, returned to Cuttack happy, and victorious. All those who had assisted Bakir Khan were well punished.

Shaikh Masum, a jemadar, was appointed as deputy governor; and Ali Verdi Khan, after settling all affairs, returned to Bengal with his army. On his way he attacked the Raja of Mour Bhanj, who fled to the hills, leaving his territory to the victor. While thus engaged, the alarming news reached Ali Verdi that Bengal had been invaded by a Mahratta chief.

He lost no time in returning to Bengal, and by a long march he reached Burdwan, to find that the Mahrattas had arrived just before him. Raghuji Bonsla, son of the brother of the Raja of the Deccan, instigated by Mir Habib, had sent Bhasker Pundit at the head of forty thousand Mahrattas of Nagpur to plunder Bengal. These men were halting at Burdwan, when Ali Verdi appeared. The marauders were all round him, plundering the country right and left, and the Bengal sepoys, unacquainted with the ways of the Mahrattas, were soon in a panic, and out of hand. The Mahrattas continued their depredations; so much so that they laid their hands on the very elephant on which the Begum was riding, and were leading it away to their camp, when Musaheb Khan, eldest son of Omer Khan, unable to bear the degrading sight, fell on them and rescued the Begum and the elephant, killing many of them, but receiving wounds which proved fatal. He was buried on the field of battle.

Ali Verdi Khan, aware of their greed, scattered some bags of money and jewels in the passes, and while the Mahrattas were engaged in plundering these, he dexterously entered Burdwan.

The troops had been for three days on horseback, engaged in a running fight, and now rested. Such, however, were the privations they had to suffer, that they were glad to accept, for food, half-burnt grain, that was saved from the wreck of the grain magazines that the Mahrattas had set on fire. The Mahrattas during 1742 laid the whole country round waste, with fire and sword. Ali Verdi Khan, with gloomy prospects before him, resolved to push his way to Murshidabad. His troops were quite unable to cope with the hardships, and after many skirmishes they arrived at Cutwah, only to find that there also Mahrattas had preceded them, and had burnt the stores of grain They were glad, however, to pick up and eat the half-burnt remnants.

Haji Ahmad, however, sent a large amount of bread and grain, and thus saved them from starvation. Mir Sharif, brother of Mir Habib, with the assistance of a number of Mahrattas, was on the point of plundering the city of Murshidabad, but the timely arrival of Ali Verdi Khan prevented this disaster. Ali Verdi neither ate nor slept for days, but worked hard collecting the army, and devising means of freeing the country from the invaders. Having raised new levies, he threw a bridge of boats across the Bhagirathi, crossed the river with a large army ; and such was the ardour of the troops and the spirited conduct of the Nawab, that though six hundred men were lost by several boats sinking under the weight of passengers, the breach was soon repaired, and the whole army crossed, unperceived by the enemy, who were quite ignorant of Ali Verdi Khan's movements. The army, headed by chosen officers, now fell upon the Mahrattas, who were sleeping with a sense of perfect security. Mir Habib, Bhasker, and the other Mahratta chiefs, were so panic-stricken by this bold and unexpected measure, that they fled. The Nawab closely followed them, and killed large numbers of them. At Cutwah they tried to make a stand, but their troops fled on the Nawab's approach.

At Ramgurh, Bhasker recruited his scattered force, and suddenly attacked Orissa, where the Governor, Masum Khan, bravely met them, but having only a small number of troops with him, he was defeated and slain, together with his followers.

The Nawab having heard the news of this disaster, hastened back to Burdwan, and having paid his men the promised reward for the victory at Cutwah, started for Cuttack, defeated the Mahrattas and regained Orissa.

Bhasker Pundit, notwithstanding these repeated defeats, led his men to plunder Behar and Bhagalpur, and the Nawab immediately went to meet them. On hearing of the approach of the Nawab, they changed their course, and marched south towards Bengal. They were engaged in plundering Baluchar, near Murshidabad, but Ali Verdi Khan followed them there, and they fled with such haste that they left behind the booty already taken. The Nawab pursued them as far as Ramgurh.

Towards the end of 1742, the Subahdar of Oude came, under the orders of the Emperor, to assist Ali Verdi Khan in expelling the Mahrattas. Ali Verdi Khan now saw no need of his assistance, as he found himself fully equal to the task, without help from outside. He wrote to the Emperor, thanking him for the help sent, and requesting him to recall the army. The Emperor accordingly recalled the Subahdar. As a reward for the valorous deeds of Ali Verdi Khan against the Mahrattas, the Emperor sent him a robe of honour, a sword, a dagger, and a string of pearls.

Although peace was restored after the departure of Raghuji, yet Ali Verdi Khan could not rest in security, so long as these marauders were in Cuttack and Balasore. He therefore, in consultation with his nobles and officers, appointed "Sowlat Jang" as Nazim of Orissa, and Mir Jaffer as his deputy. Mir Jaffer was also paymaster and Foujdar of Midnapur and Hijli. "Sowlat Jang," on his own account, honoured his deputy and set him at the head of seven thousand horse and twelve thousand infantry, with orders to expel the Mahrattas. Mir Jaffer, leaving Mir Mahomed Ismail, the son of his brother, as deputy paymaster, and Sujan Singh as deputy Foujdar of Hijli, started for Orissa with his forces, and reached Midnapur. There he met the Mahrattas and Afghans, and drove them off with great slaughter.

Mir Habib, the Mahratta, sent his trustworthy agents to Mir Jaffer with proposals for peace, which were reported to Ali Verdi Khan. The Nawab, now in his eightieth year, thought that the termination of war was for the welfare of the people at large, and accordingly gave his consent. Mir Jaffer therefore sent Mir Hassan Ali and Mir Gous Ali to Mir Habib, who, after twelve years' warfare, now talked of peace. They settled the conditions of peace, and in 1751 (1164 A.H.) a treaty was drawn up, by which the Nawab agreed to pay as *Chouth** of the three provinces, Bengal, Behar, and Orissa, one crore and

* Fourth part of the revenue (*v.* p. 6).

twelve lakhs, in two instalments, to Raghuji, or his descendants. Of this sum twelve lakhs was due in cash, and the remaining one crore from the revenue of Orissa, which was wholly yielded to the Mahrattas up to a boundary fixed by the river Subarun Rekha. Orissa continued detached from Bengal for eighteen years, but it was again annexed to Bengal by the treaty of 1768 A.D., by which the reigning Nawab had to pay sixteen lakhs, for which the English stood security.

Ali Verdi Khan, though very intelligent and a most prudent administrator, showed great weakness in taking Suraj-u-Dowlah as his heir and successor. The nature and character of the boy were totally unknown to him, and he only became aware of his nature at a time when all remedy was out of his power.

Ali Verdi died of dropsy in 1756, in his eightieth year, after a reign of sixteen years over the three provinces of Bengal, Behar, and Orissa. Khush Bagh Cemetery is his last resting-place.

Ali Verdi Khan was very regular in his devotions and assiduously abstained from all things forbidden by the divine law. He always rose two hours before daybreak, and after ablution and prayers drank coffee with his select companions. Then for two hours he gave public audience and attended to the affairs of the people in general. At the expiration of that time he retired with Shahamut Jang, Sowlat Jang, and his favourite, Suraj-u-Dowlah, to his private apartments, where such as were invited came. Pieces of poetry were recited, or history or anecdotes read to him. He liked good food, so that if anybody knew any new *recipe*, he would have it cooked before him, and would himself give directions to cook particular dishes according to his taste. The officers of different departments, if necessary, also came for orders. He then sat down to eat with his friends, and many shared the bounties of his table. Each man at the table would surely receive what he liked. Thus he not only fed the poor; the rich also got a share of his bounty. After the second prayer, he would drink cold, or iced, water. This is the only water that he drank in the twenty-four hours. Then he received learned men, to whom he paid the utmost respect, and heard their discussions and listened to the books of Kalini and Kafi that were read to him. Then came the revenue officers with the Jaggat Seth and others, and gave him the news from all countries and provinces of his kingdom, and he issued necessary orders to them. After sunset, lights were brought; after the evening prayers, he received his wife and other female relatives; after the night prayers, the women retired and men were admitted, and as he took no supper, some dried fruits were served with sweetmeats and other light food. Then he retired to rest. In this way he passed his time, having stated hours for every employment.

He was unequalled in his benevolence towards his relations, friends, and people in general—particularly to those who had shown him the smallest kindness during his distress in Delhi in his early youth—sending for them, if alive, or, if not, for their children, and conferring favours on them beyond their expectations. The people at large, during his lifetime, lived a life of utmost ease and security; the lowest servants on his establishment possessed lakhs of rupees. He encouraged the deserving of every profession. He was intelligent in all affairs, affable in manners, and possessed many noble qualities.

V.

SURAJ-U-DOWLAH.

1756-1757.

SURAJ-U-DOWLAH was the eldest son of Zain-ul-Din, nephew and son-in-law of the late Nawab. His real name was Mirza Mahomed, but his grandfather, on his own accession to the Government had procured for him, from Delhi, the title of "Suraj-u-Dowlah," by which he is known in history.

He was early adopted by Ali Verdi Khan as his heir, and from a child was indulged in the gratification of every caprice. In 1753 Ali Verdi Khan placed him by his side on the *Musnud* as his successor, when the boy was only fifteen years old. This is the date given by Stewart (15) (1847, p. 308). It is stated, however, in Mr. Long's "Records" (13), August, 1752, that the Nawab Suraj-u-Dowlah, whom Ali Verdi Khan had appointed to be his successor, had arrived at Hughli. The President, accompanied by two other members of Council and the Commandant, went to greet him with a present. The various articles which composed the presents were valued at nearly Rs. 16,000. The President was received by the Nawab with the utmost politeness and distinction, far superior to that paid to the Dutch or French. "If these peoples' words are ever to be confided in," continues the dispatch to the Court of Directors, "we flatter ourselves that the expense we have been at on this occasion has procured you great favour, and will be the means of your business being conducted without any interruption from the Government for some time to come." From this time he was permitted to interfere in the affairs of Government, though his grandfather did not die till 1756. His uncle, Nuazish Mahomed, was then the Governor of Dacca and the eastern districts, and the most influential man in the State. His power and wealth excited the envy of Suraj-u-Dowlah, and his two deputies were murdered. Nuazish Mahomed himself died without leaving any children. His widow, Gheseeta Begum, inherited his palace on the bank of the Moti jhil, and the treasures which it contained. The first act of Suraj-u-Dowlah on finding himself freed from restraint by the death of Ali Verdi Khan, was to storm this palace and seize the property of his aunt. Her treasury is said to have contained no less than sixty-one lakhs of rupees in gold and silver, and the value of the jewels, plate, elephants, etc., amounted to as much more. The next act, within two months after his accession, was his rupture with the English on some slight pretext, and his march on Calcutta. After his defeat at Plassy the Nawab fled up the Ganges towards Patna; when opposite Rajmehal, he was betrayed by a fakir whom he had maltreated in his day of prosperity, and was sent back a prisoner to the house of Mir Jaffer in Murshidabad. Immediately on his arrival he was murdered by the orders of Miran, the son of Mir Jaffer.*

* See chapter on History for further particulars; and read "grandson" for "son," p. 8, line 21.

VI.

MIR MAHOMED JAFFER.

SUJAH-UL-MULK, HISAM-U-DOWLAH, NAWAB MIR MAHOMED JAFFER, KHAN BAHADUR, MAHABAT JANG.

PART I.—1757-1760.

On the 29th June, 1757, Mir Jaffer ascended the Nizamat *Musnud*, and began to govern the three provinces with Raja Dulhab Chand as Diwan. He devoted himself to the management of State affairs, and tried to set right the disorder caused by Suraj-u-Dowlah's bad government. He won the hearts of the people by his impartial administration. He showered presents and rewards on the chief English officers, and followed out the agreement between himself and the East India Company, which was signed twenty-five days previous to the battle of Plassy, and of which the following is a copy :—

TRANSLATION OF THE PUBLIC TREATY MADE WITH ADMIRAL WATSON, COLONEL CLIVE AND THE OTHER COUNCILLORS, MR. DRAKE AND MR. WATTS, AS WRITTEN IN PERSIAN, ETC., ETC., AND SIGNED BY MIR JAFFER ALI KHAN WITH HIS OWN HAND, JUNE, 1757.

I swear by God, and the Prophet of God, to abide by the terms of this Treaty whilst I have life.

Article 1.—Whatever articles were agreed to in the time of peace with the Nawab Suraj-u-Dowlah, I agree to comply with.

Article 2.—The enemies of the English are my enemies, whether they be Indians or Europeans.

Article 3.—All the effects and factories belonging to the French in the province of Bengal, the paradise of nations, and Behar and Orissa, shall remain in the possession of the English, nor will I ever allow them any more to settle in the three provinces.

Article 4.—In consideration of the losses which the English Company has sustained by the capture and plunder of Calcutta by the late Nawab, and the charges occasioned by the maintenance of the forces, I will give them one crore of rupees.

Article 5.—For the effects plundered from the English inhabitants at Calcutta, I agree to give fifty lakhs of rupees.

Article 6.—For the effects plundered from the Gentoos, Moors, and other inhabitants of Calcutta, twenty lakhs of rupees shall be given.

Article 7.—For the effects plundered from the Armenian inhabitants of Calcutta, I will give the sum of seven lakhs of rupees. The distribution of the sums allotted to the English, Gentoos, Moors, and other inhabitants of Calcutta, shall be left to Admiral Watson, Colonel Clive, Roger Drake, William Watts, James Kilpatrick, and Richard Becher, Esquires, to be disposed of by them to whom they think proper.

Article 8.—Within the ditch which surrounds the borders of Calcutta, are tracts of land belonging to several zemindars; besides these I will grant to the English Company six hundred yards without the ditch.

Article 9.—All the land lying south of Calcutta, as far as Culpee, shall be under the zemindari of the English Company, and all the officers of these parts shall be under their jurisdiction. The Revenues to be paid by the Company in the same manner as other zemindars.

Article 10.—Whenever I demand the assistance of the English, I will be at the charge of the maintenance of their troops.

Article 11.—I will not erect any new fortifications near the river Ganges below Hughli.

Article 12.—As soon as I am established in the three provinces, the aforesaid sums shall be faithfully paid.

Dated the 15th of the month of *Ramzan*, in the first year of the present reign.

This treaty, as written and signed by the English, contained the sense of the above articles, though in different words and concluded with an additional clause to the following effect :—

Article 13.—On condition, Mir Jaffer Khan Bahadur solemnly ratifies and swears to fulfil the above Articles, we, the underwritten, do, for and on behalf of the Honourable East India Company, declare on the Holy Evangelists, and before God, that we will assist Mir Jaffer Khan Bahadur with our whole utmost force to obtain the Subahships of the provinces of Bengal, Behar, and Orissa, and further that we will assist him to the utmost against all his enemies whatever, whensoever he calls upon us for that purpose, provided that when he becomes the Nawab, he fulfils the above Articles.

This Treaty was agreed to by :—

ADMIRAL WATSON.	MR. DRAKE.	MAJOR KILPATRICK.
COLONEL CLIVE.	MR. WATTS.	MR. BECHER.

Nawab Jaffer Khan conferred on his son, Miran, the title of "Nasir-ul-Mulk, Ala-u-Dowlah, Nawab Mir Mahomed Sadik Ali Khan," and also the Revenue Stewardship of the three provinces. All the chiefs, subjects, and administrative officers submitted to the Nawab except Hazir Ali Khan, Darogah-Diwan, and Achal Sing, Diwan of Sowkat Jang, who raised an army of their own in Purnea and headed a rebellion. Nawab Jaffer Khan, leaving his son Miran at Murshidabad, as his representative, started with a large army of his own, and that of the English under Colonel Clive. He sent Syud Khadan Ali Khan from Rajmehal to Purnea, and he himself went towards Behar. Khadan Ali Khan, after hard fighting, captured Achal Sing and drove Hazir Ali Khan to the mountains. He entered Purnea with triumph, and devoted himself to the management of the affairs entrusted to him. Mir Jaffer halted at Patna. Having settled the affairs of the District with the help of Raja Ram Narain Naib Bahadur, and other officers, he returned to his capital at Murshidabad, after a three months' tour in Behar. The usual presents to the Court of Delhi had been discontinued. In 1758 Prince Ali Gowhar, the Shahzada, without the permission of his father, Alumgir II., being advised by Mahomed Kuli Khan, Subahdar of Allahabad, came to Behar with the intention of taking possession of that province. Raja Ram Narain having informed the Nawab of the matter, attacked the Shahzada. After much fighting, Ram Narain came off victorious. Nawab Miran and Colonel Clive, who went from Murshidabad to help Raja Ram Narain, hearing of the defeat of the enemy before their arrival, were glad to halt at Azimabad. The Prince and his followers being informed of the large army with Miran, did not venture to face him, and fled to Allahabad. Nawab Miran and Colonel Clive having nothing further to do, returned to Murshidabad.

Mir Jaffer, after this victory, gave to Lord Clive a *Jaghir* (land) worth three lakhs, and also the twenty-four Pergunnahs, which had been hitherto held by the East India Company as tenants.

On the night of Thursday, July 2nd, 1760, it began to rain heavily, with thunder and lightning. The lightning struck Miran, and killed him. Raja Raj Ballab took over the command of the army of the deceased Prince, and, by the advice of Colonel Clive, kept the news of Miran's death from the public, and sent his body to Rajmehal for interment. Colonel Clive and Raja Raj Ballab then left for Patna. Nawab Miran was brave and had great administrative power, but his character was spoiled by vice and cruelty. Villain that Suraj-u-Dowlah undoubtedly was, the way in which Miran had him killed was most unchivalrous.

Nawab Mir Jaffer Khan was overwhelmed with grief at the death of his son Miran. He appointed Mir Kasim in place of Miran, sending a letter to Calcutta, of which the following is a translation :—

"Before this the command of the army, the administration of the State affairs, and the other financial business were entrusted to my deceased son, Nawab Miran. Now, except Mir Kasim, I could not find anyone among my relatives fit to manage these momentous affairs. He (Kasim Ali Khan) has hitherto served me faithfully, and has been faithful to my cause. I have therefore appointed him in place of the deceased Nawab Miran. There is no doubt that you too will approve of the appointment, as I know you are well acquainted with the aforesaid relative of mine. I hope you will order Maharaja Ram Narain to submit to his every order. I further hope you will accord the same indulgence and help to Mir Kasim, as you have done in the case of Miran, to keep the Nizamat affairs on a sound basis. By doing so, the bonds of friendship between you and me will be daily strengthened, and will be a constant source of pleasure to me."

In 1758 Clive discovered that Mir Jaffer, through an agent, Khojah Wajid, had made a treaty with the Dutch at Chinsurah. Dutch ships of war were seen in the Hughli. Peace existed between the Dutch and English, but Clive heard that Dutch troops had been sent for from Batavia. Mir Jaffer was asked to direct the withdrawal of the Dutch. The Nawab went to Hughli (Chinsurah), and from there sent word to Clive that at the proper season the Dutch ships would depart. Clive was suspicious, and when the Dutch ships attacked Fort Tanah, south of Calcutta, he was ready for them and repulsed them. They next attacked Captain Forde in a fort below Chinsurah. With an order from Clive to back him up, Forde engaged the Dutch and defeated them. Clive left India in 1760, and shortly after his departure Mir Kasim, as Mir Jaffer's Diwan, visited Calcutta. The governor, Mr. Vansittart, proposed that as the Nawab was old and not able to cope with the difficulties of administration, Mir Kasim should act for him as Deputy-Nazim. Mir Kasim agreed, and Hastings and Vansittart, with a strong escort, accompanied him back to Murshidabad. The Nawab did not receive their proposal favourably, he was afraid of his son-in-law. The position was a difficult one, for Mir Kasim's life would not have been safe in the city, under the Nawab's displeasure. He was, in fact, preparing to escape to Delhi. Mr. Vansittart, however, convinced that the change was necessary, directed the Company's troops to seize the palace. The Nawab then gave way, but was disinclined to remain in Murshidabad, Nawab only in name. Mir Jaffer and his wife, Muni Begum, with servants, treasure, etc., went to Calcutta. Thus Mir Jaffer gave up the reins of Government, and shortly after was deposed by the Council. The Deputy became Nawab Nazim *de facto* in March, 1760. Mir Jaffer bought land in Maidapathi (Calcutta) and built a house. His senior wife, Nawab Shah Khanum, remained with her daughter in Murshidabad.

VII.

KASIM ALI.

Nasir-ul-Mulk Imtiaz-u-Dowlah Nawab Mahomed Kasim Khan Bahadur Nasirat Jang.

1760—1763.

Mir Kasim Ali Khan, son-in-law of Mir Jaffer, raised to power after Miran's death, began to plan mischief. The Murshidabad army, which, after the death of Nawab Miran, was commanded by Raja Raj Bullab, waited in Behar till the rainy season was over, and Mir Jaffer, at Murshidabad, being grieved by his son's death, kept himself shut up. Mir Kasim, availing himself of this opportunity, made an arrangement with the Governor of Calcutta, Mr. Vansittart, and other English and Nizamat officers, and, as we have learned, in 1760, was made absolute ruler of the country, under the title of "Nasir-ul-Mulk Imtiaz-u-Dowlah Mir Mohamed Kasim Khan Bahadur."

Mr. Vansittart and Warren Hastings came to Murshidabad to place him on the *musnud*, and Mir Kasim, in accordance with the agreement which was signed on Safar 18th, 1760, made over to the Company the revenues of Burdwan, Midnapur, and Chittagong for the maintenance of the English army, and gave them a *Sanad*, granting them permission to trade in lime, etc.

Nawab Mir Kasim fixed an allowance for the expenses of his father-in-law, and devoted himself to the management of the Nizamat affairs. Ali Ibrahim Khan was appointed Diwan, and Sustab Ram Diwan of the household affairs. Hafiz Israr Khan was made Mir Munshi and Private Secretary, and had also the title of "Khan" conferred on him. An Armenian named Gregory, formerly a cloth merchant, became Darogah of the Topekhana (artillery park), with the title of "Khan Bahadur," and was also entrusted with the duty of teaching the soldiers English war tactics. After placing the revenue affairs on a sound basis, Mir Kasim paid to the Company the amount due in accordance with his agreement.

The Bengal army which was in Behar at the time of the invasion by the Emperor, had returned after the rainy season. After being reviewed by Mir Kasim, it was sent to Kaipur, under Major Carnac. The Emperor was still in the field, but was driven off by Major Carnac. Monsieur Laws,* a Frenchman of the Emperor's army, was captured by the Nizamat army. The Emperor then made peace with the Nazim. He consequently begged an interview with the Nazim. The Nizamat officers sent Rao Shitab Rai to the Emperor for the peace conference. The next day was fixed by him for the interview of the Emperor with Ram Narain and other Nizamat officers. On the day fixed for the Emperor's arrival Major Carnac and Rao Shitab Rai went to receive him, and brought him to the garden of Gainpur, and paid due respect to him. Raja Ram Narain, Raja Raj Ballab, Major Carnac, and other native and English officers entertained the Emperor. Raja Ram Narain assured the Emperor that the Nazim would soon come to see him, and that peace would soon be established. The Emperor returned to his camp highly pleased. The next day Raja Ram Narain, with other officers, again waited upon the Emperor, and brought him to Patna. In the meantime, Mir Kasim had come to Patna. The interview between the Emperor and the Nazim was so arranged that the Emperor went to the English Residence alone, *i.e.*, without his army. The English and native officers received the Emperor, and conducted him to the throne, which was set up specially for him. Mir Kasim arrived an hour later, and saluted him, presenting one thousand and one asarfis (gold mohur) as "Nazar." The Emperor in return bestowed on Kasim Ali a pearl necklace, a head-dress, and an *aigrette*. After the ceremony they sat in two different rooms. The peace conference decided that Mir Kasim should pay twenty-four lakhs of rupees yearly to the Emperor, and that the Emperor should confer on the Nazim the patent of the Governorship of the three Provinces. Orissa was still in the hands of the Mahrattas and their Afghan allies, under the agreement of 1768 (?). After staying some days, the Emperor left for Delhi.

Mir Kasim peacefully settled the affairs of Behar. Suspecting Raja Ram Narain's fidelity, he deprived him of his office on the pretext of ill-government, imprisoned him, and confiscated his property, appointing Raja Raj Ballab in his place as Governor of Patna (Behar). He imprisoned Raja Murali Dhar, Mahomed Afag, Katwal Mustafa Ali Khan, brother of Eruj Khan, and others supposed to be faithful to the cause of Mir Jaffer. Nasir Ali was entrusted with the charge of the fort of Rhotas, and Shah Ali was appointed as his (Nasir Ali's) Peshkar. The Nawab Nazim made a tour through Tikari, and other parts of Behar, to see the state of the country and its subjects. By agreement, the East India Company was freed from the numerous "duties" on articles of commerce

* Called General Gurghin Khan. Fought against Clive at Plassy. He was murdered by Mir Kasim's agents.

Mir Kasim received many complaints from his revenue officers that this favour was very often abused by both civil and military officers of the Company, trading on their own account. The Nawab's influence, and revenues, were injured by these unfair practices. He complained to the Company's Council at Calcutta. As no notice was taken, Mir Kasim sent word that unless his orders were backed up by the Council he must resign. Vansittart and Hastings both tried to stop the abuses complained of, but, as certain members of the Council were by this very means amassing wealth, these two found no supporters. Indeed, oppression went so far that many merchants were ruined by the prices fixed by the Company's servants.

In 1762 Mir Kasim went to Monghyr, made it the temporary capital of Bengal, and began to erect stately buildings.* Previous to his departure, he had imprisoned some of the offenders, and Mr. Amyatt and Mr. Hay went to his Court to ask him to release these English agents and the English merchants, and, as regards the "duties," to do as was mentioned in the agreement, but nothing, except dispute and quarrel, came of the interview. The Nawab kept Mr. Hay in custody till the release of the Nizamat officers, viz., Mirza Mahomed Ali and others, who were in prison at Calcutta. These men, acting under orders, had tried to stop the evasion of "duty" by private traders at Dacca and Patna. Mr. Amyatt, at the time of his departure from the Court of Mir Kasim, wrote to Mr. Ellis at Patna that the bond of friendship between them and the Nizam had given way, and their mission had come to nothing. Mr. Vansittart visited Monghyr to try to prevent a rupture. The Nawab wanted customs "duty" paid at 9 per cent., but Vansittart and Hastings were the only members of Council who agreed. The rest wanted the rate fixed at 2½ per cent. Mir Kasim then abolished all "duties," and to this the English objected, as they thereby ceased to have any advantage over the native merchants.

Mr. Ellis and Major Carnac being informed of the matter, at the head of the English army assigned to Patna, on Zil Haj 12th, 1176 A.H., declared war, and put Mir Mehdi Khan, Naib of Behar, to flight. Mir Kasim being informed of the occurrence, sent an army to help the Naib. Till after the massacre, the Nizamat armies were victorious. The English army advanced from Patna towards Bankipur, and from thence towards Chapra. The Foujdar of Sarkar Saran, falling upon the English army, made Mr. Ellis and some of his followers captive. Mir Kasim, being informed of the matter, issued firmans to all parts of his dominion for the wholesale massacre of the English wherever they could be found. Mr. Amyatt, who came to Murshidabad from Monghyr, by way of Calcutta, was, with all his followers, put to death by Shah Sowar Beg and other Nizamat officers; and at Kasimbazar the English Residence was looted. The Governor of Calcutta, together with the members of his Council, then went to Mir Jaffer Khan and asked his help in their task of deposing Mir Kasim, and promised to re-place him on the *musnud* of the Subahdari. After much discussion, they came to the conclusion that two agreements were to be signed afresh on July 10th, 1763. In the first, the English promised to try their best to depose Mir Kasim and to seat Mir Jaffer on the *musnud*. Mir Jaffer, in addition to his attestation to the Plassy agreement, was to make over the Chaklas of Burdwan, Midnapur, and Chittagong to the Company for the maintenance of the English army, as Mir Kasim had done, and was to abolish all the "duties" *only* on English merchandise, except that on salt. For others, "duty" was not to be abolished. He also promised not to keep more than twelve thousand cavalry and an equal number of infantry under him in all his dominions without the approval of the Company, and that the English money should be circulated with the Murshidabad coin, and that he should pay thirty lakhs of rupees as the cost of the war. The conditions are shown in the following Treaty :—

* Now forming part of the district jail of Monghyr.

ARTICLES OF A TREATY AND AGREEMENT BETWEEN THE GOVERNOR AND COUNCIL OF FORT WILLIAM, ON THE PART OF THE ENGLISH EAST INDIA COMPANY, AND THE NAWAB SUJAH-UL-MULK, HISAM-U-DOWLAH, MIR MAHOMED JAFFER KHAN BAHADUR, MAHABAT JANG, 1763.

On the part of the Company.

We engage to reinstate the Nawab, Mir Mahomed Jaffer Khan Bahadur in the Subahdari of the provinces of Bengal, Behar, and Orissa by the deposal of Mir Mahomed Kasim Ali Khan; and the effects, treasure, and jewels, etc., belonging to Mir Mahomed Kasim Ali Khan, which shall fall into our hands, shall be delivered up to the Nawab aforenamed.

On the part of the Nawab.

Article 1.—The treaty which I formerly concluded with the Company upon my accession to the Nizamat, engaging to reward the honour and reputation of the Company, their Governor and Council as my own, granting *Perwannahs* for the currency of the Company's business, the same Treaty I now confirm and ratify.

Article 2.—I do grant and confirm to the Company, for defraying the expenses of their troops, the Chaklas of Burdwan, Midnapur, and Chittagong, which were before ceded for the same purpose.

Article 3.—I do ratify and confirm to the English the privilege granted them by their Firman and several Husbulhukums, of carrying on their trade by means of their own *dustuck*, free from all "duties," taxes, or impositions, in all parts of the country, excepting as to the article of salt, on which a "duty" of 2½ per cent. is to be levied on the "rawana" or Hughli market price.

Article 4.—I give to the Company half the saltpetre which is produced in the country of Purnea, which their Gomastahs shall send to Calcutta. The other half shall be collected by my Foujdar, for the use of my offices; and I will suffer no other person to make purchases of this article in that country.

Article 5.—In the Chakla of Sylhet, for the space of five years, commencing with the Bengali year 1170, my Foujdar and the Company's Gomastah shall jointly prepare *chunam* (lime), of which each shall defray half the expense, and half the *chunam* so made shall be given to the Company, and the other half shall be for my use.

Article 6.—I will maintain twelve thousand horse and twelve thousand foot in the three Provinces. If there should be occasion for any more, the number shall be increased by consent of the Governor and Council, proportionately to the emergency; besides these, the force of the English Company shall always attend me when they are wanted.

Article 7.—Wherever I shall fix my Court, either at Murshidabad or elsewhere, I will advise the Governor and Council; and what number of English forces, I may have occasion for in the management of my affairs, I will demand, and they shall be allowed me, and an English gentleman shall reside with me to transact all affairs between me and the Company, and a person shall also reside, on my part, at Calcutta to negotiate with the Governor and Council.

Article 8.—The late *Perwannahs* issued by Kasim Ali Khan, granting to all merchants the exemption from all "duties," for the space of two years, shall be reversed and called in.

Article 9.—I will cause the rupees coined in Calcutta to pass in every respect as equal to the *siccas* of Murshidabad, without any deduction of *batta*, and whosoever shall demand *batta* shall be punished.

Article 10.—I will give thirty lakhs of rupees to defray all the expenses and loss occurring to the Company from the war and stoppage of their investments; and I will reimburse to all private persons the amount of such losses, proved before the Governor and Council, as they may have sustained in their trade in the country. If I should not be able to discharge this in ready money, I will give assignments of land for the amount.

Article 11.—I will confirm and renew the Treaty which I formerly made with the Dutch.

Article 12.—If the French come into the country, I will not allow them to erect any fortifications, maintain forces, hold lands, zemindaries, etc., but they shall pay tribute, and carry on their trade as in former times.

Article 13.—Some regulations shall be hereafter settled between us for deciding all disputes which may arise between the English Agents and Gomastahs, in the different parts of the country, and my officers.

In testimony whereof, we, the said Governor and Council, have set our hands and affixed the seal of the Company to one part hereof and the Nawab aforesaid hath set his hand and seal to another part hereof which were mutually done and interchanged at Fort William, the 10th day of July, 1763.

(*Signed*) HENRY VANSITTART. WARREN HASTINGS.
JOHN CARNAC. RANDOLPH MARRIOT.
WILLIAM VILLIERS. HUGH WATTS

VIII.

MIR MAHOMED JAFFER (Re-instated).

Part II.—1763-1765.

Mir Jaffer Khan, being re-instated as Nawab, thus gave up to the English the revenues of Burdwan, Midnapur, Chittagong, and paid five lakhs of rupees per month, as the pay of the English soldiers up to the end of war with Sujah-u-Dowlah, Subahdar of Oude. Three lakhs of this sum from the revenues of Bengal were allotted from the Murshidabad treasury, and two lakhs from the Behar revenue from the Patna treasury.

The contest with Mir Kasim, his defeat, and flight, have been described (p. 16). Mir Jaffer, worn out with disease,* and too old for much active work, was escorted by English troops to Murshidabad. Eruj Khan, the father-in-law of Suraj-u-Dowlah, and an old friend of Mir Jaffer, went out with the other nobles of the city to receive Mir Jaffer. After the meeting, Eruj Khan returned to Murshidabad as directed, and proclaimed Mir Jaffer Nawab Nazim of the three provinces. Mir Jaffer entered Murshidabad on Sunday, July 24th, 1763. After remaining six days at Murshidabad, and taking a loan of twenty-one lakhs of rupees from the "Jaggat Seth" for the expenses of the war, and making Eruj Khan his representative, he set out with the Nizamat and English army to punish and quell Mir Kasim. Mir Jaffer was at the head of nearly nineteen thousand soldiers, of which twelve thousand were from the English army. The Governor of Calcutta wrote a letter of congratulation to the re-instated Nawab on his success in the contest with Mir Kasim: "Bengal now has come into your hands, and the inhabitants, being freed from the oppression of Mir Kasim, have come under your protection. If God please, the country will again flourish."

After Mir Kasim had been driven as far as Buxar, Mir Jaffer, with Major Carnac, came to Calcutta

* Leprosy ?—Marsham (31).

on December 3rd, 1764, to receive instructions regarding their future movements. The English received the old Nawab with great respect, and civil and military heads of departments presented "nazar" (presents of homage, given and returned) of ninety-one *asrafis* (gold mohurs), and other presents, to him.

The Emperor now sought an alliance with the English and the Nazim. He asked Mir Jaffer, through the Governor of Calcutta, to pay the tribute of twenty-four lakhs of rupees promised by Mir Kasim when he concluded a treaty with the Emperor. At the instance of Mir Mahomed Jaffer Khan, the Governor of Calcutta replied that at that time, as the wealth of the country had been drained by Mir Kasim, it was impossible for Mahomed Jaffer to pay the tribute or until after the establishment of peace and tranquillity in the country. Mir Jaffer was not disposed to disobey the Emperor's wish, but, owing to the enormous expenses of the war, he had no funds for other purposes. Mir Jaffer, on completing his business at Calcutta, returned to Murshidabad. He called upon Mir Mahomed Reza Khan, Naib of Dacca, to settle his accounts in Murshidabad, and on his arrival cast him into prison, on the advice of Nunda Kumar.

Mir Jaffer died at the age of seventy-four, on January 17th, 1765. He was, in the main, brave, thoughtful, provident, and wise. He was a good rider, and respected as a soldier, for Broome relates that the Commander-in-Chief of the English forces issued an order requesting his officers to wear a crape band as mourning, as a mark of respect to the memory of Mir Jaffer. Mir Jaffer Khan was the second son of Syud Ahmad Najafi. He married Shah Khanum, step-sister of Ali Verdi Khan, in 1726 (?) In 1740 Mir Jaffer became Commander-in-Chief of Bengal, with the title of "Khan Bahadur." In 1744, for his valour and bravery in the Mahratta war, he was raised to the rank of the commander of four thousand horse. In 1746, Mir Jaffer, in addition to his Commander-in-Chiefship, became Naib Subahdar (Deputy Governor) of Orissa and collector of revenue and magistrate of Midnapur and Hijli. In 1756, Mir Jaffer, to protect them from Suraj-u-Dowlah, sheltered some European ladies in his own quarters, and sent them, on the first opportunity, with his trustworthy companion, Mirza Amir Beg, to Governor Drake, in his own special boat, at night. This was the original cause of the friendship between the English and Mir Jaffer.

IX.

NAJIM-U-DOWLAH.

SUJAH-UL-MULK NAJIM-U-DOWLAH NAWAB NAJIM-U-DIN ALI KHAN BAHADUR MAHABAT JANG.

1765-1766.

THE son of Mir Jaffer and Muni Begum, Nawab Najim-u-Dowlah, became Nawab at the age of fifteen. Mr. Middleton, the English Resident at Murshidabad, and Mr. Johnstone, a member of the Governor's Council, represented the East India Company at the succession ceremony. They paid their respects in the customary manner, and received *khilats* and rewards. Also at this Durbar Mahomed Reza Khan, on the recommendation of the English, received the appointment of Naib-i-Nizamat as Deputy Governor, and the title "Moin-u-Dowlah Mozuffer Jang."

Before the installation of Najim-u-Dowlah a written agreement was made between the Nawab and the East India Company.

Mr. Johnstone and Mr. Leycester, members of the Council, being ordered by the Governor, came to Murshidabad, bringing with them a copy of the draft of the agreement, which ran as follows :—

COPY OF A LETTER FROM FRANCIS SYKES, ESQUIRE, RESIDENT AT THE DURBAR, TO THE SECRET COMMITTEE AT CALCUTTA, DATED THE 24TH JULY, 1765.

To William Brightwell Sumner, Esquire, etc., Gentlemen of the Select Committee.

"GENTLEMEN,—By the great, sudden fall of rain, and the rapidity of the river, I have been prevented from arriving here till yesterday : I shall directly proceed on my business with all possible despatch, and you may depend upon it, that nothing shall be wanting on my part to finish the affairs which I am commissioned on, as well as any others which may fall to my management during my stay here, to the entire satisfaction of the Committee.

"I have had the pleasure to receive several letters from Lord Clive since I left Calcutta, wherein his Lordship represents to me the inconveniences and difficulties the present Ministers find in carrying on the affairs of the Government; owing to the Nawab's ignorance, and his being totally unacquainted with any kind of business whatever; and to obviate and effectually remove an evil of so dangerous a tendency his Lordship recommends to me to endeavour to get the Nawab to throw the management of affairs entirely into the hands of the Ministers now in power; to make over all the revenues arising from the Subahship, in order to enable us to pay the expenses of the army, discharge the demands for restitution, army, etc., and for an annual stipend to the King, with other contingent expenses, in consideration of our paying him a sum of about fifty lakhs per annum, for his horses, sepoys, Begum, brother's zenana, household charges, and every other expense which may attend himself, provided this affair be sanctified by a *Sanad* from the King. This undoubtedly will be a grand point: and to obtain it I shall certainly exercise my endeavours, as I esteem it to be equally for the Nawab's ease and our own interest; for it is certain the share of influence we enjoy in these provinces, however great in appearances, does not carry with it those real advantages and weighty effects which are necessary, not to leave that power in danger of being disputed, and failing us at a time when the Company is in most want of it; besides, it will be attended with many further good consequences, particularly that of effectually putting a stop to that dissipation of revenues which hath reduced the Nawab, the Company, and the country so frequently to a distressed condition.

"I am getting an account of the Nawab's immediate expenses, in order to be able the better to judge what stipend will be most suitable to his rank and dignity, and our honour and credit.

"Mr. Sumner having informed me that there was a deficiency in the money paid by the Nawab into our treasury, of about Rs. 40,562-2, I therefore acquaint you that an order was sent the day before yesterday for the payment of it, which I hope by this time is come safe to hand.

"I am, with greatest respect,
"GENTLEMEN,
"Your most obedient and humble Servant,
(*Signed*) "FRANCIS SYKES.

"MORADBAGH,
"*The 24th July*, 1765."

COPY OF THE NEW AGREEMENT, OR TREATY, JOINTLY ENTERED INTO BETWEEN THE NAWAB NAJIM-U-DOWLAH, THE NAWAB SUJAH-U-DOWLAH, THE EMPEROR SHAH ALUM AND LORD CLIVE AND THE SECRET COMMITTEE OF CALCUTTA, UPON THE LATTER REVOKING ALL FORMER TREATIES, AND NEW MODELLING THE AFFAIRS OF THE COMPANY, BY ASSUMING THE DIWANNI, DATED THE 16TH AUGUST, 1765. (SEALED AND APPROVED BY THE EMPEROR.)

Whereas the Right Honourable Robert Lord Clive, Baron Clive of Plassy, Knight Companion of the Most Honourable Order of the Bath, Major-General and Commander of the Forces, President of the Council, and Governor of Fort William, and of all the settlements belonging to the United Company of Merchants of England trading to the East Indies, in the Provinces of Bengal, Behar, and Orissa; and John Carnac, Esquire, Brigadier-General, Colonel in the service of the said Company, and Commanding Officer of their forces upon the Bengal Establishment, are invested with full and ample powers, on behalf of His Excellency the Nawab Najim-u-Dowlah, Subahdar of Bengal, Behar, and Orissa, and likewise on behalf of the United Company of Merchants of England trading to the East Indies, to negotiate, settle, and finally to conclude a firm and lasting peace with his Highness the Nawab Sujah-u-Dowlah, Vizier of the Empire. Be it known to all those to whom it may or shall in any manner belong, that the above-named plenipotentiaries have agreed upon the following articles with His Highness :—

First.—A perpetual and universal peace, sincere friendship, and firm union shall be established between his Highness Sujah-u-Dowlah and his heirs, on the one part, and his Excellency Najim-u-Dowlah and the English East India Company, on the other, so that the said contracting powers shall give the greatest attention to maintain between themselves, their dominions, and their subjects, this reciprocal friendship without permitting, on either side, any kind of hostilities to be committed from henceforth for any cause, or under any pretence whatsoever; and everything shall be carefully avoided, which might hereafter prejudice the union now happily established.

Second.—In case the dominions of his Highness Sujah-u-Dowlah shall at any time hereafter be attacked, his Excellency Najim-u-Dowlah and the English Company shall assist him with a part or the whole of their forces, according to the exigency of his affairs, and so far as may be consistent with their own security; and if the dominions of his Excellency Najim-u-Dowlah or the English Company shall be attacked, his Highness shall in like manner assist them with a part, or the whole, of his forces. In the case of the English Company's forces being employed in his Highness's service, the extraordinary expense of the same is to be defrayed by him.

Third.—His Highness solemnly engages never to entertain or receive Kasim Ali Khan, the late Subahdar of Bengal, etc., "Sumru," the assassin of the English, nor any of the European deserters within his dominion, nor to give the least countenance, support, or protection to them; he likewise solemnly engages to deliver up to the English whatever Europeans may in future desert from them into his country.

Fourth.—The King, Shah Alum, shall remain in full possession of Cora, and such part of the province of Allahabad as he now possesses, which are ceded to his Majesty as a royal demesne for the support of his dignity and expenses.

Fifth.—His Highness Sujah-u-Dowlah engages, in the most solemn manner, to continue Bulwant Singh in the zemindari of Benares, Ghazipur, and all those districts he possessed at the time he came over to the late Nawab Jaffer Ali Khan and the English, on condition of his paying the same revenue as heretofore.

Sixth.—In consideration of the great expenses incurred by the English Company in carrying on the late war, his Highness agrees to pay them (fifty) 50 lakhs of rupees, in the following manner, *viz.:* (twelve) 12 lakhs of money, and a deposit of jewels, to the amount of eight lakhs upon the signing of this treaty, (five) 5 lakhs one month after, and the remaining (twenty-five) 25 lakhs by monthly payments, so that the whole may be discharged in (thirteen) 13 months from the date hereof.

Seventh.—It being firmly resolved to restore to his Highness the country of Benares and the other districts now rented by Bulwant Singh, notwithstanding the grant of the same from the King to the English Company; it is, therefore, agreed that they shall be ceded to his Highness in manner following, *viz.:* They shall remain in the hands of the English Company, with their revenues, till the expiration of the agreement between the Raja Bulwant Singh and the Company, being on the 27th November next; after which his Highness shall enter into possession, the fort of Chunar excepted, which is not to be evacuated until the sixth article of this treaty be fully complied with.

Eighth.—His Highness shall allow the English Company to carry on a trade "duty" free, throughout the whole of his dominions.

Ninth.—All the relations and subjects of his Highness who in any manner assisted the English during the course of the late war, shall be forgiven, and in no ways molested for the same.

Tenth.—As soon as this treaty is executed, the English forces shall be withdrawn from the dominions of his Highness, excepting such as may be necessary for the garrison of Chunar, or for the defence and protection of the King in the city of Allahabad, if his Majesty should require a force for that purpose.

Eleventh.—His Highness the Nawab Sujah-u-Dowlah, his Excellency the Nawab Najim-u-Dowlah, and the English Company, promise to observe sincerely and strictly all the articles contained and settled in the present treaty; and they will not suffer the same to be infringed directly or indirectly by their respective subjects, and the said contracting powers generally and reciprocally guarantee to each other all the stipulations of the present treaty.

CLIVE (L. S.)
JOHN CARNAC (L. S.)
SUJAH-U-DOWLAH'S (L. S.) seal and ratification.
MIRZA KASIM KHAN.
RAJA SHITAB RAI.
MIR MASHA ALLAH.

Signed, sealed and solemnly sworn to according to their respective faiths by the contracting parties at Allahabad, this 16th day of August, in the year of our Lord 1765, in the presence of us.

EDMUND MASKEYLYNE.
ARCHIBALD SWINTON.
GEORGE VANSITTART.

A true copy,
ALEXANDER CAMPBELL, *S.S.C.*

FORT WILLIAM,
September 30th, 1765.

Mr. Saxon told the Nazim that, as the Company had taken upon themselves the protection of the country, it was useless to maintain so large an army at a cost of so large a sum, eighteen lakhs a year; and, therefore, he ought to disband his own army. Calcutta coin was to circulate in the same manner as the Murshidabad coin.

Before the arrival of Mr. Johnstone and Mr. Leycester, Raja Naba Krishna, the Nizamat Agent, deputed to Calcutta, informed the Nawab that there had been a discussion in the Council regarding the appointment of the Naib, and Diwan of the Nizamat, and that Mahomed Reza Khan was selected for the post. On receiving this information, the Nawab raised objection to the appointment of Reza Khan; but previous to this the members of the Council had summoned Reza Khan from Dacca. The Nawab favoured Nunda Kumar. At this time Mr. Vansittart was still Governor of Calcutta, but it was reported that Lord Clive, vested with more power than before, had sailed from England, being appointed Governor of Calcutta. Messrs. Johnstone and Leycester from Calcutta, and Mahomed Reza Khan from Dacca, reached Murshidabad in Ramzan, 1178 A.H., and these gentlemen, together with Mr. Middleton, who was also deputed by the Council, presented themselves before the Nazim and appointed a Council meeting for the settlement of the terms of agreement. Maharaja Nunda Kumar and Munshi Sudder-u-Din were present in the court on behalf of the Nazim. After much discussion, owing to the Ramzan,* the meeting was adjourned till next day. At the next meeting Munshi Sudder-u-Din requested that the new agreement might be written in the same manner as the last one, and also said that the appointment of Reza Khan had been disapproved by the Nazim for several reasons: firstly, there were arrears of twenty-two lakhs of rupees, due by him to the Government; and, secondly, because, for suspected embezzlement of this money, he had been cast into prison, and on that account he bore ill-feeling towards the Nazim; thirdly, his residence in the city would upset the affairs of Dacca, which had been in his charge; fourthly, his abilities were not such as to make him competent to fill such a responsible post, because his family, excepting in medical science, had never been in any way concerned with State affairs, and because he himself had not done well in his appointment as Foujdar of Cutwah and Islamabad during the time of Mir Jaffer. Mr. Johnstone asked who had sent the Munshi to the meeting. Munshi Sudder-u-Din replied that the servants of the Nazim could not but be faithful to the Nazim's cause. Mr. Johnstone angrily told him that they did not want his co-operation in the matter. Munshi Sudder-u-Din then left the meeting, and sat outside. Mr. Johnstone at last won over the Nawab to his side, and settled the agreement under the Nazim's signature and seal. At the instance of the members of the Council, Raja Dulhab Ram and the "Jaggat Seth" were appointed assistants of Reza Khan for the period of the Nawab's minority. Reza Khan having got the full administrative power into his hands, sent Maharaja Nunda Kumar in custody to Calcutta, and began to conduct peaceably the State affairs. He assigned Aga Rezi, with the title of "Rezi-u-Din Khan," to the district of Nadia, and Reza Ali Khan to Khas Taluq. He appointed Ahmad Ali Khan Bukshi darogah of Pachotara at Murshidabad, and Hussain Ali Khan, Syud Rufiuddin Khan, and Kasim Ali Khan, Foujdars of Akbar Nagar, Purnea, and Hughli respectively; and Askar Ali Khan to the post of Kazi-ul-Kuzzat. He sent Ram Nath Bhaduri to Rajshaye and made Sher Ali Khan darogah of Dasti Topekhana, and Nasir Ali Khan darogah of Juisi Topekhana.

The war yet continued between Bengal and the Vizier of Oude's armies. Major Munro (in the lifetime of Mir Jaffer) succeeded Major Carnac in the command of the forces at Patna, which had been assigned to Behar. After making great military preparations, in September, 1764, he encroached upon the territories of the Vizier of Oude. The armies of the Nazim and the Vizier met at Buxar (on the banks of the Sone, within the boundaries of Gourpur). After much fighting and bloodshed, the Bengal army came off victorious on the 23rd of October, 1764. The Vizier with his army fled to Allahabad, leaving his baggage behind. The Bengal army obtained immense booty in this battle. The Emperor, also, was in the same field, at some distance, with an army to help the Vizier. Being informed of the valour and bravery of Major Munro, and the strength of the Bengal army, and the flight of the Vizier, the Emperor gave up the

* Month of fasting, *v.* p. 66.

alliance with the Vizier and sued for peace with the English and the Nazim. He encamped on this side of Benares, and summoned the Bengal officers before him. In this interview peace was concluded between them. Availing himself of this opportunity, Raja Beni Behadur, one of the premier Omrahs of the Vizier, who was at this time with the Emperor, requested the Bengal officers, on behalf of his master, to make peace.

Mir Kasim Ali Khan, who was a captain in the army of the Vizier, fled from the Vizier's army, then at Benares, while it was in a state of confusion; and taking his family with him from Allahabad, he safely reached the land of the Rohillas. The Vizier, being defeated, sent off his family and property from Allahabad to Faizabad, in the care of Hafiz Rahamatulla. He entered into a league with Hafiz, and began to collect an army. On Major Munro's resigning, Major Fletcher officiated for him till the arrival of Carnac, who had been made Brigadier-General of the Bengal army.

Lord Clive reached Calcutta on May 3rd, 1765, and wrote a letter of condolence to Najim-u-Dowlah and Muni Begum, expressing sympathy. In reply to Clive's letter, the Nazim informed him of his (Nazim's) intended visit to consult with him regarding the conclusion of peace with the Vizier. After some days the Nawab, accompanied by Mahomed Eruj Khan, Nawab Asadulla Khan and Ashruf Ali Khan, started for Calcutta. Clive sent two members of the Council, Mr. Sykes and Mr. Watson, to receive them, and he himself, with the other members of the Council, waited upon the Nazim when he arrived. Clive paid him a visit of ceremony and presented "Nazars," etc. The next day Lord Clive, with the members of the Council, again attended upon the Nazim, and brought up the questions of the giving of the *Diwanni* to the Company and of the peace with the Vizier and Emperor. The Nazim, at the request of Lord Clive, summoned Reza Khan, who was then at Murshidabad at the head of affairs, to Calcutta.

After much discussion, it was settled that the revenue only would be given up to the Company, and that a treaty would be made regarding the alliance of the three parties, namely, the Company, the Nazim, and the Vizier, and would be signed. In *lieu* of the Jaghirs an allowance was to be fixed for the Nazim, and for the Nizamat expenses. But the Nazim bore malice against Mozuffer Jang; and Munshi Sudder-u-Din and Maharaja Nunda Kumar further irritated the Nazim against Mozuffer Jang. Clive determined to make up the quarrel between the Nazim and Mozuffer Jang, but owing to the obstinacy of the Nazim, he found it difficult. Clive consulted Reza Khan, Mr. Sykes, and Raja Naba Krishna, who had been, from the time of Mir Jaffer, the Nizamat's agent in the Calcutta Council, on the subject. They were of opinion that, on account of Munshi Sudder-u-Din and Raja Nunda Kumar, the Nazim was now pleased with Reza Khan, and that by winning the Munshi to Reza Khan's views, the Nazim's displeasure could be removed. Lord Clive asked Reza Khan to win the Munshi to his side. If he could do so it was all right, if not, he himself would try to pacify the Munshi. Being ordered by the Governor, Mahomed Reza Khan asked the Munshi to come to him, and requested him to do everything in his power to restore him to the favour of the Nazim; and in return for these services he promised to give him a lucrative post. The Munshi replied that without the Nazim's permission he (the Munshi) could not wait upon him. Reza Khan sent Ismail Ali Khan to the Nazim to get his permission. On being permitted by the Nawab, the Munshi went to see Reza Khan, who tried his utmost to win the Munshi to his side. The next day Mr. Sykes paid a visit to the Munshi for the same purpose. If the Nazim followed the advice of Nunda Kumar, who was in reality an ill-wisher (but who professed to be a well-wisher) of the Nazim, in his doings they felt they could not do any good to the Nazim. Lord Clive asked the Munshi to induce the Nawab to follow their advice. The Munshi replied that as the Nawab regarded Clive as his elder brother, and entertained great regard for him, he would do anything which Clive requested him to do. But he hesitated only in respect of the appointment of Reza Khan to the Nizamat. Clive asked the Munshi whether there had been any talk between him and Reza

Khan on the subject. The Munshi fully related what had occurred. Clive assured the Munshi that if Reza Khan proved false to his words he (Clive) himself would take the Munshi's part. Clive also told the Munshi that at that time certain arrangements were desirable. The Munshi then consented to the proposal. After this Clive mentioned the advantages of making peace with the Vizier and Emperor, and asked for six lakhs of rupees as a loan from the Nazim. Clive then asked the Munshi to withhold his communication from Nunda Kumar, and informed him that if he disobeyed this order he would incur the displeasure of the Company, which would be a great source of misfortune to him. The Munshi promised that he would see Nunda Kumar only once more, to take leave of him. The Governor gave his consent, and bade the Munshi good-bye. The Munshi then went to the Nazim, and after fully relating the circumstances to him, persuaded him to act as requested by Lord Clive. Najim-u-Dowlah ordered preparations for his departure to Murshidabad. The next day Mr. Sykes waited upon him and obtained his approval of the loan of six lakhs of rupees. It was settled that Munshi Sudder-u-Din should be appointed representative between the Naib and the Nazim for carrying on State affairs.

The Governor paid another visit to the Nawab, and, after adjusting the afore-mentioned affairs, returned highly pleased. Lord Clive expressed his intention of visiting the Nawab again at Murshidabad, after the *Ashura* (10th day of Mohurram)* so that he might settle the remaining affairs relating to the treaty with the Vizier and the Emperor, and the fixing of the Nizamat stipend. The allowance was to be fifty lakhs of rupees. Najim-u-Dowlah now returned to Murshidabad. Previous to his arrival, Lord Clive wrote to Mr. Francis Sykes, Resident at the Murshidabad Court, to prevail upon the Nawab to keep faithful to their policy, and to endeavour to get the Nawab to throw the management of affairs entirely into the hands of the Ministers then in power; to make over all the revenues arising from the three provinces, in order to enable the Company to pay the expenses of the army, the annuity to the Emperor, and other contingent expenses, etc., in consideration of their paying him a sum of fifty lakhs per annum for his horses, sepoys, household charges, etc.; this to be sanctioned by a *sanad* from the Emperor.

Clive reached Murshidabad on July 5th, 1765, and the Nazim, accompanied by the State Officers, accorded him a grand reception. Lord Clive, at the intervention of Nawab Mozuffer Jang, Raja Dulhab Ram, and Jaggat Seth, and Munshi Sudder-u-Din, after going through the State papers estimated a monthly pension for the Nazim and Nizamat expenses, and settled on what terms the peace with the Vizier and Emperor was to be concluded. Preparations were made for sending the usual presents to the Emperor, in order to procure for Nawab Najim-u-Dowlah certain titles. Clive procured for Carnac and Shitab Rai the necessary *sanads* (authority) for their deputation to the Court of Delhi from the Nazim. Previous to the deputation, Clive sent Carnac to bring the Vizier from Faizabad to Allahabad. Before this Rao Shitab Rai, Diwan of Behar, had been for some time in communication with the Omrahs of the Emperor and the Vizier about the peace negotiations. At the request of Rao Shitab Rai, Clive, and Carnac, on behalf of the Nazim, and the Company, immediately repaired towards Allahabad. Najim-u-Dowlah sent the usual present to the Emperor of Delhi, and addressed a letter to Lord Clive, who was then at Patna on his way to Allahabad, stating that in consultation with Mozuffer Jang, Sykes, etc., another sum of Rs. 3,86,131-9 had been estimated in addition to the fifty lakhs for the Nizamat expenses and the Nazim's stipend.

The Emperor and the Vizier, who had been overpowered by their party, acceded to the proposal that Nawab Najim-u-Dowlah should pay a yearly offering of twenty-six lakhs to the Emperor, and the Company, in the capacity of Diwan, should be security for the realisation of the said amount, and that the Company would pay the Nazim the necessary allowance for the Nizamat and his private expenses. The Emperor granted the *sanads* and *firmans* to Najim-u-Dowlah, conferring upon him the Subahdari of the three provinces, and gave him the rank of Hast Hazari (commander of eight thousand soldiers), and a Jaghir.

* *Vide* p. 67.

To the East India Company the Emperor granted the Diwanni of the three Provinces, and also gave them a firman, granting them the zemindari rights over the Chaklas of Burdwan, Midnapur, Chittagong, and the twenty-four Pergunnahs, which had been given to them by Mir Jaffer and Mir Kasim. An agreement, dated August 18th, 1765, was made between the Vizier, Sujah-u-Dowlah, Nawab Najim-u-Dowlah, and the Company, under the hands and seals of the three parties, and with the approval of the Emperor. The dispute, which hitherto had been lingering between the Emperor and the Nazim, thus came to an end, and thus the financial affairs and military defences of the country being separated from the Nizamat, came into the hands of the Company, and only the civil administration was left to the Nazim. Colonel Smith on behalf of the Company, and another on behalf of the Nazim, were appointed as agents at the Court of Delhi, and Lord Clive, accompanied by General Carnac and Rao Shitab Rai, came back to Murshidabad. Immediately, for the execution of the above-mentioned estimate for stipend, an agreement, dated September, 1765, was made between the Company and the Nazim, each of the parties taking a copy of the same. It ran as follows :—

ARTICLES OF TREATY AND AGREEMENT CONCLUDED BETWEEN THE GOVERNOR AND COUNCIL OF FORT WILLIAM ON THE PART OF THE ENGLISH EAST INDIA COMPANY, AND NAWAB NAJIM-U-DOWLAH.

On the part of the Company.

We, the Governor and Council, do engage to secure to the Nawab Najim-u-Dowlah all the Subahdari of the Provinces of Bengal, Behar, and Orissa; and to support him therein with the Company's forces against all enemies. We will also, at all times, keep up such forces as may be necessary effectually to assist and support him in the defence of the Provinces; and as our troops will be more to be depended on than any the Nawab can have, and less expensive to him, he need, therefore, entertain none but such as are requisite for the support of the civil officers of his Government, and the business of his collections through the different districts.

We do further promise, that in consideration the Nawab shall continue to assist in defraying the extraordinary expenses of the war now carrying on against Sujah-u-Dowlah with five lakhs of rupees per month which was agreed to by his father, whatever sums may be hereafter received of the King, on account of our assistance afforded him in the war, shall be repaid to the Nawab.

On the part of the Nawab.

In consideration of the assistance the Governor and Council have agreed to afford in securing to me the succession in the Subahdari of Bengal, Behar, and Orissa, heretofore held by my father, the late Nawab Mir Jaffer Ali Khan, and supporting me in it against all my enemies, I do agree and bind myself to the faithful performance of the following Articles :—

Article 1.—The treaty which my father formerly concluded with the Company upon his first accession to the Nizamat, engaging to regard the honour and reputation of the Company and of their Governor and Council as his own, and granting *perwannahs* for the currency of the Company's trade, the same Treaty, as far as is consistent with the Articles hereafter agreed to, I, too, do hereby ratify and confirm.

Article 2.—Considering the weighty charge of Government and how essential it is for myself, for the welfare of the country and for the Company's business, that I should have a person who has had experience therein to advise and assist me, I do agree to have one fixed with me, with the advice of the Governor and Council, in the station of Naib Subah, who shall accordingly have, immediately under me, the chief management of all affairs; and as Mahomed Reza Khan, the Naib of Dacca, has in every respect my approbation and that of the Governor and Council, I do further agree that this trust shall be conferred on him, and I will not displace him without the acquiescence of those gentlemen; and, in case any alteration in this appointment should hereafter appear advisable, that Mahomed Reza Khan, provided he has acquitted himself with fidelity in his administration, shall in such case be reinstated in the Naibship of Dacca, with the same authority as heretofore.

Article 3.—The business of the collection of the revenues shall, under the Naib Subah, be divided into two or more branches, as may appear proper; and as I have the fullest dependence and confidence on the attachment of the English and their regard to my interest and dignity, and am desirous of giving them every testimony thereof, I do further consent, that the appointment and dismissal of the Muttasuddis of those branches, and the allotment of their several districts shall be with the approbation of the Governor and Council; and considering how much men of my rank and station are obliged to trust to the eyes and recommendations of the servants about them, and how liable to be deceived, it is my further will that the Governor and Council shall be at liberty to object and point out to me when improper people are entrusted, or where my officers and subjects are oppressed, and I will pay a proper regard to such representations, that my affairs may be conducted with honour, my people everywhere be happy, and their grievances be redressed.

Article 4.—I do confirm to the Company, as a fixed resource for defraying the ordinary expenses of their troops, the Chaklas of Burdwan, Midnapur and Chittagong, in as full a manner as heretofore ceded by my father. The sum of five lakhs of sicca rupees per month for their maintenance was further agreed to be paid by my father; I agree to pay the same out of my treasury, while the exigency for keeping up so large an army continues. When the Company's occasions will admit of diminution of the expenses, they are put to on account of those troops, the Governor and Council will then relieve me from such a proportion of this assignment as the increased expenses incurred by keeping up the whole Force necessary for the defence of the provinces will admit of; and, as I esteem the Company's troops entirely equal thereto and as my own, I will only maintain such as are immediately necessary for the dignity of my person and Government, and the business of my collections throughout the Provinces.

Article 5.—I do ratify and confirm to the English the privilege granted to them by their Firman and several Husbulhukums of carrying on their trade by means of their own *dustuck*, free from all "duties," taxes, or impositions, in all parts of the country, excepting in the article of salt, on which a "duty" of 2½ per cent. is to be levied on the Hughli market price.

Article 6.—I give the Company the liberty of purchasing half the saltpetre produced in the country of Purnea, which their Gomastahs shall send to Calcutta; the other half shall be collected by my Foujdar for the use of my offices; and I will suffer no other persons to make purchases of this article in that country.

Article 7.—In the Chakla of Sylhet, for the space of five years, commencing with the Bengali year 1171, my Foujdar, and a Gomastah on the part of the Company, shall jointly provide *Chunam*, of which each shall defray half the expenses, and half the *Chunam* so made shall be given to the Company.

Article 8.—Although I should occasionally remove to other places in the Provinces, I agree that the books of the Sirkar shall be always kept, and the business conducted at Murshidabad, and that it shall, as heretofore, be the seat of my Government; and wherever I am, I consent that an English gentleman shall reside with me to transact all affairs between me and the Company, and that a person of high rank shall also reside, on my part, at Calcutta, to negotiate with the Governor and Council.

Article 9.—I will cause the rupees coined in Calcutta to pass in every respect as equal to the siccas of Murshidabad, without any deduction of *batta*; and whosoever shall demand *batta* shall be punished; the annual loss on coinage, by the fall of *batta* on the issuing of the siccas, is a very heavy grievance to the country ; and after mature consideration, I will, in concert with the Governor and Council, pursue whatever may appear the best method for remedying it.

Article 10.—I will allow no Europeans whatever to be entertained in my service, and if there already be any, they shall be immediately dismissed.

Article 11.—The Kistbundi for payment of the restitution to the sufferers in the late troubles, as executed by my father, I will see faithfully paid. No delays shall be made in this business.

Article 12.—I confirm and will abide by the Treaty which my father formerly made with the Dutch.

Article 13.—If the French come into the country, I will not allow them to erect any fortifications, maintain forces, or hold lands, zemindaries, etc., but they shall pay tribute, and carry on their trade as in former times.

Article 14.—Some regulations shall be, hereafter, settled between us for deciding all disputes which may arise between the English Gomastahs and my officers, in the different parts of the country.

In testimony whereof, we, the said Governor and Council, have set our hands, and affixed the seal of the Company to one part hereof, and the Nawab, before-named, hath set his hand and seal to another part.

W. MAJENDIE, *Secretary.*

TRANSLATION OF AN AGREEMENT CONCLUDED BETWEEN NAWAB NAJIM-U-DOWLAH BAHADUR AND THE HONOURABLE EAST INDIA COMPANY, IN THE YEAR 1172 BENGALI. (SEPTEMBER, 1765.)

I am Nawab Sujah-ul-Mulk Hisam-u-Dowlah Mir Najim-u-Din Ali Khan Bahadur Mahabat Jang.

Whereas His Majesty, the shadow of God, has, through the most gracious Royal favours, bestowed the office of *Diwan* of the Provinces of Bengal, Behar, and Orissa, with the revenues of the aforesaid provinces, in the shape of an *altumgha*, reward, etc., to the English Company of noble and honourable rank, of grand and dignified position, subject to several conditions ; and one of those conditions is, that the expenses of the *Nizamat* shall be paid in a suitable manner ; I do declare, and give in writing, that the said Company, of noble rank, shall pay, towards the said expenses, the sum of *sicca* rupees fifty-three lakhs eighty-six thousand one hundred and thirty-one, annas nine—out of which seventeen lakhs twenty-five thousand eight hundred and fifty-four rupees are for all the household expenses, inclusive of dependants and attendants, etc.—and thirty-six lakhs sixty thousand two hundred and seventy-seven rupees, and nine annas, for the expenses of horsemen, *Telangas* (sepoys) peons, *burkundazis*, etc., whatever may be required for the purpose of *Sawari* (retinue), provided they shall pay the sum of thirty-six lakhs sixty thousand two hundred and seventy-seven rupees, nine annas for the above expenses, if considered necessary in future ; but nothing whatever shall be increased to it. As I have entire confidence in Nawab Moin-u-Dowlah Syud Mahomed Reza Khan Bahadur Mozuffer Jang, it is laid down that the expenses under the last-mentioned head for horsemen, etc., shall be defrayed through the said Nawab. It is strongly hoped that, so long as, by the help of God, the factories of the said English Company, of high rank, shall exist in the Provinces of Bengal, etc., there shall be no deviation whatsoever from this Covenant and Agreement.

The year 1172, one thousand one hundred and seventy-two, Bengali.

Memorandum of Details of the *Nizamat* expenses of *Sirkar* Nawab Najim-u-Dowlah Bahadur.

As per former Estimate Rs. 45,71,239-5 }
" " present " " 8,14,892-4 } ... Rs. 53,86,131-9.

Expenses of *Mir Samani* (Household Department) etc., under the control of Nawab Najim-u-Dowlah Bahadur, per annum ... Rs. 17,25,854

As per former Estimate ... Rs. 9,10,961-12 }
" " present " ... " 8,14,892-4 }

Mir Samani (Household Department) Rs. 8,49,854 }
As before }

Salaries of servants attached to the *Mahal* at Rs. 6,000 monthly.
Rs. 72,000 annually.

Former (account) at Rs. 3,491-5 monthly, Rs. 41,895-12 annually.
Present (account) at Rs. 2,508-11 monthly, Rs. 30,104-4 annually.

Deori of Jaffraganj in charge of Mir Syud Saheb at Rs. 5,000 monthly.
Rs. 60,000 annually.

Former (account) at Rs. 1,601 monthly, Rs. 19,212 annually.
Present (account) at Rs. 3,399 monthly, Rs. 40,788 annually.

Nawab Saif-u-Dowlah Bahadur at Rs. 7,000 per month, Rs. 84,000 annually henceforward.

Nawab Mobarak-u-Dowlah at Rs. 5,000 per month, Rs. 60,000 annually henceforward.

Necessary personal expenses besides the amount fixed at Rs. 50,000 monthly, Rs. 6,00,000 annually henceforward.

Salaries of servants attached to the retinue and persons employed for the duties of officers, artillerymen, menial servants, etc., under the control of Nawab Moin-u-Dowlah Bahadur, etc., Rs. 30,60,277-9 as before.

(*On the back.*)

Agreement concluded between Nawab Najim-u-Dowlah and the Honourable East India Company of England, being dated and signed in presence of the Right Honourable Lord Clive and Francis Sykes, Esq.

The 6th Year. The devoted servant of Shah Alum, the Victorious King, Sujah-ul-Mulk Hisam-u-Dowlah Syud Najim-u-Din Ali Khan Bahadur Mahabat Jang.

We, whose names are under-written, do promise on the part of the English Company, faithfully to adhere to this agreement, and in token thereof, have hereunto affixed our hand and seals.

(*Signed*) { WM. B. SUMNER, JOHN CARNAC, H. VERELST } *Seals.*

(*Signed*) CLIVE (*Seal*) (*Signed*) FRANCIS SYKES (*Seal*).

(Signature of Nawab Najim-u-Dowlah, in Persian.)

What is written in the text is agreed to, and accepted.

Rao Shitab Rai, in reward for his good services, was appointed Naib Subahdar of Behar, in place of Nawab Kasim Ali Khan, on behalf of the Nazim, and Diwan on behalf of the Company. For sometime Raja Dhiraj Narain, brother of Raja Ram Narain, served under him as his assistant. A pension of one lakh yearly was fixed on Kasim Ali Khan. Nawab Reza Khan Mozuffer Jang was confirmed in his post as Naib of the Nizamat, and was made Naib of the Diwanni of the Company. Mr. Sykes was also to work with Mozuffer Jang.

The Governor, after these arrangements, left for Calcutta. Again, in May, 1766, Lord Clive, with the intention of going to Allahabad to see the Vizier, started for Murshidabad in order to celebrate the "Punya" ceremony. The Nawab, with Mozuffer Jang and Eruj Khan, advanced as far as Plassy to receive him. The Governor gave the usual present to the Nazim. The Nazim and the Governor then went on the same same elephant on a hunting party; a large tiger appeared before them; the Nazim shot four arrows at the tiger, all of which hit at one and the same place. The Governor was astonished at the dexterity of the Nazim, and from there the Governor and the Nazim came to Murshidabad.

Muni Begum wrote to Lord Clive that she wanted to convey a testament of the late Mir Jaffer to him, and requested him to see her. Clive waited upon her at Ainamahal. Haji Sadatmund and Munshi Sudder-u-Din were employed as messengers, and Saheb-u-Din as interpreter.

According to Mir Jaffer's will, jewels and cash to the value of five lakhs of rupees had to be paid to Lord Clive. At his death, Mir Jaffer also enjoined his son to pay the amount to Clive if he came back to India, and if he did not come, to send the amount to England by "bill of exchange." According to the writ, the amount to be paid to Clive was five lakhs, including jewels, notes, etc. Clive, after many requests, accepted, on this condition, that instead of the gold mohurs and jewels a Nizamat cheque to the Company for two lakhs of rupees be given to him with the cash. The will was executed so late, because Lord Clive up to that time had been so busy with affairs relating to war, etc., that he had little or no leisure to attend upon the Begum.

Previous to this Nawab Najim-u-Dowlah wrote a letter to Clive, informing him of Mir Jaffer's will, bequeathing to him three lakhs of rupees in cash, and mohurs and jewels to the value of two lakhs. Finally, three lakhs of rupees and a cheque for two lakhs were sent through Munshi Sudder-u-Din to Lord Clive. Lord Clive with that money established a fund for helping the orphans and the widows of English soldiers, to perpetuate the memory of Mir Jaffer and himself. Nawab Najim-u-Dowlah requested Clive to repay the six lakhs of rupees which the Company borrowed from the Nizamat treasury. Clive issued a cheque, and asked Mozuffer Jang to pay the amount to the Nazim. On April 23rd, 1766, Clive, on his way to Lucknow, halted at Sadaqbagh. The Nazim attended with his courtiers, and paid him a visit. On the day of his departure the Nazim gave a party, during which the Nazim was attacked with a "fever." The guests were dismissed. On Wednesday morning at four o'clock the Nazim arrived at the Murshidabad Fort. Nawab Asadulla Khan, aided by Hakims Maktate Ali Khan, and Yusuf Ali Khan, prescribed for the Nazim a purgative. For some time the malady showed signs of abatement. He dismissed the officers who were with him at four o'clock. At this time he was a little better; but again at 9 p.m. the "fever" renewed its attack still more vigorously. He called for Mozuffer Jang and Hakim Mahomed Hussain. The whole night passed, neither did Mozuffer Jang come nor did he send the Hakim to the Nazim. Munshi Sudder-u-Din related that the Nazim passed the whole night on his lap. The next morning Mozuffer Jang came to attend, with all the courtiers, and found the Nazim insensible. Hakims (Mahomedan physicians) tried their best, but could do nothing. On the 3rd May, 1766,

Najim-u-Dowlah breathed his last. He was childless. He was buried in the Jaffraganj cemetery. Mr. Sykes, Resident at Murshidabad, sent watchmen to all the departments to keep guard over the effects of the Nazim.

X.

SAIF-U-DOWLAH.

SAIF-UL-MULK, SAIF-U-DOWLAH, NAWAB SYUD NAJABUT ALI KHAN BAHADUR, SHAHAMUT JANG.

1766-1770.

NAWAB NAJIM-U-DOWLAH had no son. Lord Clive received the news of Najim-u-Dowlah's death when he was on his way to Lucknow. He wrote letters to the members of the Calcutta Council to place Nawab Saif-u-Dowlah, the brother, and, according to the Mahomedan law, the rightful successor of the late Nawab, on the throne. Saif-u-Dowlah was installed as Governor of the three provinces on the 22nd May, 1766. The members of the Calcutta Council came to Murshidabad, and requested the Nazim to sign the following treaty, dated May 19th, 1766:—

ARTICLES OF TREATY AND AGREEMENT CONCLUDED BETWEEN THE GOVERNOR AND COUNCIL OF FORT WILLIAM, ON THE PART OF THE ENGLISH EAST INDIA COMPANY AND NAWAB SAIF-U-DOWLAH, MAY 19TH, 1766.

On the part of the Company.

We, the Governor and Council, do engage to secure to the Nawab Saif-u-Dowlah, the Subahdari of the Provinces of Bengal, Behar, and Orissa, and to support him therein with the Company's forces against all his enemies.

On the part of the Nawab.

Article 1.—The Treaty which my father formerly concluded with the Company upon his first accession to the Nizamat, engaging to regard the honour and reputation of the Company and of the Governor and Council as his own, and that entered into with my brother, Nawab Najim-u-Dowlah, the same Treaties, as far as is consistent with the spirit, intent, and meaning thereof, I do hereby ratify and confirm.

Article 2.—The King has been graciously pleased to grant unto the English East India Company the Diwanship of Bengal, Behar, and Orissa, as a free gift for ever; and I, having an entire confidence in them, and in their servants settled in this country, that nothing whatever be proposed or carried into execution by them, derogating from my honour, dignity, interest, and the good of my country, do therefore for the better conducting the affairs of the Subahdari and promoting my honour and interest, and that of the Company, in the best manner, agree that the protecting the Provinces of Bengal, Behar, and Orissa, and the force sufficient for that purpose, be entirely left to their discretion and good management, in consideration of their paying the King, Shah Alum, by monthly payments, as by Treaty agreed on, the sum of Rs. 2,16,567-10-9, and to me, Saif-u-Dowlah, the annual stipend of Rs. 41,86,131-9, *viz.* :—the sum of Rs. 17,78,854-1 for my house, servants, and other expense indispensably necessary; and the remaining sum of Rs. 24,07,277-8 for the support of such sepoys, peons, and burkundazis as may be thought proper for my *Sawari* only; but on no account ever to exceed that amount.

Article 3.—The Nawab Moin-u-Dowlah, who was, at the instance of the Governor and gentlemen of the Council, appointed Naib of the Provinces, and invested with the management of affairs, in conjunction with Maharaja Dulhab and Jaggat Seth, shall continue in the same post and with the same authority; and having perfect confidence in him, I, moreover, agree to let him have the disbursing of the above sum of Rs. 24,07,277-8 for the purposes above mentioned.

This Agreement (by the blessing of God), I hope, will be inviolably observed as long as the English Company's factories continue in Bengal.

Dated this 19th day of May, in the year of our Lord, 1766.

(*Signed*) W. B. SUMNER.
H. VERELST.
RANDOLPH MARRIOTT.
H. WATTS.
CLAUD RUSSELL.
W. ALDERSEY.
THOMAS KELSALL.
CHARLES FLOYER.

Saif-u-Dowlah, after sending the usual Nazars, procured from the Emperor of Delhi *sanads* and *firmans* for the Subahdari and Foujdari of the three provinces, and the rank of "Hast Hazari" (commander of eight thousand horse). His supremacy over the three *Subahs* was acknowledged without any resistance. Nawab Mozuffer Jang, as before, owing to the minority of the Nawab, held the post of Naib, and, obtaining more powers than before over the Nizamat affairs, directed his attention to the government of the estate. The Governor and his Councillors took upon themselves the superintendence of the State affairs and the protection of the country. Mozuffer Jang appointed his own favourites, Ismail Ali Khan and Mir Abdul Ali and others, aides-de-camp and tutors to the young Nazim.

Lord Clive left again for England in 1767 A.D. Mr. Verelst succeeded Clive as Governor. From the Nizamat records it is found that through the Mahanta of Udypur and the Maharaja's special Minister, a treaty was concluded between Maharaja Janaji Bhonsla and the Nawab Saif-u-Dowlah on Shawal 19th, 1181 A.H. By this treaty, Janaji Bhonsla ceded the province of Orissa, by the cession of which, and an annuity of two lakhs of rupees, Ali Verdi Khan had concluded his peace with the Mahrattas, in return for sixteen lakhs of rupees yearly, on the Company's security.

At that time the affairs of the Government were conducted in the following manner:—Mozuffer Jang, Shitab Rai, and Jisarut Khan, in Bengal, Behar, and Dacca respectively, after discharging their State duties, submitted twice a week their administration reports and other papers to the Governor. The Foujdars and other officers of every place, after conducting the Nizamat affairs, submitted reports to the Naib Nazim, and the Naib conducted the affairs with the advice of the Political Resident. And also from that time, at the intercession of Mozuffer Jang, the Naibs, Diwans, Kanongoes, and Mohurrirs, etc., who had hitherto been paid by percentage commission, began to receive fixed monthly pay. Mozuffer Jang received three lakhs, and Raja Mahendra, and Dulhab Ram, Diwan, two lakhs each, and Shitab Rai one lakh yearly. The system of paying by commission was abolished altogether. After taking the Diwanni, Clive removed the Supreme Kutcheri (Court) from the Nizamat Kila (Fort) to the Moti Jhil garden-house of Shahamut Jang, son-in-law and nephew of Ali Verdi Khan, and there celebrated the "Punya" ceremony. Mozuffer Jang carried on the Diwanni business alone till the year 1770 A.D., when Mr. Becher succeeded Mr. Sykes, and a second Resident (Mr. Morrison) was appointed, and put limits to his power and authority. Mozuffer Jang, finding himself reduced in power, tried to extricate himself from their hands. From this year the date of the payment of Nizamat pensions, etc., and the regulation of other State affairs, were transferred from the lunar to the solar year.

In the same year, according to the advice of the second Resident, the Nazim complained of the conduct of the Mozuffer Jang to Mr. Verelst, the Governor. The Governor summoned Mozuffer Jang to Calcutta, and told him that he (Mozuffer Jang) would have to give up the charge of the "Behla" and other household affairs to the Nazim, and, as before, carry on the administration of the State affairs. The Nazim, who had hitherto been excluded from the government, took this decision of the Governor to be highly favourable to him. At that time, also, the Governor and his Councillors, with the approval of the Nazim and Mozuffer Jang, planned the appointment of an English officer for the management of the financial department. After this the Governor, Mr. Verelst, bidding farewell to the Nazim, left for England in 1769 A.D. Mr. John Cartier succeeded him as Governor, and came to Murshidabad. Mr. Morrison died at that time. As the Europeans privately imported into this country ammunition and weapons at this time, a custom house was erected for the Nizamat, and perwannahs were sent to the English, French, and Danish officers, directing them to examine all ships, and to put a stop to the import of the offensive weapons. Also, during the same period, a great famine and an epidemic of small-pox broke out in the country. Mortality was very high during three months. Nawab Saif-u-Dowlah and his brother, Syud Ashrab Ali Khan, died of small-pox* Both of them were childless. Saif-u-Dowlah, during his short reign of three years two months and some days, never flinched from the path of duty. Though he had practically no hand in the affairs of his estate, yet he did much for the welfare of his dependants. He subscribed three lakhs to the fund for helping the widows of English soldiers, a fund which Clive had established with the money Mir Jaffer had left him. The year 1770 and its calamities has been alluded to in Part I.

TRANSLATION OF A FIRMAN FROM THE EMPEROR SHAH ALUM GRANTING TO NAWAB SAIF-U-DOWLAH THE TITLE AND RANK, OR MONSUB, OF "HAST-HAZARI," ON THE 3RD DAY OF MOHURRAM IN THE YEAR 1180 A.H., CORRESPONDING WITH THE 15TH OF JUNE, 1766 A.D.

Let this be re-submitted.

The whole (of this) is (found correct) according to the *Waquia* (Register).

Re-submitted to His Gracious Majesty on the 17th day of the holy month of Mohurram in the auspicious year of *Juloos*.

On Thursday, the 3rd of the holy month of Mohurram, in the auspicious seventh year (*Juloos*), corresponding with the year 1180 A.H., in the *Risala* of the seat of nobility and respectability, the centre of courage and bravery, the possessor of knowledge as to matters connected with religion and kingdom, proficient in matters concerning the state and faith, the bearer of the standard of pomp and dignity, the adorner of the carpet of rank and greatness, the giver of strength to kingdom and royalty, the confidential officer of the state and kingdom, the contributor of success in battle-fields for conquest of the world, the means of affording pleasure to assemblies of merriment and gaiety, experienced in matters concerning kingdom and wealth, the founder of the basis of riches and prosperity, the possessor of secrets of royalty, the initiated into the mysteries of human nature, the jewel of the mirror of truth and loyalty, the light of the lamp of true friendship and sincerity, the open-hearted companion in assemblies of select friends, the confidential coadjutor, bearing feelings of sincere friendship, the wielder of the sword and the pen, the counsellor of affairs of the world, the cream of the Khans [Chiefs] of high position, the best among the Emirs [Chiefs] of noble rank, the disciple of the guide, without show

* Called in Bengali, *Basanta-rog*, or spring disease. It is at its worst during the early months of the year.

and hypocrisy, the select among the devoted servants, possessed of wisdom, the support of warriors of indomitable courage, the pride of heroes of the field of battle, the *Emir* skilled in the affairs of administration, the wise counsellor of noble rank, deserving of honour and respect, worthy of esteem and regard, the pillar of the kingdom of the Solomon-like sovereign, Bukhshi-ul-mamalik Amir-ul-Omrah Nasir-ul-Mulk Najib-u-Dowlah Najib Khan Bahadur Sabatjang Sipah Sirdar [Commander-in-Chief], and during the incumbency of *Waqia** of the most humble and faithful slave of the sky-like threshold of (royalty), *viz.*, Anund Ram,—it is (hereby) written and orders are issued (to the effect that) Saif-u-Dowlah Syud Najabut Ali Khan Bahadur Shahamutjang has been honoured with the rank *(appointment) of the office* of "Hast Hazari" [eight thousand] for self, with eight thousand for troopers, inclusive of the amount originally fixed and the amount newly added, out of which three thousand and one hundred troopers are to have two horses (each),—subject to the condition of *Subahdari* of Bengal and *Foujdari* of Muxsudabad, etc., as also the title of "Saif-ul-Mulk," and the order of *Mahi Maratib.* Dated the 10th day of the holy month of Mohurram in the auspicious seventh year (of *Juloos*). Written out on being found correct according to memorandum.

Particulars of the signature—of the seat of nobility and respectability, the centre of courage and bravery, the possessor of knowledge as to matters connected with religion and kingdom, proficient in matters concerning the state and faith, the bearer of the standard of pomp and dignity, the adorner of the carpet of rank and greatness, the giver of strength to kingdom and royalty, the confidential officer of the state and kingdom, the contributor of success in battle-fields for conquest of the world, the means of affording pleasure to assemblies for merriment and gaiety, experienced in matters concerning kingdom and wealth, the founder of the basis of riches and prosperity, the possessor of secrets of royalty, the initiated into the mysteries of human nature, the jewel of the mirror of truth and loyalty, the light of the lamp of true friendship and sincerity, the open-hearted companion in assemblies of select friends, the confidential coadjutor bearing feelings of sincere friendship, the wielder of the sword and the pen, the counsellor of affairs of the world, the cream of the *Khans* of high position, the best among the *Emirs* of noble rank, the disciple of the guide, without show or hypocrisy, the select among the devoted servants, possessed of wisdom, the support of warriors of indomitable courage, the pride of the heroes of the field of battle, the *Emir* skilled in the affairs of administration, the wise counsellor of noble rank, deserving of honour and respect, worthy of esteem and regard, the pillar of the kingdom of Solomon-like sovereign, Bukhshi-ul-mamalik Amir-ul-Omrah Nasir-ul-Mulk Najib-u-Dowlah Najib Khan Bahadur Sabatjang Sipah Sirdar [Commander-in-Chief]:—Let this be entered in the *Waqia* [Register].

Copy of Signature in His Majesty's own handwriting.

Scheme (prepared) under the seal of Syud Najabut Ali Khan Bahadur, and received in the office, regarding addition to pay of the office and title of him, who is the most humble slave of His Majesty expectant of His Royal favours.

Addition of pay, inclusive of the amount originally fixed and the amount newly added. Eight thousand for self, and eight thousand for troopers.	Original amount seven thousand for self and seven thousand for troopers. Added amount one thousand for self and one thousand for troopers.
Addition of title	Original (title) Saif-u-Dowlah Syud Najabut Ali Khan Bahadur Sahamutjang. Addition—Saif-ul-Mulk.

* Keeper of records.

(Order of) *Mahi Maratib.*

Let the orders be duly carried out... ... { Signature of Bukhshi-ul-mamalik Amir-ul-Omrah Bahadur.

Eight thousand for self.
Eight thousand for troopers.

Two horses for each trooper			Total estimate 7,900 troopers.
3,100 troopers			
3,000			
Original	7,000		Seven thousand for self (and) seven thousand for troopers.
Added	1,000		One thousand for self with the title of "Saif-ul-Mulk" and one thousand for troopers.

Total estimate 11,000 for troopers.
Out of this 3,100 for troopers with two horses each, subject to conditions.
For *Subahdari* of Bengal 1,000 troopers.
For *Foujdari* of Muxsudabad 2,100 troopers.
Dated as above, month as above, in the auspicious year of *Juloos.*

Seal of Amir-ul-Omrah Najib-u-Dowlah Najib Khan Bahadur Sipah Sirdar, the devoted servant of Shah Alum Badshah, 1177.	Seal of Anund Ram, the devoted servant of Shah Alum Badshah Ghazi.	Seal of the devoted servant of Shah Alum Ghazi.

Translated by WAHIDUDDIN AHMAD, *Interpreter, High Court, Original Side.*

SANAD OF APPOINTMENT TO THE OFFICE OF NAIB NAZIM OF SUBAH BEHAR, ISSUED ON THE 5TH MOHURRAM, 1180 A.H., CORRESPONDING WITH JUNE 17TH, 1766 A.D.

Seal of the Vizier Mirza Akbar Shah.

Agreeably to the gracious orders of (His Imperial Majesty), the office of *Naib Nazim* and *Foujdar* of Sarkar *Shahabad* in Subah Behar—which rests personally with the *Vakeels* (agents) of His Royal Highness, the Nawab of high rank, the illustrious and eminent Prince of noble birth and exalted rank, the new plant of the garden of sovereignty, the chosen fruit of the tree of royalty, the fresh and blooming plant of the orchard of dignity, the shining star of the forehead of religion and kingdom, the lustre of the eye of royalty and faith, the priceless pearl of the ocean of kingdom, the Prince of high rank, Mirza Jahandar Shah Bahadur—is conferred, as per endorsement on back, upon the seat of nobility and respectability, the centre of courage and bravery, Saif-ul-Mulk Saif-u-Dowlah Syud Najabut Ali Khan Bahadur Shahamutjang, on the death of the late Mir Najim-u-Dowlah Ali Khan. He should duly perform and carry out the duties and requirements of these offices, and fail not to observe due caution and vigilance. He should use his best exertions towards the checking and suppressing of mischievous and refractory persons, the extermination of highway robbers, the protection of the weak and of all rent-payers, and the prevention of blacksmiths from making guns. He should give positive instructions to the *Thannadars*, appointed by him for the management and due control (of all matters), not to make any illegal exactions, and to see that no one uses any prohibited articles and intoxicating drugs. And if the mischievous people of any of the villages should commit acts of mischief, he should, first of all, try to win over some of them, and reform their habits so that they may show penitence and repent of their disobedience and refractoriness, and turn into peaceful citizens and rent-payers ; but if, through their innate villainy and wicked nature, they do not reform themselves, he should attack such village, and punish the miscreants of that place (at the same time taking care to see) that no harm whatsoever is caused to the loyal subjects and (none of them) is imprisoned, unless it be in a *Dar-ul-Harb* [land of infidels] and any booty, which may be got in the nature of cattle, etc., should be confiscated to Government. He should cause the ways and roads to be guarded in such a manner that travellers and wayfarers may pass and repass with perfect assurance and peace of mind, and no theft and robbery may take place anywhere. And if perchance anyone's property is robbed or stolen, he should by strict search cause the thieves and robbers to be apprehended, and the property to be restored to the owner, and have the offenders duly punished; and, if he fail to get them apprehended, the responsibility in respect of those properties shall not [*sic*] rest with him. The *Choudhuris*, *Kanongoes*, *Mutasuddis*, cultivators, and tenants of that place should regard the above-named *Khan* as the permanent Nawab Nazim of the *Subah* and *Foujdar* of the above *mahal*, and recognise him as duly invested with the essential requirements of these offices. They should consider the powers of the said seal of nobility to be firm and absolute as regards the management of matters pertaining to the said offices, and the administration of affairs concerning the said *Subah* and *Foujdari mahal*. With respect to this they should regard the directions of His Gracious Majesty to be positive and imperative. Written out on the 5th day of the holy month of Mohurram, in the seventh year of the auspicious and prosperous *Juloos*.

Endorsement.—According to the gracious orders of His Majesty, the office of Nawab Nazim and Foujdar of Sarkar Shahabad, etc., in Subah Behar,—which rests personally with the *Vakeels* [agents] of His Royal Highness, the Nawab of high rank, the illustrious and eminent Prince of noble birth and exalted rank, the new plant of the garden of sovereignty, the chosen fruit of the tree of royalty, the fresh and blooming plant of the orchard of dignity, the shining star of the forehead of religion and kingdom, the lustre of the eye of royalty and faith, the priceless pearl of the ocean of kingdom, the Prince of high rank, Mirza Jahandar Shah Bahadur,—is, upon the death of the late Mir Najim-u-Din Ali Khan, conferred, as per endorsement on back, upon and entrusted to the seat of nobility and respectability, the centre of courage and bravery, Saif-ul-Mulk, Saif-u-Dowlah Syud Najabut Ali Khan Bahadur Shahamutjang.

Translated by WAHIDUDDIN AHMAD, *Interpreter, High Court, Original Side.*
2nd May, 1895.

TRANSLATION OF A SANAD FROM THE VIZIER OF THE EMPEROR SHAH ALUM GRANTING TO NAWAB SAIF-U-DOWLAH JAGHIRS IN BENGAL, DATED JUNE 19TH, 1766.

Seal of the
Vizier Mirza Akbar
Shah Bahadur.

To the seat of nobility and respectability, the centre of rank and dignity, the English (East India) Company Bahadur, may you remain the object of the Emperor's favours!

Whereas the sum of five crores eighty-two lakhs eight thousand five hundred and thirty dams, from the paradise-like *Subah* [province] of Bengal, subject to condition, and without condition, is, upon the death of Mir Najim-u-Din Ali Khan, fixed [*i.e.*, granted] as the *Jaghir* of the sea of nobility and respectability, Saif-ul-Mulk Saif-u-Dowlah Syud Najabut Ali Khan Badahur Shahamutjang, commencing from half (*i.e.*, from) *Rubee* season of *Enut Eal* [or year of the horse] as per details on back; it is, therefore, written (to you) that you should give positive instructions to the *Zemindars* [land-holders] of that place to the effect that they should pay up the Government revenue and all civil dues, duly and faithfully, according to the usual practice and custom, unto the *Amil* [Revenue Collector] of that place, and that they should not fail to act up to what is just, right, and proper. Written out on the 7th day of the holy month of Mohurram in the seventh year of the auspicious *Juloos.*

Contents of the Zimmun.

Endorsement.—Granted to Saif-ul-Mulk Saif-u-Dowlah Syud Najabut Ali Khan Badahur Shahamutjang from the paradise-like *Subah* of Bengal, upon the death of Mir Najim-u-Din Ali Khan (Najim-u-Dowlah), subject to condition, and without condition, commencing from half (*i.e.*, from) *Rubee* (season) of *Enut Eal* [or year of the horse].

Seal of the Vizier's office affixed on the 19th day of the holy month of Mohurram in the seventh year of the auspicious *Juloos.*	Copy received in the office on the 7th day of the holy month of Mohurram in the seventh year of the auspicious *Juloos.*	Corresponds with the entry in the office.

5 crores
82 lakhs
8530 dáms

5,82,08,530

In respect of the *Subahdari*, subject to condition and without condition.

10,00,000
1 crore

Subject to condition 80 lakhs of dáms

without condition 20 lakhs of dáms

In respect of *Foujdari* of Muxsudabad, etc., subject to condition, and without condition.

4,82,08,530
4 crores
82 lakhs
8,530 dáms

Subject to condition of *Foujdari* 1,68,00,000.
1 crore, 68 lakhs of dáms.

without condition
3 crores 14 lakhs.
8,530 dáms.

Foujdaris of

- Muxsudabad, 8 lakhs of dáms, (8,00,000).
- Islamabad, 64 lakhs of dáms, (64,00,000).
- Kuch-Behar, 64 lakhs, (64,00,000).
- Karimabad, 8 lakhs, (8,00,000).
- Midnapur, 12 lakhs of dáms, (12,00,000).
- Hughli, 12 lakhs of dáms, (12,00,000).

Translated by WAHIDUDDIN AHMAD, *Interpreter and Translator, High Court, Original Side.*

TRANSLATION OF A SANAD FROM THE VIZIER OF THE EMPEROR SHAH ALUM, GRANTING TO NAWAB SAIF-U-DOWLAH, JAGHIRS IN BEHAR, DATED JUNE 19TH, 1766.

Seal of the Vizier
Mirza Akbar Shah
Bahadur.

To the Choudhuris, Kanongoes, Mukuddams, tenants and cultivators of Pergunnah Palain, etc., appertaining to Subah Behar.

Let it be known to you.—Whereas the sum of four crores forty-five lakhs ninety thousand and twenty dáms (4,45,90,020), subject to condition and without condition, is, upon the death of Mir Najim-u-Din Ali Khan, fixed (*i.e.*, granted) as the Jaghir of the seat of nobility and respectability, Saif-ul-Mulk Saif-u-Dowlah Syud Najabut Ali Khan Bahadur Shahamutjang, commencing from half (*i.e.*, from) *Rubee* season of *Enut Eal* [or year of the horse], as mentioned in Zimmun (as per details on back). It is necessary that you should pay up the revenue and all civil dues, duly and faithfully, according to the usual practice and custom, unto the *Amil* (Revenue Collector) of that place; and that you should not fail to act up to what is just, right, and proper. Written out on the 7th day of the holy month of Mohurram in the seventh year of the auspicious *Juloos.*

Seal of the Vizier's office affixed on the 19th day of the holy month of Mohurram in the seventh year of the auspicious *Juloos.*

Granted in favour of the seat of nobility and respectability, Saif-ul-Mulk Saif-u-Dowlah Syud Najabat Ali Khan Bahadur Shahamutjang, Pergunnah Palain, etc., in *Subah* Behar, upon the death of Mir Najim-u-Din Ali Khan (Najim-u-Dowlah) subject to condition and without condition, commencing from *half Rubee* season of *Enut Eal* [or year of the horse].

4,45,90,020 dáms.

In respect of Naib Subahdari—
Subject to condition,

1,60,00,000.
Palain in Sarkar Behar,
56,00,000.
Borai in Sarkar Sarun,
4,00,000.
Sassaram in Sarkar Rohtas,
8,00,000.
Havili Shahabad,
84,69,440.
Mahsi in Sarkar Champarun,
7,30,560.

In respect of Foujdari Shahabad—

2,00,00,000.
Havili Azimabad,
42,12,214.
Havili Shahabad,
1,30,786.
Arrah,
85,39,000.
Bonoarah,
3,11,850.
Havili Durbhanga, Sarkar Tirhut,
18,980.
Khalilpur, Sarkar Tirhut,
3,20,000.

Jabdi, Sarkar Tirhut,
40,980.
Nouton, Sarkar Tirhut,
1,048.
Koradi, Sarkar Tirhut,
1,00,000.
Chukmani, Sarkar Tirhut,
5,35,000.
Mokrabpur, Sarkar Tirhut,
75,000.
Ughara, Sarkar Tirhut,
1,57,000.
Thatar, Sarkar Tirhut,
50,000.
Dharur, Sarkar Tirhut,
1,00,000.
Saleenpur, Sarkar Tirhut,
1,50,000.
Parkarpur, Jabdi, Sarkar Tirhut,
40,000.

Gaur, Sarkar Tirhut,
10,480.
Nursia, Sarkar Tirhut,
4,25,000.
Nowa Noan, Sarkar Tirhut,
1,50,000.
Khand, Sarkar Tirhut,
60,000.
Gudsind, Sarkar Hajipur,
1,00,000.
Mahsi, Sarkar Champarun,
5,62,500.
Without condition—
85,29,000.
Bhalowar, Sarkar Behar,
1,15,200.
Bal, Sarkar Sarun,
43,07,904.
Baloguch, Sarkar Hajipur,
11,66,916.

TRANSLATION OF A SANAD FROM THE VIZIER OF THE EMPEROR SHAH ALUM GRANTING TO NAWAB SAIF-U-DOWLAH JAGHIRS IN ORISSA, DATED JUNE 19TH, 1766.

Seal of the Vizier
Mirza Akbar Shah
Bahadur.

To the seat of nobility and respectability, the centre of rank and dignity, the English (East India) Company Bahadur, may you remain the object of the Emperor's favours!

Whereas the sum of two crores thirty-eight lakhs twenty-five thousand and three hundred dáms, from the *Subah* [Province] of Orissa, subject to condition and without condition, is, upon the death of Mir Najim-u-Din Ali Khan, fixed (*i.e.*, granted) as the Jaghir of the seat of nobility and respectability, Saif-ul-Mulk Saif-u-Dowlah Syud Najabut Ali Khan Bahadur Shahamutjang, commencing from half (*i.e.* from) *Rubee* season of *Enut Eal* [or year of the horse], as per details on back; it is, therefore, written (to you) that you should give positive instructions to the Zemindars [land-holders] of that place to the effect that they should pay up the Government revenue and all civil dues, duly and faithfully, according to the usual practice and custom, unto the *Amil* [Revenue Collector] of that place; and that they should not fail to act up to what is just, right, and proper. Written out on the 7th day of the holy month of Mohurram in the seventh year of the auspicious *Juloos*.

Contents of the Zimmun.

Endorsement.—Granted to Saif-ul-Mulk Saif-u-Dowlah Syud Najabut Ali Khan Bahadur Shahamutjang from the *Súbah* of Orissa, upon the death of Mir Najim-u-Din Ali Khan (Najim-u-Dowlah) subject to condition and without condition, commencing from half (*i.e.*, from) *Rubee* season of *Enut Eal* [or year of the horse].

2,38,25,300 dáms.

Conditional,	Without condition,
80,00,000.	1,58,25,300.

Seal of the Vizier's office affixed on the 19th day of the holy month of Mohurram in the seventh year of the auspicious *Juloos.*	Copy received in the office on the 7th day of the holy month of Mohurram in the seventh year of the auspicious *Juloos.*	Corresponds with the entry in the office.

TRANSLATION OF A SANAD FROM THE VIZIER OF THE EMPEROR SHAH ALUM, GRANTING TO NAWAB SAIF-U-DOWLAH JAGHIRS, FOR KILADARI OF ROHTAS, DATED JUNE 19TH, 1766.

Seal of the Vizier
Mirza Akbar Shah.

To the Choudhuris, Kanongoes, Mutasuddis, tenants and cultivators of Pergunnah Havili, in Sarkar Rohtas, appertaining to *Subah* Behar.

Let it be known to you:—Whereas the sum of four lakhs of dáms, from the aforesaid Pergunnah has been fixed (*i.e.*, granted) as the *Jaghir* of the seat of nobility and respectability, Saif-ul-Mulk Saif-u-Dowlah Syud Najabut Ali Khan Bahadur Shahamutjang, subject to condition of *Kiladari* [command of fort], commencing from half (*i.e.*, from) *Rubee* season of *Enut Eal* [or year of the horse], as per details on back; it is necessary that you should pay up the revenue and all civil dues, duly and faithfully, according to usual practice and custom, unto the *Amil* [Revenue Collector] of that place; and that you should not fail to act up to what is just, right, and proper. Written out on the 7th day of the holy month of Mohurram in the seventh year of the auspicious *Juloos.*

Let the Endorsement be written out.

Contents of the Zimmun.

Endorsement.—Granted in favour of the seat of nobility and respectability, Saif-ul-Mulk Saif-u-Dowlah Syud Najabut Ali Khan Bahadur Shahamutjang from Pergunnah Havili, Sarkar Rohtas, *Subah* Behar, subject to condition of *Kiladari*, which was (previously) granted unto Raja Shahmull.

4 lakhs.
dáms 400,000.

Seal of the Vizier's office affixed on the 19th day of the holy month of Mohurram in the seventh year of the auspicious *Juloos.*	Copy received in the office on the 7th day of the holy month of Mohurram in the seventh year of the auspicious *Juloos.*	Corresponds with the entry in the office.

Translated by WAHIDUDDIN AHMAD, *Interpreter and Translator, High Court.*

Translation of the Firman from the Emperor Shah Alum granting to Nawab Saif-u-Dowlah the Subahdari of Bengal, dated June 27th, 1766.

**Seal of Emperor
Shah Alum.**

To the Seat of Chiefship and gentility, the centre of respectability and nobility, the focus of rank and dignity, the cream of the Emirs [Chiefs] of distinguished position, the best among the Khans [Chiefs] of high rank, the helper at the battlefield of success and prosperity, the support of the pillar of the throne of dignity and magnificence, the administrator of affairs of the kingdom, the manager of matters of importance (concerning the State), the founder of the basis of the affairs of sovereignty, the giver of strength to the foundation of devotion and royalty, the asylum of true and sincere friends, the pride of the select persons of sincere feelings, the splendour of the sword of kingdom, the polish of the scimitar of the battlefield for discomfiture of enemies, the chosen among the devoted servants, worthy of (royal) favours and kindness, deserving of unbounded grace and bounties, the object of boundless munificence, the centre of many loyal wishes, Saif-ul-Mulk (sword of the kingdom), Saif-u-Dowlah Syud Najabut Ali Khan Bahadur Shahamutjang.

Be it known to you, while you are favoured and honoured with our manifold royal favours, as follows:—In these auspicious and happy days we, being disposed to show our royal favours and kindness towards our servants and protéges, have been pleased to confer upon you, who are worthy of (our) favours and bounties, the honour and distinction of *Subahdari* of the paradise-like province of Bengal, with *Foujdaris* upon the death of the late Mir Najim-u-Din Ali Khan (Najim-u-Dowlah). You should, by showing your thankfulness towards our exalted self for these unbounded favours, use your best exertions and endeavours in administering and conducting (the affairs of) the said *Subah* [province], and in according kind and good treatment towards the rent-payers, as also in suppressing and punishing bad characters, and turning out and expelling mischievous people from the precincts of your territory. And you should exert your best efforts in dealing gently with our subjects and people in general, and in putting a stop to (the use of) intoxicating drugs and other prohibited articles, preventing mischief, disposing of claims, and deciding litigations in accordance with the holy Mahomedan law and the noble principles of justice, so that the inhabitants of that place may, with perfect assurance and peace of mind, engage themselves in their respective occupations and avocations, and no oppression and injury may be suffered by the weak, and no new practices may be introduced. On this subject our royal directions must be considered as imperative. Written out on the 15th day of the holy month of Mohurram in the seventh year of the auspicious *Juloos*.

Seal of Vizier Mirza Akbar Shah of Gurkani family.

Seal affixed on the 18th day of the holy month of Mohurram in the seventh year of the auspicious *Juloos*.

Contents of the Zimmun.

In the *Risala* of the blossom of the garden of kingdom and royalty, the flower of the orchard of justice and wise rule, the gentle breeze of the flower garden of good nature and world-adorning qualities, the drawn sword of sovereignty and royalty, the polished arrow of the battlefield for discomfiture of enemies and vanquishment of foes, the lion of the forest of manliness and bravery, the horseman of the field of lion-like courage and intrepidity, the light of the sanctuary of kingdom, the priceless pearl of sovereignty, the centre of the circle of state and dignity, the lustre of the eye of ample good fortune, the shining star of the forehead of greatness and dignity, the wielder of the sword as well as the pen, the bearer of the standard of pomp and dignity, the letters patent of the Council of State and grandeur, the binding of the book of wealth and prosperity, the illuminator of the world of distinction, the pearl of the crown of royalty, the defender of the holy religion, the propagator of the commands of the immutable Mahomedan law, the ever-burning lamp of royalty, the best of the descendants of the Gurkani (family), the light of the eye of auspiciousness, the Vizier of the kingdom, the honoured Mirza Mahomed Akbar Shah Bahadur.

Seal of the Vizier's office affixed on the 19th day of the holy month of Mohurram in the seventh year of the auspicious *Juloos*.

Copied on the 21st day of the holy month of Mohurram in the seventh year of the auspicious *Juloos*.

Seal of the State.

Copy received in the office of the *Khalsa Sharifa* on the 23rd day of the holy month of Mohurram in the seventh year of the auspicious *Juloos*.

The august *Firman* was written out according to the entry in the records of *Khalsa Sharifa* office.

Translated by WAHIDUDDIN AHMAD, *Interpreter and Translator, High Court, Original Side.*

TRANSLATION OF THE FIRMAN FROM THE EMPEROR SHAH ALUM GRANTING TO NAWAB SAIF-U-DOWLAH SUBAHDARI OF ORISSA, DATED JUNE 27TH, 1766.

Seal of Emperor
Shah Alum.

To the seat of chiefship and gentility, the centre of respectability and nobility, the focus of rank and dignity, the cream of the Emirs [chiefs] of distinguished position, the best among the Khans [chiefs] of high rank, the helper at the battlefield of success and prosperity, the support at the pillar of the throne of dignity and magnificence, the administrator of affairs of sovereignty, the giver of strength to the foundation of devotion and loyalty, the asylum of true and sincere friends, the pride of the select persons of sincere feelings, the splendour of the sword of kingdom, the polish of the scimitar of the battlefield for discomfiture of enemies, the chosen among the devoted servants worthy of (royal) favours and kindness, deserving of unbounded grace and bounties, the object of boundless munificence, the centre of many loyal wishes, Saif-ul-Mulk (sword of the kingdom), Saif-u-Dowlah Syud Najabut Ali Khan Bahadur Shahamutjang.

Be it known to you, while you are favoured and honoured with our manifold royal favours, as follows:—In these auspicious and happy days, we, being disposed to show our royal favours and kindness towards our servants and protéges, have been pleased to confer upon you, who are worthy of (our) favours and bounties, the honour and distinction *of Subahdari of Orissa with Foujdaris* upon the death of the late Mir Najim-u-Din Ali Khan (Najim-u-Dowlah). You should, by showing your thankfulness towards our exalted self for these unbounded favours, use your best exertions and endeavours in administering and conducting (the affairs of) the said *Subah* [province], and in according kind and good treatment towards the rent-payers, as also in suppressing and punishing bad characters and turning out and expelling mischievous people from the precincts of your territory. And you should exert your best efforts in dealing gently with our subjects and people in general, and in putting a stop to (the use of) intoxicating drugs and other prohibited articles, preventing mischief, disposing of claims, and deciding litigations in accordance with the holy Mahomedan law and the noble principles of justice, so that the inhabitants of that place may with perfect assurance and peace of mind, engage themselves in their respective occupations and avocations, and no oppression and injury may be suffered by the weak, and no new practices may be introduced. On this subject our royal directions must be considered as imperative. Written out on the 15th day of the holy month of Mohurram in the seventh year of the auspicious *Juloos.*

Contents of the Zimmun.

Seal of Vizier Mirza Akbar Shah of Gurkani family.	Seal affixed on the 18th day of the holy month of Mohurram in the seventh year of the auspicious *Juloos.*

In the *Risala* of the blossom of the garden of kingdom and royalty, the flower of the orchard of justice and wise rule, the gentle breeze of the flower garden of good nature and world-adorning qualities, the drawn sword of sovereignty and royalty, the polished arrows of the battlefield for discomfiture of enemies and vanquishment of foes, the lion of the forest of manliness and bravery, the horseman of the field of lion-like courage and intrepidity, the light of the sanctuary of kingdom, the priceless pearl of sovereignty, the centre of the circle of state and dignity, the lustre of the eye of ample good fortune, the shining star of the forehead of greatness and dignity, the wielder of the sword as well as the pen, the bearer of the standard of pomp and dignity, the letters patent of the Council of State and grandeur, the binding of the book of wealth and prosperity, the illuminator of the world of distinction, the pearl of the crown of royalty, the defender of the holy religion, the propagator of the commands of the immutable Mahomedan law, the ever-burning lamp of royalty, the best of the descendants of the Gurkani family, the light of the eye of auspiciousness, the Vizier of the kingdom, the honoured Mirza Mahomed Akbar Shah Bahadur.

			Seal of the State.
Seal of the Vizier's office affixed on the 19th day of the holy month of Mohurram in the 7th year of the auspicious *Juloos.*	Copied on the 21st day of the holy month of Mohurram in the 7th year of the auspicious *Juloos.*	Copy received in the office of the *Khalsa Sharifa* on the 23rd day of the holy month of Mohurram in the 7th year of the auspicious *Juloos.*	The august Firman was written out according to the entry in the record of *Khalsa Sharifa* office.

TRANSLATION OF THE FIRMAN FROM THE EMPEROR SHAH ALUM GRANTING TO NAWAB SAIF-U-DOWLAH THE KILA OF ROHTAS, DATED JUNE 27TH, 1766.

Seal of Emperor
Shah Alum.

In these auspicious times our Royal Mandate, worthy of being obeyed, is issued to this effect:—That upon the death of the late Mir Najim-u-Din Ali Khan (Najim-u-Dowlah), we have been pleased to confer the office of *Kiladar* [Commander of Fort] of Kila Rohtas in the Province of Behar, subject to conditions, upon him who is the seat of chiefship and gentility, the centre of respectability and nobility, the focus of rank and dignity, the cream of the Emirs [chiefs] of distinguished position, the best among the Khans [chiefs] of high rank, the helper at the battlefield of success and prosperity, the support of the pillar of the throne of dignity and magnificence, the administrator of affairs of the kingdom, the manager of matters of importance (concerning the State), the founder of the basis of affairs of sovereignty, the giver of strength to the foundation of devotion and royalty, the asylum of true and sincere friends, the pride of the select persons of sincere feelings, the splendour of the sword of kingdom, the polish of the scimitar of the battlefield for the discomfiture of enemies, the chosen among the devoted servants, worthy of (royal) favours and kindness, deserving of unbounden grace and bounties, the object of boundless munificence, the centre of many royal wishes, Saif-ul-Mulk (sword of the kingdom), Saif-u-Dowlah Syud Najabut Ali Khan Bahadur Shahamutjang. He should do what is needful and customary for the purpose of protecting and guarding the fort, and should not fail to observe due caution and vigilance. He should appoint and employ trustworthy and experienced persons at the gates of the fort, and see that they keep watch and ward in due manner day and night, and do all that is necessary for guarding and protecting the same; and that they shut and open the doors of the fort according to usual practice, and not give admittance to anybody within the fort without permission. He should give positive orders to the servants and dependants to properly guard and watch over the towers and bastions (of the fort), and to replenish the store of grain every year by replacing (the old) grain with new. He should keep the officers and employés of that place content and satisfied, and pay off their wages every two months, according to usual practice, and despatch the records relating thereto, together with a report as to deceased and absconding persons, to the office of the Diwan of the *Subah*. The officers and employés of the said fort, in their turn, should regard the above-named centre of nobility as the permanent *Kiladar*, and consider the powers of the said seat of dignity as regards the administration of affairs pertaining to the said office to be general and absolute, as also consider any praise or complaint made by him to hold good with regard to themselves. Written out on the fifteenth day of the holy month of Mohurram in the seventh year of the auspicious *Juloos*.

In the *Risala* of the blossom of the garden of kingdom and royalty, the flower of the orchard of justice and wise rule, the gentle breeze of the flower garden of good nature and world-adorning qualities, the drawn sword of sovereignty and royalty, the polished arrow of the battlefield for the discomfiture of enemies and vanquishment of foes, the lion of the forest of manliness and bravery, the horseman of the field of lion-like courage and intrepidity, the light of the sanctuary of kingdom, the priceless pearl of sovereignty, the centre of the circle of state and dignity, the lustre of the eye of ample good fortune, the shining star of the forehead of greatness and dignity, the wielder of the sword as well as the pen, the bearer of the standard of pomp and dignity, the letters patent of the Council of state and grandeur, the binding of the book of wealth and prosperity, the illuminator of the world of distinction, the pearl of the crown of royalty, the defender of the holy religion, the propagator of the commands of the immutable Mahomedan law, the ever-burning lamp of royalty, the best of the descendants of the *Gurkani* family, the light of the eye of auspiciousness, the Vizier of the kingdom, the honoured Mirza Mahomed Akbar Shah Bahadur.

Seal of Vizier Mirza Akbar Shah.

Seal affixed on the 18th day of the holy month of Mohurram in the seventh year of the auspicious *Juloos*.

Seal of the Vizier's office affixed on the 19th day of the month of Mohurram in the seventh year of the auspicious *Juloos*.

Copy received in the *Khalsa Sharifa* office on the 23rd day of the month of Mohurram in the seventh year of the auspicious *Juloos*.

Filed on the 21st day of the holy month of Mohurram in the seventh year of the auspicious *Juloos* (illegible).

The august *Firman* was written out according to the entry in the *Khalsa Sharifa* (office).

Translated by WAHIDUDDIN AHMAD, *Interpreter and Translator, High Court, Original Side.*

NAWAB NAZIM MOBARAK-U-DOWLAH.

XI.

MOBARAK-UD-DOWLAH.

MUTAMUN-UL-MULK, MOBARAK-U-DOWLAH, SYUD MOBARAK ALI KHAN BAHADUR, FEROZE JANG.

1770-1793 A.D.

ON March 26th, 1770, Nawab Mobarak-u-Dowlah, the third son of Mir Jaffer, by his wife Bubbu Begum, at the age of eleven succeeded, according to Mahomedan law, his brother Saif-u-Dowlah. The Company drew up the following agreement, which corresponds, with slight changes only, with the treaties signed by previous Nawabs Nazim :—

ARTICLES OF TREATY AND AGREEMENT BETWEEN THE GOVERNOR AND COUNCIL OF FORT WILLIAM, ON THE PART OF THE EAST INDIA COMPANY AND NAWAB MOBARAK-U-DOWLAH, DATED MARCH 21ST, 1770.

On the part of the Company.

We, the Governor and Council, do engage to secure to the Nawab Mobarak-u-Dowlah, the Subahdari of the Provinces of Bengal, Behar, and Orissa, and to support him therein with the Company's forces against all his enemies.

On the part of the Nawab.

Article 1.—The Treaty, which my father formerly concluded with the Company upon his first accession to the Nizamat, engaging to regard the honour and reputation of the Company, and of the Governor and Council as his own, that entered into by my brothers, the Nawabs Najim-u-Dowlah and Saif-u-Dowlah, the same Treaties, as far as is consistent with the true spirit, intent, and meaning thereof, I do hereby ratify and confirm.

Article 2.—The King has been graciously pleased to grant unto the English East India Company, the Diwanship of Bengal, Behar, and Orissa as a free gift for ever; and I, having an entire confidence in them and in their servants, settled in this country, that nothing whatever be proposed or carried into execution by them derogating from my honour, interest and the good of my country, do therefore, for the better conducting the affairs of the Subahdari and promoting my honour and interest and that of the Company, in the best manner, agree that the protecting of the Provinces of Bengal, Behar, and Orissa and the force sufficient for that purpose, be entirely left to their direction and good management, in consideration of their paying the King, Shah Alum, by monthly payments, as by Treaty agreed on, the sum of rupees two lakhs sixteen thousand six hundred and sixty-six, ten annas, and nine pie (Rs. 2,16,666-10-9): and to me, Mobarak-u-Dowlah, the annual stipend of rupees thirty-one lakhs eighty-one thousand nine hundred and ninety-one, and nine annas (Rs. 31,81,991-9) *viz.* :—the sum of rupees fifteen lakhs eighty-one thousand nine hundred and ninety-one, and nine annas (Rs. 15,81,991-9) for my house, servants, and other expenses, indispensably necessary, and the remaining sum of rupees sixteen lakhs (Rs. 16,00,000) for the support of such sepoys, peons, and burkundazis, as may be thought proper for my Sawari only, but on no account ever to exceed that amount.

Article 3.—The Nawab Moin-u-Dowlah, who was at the instance of the Governor and gentlemen of the Council, appointed Naib of the Provinces, and invested with the management of affairs, in conjunction with Maharaja Dulhab Ram and Jaggat Seth, shall continue in the same post and with the same authority, and having a perfect confidence in him, I moreover agree to let him have the disbursing of the above sum of rupees sixteen lakhs for the purposes above mentioned.

This Agreement (by the blessing of God) shall be inviolably observed for ever.

Dated the 21st day of March in the year of our Lord, 1770.

JOHN CARTIER.	CHARLES FLOYER.	JOSEPH JEKYELL.
RICHARD BECHER.	JOHN REED.	THOMAS LANE.
WILLIAM ALDERSEY.	FRANCIS HARE.	RICHARD BARWELL.
CLAUD RUSSELL.		

Mobarak-u-Dowlah, when sending an offering of three lakhs of rupees to the Emperor of Delhi, asked for the usual *sanads* and *firmans* for the Subahdari and Foujdari of the three provinces, and for the jaghir and for the title and rank of "Hast Hazari" (the commander of eight thousand horse), etc.

Under the supervision of the English, Mozuffer Jang now had more power than before in every department, with the exception of the household, which was given into Muni Begum's charge. Maharaja Shitab Rai continued in his office as Naib (Deputy) of Behar. In 1771 famine still extended her ravaging hands over this country. Englishmen were appointed as counsellors to Mozuffer Jang to various districts for collection duties, etc. In addition to the Naibship of the Subahdari (Deputy Subahdarship), and Diwanni, Mozuffer Jang had in his hands the collection duty of Murshidabad and Rajshaye. From January, 1772, by order of the Court of Directors, seventeen lakhs was fixed for the Nazim's personal expenses during his minority. In this year, in April, Mr. Hastings, who had been in the time of Mir Jaffer, English Agent at Murshidabad, came from Madras to Bengal as Governor of Calcutta, and Mr. John Cartier sailed for England. In this year also the Naib Diwanship of Bengal and Behar, respectively, were taken away from the hands of Mozuffer Jang and Rao Shitab Rai. The Revenue department, hitherto in the hands of native officers, was now worked by men appointed by the English. Two councils, consisting of one chief English officer, and some three or four Englishmen, as subordinates, were appointed, one at Murshidabad, and another at Patna. This notice, dated May 11th, 1772 (?), was issued to the Nazim.

DETAILS OF THE REVENUE WORK.—1. To appoint rural collectors. 2. To collect the revenues of Khas Mahals (Government estates). 3. To settle and manage the Pergunnahs. 4. To examine the income of the Mahals. 5. To supervise the accounts, income, and expenses. 6. To instal and depose the zemindars, with the Nazim's approval. 7. To better and improve the condition of the country. 8. To investigate and settle demands of the Revenue Department. 9. To decide the rights and claims of the Talukdars.

Mozuffer Jang and Shitab Rai still remained in their posts of Deputy Nazimship for the civil and criminal duties, which were in the hands of the Nazim.

The Governor, Warren Hastings, came to Murshidabad in July, 1772 A.D., to examine the work of the newly appointed Council. With the sanction of the Nazim, a Nizamat Adalut (Supreme Court) was established at Calcutta as described *pp.* 27, 28. During his two months' and some days' stay at Murshidabad, Hastings dismissed Mozuffer Jang and Shitab Rai from their posts in Bengal and Behar respectively, and appointed Raja Guru Das, son of Nunda Kumar, in place of Mozuffer Jang, and Babu Jaggat Chandra as Nizamat Peshkar, and vested Muni Begum with full powers over the education of the Nazim, and over the household affairs. He returned to Calcutta on September 10th, 1773 A.D., and summoned Mozuffer Jang and Shitab Rai there.

Mobarak-u-Dowlah, at the request of the Governor, dismissed Syud Ali Khan, from whom no good either to the Nizamat or to the Company could be expected, from the Foujdari of Hughli, and appointed

Khan Jehan Khan in his place. The French and the Dutch raised objection to this appointment. The Governor, bringing the matter to the notice of the Nazim, requested him, if it was not against the rules and regulations of the country, to issue *Perwannahs*, in the name of the French, and the Dutch, informing them of the appointment of Khan Jehan Khan to the Foujdari of Hughli; and asking them to acknowledge him. The Nazim addressed letters of information to the Directors of the three Companies, and they were compelled to acknowledge Khan Jehan as the Foujdar of Hughli. The Governor being satisfied with Shitab Rai, recommended him to the Nazim for re-appointment to the Naibat of the province of Behar. The Nizam did so, to oblige the Governor. After receiving the *sanads*, etc., he proceeded to Patna and died there in 1773 A.D. His son, Kalian Singh, succeeded him in the Naibat, with the title of "Maharaja."

In the same year, by *Act* No. iii. of December, 1773, of the English Parliament, it was enacted that the Governor-General of Bengal should be Governor-General of the Indian possessions of the Company, and that he should have four Councillors to advise him in the government of the country. By this law Hastings became the first Governor-General, and Mr. Barwell, General Clavering, Colonel Monson, and Sir Philip Francis, the first four Councillors of the Governor-General. Also, in this year, Mr. Martin succeeded Mr. Middleton as Resident, at Murshidabad.

The Governor-General requested the Nazim to degrade Maharaja Guru Das from the post he then held to that of "Roy Royan," and recommended Mozuffer Jang's re-appointment to his post as Naib Subahdar. On November 10th, the same year, the Nazim acted according to the request of the Governor-General. Mozuffer Jang, on returning to power, made Ali Ibrahim Khan, one of the nobles of Mir Kasim, Diwan of the Nazim's household affairs, and he himself directed the civil and criminal affairs. Mozuffer Jang and Ali Ibrahim Khan soon quarrelled, and Mozuffer Jang, on some pretext, dismissed him, and appointed his own son, Bahrum Jang, to the post.

The French envied the English for their power and authority in the country. This led to hostilities and disputes, which reached a crisis in 1775, when the French erected several factories without the sanction of the Nazim. The Governor-General, informing the Nazim of the matter, to maintain the dignity and authority of the Nazim, razed the newly built French factories to the ground.

In the year 1777 Nawab Mobarak-u-Dowlah abolished the Murshidabad mint at the request of the Governor-General. The Nazim issued *Perwannahs* to the French and Dutch, asking them to have their money coined at Calcutta.

About this time Mr. William Jones, an English merchant, came to Bengal in hopes of carrying on his trade here, side by side with the East India Company. The Governor-General, at the instance of the Court of Directors, requested the Nawab to forbid Mr. Jones to land his merchandise in his (the Nazim's) dominions. The Nawab directed the different Foujdars to enforce this order, and Mr. Jones had no alternative but to go back, disappointed. In this year also the Nazim, at the age of eighteen, took the household affairs into his own hands, and sent *firmans* to the Foujdars of the different places under him, to check the high-handedness of the French in respect of their erecting factories at Birbhum, and Rajshaye, and maintaining soldiers in them.

In 1778 A.D., Rana Chater Singh, Maharaja of Gohud, sent his agent and representative to the Nazim with letters, seeking the Nazim's alliance and friendship, and also requesting the Nawab to recommend the Company to be on good terms with that State. The Nazim acceded to these requests.

In 1779 A.D. Mr. Martin resigned his Murshidabad Residentship. The Governor-General sent Sir John Daly in his place. Also in the same year a dispute arose regarding the salt "duty," and, according to the decision of the Governor-General and Council, the Nazim sent *Perwannahs* to the Foujdars, ordering them to raise the "duties" on *Kar-cutch* salt, imported into Behar and Orissa, to Rs. 30, per hundred maunds, from March, 1780.

In 1781 A.D. the Nazim, at the request of the Governor-General in Council, replaced all the principal native Foujdars, Thannadars, and other Nizamat officers by Europeans.

The East India Company had obtained the military power of the country from Mir Jaffer and Najim-u-Dowlah, and during Najim-u-Dowlah's reign, the revenues came into their hands; now the civil administration, which had hitherto been in the Nazim's hands, was made over to the Company.

In 1783 Maharaja Sundar Singh was appointed Nizamat Diwan. In 1784 the Governor-General sent General Carnac to Mobarak-u-Dowlah, for some reward for the services he had rendered to the State at the time of the war with the Vizier, and the Emperor, as already related. The Nawab, in spite of the heavy pressure on his finances, paid him a lakh of rupees.

In 1785 Warren Hastings left India, and Sir John Macpherson became Governor-General. In the same year the Directors of the Dutch Company put the following questions to the Nazim:—

1. "Whether the East India Company were, as subjects, like the other natives in this country, and if not, as what?"

2. "In whose hands is the government of the country?"

3. "If the East India Company, known as the Diwan, had equal rights in respect of trade as other natives, or what?"

The Governor-General informed the Nazim that what the Hollanders had done, the French and other foreign nations also might do. Consequently he should reply in the following manner:—"That Khan Jehan Bahadur had been appointed from the side of the Nazim, Foujdar of Hughli, for the management of affairs relating to the French, Dutch," etc. An Englishman named Lock had also been deputed for the final settlement of these affairs.

In 1786 the misunderstanding between the English and the French was settled under the following conditions: "That a native custom-house, with Nizamat police, be established on the bank of the river for examining and counting the ships that were expected at, or sailed from, the port of Hughli." On July the 20th, the Nizamat passed the following regulations regarding the management of the custom-house:—

1. "That the Darogah should inform the Nawab fortnightly of the arrival and departure of the ships."

2. "That he should always watch how many ships sailed from, or came to, the port during that time."

3. "And that if prohibited cargoes, such as salt, more than the quantity needed for their own use, and war implements and the like, were found on board any ship, that ship should be held back from either entering, or going out of, the port; and if the master raised objection he should immediately send information to the Commander of the English forces in the vicinity and to other garrisons. In case of finding excess of salt, he should send information to the head of the Salt Department."

In short, after so much adjustment, allowing the establishment of French factories at Saidabad (part of Kasimbazar), etc., kept them (the French) content in their own place.

In 1786 Lord Cornwallis came to India as Governor-General. The Nazim, being informed, wrote a letter of welcome, dated September 13th, 1786, to the new Governor-General. The Governor-General, Lord Cornwallis, addressed a letter of introduction to the Nawab, dated October 2nd, 1786, announcing his arrival in Calcutta and acknowledging the Nazim's friendship, and alliance with the Company, assuring him that the bonds of friendship between him and the Governor would go on increasing daily.

On the 3rd of October the Governor-General wrote, in reply to the Nazim's congratulatory letter, the following:—"I have been sent to the country to maintain the peace and safety of its people and for the welfare of the well-wishers of the Company; so it is my bounden duty to devote myself to the same. I shall try to maintain the friendly relation which has existed between us and your family, for a long time." The Governor-General sent another letter to the Nazim on the 17th of October, in which he spoke highly of the friendship of the Nawab to the Company, and the friendship they had for him. The Nawab, after receiving these friendly letters from the Governor-General, intimated his intention to visit Calcutta in November, 1786.

The Governor-General, as usual, issued orders to the zemindars, etc., asking them to present "Nazars" to the Nawab on his way to Calcutta. The Nawab proclaimed to the zemindars, etc., that he would accept no presents whatever from them, and prohibited any gift, or offering, to him. The Governor-General wrote in reply that the Nawab professed so great friendship for the Company that it was impossible for him to describe it. His refusal to accept presents, which was purely owing to kindness to the people, had been against their wishes, although these presents from the Rajas and Zemindars, proving their prosperity and riches, were of no intrinsic value to the Nazim.

The Nawab reached Calcutta, and the Governor-General and his Councillors paid him great honour. After staying there for some time, he came back to his capital at Murshidabad on December 14th, 1786. The Governor-General, in 1787, directed the Nawab to do away with his soldiers, and to economize his expenditure. In the same year, at the express order of the Court of Directors, the post of the English agent at Murshidabad was abolished, and the Collector of Rajshaye was appointed to carry on the Nizamat affairs.

The Governor-General, in reply to one of the Nawab's applications, through Sir John Daly, for an increment in his stipend, wrote that he was charged by the Directors of the Company to convey to the Nawab that, owing to the friendship that had existed between his father, the late Mir Jaffer, and his brothers, the deceased Najim-u-Dowlah and Saif-u-Dowlah, and owing to the sincerity of the esteem they had for him, they heartily wished to promote his dignity. But on account of the wars (with Tippu Sultan), in which the Company had to take part, for the protection of Bengal and their allies, the expense of which had fallen on their Bengal resources, they were at that time unable to do anything to increase the Nawab's wealth. He should, somehow or other, by retrenching his expenditure, free himself and his dependants from the difficulty of debt, and from the importunities of his creditors. An officer was sent to help him, and a wish expressed that he should, for his own sake, and that of the Company, assist this gentleman in his duties. The Nawab had no alternative but to quietly submit to the policy of Lord Cornwallis.

In 1787 Lord Cornwallis paid a visit to Murshidabad. The Nawab and his courtiers went out as far as ten miles from the city to receive him. After staying for some hours at Murshidabad, the Governor-General proceeded on his tour to Lucknow, Allahabad, and Faizabad.

In 1790 the Queen of the Emperor, Shah Alum of Delhi, asked, through Lord Cornwallis, for one of Nawab Mobarak-u-Dowlah's daughters in marriage for her son. The Nawab rejected the offer in the following terms, in a letter to the Governor-General:—"Please request the Queen to pass over the matter. I cannot, by any means, accede to the proposal. There are many obstacles in the matter. Moreover, there is a long-standing usage in my family, that our daughters can never be given in marriage to any one other than Syuds.* If I act contrary to this, my family custom, I shall be ruined. At all events, my mother and I cannot accept the offer."

Although Nawab Mobarak-u-Dowlah had thirteen daughters, and to some extent regarded himself as a servant of the Emperor, he, for family reasons, did not allow the marriage of one of the thirteen with even such an honourable prince as the Prince of Delhi.

Nawab Mobarak-u-Dowlah died on the 6th of September, 1793. He was buried in Jaffraganj Cemetery. He had, besides the thirteen daughters just mentioned, twelve sons. He left, also,

* The highest of the principal groups of Mahomedans. The Nawabs are Fatimite Syuds.

to mourn his loss, his widows, of whom the chief was Fais-un-nissa Begum, called also Walida Begum. He paid great attention to his friends and relations. He was noted for his liberality and generosity to his dependants; indeed, it amounted at times to extravagance. He was a great lover of music. He kept great singers and music masters. He spent large sums of money on the "Ids," "Bera," "Diwali," and other ceremonies.

XII.

BABER JANG.

NASIR-UL-MULK, AZUD-U-DOWLAH, NAWAB SYUD BABER ALI KHAN BAHADUR, DELIR JANG.

1793-1810.

ON the 24th of September, 1793, Nawab Baber Ali Khan Bahadur, Delir Jang, the eldest son of Nawab Mobarak-u-Dowlah, with the approval of the Governor-General in Council, ascended the Nizamat throne under the title of "Nasir-ul-Mulk, Azud-u-Dowlah, Nawab Syud Baber Ali Khan Bahadur, Delir Jang."

At the instance of the Resident, the Notification of the Governor-General, proclaiming the Nazim's succession, already published in all the districts of the three provinces, was read in a loud voice in the Durbar Hall. It was as follows:—

"Nawab, the Governor-General, Bahadurs of high rank, and the honourable gentlemen of the Council, who have been employed by the Royal Charter, to manage the affairs, in which the Company, as Diwan of the provinces of Bengal, Behar, and Orissa, is interested, do by means of proclamation and vote acknowledge Nawab Azud-u-Dowlah, Nasir-ul-Mulk, Syud Baber Ali Khan Bahadur. Delir Jang, son of the late Nawab Mobarak-u-Dowlah, who is an uniform friend and ally, as heir and successor of the deceased Nawab. We shall not neglect in the minutest degree to help and succour him. At present the Company strictly enjoin all the subjects of the State, and request every well-wisher and dependant of the State, to acknowledge Nawab Nasir-ul-Mulk Bahadur as the true Governor of the three provinces. The nobles and subjects of Murshidabad must present themselves before the said Nawab on the day of his accession."

On September the 10th, 1793, the Governor-General addressed the following letter to the Nazim:—

"Before this, a letter of condolence was written. Now the honourable members in Council have decided that your Highness, who is the eldest son of the late Nawab, and in whose abilities and good behaviour and fitness this Government has full confidence, be acknowledged as Subahdar of the provinces of Bengal, Behar, and Orissa.

"Accordingly, Sir John Harrington has been instructed to attend the auspicious assembly of your Highness' succession to the Nizamat Musnud, and to acknowledge your Highness on behalf of this Government as Subahdar of the three provinces. He is also directed to give publicity of the same to the people at large, by notification and proclamation, and to fix the date of installation in consultation with your Highness. It has been unanimously decided in the Council that the system of the distribution of the Nizamat stipend (namely sixteen lakhs of rupees), as it now exists, in accordance with the circumstances and rules laid down in the scheme, detailing the payment of the amount of the allowance of each individual dependant of the Nizamat, and the liquidation of debts, as sanctioned by the Directors of the East India Company, will hold good and remain upon the same footing in your Highness' case.

"The authorities of this Government are fully sure that due regard and kind consideration, as shown

NAWAB NAZIM BABER JANG.

NAWAB NAZIM ALI JAH.

to all the dependants and relatives of your family, by the late Nawab, your father, and especially in the case of the Nawabs, Muni Begum, and Bubbu Begum, will also be shown by your Highness. Your Highness may be fully assured that the friendship and cordial relations, which existed between this Government and the late Nawab, have, with the greatest pleasure and happiness of this Government, and without any difference, been transferred to your Highness. And a due regard for your Highness' rank and honour, and for the protection of your Highness' dignity, according to the high position of that noble family, of which your Highness is the most honoured and dignified head, will ever be continued to, and observed towards, your Highness."

The Nawab, after the accession, dismissed Khali Fullah Khan from the Nizamat Diwanship, and appointed Rai Mahomed to the office, with a salary of Rs. 2,000 a month, and the title of "Rai Bahadur."

The Nawab died on April the 28th, 1810 A.D. He was unrivalled for his liberality and generosity, and especially for his kindness and favour to his chief dependants.

He was very fond of tonics, in the shape of *Kushta* (of gold, etc.). He always searched for and inquired after Jogis and others, who were experts in the making of "Kushtas." He always visited the sacred tombs, especially the Kadam Sharif. He performed the "Tazziadari" with great veneration.

XIII.

ALI JAH.

NAWAB SUJAH-UL-MULK, MOBARAK-U-DOWLAH, ALI JAH, NAWAB SYUD MAHOMED ZAIN-UL-ABDIN KHAN BAHADUR, FEROZE JANG.

1810-1821.

ON the death of Nawab Baber Jang a dispute arose regarding the succession. Nawab Muni Begum, wife of Mir Jaffer, and the courtiers and nobles nominated Nawab Abul Kasim Khan Bahadur, second son of the late Nawab Mobarak-u-Dowlah, who was a favourite on account of his virtues and pleasant manners.

The Resident did not agree with the Begum and her party. He said that as Nawab Baber Jang had left a son, it would be very unjust to place his brother on the "Musnud." Mr. Roche therefore paid no heed to the objections that were raised, and said that the deceased Nawab's eldest son was intelligent and fit for the post, therefore the father's estate and title should pass to him and not to his uncle, or any other relative. Besides that, the Government had to take the Mohamedan law into consideration. Nawab Muni Begum and the courtiers could find no other remedy but silence before the arguments of the Resident. In this matter the Resident was acting under Lord Minto's direction, as is shown by the following letter:—

LETTER FROM LORD MINTO TO NAWAB NAZIM ZAIN-UL-DIN ALI KHAN, DATED MAY 26TH, 1810.

"Mr. Richard Roche, in charge of Nizamat affairs, has received instructions to attend at the *Musnud* of the Subahdari in the Court of that friend on the part of this Government, to invest your Highness with the Subahdari of the three Subahs aforesaid, and publicly to proclaim the auspicious event to the people, and, in concert with your Highness, to fix a day for the ceremony.

"The stipend fixed, on the accession of your august father, by the Honourable East India Company, will be continued to your Highness without any difference; namely, the annual allowance of sixteen lakhs of rupees will be continued to your Highness in monthly issues as usual, in the mode already prescribed, or that your Highness may consider expedient hereafter to arrange in conjunction with the members of this Government for the distribution of the pensions suitably to the circumstances of the dependants of the Nizamat, and also for the liquidation of debts of the Nizamat, the burden of the responsibility whereof has now naturally devolved on your Highness.

"Above all, be assured that this person will, at all times and in all junctures, to the utmost of his power and the best of his ability, proffer his best counsel and exert his most friendly aid in supporting the rank and dignity, and promoting the ease, comfort, happiness, and welfare of that esteemed friend and all his family.

"And that friend may be assured that the friendship and regard this Government showed his honoured father will, without any difference, be freely and willingly transferred to himself, and that all the honours, consideration, and respect due to the exalted station of the family, whereof your Highness is now the head and source of dignity, will be kept in view and observed towards that friend.

"On other points, I would refer you to the gentleman above-mentioned, Mr. Roche, in whose worth and ability I have entire confidence, and favoured by whom you will ever receive renewed proofs of regard and attachment to yourself and family, and the interest I feel in their welfare. I hope that, considering this person a real friend and well-wisher, you will ever gratify him with letters of your health and prosperity. What can I say more? *(Signed)* "MINTO."

After this, on June the 5th, 1810, in the presence of all the Nizamat relations, and nobles of the city and the neighbourhood, Nawab Zain-ul-Abdin, the eldest son of Nawab Baber Jang, ascended the throne under the title of "Sujah-ul-Mulk, Mobarak-ul-Dowlah, Ali Jah, Feroze Jang," in succession to his father.

At the instance of the Resident, the following proclamation was read in a loud voice in the Durbar:—

"Nawab Zain-ul-Abdin, Ali Khan Bahadur, Ali Jah being placed, in the place of Nawab Syud Baber Ali Khan Bahadur, on the Musnud of the Subahdari of Bengal, Behar, and Orissa, has been acknowledged as Nazim. The Company will not flinch from helping and succouring the Nawab."

Khilats and rewards were bestowed on those present at the Durbar, according to their rank. In Ali Jah's time the Nizamat "Deposit Fund," for the extraordinary expenses of the Court, was established, and the Nizamat affairs were carried on as usual. After governing for eleven years and six months, Ali Jah died on Sunday, August 6th, 1821, at three p.m.

He was very fond of music, and he himself was a great musician. He was an expert marksman, and was very fond of shooting. He was extremely kind, liberal, and generous. He left three daughters, but no son.

From the Persian Secretary to Government to His Highness the Nawab Nazim of Bengal, dated April 20th, 1811.

"I have perused your Highness' letters to the Governor-General's address, on the subject of the claims which have been advanced by your Highness' uncles to participate in the property left by her Highness the Bubbu Begum, and also the whole of the correspondence which your Highness' uncles have held with Mr. Roche on that subject.

"I have considered the question to which your Highness' letter and that correspondence relates, with a due regard to *your Highness' rights and privileges, dignity, and honour*, and I have communicated my sentiments on it to Mr. Roche, by whom they will be made known to your Highness, as also certain advice of a nature calculated equally to restore confidence and harmony between your Highness and your Highness' respected uncles, and to elevate the fame of your *Highness' liberality.*"

FROM THE PERSIAN SECRETARY TO GOVERNMENT TO THE SUPERINTENDENT OF NIZAMAT AFFAIRS, DATED APRIL 20TH, 1811.

"I am directed to acknowledge the receipt of your despatches of the 10th of September, and 12th of November, the former enclosing a copy of the correspondence which had passed between you and His Highness the Nawab of Bengal and his Highness' uncles on the subject of their dispute respecting the property of her late Highness the *Bubbu Begum*, the latter transmitting a letter from his Highness the Nawab to the address of the Right Honourable the Governor-General on the same subject; and to inform you, in reply, *that Government, being bound to recognise and support the rights and privileges of the Nazim of Bengal as far as is consistent with the existing order of things*, deems it proper to refer the contested point, being a question arising strictly within his own family, to what would have been the case in the *plenitude of the Nazim's power.*

"The question therefore is simply this: Would the *Nazim at that time* have admitted of the distribution of his female ancestor's property among the heirs according to the laws of inheritance, or would he, according to the *practice of Asiatic Princes*, have considered it as *revertible to the coffers of the Sovereign?* In the opinion of his Excellency the Vice-President in Council, there can be little or no doubt of the latter, and therefore Government will not *interpose its influence to prevent* the appropriation of her late Highness' property by his Highness the Nawab. You will accordingly be pleased to signify this determination to all the parties concerned in the dispute.

"At the same time, as there is every reason to suppose that the *property left by the Bubbu Begum is very considerable*, his Excellency in Council desires that you will intimate to his Highness the Nawab that it might be *advisable* for his Highness *to consider whether it would not be creditable to his liberality* and serve to conciliate his uncles (whose disappointed hopes may be supposed to increase the vehemence of that spirit of animosity against his Highness which has characterized the present unhappy dispute), if he were to *make over to them some portion of the property of their deceased relation.*

"I am directed to transmit to you the enclosed reply from his Excellency the Vice-President to his Highness the Nawab's letter to the Governor-General's address, together with copies of it in the English and Persian languages for your information."

EXTRACT FROM PARAGRAPH 7 OF LETTER OF FEBRUARY 8TH, 1813, FROM THE PRIVATE SECRETARY TO GOVERNMENT, TO THE SUPERINTENDENT OF NIZAMAT AFFAIRS.

"You may state, as the ruling principle adopted in the most unqualified manner by the Governor-General in Council, that *no part of Muni Begum's property* should, in any event, be appropriated to the use or *benefit of the Company*, but that the *whole*, without any reservation, shall be faithfully *applied to the personal advantage of his Highness, to that of the principal members of his family, and to the general accommodation of the Nizamat.*"

LETTER FROM J. MONCKTON, ESQ., AGENT, GOVERNOR-GENERAL, TO JOHN ADAM, ESQ., ACTING CHIEF SECRETARY TO GOVERNMENT, DATED DECEMBER 26TH, 1816.

Paragraph 15. "The sum of Rs. 16,053 being deducted from the *property found in the late Muni Begum's* apartments, the treasure which actually belonged to her Highness, amounted to Rs. 14,85,454-12-0, out of which has been deducted Rs. 8,58,043-14-8, and a further sum of Rs. 44,650, resumed for the purpose of redeeming jewels mortgaged on bond, to the amount of Rs. 50,000, leaving a surplus of Rs. 5,82,760-13-4, which *has been formally made over to his Highness, together with the whole of the jewels, gold and silver utensils, and other property*, amounting, collectively, to about Rs. 8,50,000. *Thus, by the death of her Highness the Muni Begum, the Nawab has acquired personal property to the extent of nearly fifteen lakhs of Rupees, besides the possession of lands and houses, and the chauk* [market] *adjoining the Palace, which alone yields a revenue of* Rs. 12,000 *per annum.*"

EXTRACT FROM LETTER FROM THE ACTING SECRETARY TO GOVERNMENT TO JOHN MONCKTON, ESQ., AGENT, GOVERNOR-GENERAL, DATED JANUARY 4TH, 1817.

2. "The Governor-General in Council has derived satisfaction from learning that the transfer of the treasure of the late *Muni Begum* after effecting the prescribed deductions, and of the other valuable property of the Begum, to the Nawab, has been effected in a manner entirely satisfactory and acceptable to His Highness. Your proceedings with regard to the property ascertained to belong to the Nawasi Begum were entirely proper and consistent with equity, and the Governor-General in Council *approves* and *confirms* the arrangement you adopted *for compensating to the Nawab for the deduction of that sum from what he had been taught to expect was the amount of the Muni Begum's treasure by charging the resources of the Nizamat with the payment of the sum* awarded to the wife of Shums-u-Dowlah on account of the interest on the amount of the stoppages of her stipend."

XIV.

WALAH JAH.

BURHAN-UL-MULK, IHTISHAM-U-DOWLAH WALAH JAH, NAWAB SYUD AHMAD ALI KHAN BAHADUR, MAHABAT JANG.

1821-1824.

OWING to Nawab Ali Jah having no male issue, his brother, Nawab Walah Jah, succeeded him. The Representative of the Governor-General read a proclamation in the presence of those attending the Durbar:—

"Nawab, the Governor-General, Bahadur, the master of the affairs of the East India Company, in the Council, acknowledges and proclaims Nawab Burhan-ul-Mulk, Ihtisham-u-Dowlah Walah Jah, Syud Ahmad Ali Khan Bahadur, Mahabat Jang, younger brother of the deceased Nawab Sujah-ul-Mulk, Mobarak-u-Dowlah, Ali Jah, Syud Zain-ul-Abdin Khan Bahadur, Feroze Jang, who is an uniform friend and faithful ally of the said Company, as Subahdar of the Provinces of Bengal, Behar, and Orissa, and will try his best to help and succour the Nawab. The Company urges all the subjects and officers, and requests all the dependants and allies to acknowledge Nawab Ahmad Ali Khan, Walah Jah as Subahdar of the three Provinces."

The Nawab received on this occasion the following letter, dated August 10th, 1821, from the Marquis of Hastings:—

LETTER FROM THE MARQUIS OF HASTINGS TO NAWAB SYUD AHMAD ALI KHAN BAHADUR, NAWAB NAZIM OF BENGAL, BEHAR, AND ORISSA, DATED AUGUST 10TH, 1821.

"On the receipt of the mournful intelligence of the demise of the late Nawab Zain-ul-Din Ali Khan Bahadur, the elder brother of that friend, no time was lost in transmitting a letter of condolence expressing

Nawab Nazim Walah Jah.

the grief and regret of this person, on the sad and important occasion. This person in Council has now resolved to seat that friend, the dear brother of the deceased Nawab of pious memory, on the Musnud of the Subahdari of the Subahs of Bengal, Behar, and Orissa. Instructions have been accordingly issued to Mr. Francis Russell to repair to the Court where that friend presides, and on the part of this Government to invest your Highness with the Subahdari of the three Subahs aforesaid, and in concert with that friend, to fix a day for the ceremony, and to determine the style and title, and to report to this person.

"The fixed allowances, and other mutually established points, will continue and endure, as approved and sanctioned by the Home authorities in the lifetime of the late Nawab; namely, sixteen lakhs of rupees annually, according to mode and arrangement settled, and that friend, in unison with the members of this Government, may consider proper for the distribution of the pensions, and each Sirkar may deem right with advertence to the position and circumstances of the connections and dependants of the Nizamat, will be, as usual, remitted in monthly issues to that friend; and be assured that the Government will, to the utmost of its power, afford its friendly counsel and aid in promoting the honour and dignity, ease, comfort, happiness, and welfare of that good friend, personally, and of all members of this family.

"And that friend may be assured that the friendship and good-will evinced by the Government for the late Nawab will, without difference, be joyfully and cheerfully continued to himself. And that the honours and distinctions due to the exalted rank of your Highness' family, whose credit, consequence, dignity, and splendour are now combined in that friend will be always paid and faithfully observed.

(Signed) "HASTINGS."

The usual treaty between the Nawab and the East India Company was also signed.

All those present, after presenting "Nazars" and offerings to the Nawab, received from him "khilats" according to their rank. After this the assembly was dismissed. The Nizamat affairs were conducted as usual. The Nawab's law officers were enjoined not to keep any case pending in the Court for more than fifteen days from the date of filing of the application. Certain rules of etiquette of the Court may here be mentioned. It was a rule that the Nawab's relatives after advancing up to a hundred paces within the fort from the gate, must dismount from any horse, or carriage, they might be using. The "Jaggat Seth" and his descendants must dismount at fifty paces, and "Naib Diwans" and "Roy Royans" at twenty-five paces. Other officers and the general public had to come down from their conveyances at the gate. It was also decreed that every morning some elephants with their howdahs, and some horses fully equipped with harness and ornaments, and other equipages befitting a procession, with "alum" (standard) and flags, etc., should be present in the courtyard, or within the kila (fort). They were not allowed to return to their respective departments until the evening. This was an old custom, and one of the few customs of the former Nazims that still prevailed in the Nizamat, kept up by Nawab Walah Jah.

Nawab Walah Jah died on October the 30th, 1824. He always kept in mind the duty of promoting the dignity of his dependants and servants, and of helping the poor and the afflicted. He left one son behind him.

LETTER FROM F. MAGUIRE, ESQ., IN CHARGE OF THE AGENT'S OFFICE, TO A. STERLING, ESQ., ACTING PERSIAN SECRETARY TO THE GOVERNMENT OF INDIA, DATED SEPTEMBER 2ND, 1822.

"I beg to forward a copy of a letter from his Highness the Nawab Nazim to my address on the subject of the property of her late Highness *Fais-un-nissa*, the Walida Begum. As the season of the Mohurram is approaching, his Highness is desirous that the articles appertaining to the 'Tazziadari' should *be made over* to him for the purpose of being employed on the approaching occasion. The letters refer to the whole of the property, but that part of it which his Highness is most anxious about at present are the articles above."

LETTER FROM A. STERLING, ESQ., ACTING PERSIAN SECRETARY TO GOVERNMENT, TO F. MAGUIRE, ESQ., IN CHARGE OF THE OFFICE OF AGENT TO THE GOVERNOR-GENERAL AT MURSHIDABAD, DATED SEPTEMBER 13TH, 1822.

"I am directed to acknowledge the receipt of your letter dated 2nd instant, and, in reply, to inform you that his Excellency, the Most Noble the Governor-General in Council, authorises you to *make over to the charge of his Highness the Nawab Nazim* the whole of the articles in the Mahal of the late *Walida* Begum appertaining to the Tazziadari."

RESOLUTION OF GOVERNMENT DATED OCTOBER 25TH, 1822, UPON MR. AHMUTY'S REPORT, DATED SEPTEMBER 17TH.

* * * * * *

7. "It will be convenient in the first place to notice that the property proved to have been transferred by gift, previous to his late Highness' demise, was of two descriptions:—

First, *property inherited from the Muni and Bubbu Begums*, consisting of—	
Jewels, and silver and gold utensils, valued at	Rs. 6,93,500
Cash	4,23,360
Gunge mahals and other landed property estimated to yield per annum ...	12,000
And secondly, *property of a private and personal nature*, comprising—	
Savings from the Privy Purse	14,00,000
Proceeds of the sale of female wearing apparel	34,000
Accumulation of the Dulin Begum's personal allowances	56,000
Total	Rs. 26,18,860

8. "*The valuable property in cash, jewels, and land left by the Muni and Bubbu Begums was made over by the Government to the Nawab Zain-ul-Din expressly in virtue of his capacity of Nazim of Bengal, and has been always viewed in the light of the public property appropriable only for the general benefit of the Nizamat.* His Lordship in Council has accordingly, from the commencement of the present litigation, seen reason to resolve that whatever might be decided regarding the late Nawab's state of mind during his last sickness, his title to alienate *the state property which had descended to the Nizamat, rather than to him personally, from his ancestors*, should not be admitted. Government discerns abundant ground for adhering rigidly to that resolution, when it considers the real character and circumstances of the alienation attempted, and all the information which has been brought to light by the Commissioner's investigation."

9. "The letter to the address of the Governor-General, about which so much has been said, is very vaguely and suspiciously worded, and relates solely, it should be observed, to transfer, made and completed, of the *property inherited from the Muni and Bubbu Begums.* It runs thus: 'As I have wished after my marriage to purchase for the Amir-un-nissa Begum, my wife, sets of jewellery and other appropriate ornaments, with your Lordship's sanction, there being no set of jewels suited to the rank and dignity or requisite expenditure of the ladies of the household purchased from the Privy Purse of the Nizamat establishment, though my predecessors had given to their ladies everything of the best kind. Reflecting, therefore, on the matter, I had given over to Amir-un-nissa Begum, all the money, golden ornaments, and sets of jewellery left by the late Muni Begum Saheba, my grandmother, which, in your Lordship's spirit, equity, and generous regard for my claims, *were made over to me by the Agent, Mr. Monckton.*'"

LETTER FROM THE ACTING PERSIAN SECRETARY TO GOVERNMENT TO THE AGENT, GOVERNOR-GENERAL, MURSHIDABAD, DATED OCTOBER 25TH, 1822.

Paragraph 5.—"The disposal of the effects and property left by the *Fais-un-nissa, or Walida, Begum* remains still to be determined on. On that subject, no orders can be passed by Government, until a full report shall have been furnished by yourself of their value and description, distinguishing what portion appertains to the office of Chief Lady of the Mahals, and what should be considered private and personal property. You are desired, therefore, to take these points into consideration, and to submit the requisite information as early as possible."

TRANSLATION OF A LETTER FROM THE GOVERNOR-GENERAL TO NAWAB NAZIM WALAH JAH, DATED NOVEMBER 1ST, 1822.

Paragraph 1.—"According to the decision of the aforesaid gentleman (Mr. Ahmuty), it clearly appears that the late Nawab Syud Zain-ul-Din Ali Khan Bahadur, may God show mercy to him and pardon his sins, was in the perfect enjoyment of his senses at the time when he signed the letter addressed to me, as also at the time when *he gave the properties* and the articles in question to the *Begum* Saheba. But those properties and goods are of two descriptions, that is, a portion of those articles belonging to the estate of the late Nawab *Muni Begum* Saheba and *Bubbu Begum* Saheba, may God have His mercy on them, and the other portion was the personal property owned and held by the late Nawab. Accordingly, in my opinion, the properties that formed the *estate of the two Begums exclusively belong to the Nizamat, and cannot be transferred to any one.* The late Nawab Saheb had not the authority to give those articles, in any way or shape whatever, to the Begum Saheba. Under such circumstances, *the jewellery, cash, articles, and the Mahals,* as per details given, in a separate sheet, fall under the head and classification No. 1; and *your Highness has got them back from the Deorie of the Begum Saheba, and those shall remain in the custody and control of your Highness, who is the Rais (head) of that noble family and the present Nazim.*

"Details of property, articles and jewellery and Mahals in dispute, which are divided into two classes :—

"Class 1 includes those properties and articles that, according to the decision of the officers of the Government, are the *properties of the Nizamat, and should remain in the custody of Nawab* Burhan-ul-Mulk Walah Jah, Syud Ahmad Ali Khan Bahadur Mahabat Jang, the present Nazim.

(1) "Jewellery and articles of the estate of the late Nawab Muni Begum Saheba.

(2) "Cash, value Rs. 4,13,360.

(3) "Mahals of the estate of Nawab Muni Begum Saheba and Bubbu Begum Saheba."

LETTER FROM THE AGENT TO THE GOVERNOR-GENERAL TO THE ACTING PERSIAN SECRETARY TO GOVERNMENT, DATED NOVEMBER 29TH, 1822.

"Her Highness *(Fais-un-nissa Begum)* expired on the night of December 30, 1820. . . . The whole of the articles appertaining to the 'Tazziadari' *were made over* by the acting Agent *to the charge of his Highness* the Nazim. . . . With reference to the instructions contained in the fifth paragraph of your letter, and dated the 25th ultimo, relative to what part of the property left by Fais-un-nissa Begum appertaining to the office of Chief Lady of the Mahals, it clearly appears, from any information that can be obtained on this subject, that the whole must be considered personal property. The jewels were given to her by the late Mobarak-u-Dowlah; the plate and the various *articles appertaining to the 'Tazziadari' were provided from her own funds, the cash savings from her personal stipend*, and revenue of her lands, and these also she had become possessed of prior to her succession to the Jainashin of the *Deories*.

"It appearing, therefore, that the Walida Begum has made no specific bequests, *that her three daughters* are amply provided for, that all the effects and property can but be considered private and personal, and that His Highness is ready and anxious to meet her wishes with regard to her old servants, and the religious rites, I am not aware of any reason for deviating from the *precedent established by Mr. Pattle and Mr. Monckton, in the cases of the Bubbu and Muni Begums*, and submit, therefore, to the consideration of Government the expediency of transferring the effects of the late *Walida Begum* as they were, *to the reigning Nazim*, with proviso that if Moti Begum makes good her claim on the bonds, and they are proved to be legal ones, the several amounts are to be paid by His Highness."

LETTER FROM THE ACTING PERSIAN SECRETARY TO GOVERNMENT TO THE AGENT, GOVERNOR-GENERAL, AT MURSHIDABAD, DATED JANUARY 31ST, 1823.

"I am directed to acknowledge receipt of Mr. Ricketts' report on the effects and property of the late *Walida Begum*, dated November 29th last, and his subsequent letter in continuation, dated 21st instant.

"The following appears to be a rough statement of the amount of that property:—

	Rs.	as.	ps.
Cash	54,879	12	0
Jewels and plate	80,000	0	0
Shawls, etc.	12,000	0	0
Total Rupees ...	1,46,879	12	0

3. "The Honourable the Governor-General in Council concurs with the late Agent in opinion that His Highness the *Nawab Nazim is entitled to be recognised as the Begum's heir both as being her grandson and nearest male relation, and likewise on the ground of the usage of the Nazim's family and the precedents established in the cases of the Muni and Bubbu Begums.* It appears clear also from the style and tenour of the letters addressed to the Nawab Zain-ul-Din Ali Khan and to Mr. Ricketts by Her Highness, that she contemplated the Nazim's succeeding to her property as a matter of course. It will, of course, be incumbent on His Highness to fulfil the bequests of the Walida Begum by providing for her servants and by assigning funds for the maintenance, on a proper footing, of the religious ceremonies and observances specified in the above letters.

4. "Entertaining these sentiments, the Governor-General in Council desires you will inform the Nawab Nazim that *Government has no objection to offer to his taking possession of the property of his deceased grandmother as her legal heir.*"

TRANSLATION OF A LETTER ADDRESSED BY THE AGENT, GOVERNOR-GENERAL, ON MARCH 1ST, 1823, TO HIS HIGHNESS THE NAWAB WALAH JAH.

"His Highness Nawab Saheb, the high in dignity, the bestower of favour, the recogniser of merits and the benefactor of those who seek bounty, may his favours increase.

"After expressing a desire for meeting, which is capable of creating good results, the substance of what this well-wisher thinks, is submitted to your Highness. The very kind and good Mr. M. Raikes had submitted to his Excellency the Governor-General a report of the estate left by the late Nawab *Fais-un-nissa Begum* Saheba, may God pardon her sins. Upon that an intimation has been received to the effect that *His Excellency gives to your Highness, the head and representative of the family, the properties left by the deceased in the same way as the predecessor of your Highness, the late Nawab Ali Jah*, may God pardon his sins, *received the estate left by the deceased Bubbu Begum Saheba*, may God pardon her sins."

XV.

HUMAYUN JAH.

SUJAH-UL-MULK, IHTISHAM-U-DOWLAH HUMAYUN JAH, NAWAB SYUD MOBARAK ALI KHAN BAHADUR, FEROZE JANG.

1824-1838.

NAWAB WALAH JAH'S son, Nawab Syud Mobarak Ali Khan Bahadur Humayun Jah, at the age of fourteen, ascended the Nizamat throne in succession to his father. The ceremony of installation took place at 10 a.m. on Thursday, December the 23rd, 1824. His titles were "Sujah-ul-Mulk, Ihtisham-u-Dowlah Humayun Jah, Nawab Syud Mobarak Ali Khan Bahadur, Feroze Jang." The relatives of the Nawab, the officers and other nobles of the city and the neigbourhood, presented "Nazars" and received, in return, "Khilats," and rewards, according to their rank. At the instance of the Agent, Babu Pran (?) Nath, Mir Munshi, read the usual proclamation of the Government to the assembly. At this time Mr. Lock was Agent to the Governor-General.

The Nawab received the following letter, dated January 14th, 1825, from Lord Amherst, on this occasion:—

LETTER FROM LORD AMHERST TO NAWAB SYUD MOBARAK ALI KHAN BAHADUR, FEROZE JANG, NAWAB NAZIM OF BENGAL, BEHAR, AND ORISSA, DATED JANUARY 14TH, 1825.

"Truly, on receiving the joyful intelligence of the happy installation of your Highness on the 'Chahar Balish' (throne) of ancestral authority, the budding of joy of this friend so bloomed with delight that to describe one of its thousand blossoms or to dress a single rose from the bough in just array is beyond the flowers of rhetoric.

"May He who is High and Holy, consecrate and prosper this auspicious event, so happily commenced and completed to the credit and honour of your Highness, and the dependants of your exalted family, and long preserve you in health and felicity.

"Your Highness may be assured that the regular fixed allowances and other mutually settled points will remain and continue, as approved and sanctioned by the Home authorities in the time of the late Nawab Syud Ahmad Ali Khan Bahadur, that good friend's noble father, namely:— sixteen lakhs of rupees per annum in reference to the regulation and arrangement which have been fixed, and your Highness may, in future, consider proper to concert with the members of this Government for the distribution of the pensions according to the judgment of both Sirkars, suitable to the condition of the dependants of the Nizamat, will be issued, as usual, in monthly portions, to that friend.

"And every mark of friendship and regard shown by this Government to the late Nawab will, without difference, be cheerfully and joyfully continued to your Highness, and the respect due to the rank and the honours and distinctions appropriate to the high and eminent family of your Highness, whereof the elevation, splendour, conduct, and direction, now centred in your Highness, will be always kept in view and observed.

(Signed) "AMHERST."

In 1826, the second year of his rule, Humayun Jah married a daughter of the late Nawab Ali Jah, his uncle. In the same year he undertook a journey to Patna for a change.

When he attained his majority and took the management of his affairs into his own hands, his first act was to dismiss Raja Ganga Dhur from the Nizamat Diwanship.

At Findal Bagh, or, as it is now called, Mobarak Munzil, had been erected the Courts of Justice of the Company, unused, after the administration of law and justice was removed to Calcutta. There were three buildings on this spacious property. In May, 1830, the Nawab bought the garden then called "Findal Bagh" and the house "Findal Kothi," from Raja Kissen Chand Bahadur and Kumar Ram Chand of Nashipur for Rs. 35,000. He made it into a pleasure garden and erected the "Red Bungalow," known also as "*Moti Mahal.*" He named the garden "*Mobarak Munzil.*"

In August, 1831, the Nawab also acquired from the English, through Mr. Pringle, Agent to the Governor-General and acting Magistrate of the city of Murshidabad, the other buildings and the rest of the land forming the Mobarak Munzil Estate.*

From the time of the removal of the Sudder Diwanni Adalut to Calcutta to the time of its coming into the Nawab's hands, the Foujdari Katcheri was held in one of the buildings. The buildings in which these and other offices were held are still in existence.

In the fifth year of his rule, during the administration of Lord William Bentinck, on August the 9th, 1829, the Nawab Nazim laid the foundation of the main palace, near the river bank. It was completed during the administration of Lord Auckland, in 1837. It is known as *the* palace or "*Bara Kothi,*" to distinguish it from the old fort, the *Kila*, and the new palace, built much later.

In 1833 Nawab Humayun Jah sent Mr. W. Chinnery, with numerous presents and gifts, to William IV, King of England. The King, in return, by a letter dated September 14th, 1856, which is still in the palace, and of which we give a photographic *facsimile*, showing the autograph of William IV, conferred on the Nazim the Grand Cross of the Royal Hanoverian Guelphic Order, with the Insignia. The King sent, also, a life-size portrait of himself. Mr. Chinnery brought with him from England various pictures, and handsome furniture, purchased for the Nawab's new palace.

Nawab Humayun Jah, by his luxuriousness and ambition, brought to memory some of the former Nazims. He died on Wednesday, October 3rd, 1838. He had one son, Nawab Feradun Jah, and one daughter, Sultana Satiara Begum.

* This is now some three and a half miles from the city, and is used as a country residence, and polo ground. There are also some good lawn tennis courts in the gardens.

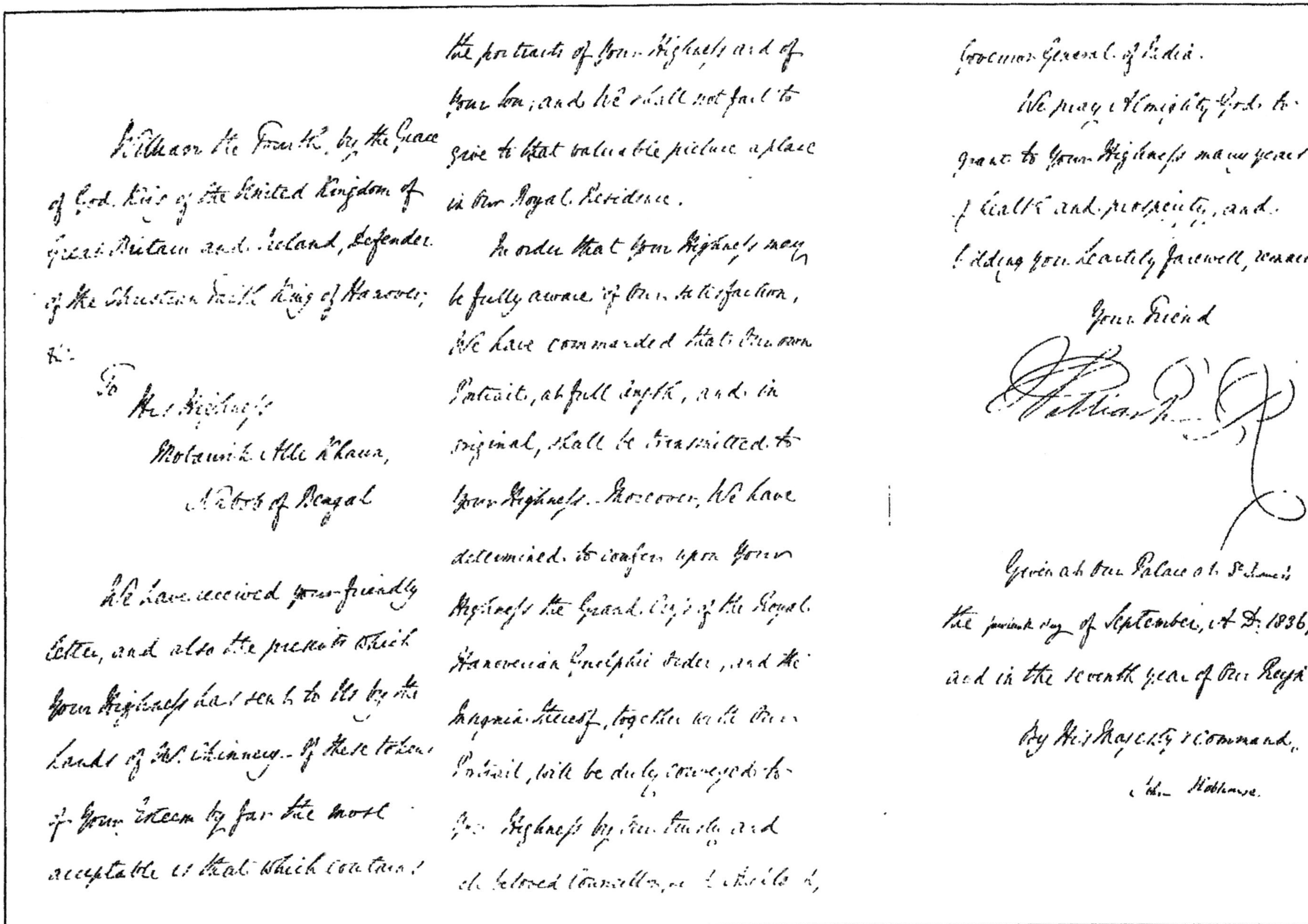

William the Fourth, by the Grace of God, King of the United Kingdom of Great Britain and Ireland, Defender of the Christian Faith, King of Hanover, &c.

To His Highness
Mobarik Ally Khaun,
Nabob of Bengal

We have received your friendly Letter, and also the presents which Your Highness has sent to Us by the hands of Mr. Chinnery. Of these tokens of Your esteem by far the most acceptable is that which contains the portraits of Your Highness and of Your Son; and We shall not fail to give to that valuable picture a place in Our Royal Residence.

In order that Your Highness may be fully aware of Our satisfaction, We have commanded that Our own Portrait, at full length, and in original, shall be transmitted to Your Highness. Moreover, We have determined to confer upon Your Highness the Grand Cross of the Royal Hanoverian Guelphic Order, and the Insignia thereof, together with Our Portrait, will be duly conveyed to Your Highness by Our trusty and well beloved Counsellor [illegible], Governor General of India.

We pray Almighty God to grant to Your Highness many years of health and prosperity, and bidding you heartily farewell, remain

Your Friend

William R.

Given at Our Palace at St. James's the [illegible] day of September, A.D. 1836, and in the seventh year of Our Reign.

By His Majesty's Command,

John Hobhouse.

Facsimile of Autograph Letter of William IV. to Nawab Nazim Humayun Jah.

NAWAB NAZIM FERADUN JAH.

XVI.

FERADUN JAH.

NAWAB NAZIM MUTIZUM-UL-MULK, MOSHIN-U-DOWLAH FERADUN JAH, SYUD MUNSUR ALI KHAN BAHADUR, NASIRAT JANG.

1838-1881.

NAWAB NAZIM FERADUN JAH was born in October, 1830, and succeeded his father on December the 19th, 1838. He was then eight years old. Like all the Nawabs Nazim, he possessed a long train of titles, viz.: "Mutizum-ul-Mulk, Moshin-u-Dowlah Feradun Jah, Nawab Nazim, Subahdar of Bengal, Behar, and Orissa." His first tutor and guardian was General Showers. The boy was clever and well educated, and extremely fond of books, adding, as he grew up, many volumes to the fine library in the Nizamat Palace.

In February, 1869, he went to England and stayed there for twelve years, returning in 1881. His journey was not altogether one of pleasure, and much of his time was spent pleading his case against certain orders of the Government of India. His excessively generous nature had at times led him into extravagance and debt. In the end he was obliged to sell many of the family jewels and to relinquish the higher title of "Nazim." Worn out with trouble and disappointment, he abdicated in favour of his son, the present Nawab Bahadur, in 1881. His remaining years were spent in the privacy of his family. He died in 1884. The last of the Nawabs Nazim was a fine horseman and all-round sportsman, whose spear had cut short the career of many a wild boar, and whose rifle had accounted for many a tiger.

When the Nawab Nazim Humayun Jah died in 1838, his only son, then a minor, became, as noted, his successor at Murshidabad. Mr. W. H. Elliott, appointed Agent to the Governor-General in December, 1838, relinquished charge of the Nizamat affairs in February, 1839, and the care of the boy Nawab passed into the hands of Colonel Caulfield. During the period from January, 1840, to December, 1846, there were many changes, three Agents being appointed and relieved. The affairs of the family must have become somewhat disordered by all these changes, and the lot of Mr. Torrens, appointed Agent to the Governor-General, December 17th, 1846, was, no doubt, not a happy one. The young Nawab Nazim could not take any part in the management of his affairs, and there is no doubt that he was surrounded by many intriguers, whose only idea was that of self-interest. Mr. Torrens was absent from April to December, 1851; in 1852, on August 15th, he died. When the Nawab Nazim came of age and began to inquire into matters, he found that confusion reigned in all departments. Money could not be accounted for, and there was a want of friendly co-operation between the native officials and the European Agent, and his officers. The Government had found it necessary to appropriate certain so-called "Nizamat funds," and had made new arrangements with regard to the Nawab's stipend. It is not unnatural that the Nawab should want explanations, and he resented what, for want of full information, he regarded as acts of injustice. The Nawab began to take an active interest in matters, and, finding much to complain of, made certain inquiries during the year 1852. We must remember that he was then a young man, only twenty-two years of age, and that he spoke and wrote with the "hot blood of youth." An unfortunate occurrence in April, 1853, prejudiced him in the eyes of Lord Dalhousie. The theft of some jewels from the Nawab's camp was followed by severe punishment of the thieves, indirectly causing their death. The Nawab's officers, taking justice into their own hands, had these men beaten, and death ensued. The evidence is conflicting, and there is reason to believe that the charge of murder was a severe one, as there was no intention to kill. Although the Judge, on appeal, acquitted the chief eunuch, Aman Ali Khan, it was unwise of the young

Nawab to receive him back into favour, though we can well understand that much pressure would be put upon the Nawab in the case of such an old and trusted servant. In November, 1853, the Governor-General directed Nawab Nazim Feradun Jah to dismiss the accused eunuchs, and the Nawab, feeling that their case was a hard one, refused. It is clear that the Governor-General thought that the Nawab should be held responsible for the acts of his servants. The example would have been bad if the action of the eunuchs had been overlooked; and the position of the Governor-General was that of the representative of justice. The Nawab's salute of nineteen guns was taken from him, and he was deprived of the privilege of "non-appearance" in Civil Courts. This he must have felt deeply, as all native gentlemen consider it a degradation to appear personally before a Law Court. This privilege, granted under old *Acts* of 1805, 1806, and 1823, was bound to go in time, and was practically cleared away by an *Act* of 1854. Allowance must be made for the difference of feeling on such matters between natives of the East and the West, and such allowance will explain much of the subsequent strife of words which existed between the Nawab Nazim and the Government of India. Against Mr. Torrens the Nawab's feelings were those of dislike and distrust; and the loss of large sums of money, and the dismissal of the Diwan Raja Sitanath, only widened the gap. Death removed Mr. Torrens from the strife, and it would have been unfair to judge him or condemn him unheard.

In the confusion that reigned at Murshidabad, the jewels and insignia of the "Grand Cross of the Hanoverian Order" had been sold in Calcutta. The Order, as we have read, had been sent to Nawab Nazim Humayun Jah by William IV, and it must be evident to consideration, unclouded by anger, that no responsible European would wilfully have removed such jewels to an auction room in Calcutta. Misplaced trust in underlings is the worst supposition in the case of Mr. Torrens, and this was shown to be the case at a later period. Fortunately, most of the insignia were recovered in 1855, but two diamond stars had entirely disappeared.

In 1853 Raja Prosunno Narain Deb had been appointed Diwan, and for nearly eight years this officer managed the Nawab's affairs well, and to the satisfaction of the Agents to the Governor-General. He had, however, a rival in the Court, one Hakim Abdul Hussain, an adventurer, who had been appointed Court physician. This man, in the opinion of Colonel Mackenzie, had caused an estrangement between the Nawab Nazim and his Diwan, and the Raja was dismissed in May, or June, 1861. This led to strained relations between the Nawab Nazim and the Agent to the Governor-General, Colonel Colin Mackenzie.*

The Nawab Nazim's plastic nature was the cause of most of his troubles. He lacked self reliance and trusted too much to the opinions of those around him. His petitions to the Government of India were rejected, and one cannot help feeling that ill fortune need have pursued the Nazim no further if he had found a wise adviser among his officers. He had about this time, as private secretary, a European, Mr. Fox. This gentleman, wanting in penetration, failed to see that the claims put forward by the Nawab Nazim could not possibly be admitted. With the blind faith of ignorance, Mr. Fox added his voice to those who advised the Nawab Nazim to carry his case to England, there to lay it before the House of Commons. While I willingly admit that Mr. Fox, erred only from inability to grasp the intricacies of the question, I cannot do as much for some of the others who joined in leading the Nawab Nazim into fresh difficulties.†

The Nawab Nazim's petition found supporters in the House of Commons, and came on for discussion at the night sitting of Tuesday, July 4th, 1871. The opening speech was made by Mr. Haviland Burke. This gentleman moved for a Select Committee to consider all "Treaties and Agreements entered into between the East India Company, or any person on their behalf, with the Nawab Nazim of Bengal, Behar, and Orissa, or his predecessors, and to ascertain whether such treaties and agreements had been faithfully

* "Storms and Sunshine of a Soldier's Life." (36.)

† This Biography is written by the Editor.

observed by the said Company and by the Indian Government, and to what claims, if any, the Nawab Nazim and his family might be rightly entitled under, and by virtue of, such treaties and agreements."*

The main question was: Were the treaties made with the various Nawabs Nazim, beginning with Mir Jaffer, personal treaties, or were they continuous, hereditary, and binding for ever? The reader may, with advantage, turn back and read over the treaties again. His first conclusion will be that, if words mean anything, the treaties are hereditary, and could not lapse with the death, or deposition of the Nawabs Nazim with whom they were made. It may, I think, be safely said that any legal document wearing an apparent air of simplicity is to be regarded with suspicion. Certain it is that the more one reads these treaties and compares the situation with that in which rulers in other countries stand in regard to their claims on their country's revenues, the more we see that each treaty was never meant to have been more than personal. No people would tolerate treaties binding them to follow blindly the agreements made with, or by, previous rulers, regardless of differences in form of government, attitude of the power controlling the country's revenues, and the importance of other claims upon the said revenues. For it must first be understood that the money in question, the revenues of Bengal, Behar, and Orissa, was not *at any time* the personal property of the Nawab Nazim, any more than the revenues of England are the property of the King. And just as the House of Commons decides, in each individual case, what part of the revenues shall be set aside for the Civil List, which includes the amount voted for private and public expenses of the King, so the East India Company, and the Government of India, which superseded the Company, had a perfect right to decide in the case of each Nawab Nazim what his personal allowance should be, and also what sums were required for what we may call his Civil List. It is true that when the Emperor Shah Alum made over the revenues of Bengal, Behar, and Orissa, to Lord Clive, as representing the East India Company, he laid down certain conditions:—twenty-six lakhs out of the revenues were to be paid to him in Delhi by the Nawab Nazim on receipt of his allowance from the Company. The Emperor did not give up his share of the revenues.†

The motion was lost: for, 64; against, 121.

The Nawab Nazim, Syud Munsur Ali Khan, died in 1884, leaving, surviving him, his mother, Rais-un-nissa Begum, three widows, Mulkazamania Begum, Shumsi Jehan Begum, and Shah-un-nissa Begum; also nineteen sons, namely:—

1. Hassan Ali Mirza. H.H. the Nawab Bahadur.
2. Hussain Ali Mirza. Mujlah Huzur.
3. Mahomed Taki Mirza (deceased). Syud Amir Saheb.
4. Assad Ali Mirza. Subah Saheb.
5. Vahed Ali Mirza. Nawab Jan Saheb.
6. Nasir Ali Mirza. Chotu Saheb.
7. Iskunder Ali Mirza (deceased). Sultan Saheb.
8. Khakan Mirza. Budhan Saheb.
9. Bahram Mirza (deceased).
10. Farhad Mirza. Farhad Saheb.
11. Kaikaus Mirza (died, of cholera).
12. Daud Mirza (died, P.P.).

* Those who wish to read the speeches made during this debate will find them among the published Parliamentary Papers. I shall merely quote such portions as are essential to the narrative.

† Mr. Grant Duff (as he then was) spoke against the claim, quoting Sir R. Palmer and Mr. Leith, the Nawab's own Counsel; still there were found other law experts equally convinced of the justice of the opposite view.

13. Jaffer Mirza (deceased).
14. Bakr Mirza. Bakr Mirza Saheb.
15. Syud Ali Mirza (in England).
16. Nusrut Ali Mirza (in England).
17. Shoeb Ali Mirza (died in England).
18. Musa Ali Mirza (in England).
19. Hamed Ali Mirza.

Also twenty-one daughters:—

1. Khyrun-nissa *alias* Ramzani Begum (in Lucknow).
2. Wahidun-nissa *alias* Sahebzadi Begum.
3. Lutfun-nissa *alias* Chahiti Begum.
4. Mulkun-nissa *alias* Hurmuzi Begum (H.H.'s own sister).
5. Hedayutun-nissa *alias* Hossaini Begum.
6. Kazimi Begum (H.H.'s sister).
7. Azizun-nissa *alias* Nishani Begum (dead) (Subah Saheb's sister).
8. Wuziri Begum.
9. Gulshun-un-nissa *alias* Sakhina Begum (deceased).
10. Kobra Begum.
11. Shaherbanu *alias* Suffri Begum.
12. Nair-un-nissa *alias* China Begum (dead).
13. Rokia *alias* Kali Begum.
14. Elahi Begum (Daud Mirza's sister).
15. Gowhorun-nissa *alias* Ali Begum.
16. Afrozun-nissa *alias* Umal Fatima Begum.
17. Jowherun-nissa Ladli Begum
18. Mariam Begum.
19. Vahedun-nissa Begum.
20. Zahura *alias* Guria Begum, and
21. Razia *alias* Peari Begum (deceased).

By an Indenture, made between Her Majesty's Secretary of State for India in Council and Nawab Nazim Syud Munsur Ali Khan, on the 1st November, 1880, the Nawab Nazim abdicated his position without prejudice to such right as any member of his family might have, and his eldest son, Hassan Ali Mirza, as head of the family, inherited all his property, to the exclusion of his other heirs.

SIR SYUD HASSAN ALI MIRZA, G.C.I.E., NAWAB BAHADUR OF MURSHIDABAD.

PRINCE WASIF ALI MIRZA (HEIR)

PRINCE NASIR ALI MIRZA.

XVII.

SIR ALI KADAR SYUD HASSAN ALI MIRZA, G.C.I.E.

NAWAB IHTISHAM-UL-MULK, RAIS-U-DOWLAH, AMIR-UL-OMRAH, SIR ALI KADAR SYUD HASSAN ALI MIRZA, KHAN BAHADUR, MAHABAT JANG, G.C.I.E.*

1881—LONG LIFE TO HIM!

THE present head of the Murshidabad family was born on the 2nd of Ramzan, 1262 (August 25th, 1846), and is the eldest of a family of nineteen sons and twenty-one daughters. When the young Nawab was five months old the ceremony of *Khir Khotal*, or weaning, took place, on December 23rd, 1846. During the display of fireworks, on that occasion, the old Imambara caught fire. Being mainly built of wood, the building burnt rapidly, and the flames were soon beyond control. To replace the loss, the present splendid Imambara was built. The Nawab Bahadur's education was carried out by English tutors, and in 1865, at the age of nineteen, he and two of his brothers, the present Mujlah Huzur and the late Amir Saheb, went to England, under the care of Colonel Herbert, who has left on record a detailed account of their doings, which shows a Boswell's fondness for minutiæ.† Colonel Herbert and his charges left Calcutta on March 9th in the Peninsular and Oriental Company's s.s. "Candia." The voyage was a pleasant one, and the young Princes first went on shore at Cairo. After visiting various places of interest they proceeded by train to Alexandria. After a day spent in drives to places of interest the party embarked in the "Nyanza" on April 5th. On the 19th they reached Southampton. The object of this journey to England and the Continent was mainly to give the Princes an opportunity to visit places of interest, to give them material for thought, and to invite comparison between the ways of the East, and the West. Their education, however, was not neglected. Shortly after his arrival in England, Colonel Herbert engaged Mr. Cooper as their tutor. This gentleman had previously been tutor to Nawab Nazim Munsur Ali, and he brought a note from the Nazim when he first called upon Colonel Herbert. This recommendation ensured his appointment; but Colonel Herbert has left on record his opinion that Mr. Cooper was a success both as a tutor and as deputy guardian, for, as such, he often took Colonel Herbert's place.

The young Princes could not complain of want of variety. Every day brought some new pleasure. Picture galleries, museums, theatres, races, all and every amusement was provided for them. The Nawab Bahadur enjoyed very good health throughout the trip. His brothers were not quite so fortunate, though their ailments were not very serious. In discussing the character of each of the three boys, Colonel Herbert selected Hassan Ali Mirza as his favourite. Though shy, he was amiable, steady, and anxious to learn. The young Nawab displayed a high moral standard, and firmness, which Colonel Herbert considered hereditary characteristics descended from his mother, Nawab Mhir Luka Begum Saheba, an Abyssinian lady. The Nawab Nazim had been very loath to let his sons leave him, and was anxious to have them return after six months, but he was persuaded to let the visit extend over twice that period.

The spring and summer were spent in England. The party, on their arrival, were installed in the South Kensington Hotel. One of their earliest visits was to the Natural History Department of

* Biography written by the Editor.

† No. 10, dated Calcutta, April 6th, 1866. From Lieut.-Colonel C. Herbert to the Secretary to the Government of India, Foreign Department, with the Governor-General, Simla.

the British Museum. While the party were examining with the greatest interest the collection of birds, the Italik Saheb was heard to exclaim, with accents of surprise: "I always understood the Almighty had made ten thousand kinds of birds, but how many more are here!"

The young Nawabs met with kindness on all sides, and many influential persons exerted themselves to make every pleasure, and excursion, available. On May 20th the young Nawabs attended the Levée held by the Prince of Wales, now our gracious King and Emperor. In recognition of their rank they were granted the private entrée.

After a short stay in the South Kensington Hotel, Colonel Herbert moved, with his charges, into No. 29, Pembridge Square. When the agreement was up, on August the 8th, the party returned to the hotel. Of the many interesting persons whom the Nawab Bahadur met during this, his first visit to England, I must not omit to mention Lady Williams, a grand-daughter of Clive. This lady remarked that the meeting of a descendant of Clive with descendants of Mir Jaffer was one worthy of notice. Colonel Herbert records a number of croquet parties, the game, after the "old style," being then a great favourite. It passed out of fashion to re-emerge under more scientific conditions, and is now again in great favour. During their visit the Amir Saheb suffered from an abscess, which the family Hakim was not able to treat. Consent having been obtained, a surgeon was called in. The name of this gentleman, Mr. Culpepper, takes us back a long way, and invites a comparison between the old and the new in the arts of medicine and surgery. When the Amir Saheb was able to move, the brothers went to Sandgate. From there the Nawab Bahadur and his brothers made many excursions along the coast, and visited Dover Castle. A journey from Sandgate to Southsea and Portsmouth, with a view of the shipping, and a visit to the Royal yacht, "Victoria and Albert," came next on the programme. Colonel Herbert then took the Nawabs to Birmingham, an example of England's greatness in manufactures. The glass works of Messrs. Osler & Co., papier-maché works, brass bedsteads, steel pens, small arms, all passed under careful review. At the small arms factory the Nawab Bahadur remembers seeing part of an order for twenty thousand stands of arms ordered for the Sultan of Turkey, who had then in his mind the possibility of war with a near neighbour. All these things are but a few of the wonders which Colonel Herbert showed his pupils. The young Nawabs must indeed have been bewildered, and more so when they were whisked away to Coventry to watch the weaving of silk ribbon from silk brought, in part, from their own home, far away in Murshidabad. Then followed visits to Kidderminster carpet looms, Worcester glove factories, and the Royal Porcelain Works. From the noise and bustle of factories, the party went to the quiet of the walled city of Chester. After a glimpse at Eaton Hall and the "Sands of Dee," Colonel Herbert passed on to Manchester, and again the Nawabs found themselves watching a variety of manufactures. On the 10th of November the young Princes were back in their London quarters at the South Kensington Hotel, and began another round of theatres, opera, and gaities. It was now time to turn their faces homeward. They left London on December the 2nd to explore parts of France, Italy, and Malta, on their return journey. Want of space will not permit me to follow the party day by day, as they "did" Paris, Bologna, Genoa, Florence, and Leghorn, where they took steamer for Civita Vecchia. From Rome they wandered to Naples and Pompeii. On January the 19th, 1866, the Nawab Bahadur and his two brothers said good-bye to Europe, and on March the 2nd they landed in Calcutta, after nearly a year's absence. In Calcutta the Naib Nazim, Nawab Ali Khan, and other officers of the Nawab Nazim's suite, relieved Colonel Herbert of his charge, and prepared to escort the Nawabs home to Murshidabad. It would be of great interest to know the Nawab Bahadur's thoughts concerning this trip. Unfortunately no notes are to hand. No money was spared to make the tour enjoyable. The expenses amounted to nearly £5,000, including salaries. Colonel Herbert's accounts are as full of detail as the rest of his record. A second visit was paid to England in 1869.

As a young man, the Nawab Bahadur was good at most sports and games, but hard work, severe fasting, and anxiety concerning his father's affairs, ended in an attack of paralysis, which left his right arm and leg so weak, that for about twelve years he has been debarred from all sports. His general health is, happily, fair, and he is always cheerful. His narrow escape during the earthquake of 1897 has been noticed in Part I. The Nawab Bahadur received the G.C.I.E. from the hands of Lord Dufferin on the 4th February, 1888.

The family of the Nawab Bahadur has included five sons.

1. The Honourable Murshizada Asif Kadr Syud Wasif Ali Mirza, born January 7th, 1875. Among his family and dependants the heir to the *musnud* is generally called the *Bará Saheb*, and his European friends and acquaintances generally call him the "Wasif Saheb," as his full name and titles are rather too long for everyday use. This Prince was one of the foreign representatives who arrived in England to attend the Coronation ceremonies, postponed on account of the King-Emperor's illness.

2. Iskandar Kadr Syud Nasir Ali Mirza, born March 15th, 1876. He is generally known as the "Nasir Saheb."

3. Syud Asaf Ali Mirza, born April 26th, 1881. A shy, retiring boy, fond of music and books. He lives much by himself, and does not care much for riding or outdoor games. He is generally known as the Munah Saheb.

4. Syud Yákub Ali Mirza, born June 9th, 1885. This boy was drowned whilst bathing on Friday, June 23rd, 1899. The bath had a dressing-room in the middle, raised on arches. Yakub Ali Mirza had once or twice dived beneath the arches successfully, but during his last attempt must have misjudged his distance and struck his head against the wall. His brothers, noticing that he did not appear, sought for him, but were too late to render any assistance. His death was a great shock to all the family. The young Prince was an adept at all manly sports, although only fourteen of years when he died.

5. Syud Moshin Ali Mirza, born November 18th, 1885. A bright, intelligent boy, whose studies have unfortunately for some time past been interfered with by ill health.

In February of this year the Nawab Bahadur was honoured by a visit from Lord Curzon, Viceroy of India.

XVIII.

THE KASIMBAZAR FAMILY.

THE Kasimbazar House was founded by Babu Krishna Kanta Nandy, better known as Kanta Babu. He rose to eminence and wealth under the auspices of Warren Hastings. While Hastings was Commercial Resident of the East India Company at Kasimbazar, Suraj-u-Dowlah, then Nawab Nazim of Bengal, ordered his arrest, in order to extort money from him. The settlement was seized and Hastings sent a prisoner to Murshidabad, but he escaped while the Nawab marched on Calcutta. A re-capture was ordered, and Hastings took counsel with Kanta Babu, who was known to him in connection with his employment in the East India Company's affairs. Hastings was sheltered in Kanta Babu's house and then taken in a boat down to Calcutta. In appreciation of the service rendered him, Hastings promised Kanta Babu to advance him in life when circumstances should be favourable. On his appointment as Governor of Bengal in 1772, Warren Hastings sent for Kanta Babu, and employed him as his Diwan. About this time Kanta Babu was directly, or indirectly, the superintendent of several highly productive Zemindaries. When Hastings marched against Raja Chait Singh, of Benares, Kanta Babu accompanied him. On his return, Hastings bestowed upon Kanta Babu a jaghir, in Ghazipur, and obtained from the then Nawab Nazim the title of "Maharaja Bahadur," for his son Lokenath. Kanta Babu received as a present the *Sangin Dalai* (Marble Hall) of Benares. This was removed and re-erected at the Kasimbazar Rajbari.

Kanta Babu visited Puri to pay his homage and worship to Jagannath. On his proposing to found *atkes*, or funds for feeding the poor, the question of his incapacity, on the grounds of low "caste," was raised by the *Pandas*. Kanta Babu referred the matter to the Pandits of Nadia, Tribeni, and other seats of learning. Their unanimous verdict was that he belonged to the second class "caste" of *Navasaks*, which could make such gifts with full propriety. Accordingly *atkes* were founded by Kanta Babu.

Kanta Babu died in 1778 (Pous 1195 B.S.), leaving a vast property in several districts of Bengal, viz:—Rangpur, Dinajpur, Burdwan, Nadia, Birbhum, Pubna, Murshidabad, Faridpur, Rajshaye, Bogra, and the twenty-four Pergunnahs, besides the *jaghir* in Ghazipur (N. W. P.).

Though a man of very little education, Kanta Babu was distinguished for his sagacity and tact in business affairs, and his grasp of administrative and legislative questions. He had also many private virtues which endeared him to his neighbours and acquaintances.

His son and heir, Maharaja Lokenath, Rai Bahadur, represented the Kasimbazar House for thirteen years, during the latter half of which he suffered from an incurable disease. This prevented him from doing anything worthy of note. He died in 1804 (1211 B.S.), leaving a son, Kumar Harinath, an infant one year old.

During the minority of Kumar Harinath the estate was managed by the Court of Wards. Harinath obtained his majority in 1820 (1227 B.S.). He contributed Rs. 15,000, towards the establishment of the Hindu College, and gave away large sums in many acts of charity. Lord Amherst conferred on him the title of "Raja Bahadur," in recognition of these acts of benevolence.

Raja Harinath was soon after involved in a heavy and prolonged lawsuit with his kinsmen, Syama Charan Nandy and Ram Charan Nandy. The claim of the suit, which was instituted in the Supreme Court, was laid at half the share of the estate. The case was dismissed, but the worry and trouble incidental to the suit interfered with his projects.

Raja Harinath was fond of music, and especially of "Kabi," which at the time was a great favourite. The "Kabi" consists of songs, generally improvised for the occasion, and sung, to the accompaniment of *Dholes*, by two parties alternately. Harinath was strong and fond of athletics. He kept a gymnasium, where wrestling and sword-play were always going on.

Sanskrit learning greatly flourished in Kasimbazar, owing to the support and encouragement it received at the hands of Raja Harinath. There were several *Chatuspathis*, to which students flocked from several districts. The chief of the Pandits was Krishnanath Nyayapanchanan, a man well versed in the "Nyaya" and Smriti.

Raja Harinath was a Vishnava, and delighted in the company of pious Hindus. Raja Harinath died in 1832 (Agrahayan 1239 B.S.), leaving behind one son—a minor,—one daughter, and his widow, Rani Harasundari, who is still living at Benares, and is drawing an allowance of Rs. 1,20,000 (one lakh twenty thousand) per annnm from the present Maharaja.

The son, Krishnanath, was educated with great care. He could both write and speak English with great ease, and mixed freely with Englishmen. He was fond of European society, and was very hospitable to his European friends and acquaintances. The title of "Raja Bahadur" was conferred on him by Lord Auckland. He spent freely the accumulations of his minority, which amounted to several *lakhs*. He was extravagant to excess, and expended forty-one lakhs in four years. He was fond of hunting and shooting, and undertook hunting expeditions to Maldah and neighbouring districts, accompanied by a large number of beaters and camp-followers. His camp resembled a town in canvas, and was brilliantly illuminated at night when he dined *en prince* with his friends and companions.

The Editor of the *Bhaskar* having attacked the Raja for his free mode of living, was prosecuted, convicted of libel, and sentenced to two years' imprisonment. The Raja had an ungovernable temper, which ultimately proved his ruin. But he was forward in advancing any noble cause. On the death of David Hare, he anticipated the good wishes of his countrymen by convening a public meeting in the theatre of the Medical College, to take measures to perpetuate the memory of the deceased. He voted for a statue of David Hare, towards which he contributed the largest subscription. In his will he bequeathed the whole of his estate to Government, for the foundation of an University at Murshidabad, to be named after him. The will was set aside by the Court.

Krishnanath was extraordinarily attached to his servants, and even nominated his *Khansamah* as one of the trustees under his will. But his enlightened public spirit did not lead him to overlook the merits of those officers and *amlas* who advised and directed him aright. He bestowed the munificent gift of a *lakh* of rupees on the late Raja Digambar Mitter, C.S.I., a distinguished and well-known member of the Hindu community.

Raja Krishnanath died by his own hand, on October the 31st, 1844. On the day previous he drafted his will in his own language, and he bequeathed the bulk of his estates to educational purposes, granting his Rani (afterwards Maharani) Surnamoyi a monthly allowance of Rs. 1,500, and withholding the permission to adopt a son and heir.

The property of the Kasimbazar Raj was taken under attachment by the East India Company, under a will said to have been executed by the Raja.*

A suit was instituted. Krishnanath was proved to have been of unsound mind at the time he made the will, and the Court decreed the suit in the Rani's favour.† The estates were in a chaotic state at the time the Rani entered upon possession; but with prudent management, in which she was materially helped by her Diwan, Rai Rajiblochan Rai Bahadur, the estates were soon restored to a very flourishing condition.

MAHARANI SURNAMOYI OF KASIMBAZAR, C.I.

This well-known lady's name is a household word in Bengal, and is synonymous with all that is noble and good in woman. To her no charity appealed in vain, she was, in fact, the "Baroness Burdett Coutts of Bengal." The Maharani was born in 1838, and came into the Kasimbazar family by marriage, as the wife of Raja Krishnanath, Rai Bahadur, the last of the direct line from Krishna Kanta Nandy. They had no son, and Surnamoyi was left a widow. Her beneficence and loyalty brought her prominently to notice, and on August the 11th, 1871, the lady received, as a personal distinction, the title of *Maharani*, and, as a further reward, a promise that the title of *Maharaja* should be revived in the person of her nephew and heir, the present Maharaja Manindra Chandra Nandy.

The investiture took place at the Kasimbazar Rajbari, in the presence of the Divisional Commissioner, acting on behalf of the Government.

On March the 12th, 1875, the Government showed a further mark of its recognition of the great services rendered by her during the famine of the preceding year, by again pledging itself to extend to her successor the title of "Maharaja."

Her Most Gracious Majesty, the late Queen-Empress Victoria, further rewarded Maharani Surnamoyi, by conferring upon her the order of the Imperial Crown of India.

In January, 1878, she was made a member of this Order, and on August the 14th of that year received, at a Durbar, held at the Kasimbazar Rajbari, by the Commissioner of the Division, the Insignia of the Order, together with the Royal letters patent. The Divisional Commissioner, in the course of his address delivered on this occasion, enumerated some of her prominent acts of charity, which, up to the year 1876-77, showed an estimated expenditure of eleven *lakhs* of rupees. As many more lakhs were spent in the course of the years following this occasion.

The lady students of the Calcutta Medical College have to thank the late Maharani for the comfortable hostel in which they live during the period of their studies. In times of famine the Maharani's generosity must have saved many lives. It is not possible to enumerate all the good done by the Maharani, and her name will be handed down to posterity as the giver of a supply of pure water to the town of Berhampur. The water-works, described elsewhere, were not finished in her lifetime, but her successor carried out the scheme his aunt had inaugurated, and the

* The *Rani* applied to several leading and wealthy men for help in recovering the property. Some of them demanded half, or even two-thirds, of the property in case she succeeded in recovering it. Babu Hara Chandra Sahin, a nephew of the well-known *Goswami* family of Sirampur, came forward to help her unconditionally, and raised money to meet the expenses of a lawsuit on the mortgage of his daughter's property.

† Sometime after, Babu Hara Chandra quarrelled with the *Rani* over a small matter. He was dismissed, but the *Rani* granted a pension after his death, to his daughter-in-law and daughter, who had been left in a helpless condition.

Maharaj-Kumar Mohin Chandra Nandy.

Maharaj-Kumar Kirti Chandra Nandy.

Maharaja Manindra Chandra Nandy.

"Surnamoyi Water-works" were opened with much ceremony by the Lieutenant-Governor of Bengal, Sir John Woodburn, in July, 1899.

Maharani Surnamoyi died on August the 25th, 1897, universally mourned by the people of Bengal. Whenever any good cause wanted support, it found in the Maharani its foremost promoter. Whenever distress made itself heard, it instantly felt the touch of her relieving hand. In short, most of her vast income was spent for philanthropic purposes.

Among her acts of beneficence and liberality, too numerous to mention in full, reference may be made to the gifts of winter clothes on the *Makar Sankranti* day, when numbers of *sadhus*, Brahmins, and mendicants congregated to receive them; the heaps of eatables, formed into the shape of a pyramid on the *Annakote* day, and distributed among thousands of the poor; the feeding of the same class on the consecutive days of the *Annapurna* puja; the entertainment of the Brahmins of the Murshidabad district on the *Ekodista shradh* days of Kanta Babu, Maharaja Lokenath Bahadur, Raja Harinath Bahadur, and Raja Krishnanath Bahadur, when presents of silver were made to them; the annual grants to the Pandits of different districts; the inauguration of the Berhampur Water-works at an expense of nearly three lakhs; the maintenance of the Berhampur College, at an annual charge of twenty thousand rupees.

On the death of the Maharani, the estate reverted to her mother-in-law, Rani Harasundari, then retiring into the life of a recluse at Benares. The reversionary heir, Manindra Chandra, the only surviving son of Govinda Sundari, daughter of Rani Harasundari, succeeded to the estate by virtue of a deed of relinquishment executed by Rani Harasundari. The Rani received an *honorarium* of nine lakhs, and a monthly allowance of ten thousand rupees was to be paid to her during her lifetime. The succession of Manindra Chandra was hailed with joy by the people of all ranks throughout the district, and outside. The day of his return from Benares to take formal possession of the estate presented a unique spectacle, when high and low, rich and poor, Hindu, and Mussulman thronged on the banks of the Bhagirathi to receive him with ovations.

Manindra Chandra was born on the 17th of Jaistha, in 1267 B.S. He lost his mother at the tender age of two, his elder brother at seven, and his father at eleven. His eldest brother died in the course of the next year. He was attacked with headaches at the early age of fourteen, which compelled him to give up his school education and seek the benefit of a change of scene and air. Though relieved of its violence with care and medical treatment, the disease recurs from time to time. It has not, however, affected his mental and physical energies.

Manindra Chandra was confirmed in the title of "Maharaja" by the Government, on May the 30th, 1898, in fulfilment of its pledge to the late Maharani.

He completed the Water-works commenced by his illustrious aunt, continues to maintain the Berhampur College, at the annual charge of twenty-two thousand rupees, and keeps intact almost all the acts of charity and gifts, for which the noble lady occupied the first place among the present landowners of Bengal.

He has three sons and two daughters. The eldest son is a student in the B.A. Class of the Presidency College. His marriage was lately celebrated with great *éclat*, when there was a continual flow of gaities and festivities for about a fortnight.

XIX.

THE NASHIPUR RAJ FAMILY.

THE Nashipur Raj is of some considerable historical interest, and may be traced as far back as Tarachand Sinha of Panipat. Ajit Sinha, grandson of Tarachand, was, in recognition of distinguished services under the Moghul Emperor Jehangir, invested with the title of "Rai."*

Rai Ajit Sinha's eldest son was Amar Sinha, who left four sons, of whom the youngest was Diwali Sinha. Raja Davi Sinha Bahadur (who got the title from the Government), the founder of the Nashipur Raj family, was the second son of Diwali; the eldest was Takiram Sinha, and the youngest Bahadur Sinha. In the year 1756 A.D. he migrated from Panipat, the historical battlefield of India, to Murshidabad, capital of Bengal, and for some time carried on business as a merchant. This, however, he abandoned, and took service under the East India Company in the revenue department, and held high and responsible offices of trust in connection with the land settlement of Bengal. He was appointed to farm the revenues, inclusively of the Government of Purnea, and subsequently of Rangpur, Dinajpur, and Edracpur. In the arrangements made by Warren Hastings, in the year 1773, by which Provincial Councils were formed, Davi Sinha became the Steward, or Secretary, to the Provincial Council of Murshidabad, and to his charge were committed extensive and populous provinces, yielding an annual revenue of 120 lakhs of rupees.

The office of Diwan, then newly created for the revenue administration of Bengal, was conferred upon Raja Davi Sinha, along with that of the Farmer-General. He was a man of marked ability, and by his energy and perseverence he attained a very high and enviable position under the Government. He died without issue, and his vast estates passed into the hands of Raja Balawant Sinha, the eldest son of his brother, Bahadur Sinha. Balawant Sinha was succeeded by his son, Raja Gopal Sinha. The inheritance next fell to Raja Udmanta Sinha Bahadur, the third son of Bahadur Sinha, and an ornament of the Nashipur Raj family. Raja Udmanta held for a short time the office of Diwan to the Nawab Nazim of Bengal. He was a most pious and charitable man, kind-hearted, and forbearing. He built a magnificent temple at Nashipur, wherein is enthroned, with many others, the deity Ram Chandra Dev Thakur, and memorials of his piety and philanthropy were scattered over his vast estates. With him originated the present system of zemindari accounts, which is prevalent throughout Bengal even now. He was honoured in many ways, and a street in Calcutta bears his name to this day. He had the personal friendship and regard of the Governors-General, the Earl of Minto, and the Marquis of Hastings. The latter on one occasion wrote to him:—"Your great loyalty and deep friendship has been the cause of great satisfaction to me." He died in 1832 without issue, and was succeeded by Raja Krishna Chandra Sinha Bahadur, the only son of his elder brother, Hanumanta Sinha. Raja Krishna Chandra left two sons; the elder, who got the inheritance, was Raja Kirti Chandra Sinha Bahadur, and the younger was Kumar Udy Chandra Sinha, who died at an early age.

* Honourable.

THE RAJA BAHADUR OF NASHIPUR.

Eldest Son of the Raja Bahadur of Nashipur.

The present Raja of Nashipur is Raja Bahadur Ranjit Sinha, who succeeded his father, Raja Kirti Chandra Sinha Bahadur. He was born on the 9th June, 1865, and is therefore now in his thirty-eighth year. During his minority the estate was managed for the time being by the Court of Wards. The Raja was educated at the Berhampur College. On attaining his majority, on the 9th June, 1886, he assumed control of his extensive estates, which he still continues to manage with marked ability. His public career began in 1887, when he was appointed an Honorary Magistrate of the Lalbagh Bench. In 1888 he was elected Chairman of the Murshidabad Municipality. The Government conferred on him the title of "Raja," on the 18th of January, 1891. In 1894 he was vested with the powers of a Magistrate of the Second Class, empowered to sit singly. He served in this capacity with so much zeal and ability that the Government, in appreciation of his services, conferred on him the powers of a Magistrate of the First Class on the 18th March, 1897, with power to take cognizance of offences and receive complaints and police reports. He was also placed in entire charge of the Lalbagh Bench, and virtually discharged the duties and functions of a Sub-divisional Officer after the abolition of the Lalbagh Sub-division. On his appointment as a member of the Bengal Council, he was instrumental in bringing about the restoration of this Sub-division. In 1897 the Raja was re-elected Chairman of the Murshidabad Municipality. On the 22nd of June, 1897, he was created a "Raja Bahadur." In private life the Raja is a model of what a man in his high position ought to be. His amiability and gentleness, his lofty conception of the obligations of his rank, and his intelligence, have made him a general favourite. That the Government hold him in high esteem, is evidenced by his being appointed, in January, 1899, to a seat in the Bengal Legislative Council, in succession to the late Maharaja Bahadur of Durbhunga.

The heir to the Nashipur property is an intelligent boy, now in his thirteenth year.

XX.

FAMILY HISTORY OF RAJA ASHUTOSH NATH ROY, OF KASIMBAZAR.

THE patrimonial title of the family is *Chattopadhya,* but Ajodhya Narain Roy, the founder of the family, had the hereditary title of "Rai" conferred upon him by the then Nawab Nazim in appreciation of his meritorious services. He was succeeded by his son, Dinobundhu Roy, who received a khilat from the Nawab's Government, and the privilege of carrying a silver stick was conferred on him, which was considered a great honour in those days. The original ancestral residence of the family was at Ferozepur, a village now in the Bhogwangola thannah, where the family deity, Modon Mohunji, is still preserved and worshipped. To him succeeded Jogobundhu Roy, from whose time the family rose to eminence. He was for some time the Diwan of the East India Company attached to the Kasimbazar Factory. He was by nature an adventurous man, and became the Diwan of the Mymensing Collectorate. At the revision of the district arrears by the East India Company in 1795, Pergunnah Sarail passed to the district of Mymensing, and forms now the major portion of the estate of Raja Ashutosh Nath Roy. In 1802 the five-anna, twelve-gunda share of this Pergunnah was put up to auction in the Mymensing Collectorate, for arrears of Government revenue, and Babu Jogobundhu Roy, of Kasimbazar, who was then the sheristadar of that office, had it purchased by a *Muktiar,* Jogi Ram Choudhuri, at a very low price. In 1831 Pergunnah Sarail was transferred to Tipperah, and in 1836 the Collector of Tipperah had to bring the seven-anna share to the hammer for arrears of revenue. It was purchased by Babu Krishingha Roy, grandson of Babu Jogobundhu Roy, alluded to above. In 1885 Diwan Monohar Ali's wife put her husband's twelve-anna share up for sale in execution of her *Kabin* decree. This share was purchased by the Court of Wards on behalf of Raja A. N. Roy, then a minor. Thus it will appear that Raja Ashutosh Nath Roy is at present the owner of fifteen annas and three gundas of the entire Pergunnah, the remaining seventeen gundas belonging to the estate of the late Rai Bahadur Mohini Mohun Burdhan and his co-parceners. The area of the Pergunnah covers about one-eighth of the district of Tipperah, stretching between 23° 56′ 10″ and 24° 1′ 53″ north latitude, and 91° 2′ 15″ and 91° 21′ 23″ east longitude, altogether 304 square miles, out of which 177,439·49 acres, or 277 square miles, were under survey and settlement. It will be not uninteresting to quote the following history of Pergunnah Sarail from the reports submitted by the settlement officer to the Collector of Tipperah on March 13th, 1893:—"Pergunnah Sarail anciently formed a part of the old Tipperah Raj. How it gradually passed into the hands of the Mahomedans is a dark chapter in the history of the district. It is, however, certain that after the Mahomedans had established their capital at Sonargaon, they made frequent inroads into the territory of the Tipperah Raj, but could not make any permanent impression. It was only after they had extended their dominion to the north and conquered Sylhet that they succeeded, by gradual encroachments, in getting hold of part of Sarail, which was thus very early cut off from the Pergunnah and incorporated with the district of Sylhet. This fact is fully borne out by the "Ain-i-Akbari." It appears from the rent-roll of Todar Mull, published in the "Ain-i-Akbari," that the southern portion of Sylhet was entirely obtained during the Pathan reigns from the Tipperah State. The rent-roll likewise shows the Sarkar of Sylhet was divided into eight mahals, Satara Khondal (the part of Sarail newly obtained from the Raj was one of them). The revenue of Satara Khondal is given at 3,90,492 dáms, or 9,761 Sursahi rupees. The headquarters of the Brahmanberiah Sub-division is situated in this part of Sarail. At present Satara Khondal is altogether a separate mahal, and bears no connection with Sarail Estate. Satara Khondal was thus the only portion that had passed into the hands of the Mahomedans previous to Akbar's reign, and it was not till the reign of Shah Jehan that the whole of the Pergunnah was completely subjugated and finally parcelled out among the Mahomedan nobles of Sylhet (A.D. 1629—A.D. 1639). During Aurungzebe's reign, Shaistah Khan, the Governor of Bengal, established a navy at Kidderpur, the northern position of the present Naraınganj, to check the raids of the Portuguese and Mug* pirates. The revenue of 112 mahals, known as Kowra mahals, was specially reserved for the maintenance of the navy. The zemindars of these mahals were allowed certain deductions from fixed revenue, payable by them on condition of supplying a stipulated number of boats (buzrahs) at the time of any naval warfare. The balance of the revenue used to be remitted to the Kijarat department of Dacca, but Sarail Juansha and Taraf are the three biggest Pergunnahs in the mahals, and since the creation of the navy they had to be transferred from the Chakla of Sylhet to that of Dacca for administrative convenience. Murshid Kuli Khan prepared his elaboate revenue roll, known as "Jumma Kamal Tomra," in 1722 A.D. The revenue of Sarail was shown in this record as Rs. 1,11,084. A large deduction of Rs. 4,00,324 was, however, allowed in consideration of the Diwan's having to supply forty boats at the time of any naval warfare. The help received from the Diwans of Sarail in olden times was highly meritorious. Mr. J. S. Brown, C.S., in his report of the district, says: "The two largest portions of Sarail are still known by the peasantry as the 'Estate of fourteen and eight ships,' a denomination which indicates the ancient form of revenue paid by them to the State. It was with the aid of the fleet collected in this part of the country that Shaistah Khan, nephew of Nur Jehan, conquered Chittagong, which, in commemoration of the success of Moslem arms, was in that time called Islamabad. There is also a very ancient *musjid*, or mosque, in the village of Sarail, erected in the name of Nur Mahomed's wife, in 1670 A.D." "I have purposely given particulars of the Sarail Pergunnah on account of its being the principal zemindari of Raja Ashutosh Nath Roy, which yields a princely income to the Raja, and also on account of its historical importance." When the Court of Wards took charge of the estate in 1880-81, the rent-roll, according to the zemindars' old papers, was Rs. 1,98,660, and after the completion of the revision settlement work, when the Court of Wards made over charge to the proprietor, the rent-roll of the Pergunnah was Rs. 2,11,573, being an increase of Rs. 12,913, or 6·3 per cent. on the old rent-roll. But the total rent-roll of Sarail, including other property of the Raja, is nearly Rs. 2,50,000 in the same Pergunnah. It will not be out of place to mention here how the value of the landed property is gradually increasing. When the five-anna, twelve-gunda share of the property was purchased in 1802, it was purchased for Rs. 40,000, and the rental alone now amounts to Rs. 1,10,000. In 1836, when the seven-anna share was purchased, it was purchased for Rs. 60,000, and the rental is at present Rs. 95,000.

Babu Nursingh Roy, grandson of Diwan Jogobundhu Roy, added considerably to the ancestral property. It was at this time that Bara Behar, belonging to Kani Bishen Kumari, of the Burdwan Raj, was purchased at a revenue sale. Nursingh Roy left two sons, Nobo Krishna Roy and Raja Krishna Roy. Nursingh Roy was famous for his charity and liberality, and his name is a household word amongst the residents of Kasimbazar. His son, Nobo Krishna Roy, died without issue. Raja

* From around Chittagong.

Krishna Roy died, leaving behind him an only son, Babu Annoda Prosad Roy, father of the present Raja Ashutosh Nath Roy. Annoda Babu being then a minor, his estate was under the protection of the Court of Wards from the year 1866 to 1869, when he attained his majority. In 1875 Annoda Prosad Roy was decorated by Government with the title of "Rai Bahadur" for his various acts of liberality during the famine of 1874-75. In February, 1880, Rai Annoda Prosad went down to Calcutta to negotiate for the title of "Raja." But, unfortunately, he died there on the 24th of the same month from an attack of cholera, leaving his only son, Raja Ashutosh Nath Roy, a minor. The Government took charge of the minor and his estate, and continued to manage it till September 7th, 1897, when the estate was released on the minor's attaining his majority. For various acts of public utility and liberality during the Court's management, and the Raja having shown his public spirit by the princely gift of a lakh of rupees in aid of the construction of Lady Dufferin's* hospital at Calcutta, the Government was pleased to decorate him with the title of "Raja" on May 24th of the same year, and the *khilat* and the *sanad* were presented to the "Raja" by the Honourable Mr. C. E. Buckland, then Presidency Commissioner, at a public durbar, on April 8th, 1898, at the Raja's residence at Kasimbazar. The Raja has two daughters, aged six and three years respectively. His mother, Srinati Anar Kali Devi, the widow of the late Rai Annoda Prosad, is yet living. Her munificence and liberality are also highly spoken of by the public. The Raja being a Brahmin by "caste," holds a very high position in society; in wealth, he may be reckoned as the second or third richest man in the district. When the Court of Wards assumed charge of the estate, the rent-roll was Rs. 2,94,564, and when the estate was released the rent-roll had become Rs. 3,64,974. So there had been an increase of Rs. 70,410. The revenue and rent payable by the Raja is Rs. 1,12,110, leaving a net profit of Rs. 2,52,864 to the Raja. The Raja owns property in the following districts:—Murshidabad, Tipperah, Rangpur, Mymensing, Burdwan, Hughli, Calcutta, and Birbhum. In Monghyr he owns a very nice house known as the "Coramchordrah," a building of historical importance, which his father purchased for Rs. 40,000 from the Maharaja of Vizinagram. Throughout the Court's management, from 1880 to 1897, Babu Bogla Nand Mukherji, who belonged to the Provincial Civil Service, was in charge of the estate.

* The Editor is of opinion that the money ought to have been left for the support of the existing *Anarkali* Hospital in Berhampur. The blame rests not with the Raja, but with those who persuaded him to divert the money, making it necessary to close the hospital.

XXI.

THE LALGOLA FAMILY.

GENEALOGICAL TABLE.

MAHIMA ROY

- Dulel Roy
- Raj Nath Roy
  - Nilkant Roy
    - Rao Atma Narain Roy
      - Rao Ram Sunkar Roy
        - Rao Mahesh Narain Roy
          - Rao Jogendra Narain Roy
            - Kumar Hemendra Narain Roy
              - Kumar Dhirendra Narain Roy
            - Kumar Satyendra Narain Roy

THE founder of this house, Mahima Roy, was originally a resident of the village of Lali, in the Pergunnah Nasmabad, of the District of Ghazipur, in the North-West Provinces. He left Ghazipur and came to Sunderpur, in Rajshaye, Bengal, on the river Pudma,* many years before the downfall of the Mahomedan power. He was a Bhumihar Brahmin by "caste," and so belonged to the same "caste" as the Maharajas of Benares and Bettiah. The village of Sunderpur was washed away by the Ganges, and the two sons of Mahima Roy, Dulel Roy and Raj Nath Roy, came to, and settled at, Lalgola, in the district of Murshidabad. The village of Lalgola is eighteen miles from the city of Murshidabad, and twelve miles from the Railway Station at Azimganj.

Nilkant Roy, the grandson of Mahima Roy, married the daughter of Rao Agnu Sinha, the Subahdar of the Nawab of Bengal, and ultimately became the Subahdar himself, and the title of "Rao" was accordingly conferred on him. Rao Atma Narain Roy, the son of Nilkant Roy, when Subahdar, acquired a large fortune.

Rao Ram Sunkar Roy, the son of Rao Atma Narain Roy, resigned the office of Subahdar, but continued to pay visits to the Nawabs, who made the title "Rao" hereditary. He established a charitable institution, called *Atithasala*, for the poor, which exists to this day, and many poor people are daily fed there.

Rao Mahesh Narain Roy, the son of Rao Ram Sunkar Roy, helped Sir Ashley Eden, when Magistrate of Jangipur, with eighty chosen men, to quell the Santal rebellion. The Magistrate afterwards thanked him for the assistance he had given at that time. There was a misunderstanding between Rao Mahesh and a European manager of the Bhugwanpur factory, who, at the time of the Sepoy

* The local name for that part of the Ganges that bounds Murshidabad District on the east.

Mutiny, secretly informed the Government that Mahesh Narain Roy carried on secret correspondence with the mutineers. Thereupon, a military officer, accompanied by seven hundred armed horsemen, came to Lalgola and held an investigation, and reported to Government that the Zemindar was a peaceful and loyal subject of Government.

Rao Jogendra Narain Roy, the adopted son of Rao Mahesh Narain Roy, is now the Zemindar of Lalgola. On the 1st of January, 1877, he was presented with a certificate of honour, which reads as follows:—

"By command of his Excellency the Viceroy and Governor-General, this certificate is presented in the name of Her Most Gracious Majesty Victoria, Empress of India, to Rao Jogendra Narain Roy of Lalgola, Zemindar and Honorary Magistrate of Murshidabad, in recognition of his loyalty to Government, his considerate charity to the poor and sick, and his admirable management of his property.

(*Signed*) "RICHARD TEMPLE.

"*January 1st*, 1877."

In forwarding the above, the Magistrate of Murshidabad wrote to the "Rao" in the following terms:—

"RAO JOGENDRA NARAIN ROY OF LALGOLA,

"To you, my friend, I make over this certificate of honour with special pleasure, because I know your good works and have with my own eyes seen the proofs of your enlightened charity. I rejoice to recognise in you one of the best of Zemindars, and an honour to your native district.

(*Signed*) "A. MACKENZIE.

"*Magistrate.*

"BERHAMPUR,

"*January 1st*, 1877."

The Government was further pleased to present him with another certificate on the occasion of the Diamond Jubilee (1897). He has built the Mahesh Narain Serai,* and constructed a hall and excavated a tank (the hall with tank and garden are called "Mackenzie Park"), at Raganathganj (Jangipur). He has also established a Middle English School and a charitable dispensary at Lalgola. He has two sons and a grandson, as shown in the genealogical table given at the beginning of the chapter.

* A rest-house.

THE RAO SAHEB OF LALGOLA.

XXII.

FAMILY HISTORY OF RAI BOGLA NAND MUKHERJI BAHADUR.

THE family to which the "Rai Bahadur" belongs enjoys a high social position, being of the "Kulin" "caste." The original residence of the ancestors of the family was at Khamargatchi, a village in the district of Hughli. In ancient times it was considered a very great honour if the daughters of Brahmin Rajas were married to "Kulins." The Nadia Rajas are by "caste" Brahmins, and they were always, in those days, anxious to secure the best "Kulins" to be their sons-in-law, without reference to riches or poverty. The great-grandfather of the "Rai Bahadur" was forced to marry a daughter of the Nadia Raj family. This unhappy union compelled him to leave his ancestral residence and settle at Mognapur, a village in the district of Bankura, near Bishenpur, to which the authority of the Nadia Raja did not extend. The Rajas of Bishenpur were at that time semi-independent, and did not owe regular allegiance to the Nawabs of Murshidabad. Bishenpur was a frontier province, and the ruins of the old ramparts and other works testify to its once being a great historical place. Hunter gives a very graphic description of it in his "Rural Bengal." Mognapur was at that time the family residence of the Diwans of the Bishenpur Rajas, who were very high "caste" Brahmins. Here the great-grandfather, Nidhi Krishna Mukherji, married a daughter of the Diwan's family, and the result of this inter-marriage was a son, Chandi Charan Mukherji, created subsequently Diwan of the Bishenpur Raj. Mr. W. S. Wells, Magistrate of Bankura, in his report of December the 17th, 1861, writes thus about the "Rai Bahadur's" ancestors :—"Whose fathers were the Diwans of the Maharaja of Bishenpur." Chandi Charan Mukherji was a very pious man, and all grants of *lakhiraj*, or rent-free, lands, for religious and charitable purposes in the Pergunnah Bishenpur, bear his signature, and that was considered sufficient authority by the English Government to allow the holders of such grants to enjoy their privileges. He died on the banks of the holy Bhagirathi at Udhanpur, near Cutwah, in 1801, leaving two sons, Kali Prosad, and Tarini Prosad, who were then minors. Kali Prosad Mukherji became, eventually, Sheristadar to the Magistrate of Birbhum, and, for a time, settled at Birbhum. Afterwards he retired on a pension, and died at Benares in the year 1853-1854 A.D.

The "Rai Bahadur's" father, Tarini Prosad, was at that time Foujdari Peshkar. In 1829 he was Peshkar to Mr. Halliday (afterwards Sir Francis, the first Lieutenant-Governor of Bengal), who was then Registrar and Assistant Magistrate of Birbhum. Afterwards he became the Foujdari Sheristadar of East Burdwan, when Mr. Patten was Magistrate. In 1838 he was appointed Collectorate Sheristadar of Midnapur, under Mr. Ricketts. In June of the same year he was made Judge's Sheristadar in West Burdwan, which appointment he continued to hold till his death in February, 1871. Tarini died at the ripe old age of seventy-nine. He was born at Moynapur in the memorable year when Lord Cornwallis introduced the "permanent settlement" into Bengal. English education was then being gradually introduced, and the sons of the upper classes were more inclined to study Persian and Arabic literature than English. Both Kali Prosad and Tarini Prosad were very good Persian and Sanskrit scholars. Bengali literature was then in its infancy. Kali Prosad wrote some Bengali works, which are now out of print. Tarini Prosad had six sons, one of whom died when young.

The eldest son, Rai Jogoanand Mukherji Bahadur, was Junior Government Pleader of the Calcutta Sudder Diwanni Adalut (afterwards the High Court). His name was well known to Government, and to the public. He was held in such high estimation that several Viceroys and Governors-General, Lieutenant-Governors, and Chief Justices, honoured him with visits at his private residence at Bhowanipur. His eventful life was brought into prominence, both abroad and in India, by the auspicious visit paid to him in his private residence by the present King-Emperor, Edward VII, who was then, as Prince of Wales, on his Indian tour of 1875. He was more than once recommended by the Local Government for a Judgeship in the Calcutta High Court, which was then very newly created. He died of small-pox near Calcutta, on the banks of the sacred Ganges, on November the 17th, 1892, at the advanced age of seventy-three, greatly lamented by a large number of his friends and relatives.

The second son, Shomalanand Mukherji, was for a long time Deputy Magistrate of Kandi (Murshidabad), where he died in 1868.

The third son, Ganganand Mukherji, was for a considerable period an extra Assistant Commissioner and Sub-Judge in Perulia, and for his long and eminent services he was made a "Rai Bahadur" on his retirement in 1891. He died at Perulia a few months after his retirement, on July 14th, 1891.

The fourth son, Bemolanand Mukherji, was for many years a Deputy Magistrate and Deputy Collector, and is now enjoying a retired life in the ancestral home at Moynapur.

The youngest son is the present "Rai Bahadur," who, having served Government for upwards of forty years in various capacities, retired in January, 1898, and has settled at Berhampur, where he had been for many years manager of the Kasimbazar estate of Raja A. N. Roy under the Court of Wards, and his services are still retained by the Raja. On account of his long and meritorious services, Government decorated him with the title of "Rai Bahadur."

Among other members of the family, several grandsons of Tarini Prosad held, and are still holding, very high and prominent appointments under Government. It may be mentioned here that amongst his grandsons (daughter's son) Rai Durga Catty Banerji Bahadur, C.I.E., who for a considerable period was the Calcutta Collector, and also a member of the Bengal Legislative Council, retired only in February, 1901.

The family is well known to Government for its loyalty and devotion, and to the public for its high position in Society, and it is generally called the Great Nand Family of Bengal.

XXIII.

THE BANWARI RAJ FAMILY.

THE founder of the Banwaribad Raj family was Nityananda Dalal, born 1752. His father, Jagomohun Dalal, was a respectable gentleman of the weaver "caste," living in the village of Sonarundi, in the district of Murshidabad. Jagomohun and his forefathers never followed the occupation of their "caste." He was a broker in a kind of coarse cotton cloth, which was then very much in use in this country. When Nityananda arrived at the age of twelve or fourteen, he paid little heed to study. His father one day rebuked him much for this negligence. Annoyed at this, Nityananda left his home and went away to the city of Patna. He there studied Persian, and having a great desire to learn Arabic, he went on to Delhi to study that language. While at Delhi, his good qualities brought him to the notice of the Emperor, Shah Alum, who, pleased with his superior knowledge in the two languages, employed him in the Imperial service, and gave him the title of "Rai Danishmanda" as a reward for his literary merits.

At this time a misunderstanding arose between the Emperor and his son, which led to a war. Nityananda succeeded in bringing about a reconciliation betweeen the father and the son. At this, the Emperor was highly pleased, and made him "Mir Munshi" in the Imperial Court. The Emperor further invested him with the high-sounding title of "Maharaja Amir-ul-Mulk, Azmat-Dowlah, Jogodindra Bahadur, Sefadarjang," and promoted him to the office of *Hapta Hazari*, with the privilege of "Nahabat Saáth," and allowed the Munshi to keep five pieces of cannon.

Under the auspices of the Court of Delhi, Rai Danishmanda made himself master of a large amount of money, and purchased estates in the districts of Rangpur, Dinajpur, Bogra, Murshidabad, Nadia, Birbhum, Burdwan, Purnea, and many other districts in Bengal. He constructed a beautiful temple, which he dedicated to the god Banwariji. He placed an image of Krishna in the temple, where up to the present time about one hundred and fifty men are daily fed on the sacred food, cooked rice and bread. Adjoining Sonarandi, he founded a village, to which, in honour of the god, he gave the name of Modrolhosma Banwaribad. He furnished the village with many large tanks, and with beautiful gardens. Here he built a magnificent house, in which he lived. After his name, Nityananda opened an era, "Danishabda," the present year being its one hundred and fifty-first year. Nityananda constructed a road, leading from Berhampur to Birbhum, with an avenue of trees planted along it. He was gentle, benevolent, and kind to the poor. He died in 1821, leaving three sons.

The eldest son, Maharaja Jogodindra Bonwarilal Bahadur, born 1803, instituted many things of public utility. He gave donations to the Calcutta Hindu School, and provided free studentships. In his Excellency Lord W. Bentinck's time, Jogodindra was invested with the title of "Maharaja Jogodindra Bahadur." At Banwariganj (Udhanpur), on the Ganges, he started a fair, which is held annually in the month of January. He constructed a road and dug a canal from Udhanpur to Banwaribad. He contributed three lakhs of rupees towards the expenses of the Burma war of 1842, and fifty thousand rupees towards the construction of the Strand Road in the city of Calcutta. He was very gentle in his behaviour towards all classes of people, very polite, sociable, benevolent, and kind to all. He died in 1855, and was succeeded by his younger brother.

The second son, Maharaja Jogodindra Banwarigobinda Deb Bahadur, born 1805, was also a man of considerable merits. He also was invested with the title of "Maharaja Jogodindra Bahadur," with a *Khilat* consisting of valuable clothes, jewels, a sword, and a shield, in the time of his Excellency Lord Canning. The Maharaja opened a Higher English School at Banwaribad, and at the time of the Orissa famine contributed two thousand rupees. He was also a benevolent and kind man, and devoted most of his life to religion. Having no son born to him, he adopted Rajbullabha, the son of a near relative, to whom he gave the name of Banwari Ananda, and who was allowed by the Government to be called Kumar* Banwari Ananda Deb Bahadur.

Kumar Banwari Ananda Deb Bahadur lives a retired life, having made over all his property to his son, the present incumbent, Kumar Banwari Mukunda Deb Bahadur.

GENEALOGICAL TABLE.

MAHARAJA AMIR-UL-MULK, AZMAT DOWLAH, JOGODINDRA NITYANANDA BAHADUR, SEFADARJANG. Born 1752. Died 1821.

- Maharaja Jogodindra Banwarilal Bahadur. Born 1803. Died 1855.
  - Maharaj Kumar Narendra Banwaridoyal Bahadur. Born 1832. Died 1852.
- Maharaja Jagodindra Banwarigobinda Deb Bahadur. Born 1805. Died 1886.
  - Maharaj Kumar Banwari Ananda Deb Bahadur. Born 1856. Living.
    - Kumar Banwari Mukunda Deb Bahadur. Born 1875. Living.
      - Kumar Banwari Birendra Deb Bahadur. Born 1899. Living.
- Maharaj Kumar Banwarikisore Bahadur. Born 1812. Died 1865.
  - Unmadini.

* Prince.

Kumar Debendra Nath Rai.

XXIV.

THE KUNJAGHATTA RAJ FAMILY.

THE history of the period from the downfall of the Moghul empire to the early British administration is enveloped in some obscurity, and our knowledge of persons who figured in that period, when India was staggering under internal dissensions, is limited chiefly to traditions and incomplete family records. About three hundred and eighty years ago, the present palace, where the Raj family dwells, was founded. But the founder, as well as most of the earlier holders, is not known. Looking back to the time of the administration of Bengal by Shaistah Khan, we find traces of Lala Nunda Ram Rai, in the year 1662 a person connected with the Government of that time, and possessing no little influence in the Kulin Brahmin society. The title of "Lala Rai" was conferred upon him by the Emperor of Delhi, as an official distinction, and he was placed in charge of two thousand horse and three thousand infantry. Large additions and alterations were made in the palace by him and the grounds increased by four bigahs of land in Saidabad, Rajshaye,* acquired from Lala Udai Narain Rai, a Zemindar of Rajshaye. (This statement is proved by a document existing at Kunjaghatta.)

He left one son, Satrajit Rai, who maintained the high position and dignity of the family intact by his connection with the then Government, and acquired other *lakhiraj* (rent free) land in Saidabad, and laid the foundation of a beautiful garden on the banks of the Bhagirathi, which was washed away by that river in 1897.

The next heir was his son, Rai Jaggat Chand, a historical personage in the early period of the British rule. He was Peshkar, or Superintendent of the Nawab's household, under Muni Begum, widow of Mir Jaffer. He married Sammani, the eldest daughter of Maharaja Nunda Kumar. Thus two great "Kulin" families in Bengal, holding high posts under Government, and having great influence in the Brahmin Society of Bengal, were amalgamated. But this union did not prove to be productive of amicable relations between the two families.

The Maharaja, Nunda Kumar, was the son of Pudmalal Rai, who held some office under Government, and was Amil of two or three Pergunnahs, such as Futti Singh, etc., the total rental of which might be about Rs. 1,50,000 at that period. Pudmalal appointed his son Nunda Kumar as a kind of deputy under himself.

Some time during the reign of the Ali Verdi Khan, Nunda Kumar had been appointed Amil of the Pergunnahs of Hijli and Mahisadal. But owing to differences with Roy Royan Cheyn Khan, he was displaced. Afterwards he was appointed Diwan, under Mahomed Yar Beg Khan, Foujdar of Hughli, and afterwards, under Shaikh Umer Ulla, Foujdar of Hughli. The latter he displaced, and became himself the Foujdar.

Lord Clive conceived a close friendship for him for his help at the time of the siege of Chandernagore. After the defeat of Suraj-u-Dowlah, when, Mir Jaffer was placed on the *Musnud*

* In those days Murshidabad was included in Rajshaye.

by Clive, Nunda Kumar was appointed Munshi to Clive, and acted also as an agent. At this time he was so much beloved and favoured by Clive, that he was called the "Black Colonel." It was by the strong recommendations of Clive that Nunda Kumar was appointed Diwan to Mahomed Yar Beg Khan, Foujdar of Hughli; and when the East India Company obtained the revenues of Burdwan and Krishnagar, the collections of these two provinces were given to the Diwan, Nunda Kumar, also by the recommendation of Clive.

In connection with the despatch of the revenue collections of Burdwan and Krishnagar, direct to Hughli, instead of through Hastings at Murshidabad, differences arose between Hastings and Nunda Kumar, and thus was sown the seed which afterwards assumed prodigious magnitude and bore bitter fruit, both for Nunda Kumar and Hastings. Nunda Kumar resigned his post.

At the time when Mr. Vansittart was Governor, and Kasim Ali Khan Nazim, Nunda Kumar connected himself very closely with the deposed Nawab, Mir Jaffer. He was not a time server. Afterwards, when the East India Company and Nawab Kasim Ali Khan came to an open rupture, Nunda Kumar attended Mir Jaffer in his war against Kasim Ali Khan, with the title of Diwan to the Rai Khalsa. After the closing victory, he obtained from Shah Alum, Emperor of Delhi, the title of "Maharaja," and various presents. But when, upon the death of Mir Jaffer, Nawab Najim-u-Dowlah succeeded to the *Musnud*, his influence in the Government ceased. After the passing of the *Regulating Act*, by Lord North, the Governor of Bengal was appointed to be the Governor-General of India, with four Councillors to assist him. These Councillors, after taking their seats, began to inquire into the affairs of the Government. In this task they derived great help from Nunda Kumar. Of these four Councillors, Mr. Barwell was supporting Hastings, while the other three, Clavering, Monson, and Francis, sought the help of Nunda Kumar, to bring to light the supposed iniquities of the late Government, for which Hastings was held to be wholly responsible. Thus Nunda Kumar incurred the displeasure of Hastings. Through his instigation, one Mohun Prosad, attorney for Ganga Bissen, executor to the estate of Bolaki Das, accused Nunda Kumar of forgery in respect to some promissory notes, alleged to be executed by Bolaki Das to the advantage of Nunda Kumar. Nunda Kumar was convicted and sentenced to death. Mr. Justice Beveridge has pointed out that the execution of Nunda Kumar was a judicial murder; and the popular feeling is that he was a martyr.

Nunda Kumar left one son, Gurudas, whose rivalry with Jaggat Chand, was one of the causes of Nunda Kumar's disgrace. Raja Gurudas was Diwan under Nawab Muni Begum and Mobarak-u-Dowlah, and received the title of *Gourpati*. He was a devout Vishnav. He died 1199 B.S., sonless, and Raja Mahanunda, son of Jaggat Chand, inherited both his office and property. Jaggat Chand died 1183 B.S. Raja Mahanunda also shared the feelings of his late father, in his enmity towards Nunda Kumar. A demonstration in support of Hastings' innocence, at the time of his impeachment, was signed by Mahanunda. Mahanunda acquired from the Company, 1202 B.S., the Jaghir of Mouza Dar Gopjan in Azimnagar Pergunnah, and other mouzas.

In 1768 A.D., Jaggat Chand received the title of "Rai," and was appointed honorary Commander of five hundred cavalry and five hundred infantry.

In 1769 A.D. Gurudas Chand received the title of "Raja Bahadur," and with it the honorary post of Commander of two thousand horse and one thousand infantry, and also a palanquin and a drum.

These *firmans* were granted by Shah Alum, the Emperor, and are yet existing at the Kunjaghatta Rajbari.

With the decline of the power of the Nawab of Murshidabad, the position and influence of the

Kunjaghatta Rajas also declined. The son of Raja Mahanunda, Raja Bejoy Krishna, was, owing to circumstances, forced to sell a part of the family property, such as the Pergunnah of Tamluk, etc., and house property at Calcutta, in Beadon Square and "Raja Gurudas" Street. The next representative was Krishna Chandra, whose son, Kumar Durga Nath, a highly intelligent man (born 1843 A.D., died 1893), recovered some of the lost ancestral property.

His son, Kumar Debendra Nath Rai, the present owner of the estate, was born 1874. He has received a liberal English education. He was appointed an Honorary Magistrate in 1893, and nominated a Municipal Commissioner in 1894.

At the Durbar, held at Murshidabad, on the occasion of her late Majesty's assuming the title of "Empress of India," Kumar Durga Nath was offered a seat with the Rajas, and the present Kumar, though not a Raja, is recognised by the Government, and treated with equal respect. Kumar Durga Nath was exempted from the operations of the *Arms Act*, with ten of his retainers, and this privilege was continued to the present Kumar, Debendra Nath Rai, on July 23rd, 1894. There are many family idols in the house, such as Radha Mohun and Brindaban Chandra and Gouranga, and many "Livas." The Kunjaghatta family is respected in Hindu society, partly on account of the fact that Maharaja Nunda Kumar,* gave a feast to a lakh of Brahmins, and was afterwards known as Bhadoura Nunda Kumar, that is, the Nunda Kumar of Bhadrapur.

The house in which Nunda Kumar lived in Kasimbazar is still standing, and now occupied by one of his descendants, Kumar Debendra Nath Rai (*vide* illustration facing p. 227).

* Nunda Kumar held various offices under the Nawabs Nazim, and in the time of Suraj-u-Dowlah was Governor of Hughli. In 1764 A.D. the Emperor Shah Alum conferred upon him the title of *Maharaja*. He was in his seventieth year when he entered into a struggle with Warren Hastings, the result of which is well known. In the year 1775, after trial in the Calcutta High Court, Nunda Kumar was convicted of forgery, and sentenced to be hanged. This case has given rise to endless discussion, and to the production of a work by Sir James Fitz-James Stephen, in proof of the Maharaja's guilt. In reply to this, Mr. Beveridge, formerly of the Indian Civil Service, has published a volume which upholds the innocence of Nunda Kumar. I do not propose to enter into any controversy. Let those who wish to form an opinion read the available literature on the subject. Personally I think with Mr. Beveridge, that the execution of Nunda Kumar was a grave miscarriage of justice. It is one of the virtues of the past that it is *past*, and no good can come from a re-opening of the question.—ED.

XXV.

THE MOJUMDARS OF ISLAMPUR.

THE family of the Mojumdars of Islampur seems to have been in possession of its estates from the early part of the sixteenth century, and its founder was one Janandan Mojumdar. An inscription on one of the temples on the estate reveals the fact that the third Zemindar, Sunkar, was living in 1586 A.D. Babu Gopi Mohun Mojumdar, generally admitted to have been the most celebrated member of a family where all were worthy of respect, was born in 1822 A.D. The cares of management fell upon his shoulders when only a boy nine years old, and the estate to which he succeeded was not in a very prosperous condition, being much encumbered with debts. The estate was first placed under the care of the Court of Wards, but was subsequently made over to his relatives (maternal uncles), who managed his affairs under the general supervision of the District Magistrate of Murshidabad. This arrangement does not seem to have worked well, and the boy, with a courage and ability rare in boys of thirteen years of age, took his burden into his own hands, and justified his action by clearing the estate from its troubles. He grew up to be a man of sound business qualities, combined with a love of scholarship, and the study of languages. He is said to have been proficient in Sanskrit, Persian, and English. He possessed a powerful memory, even as a child, and at the age of seven could repeat the *Rasha Panchadhya* (Krishna's dancing festivities). He was very tolerant in religious matters, kind to his tenants, and an indefatigable worker. When rural sub-registrars were first appointed, Babu Gopi Mohun Mojumdar readily consented to assist the local Government by opening a registration office in his village. His work in this department was crowned with success, and he received the thanks it deserved.

The work of Babu Gopi Mohun Mojumdar was carried on by a son, of whom he had every reason to be proud. Babu Hari Krishna Mojumdar was created a "Rai Bahadur" in January, 1895, as a well-merited reward for years of devotion to public duties as an Honorary Magistrate, and as Chairman of the Sudder (headquarters) Local Board. This honour, unfortunately, he did not long enjoy, as in that very same year he died, at the early age of thirty-nine. In the midst of public and private duties he found time for literary work. He was the author of "The History of Ancient India," and was at the time of his death still engaged on a critical review of Sanskrit verse. He was fully conscious of the backwardness of his birthplace, and tried his best to promote the spread of higher, and primary education, among the people of his part of the district, by founding and maintaining a High School and a school for girls.

The following extract shows how greatly his death was mourned :—

"The district of Murshidabad is mourning the death of Babu Hari Krishna Mojumdar, Rai Bahadur, of Islampur, in the prime of life. He had recently returned from a visit to Calcutta, during which he had received the well-merited distinction of 'Rai Bahadur' at the Belvedere Durbar, and was apparently in perfect health when he succumbed to a fit of apoplexy. The deceased gentleman was foremost in every work tending to promote the good of his district, and enjoyed the respect and confidence of all classes. His funeral was attended by Mr. J. Kennedy, Magistrate-Collector of

RAI HARI KRISHNA MOJUMDAR BAHADUR.

Charu Krishna Mojumdar.

Murshidabad, and by a large number of leading residents of Berhampur."—*The Englishman*, December 27th, 1895. Other newspapers wrote in the same strain.

The district lost a valuable public servant as shown by the following extract from the proceedings of a meeting of the Murshidabad District Board, held on January 16th, 1896:—

"Resolved, that the Board wishes to place on record the feeling of loss it has sustained by the death of the late Rai H. K. Mojumdar Bahadur, and that the members desire to express their sympathy with the family. Memo. No. 1,016 D.B.

"Murshidabad District Board, Berhampur, January 30th, 1896.

"Copy forwarded to Babu Charu Krishna Mojumdar, brother of late Rai H. K. Mojumdar Bahadur, for information and communication to the family of the late Rai Bahadur.

(*Signed*) "J. KENNEDY, *Chairman*."

The present representatives of this family are two brothers, Babu Charu Krishna Mojumdar and Babu Priya Krishna Mojumdar, good types of well-educated Bengali gentlemen. While relinquishing no important features of racial custom and religion, they have adopted all Western methods and ideas which could be useful to them in their zemindari affairs. Seeing that the estate did not provide sufficient work for both of them, the younger brother wisely sought and obtained an appointment as manager to the Maharaja of Gidhour. His work is highly spoken of. The family property is managed by Babu Charu Krishna Mojumdar with success, and a note on certain improvements and experiments in agriculture carried out on the Islampur estates, which he has kindly furnished for this work, is given below:—

REPORT ON AGRICULTURAL EXPERIMENTS.

Potatoes.

The cultivation of potatoes being unknown to the peasants of the eastern part of this district, Babu Charu K. Mojumdar tried experiments with the Naini Tal seed potatoes, to induce them to follow his example in case the experiments succeeded. The "Sehai Devi" tree and fruit gardens at Almorah supplied him with the seed potatoes at a very favourable rate, and they were planted on ordinary land, only ploughed, and manured with two or three cartloads of ashes. The potatoes were planted in lines a foot and a half apart, and the distance between each row was nine inches. About three inches of the earth was removed from the surface, the seed put in, and fresh earth thrown over it sufficient to cover it. From the date of the sowing, which was towards the beginning of November, until the potatoes germinated, the surface was sprinkled with water every evening. The whole land was subsequently thoroughly watered by means of that excellent system of irrigation so very common in Behar, but which was totally unknown in this part of the country, by an "indigenous" structure known by the name of *Lâthas* (water-lifting levers). This system was introduced, and people have since resorted to it, as they find it as little expensive as it is highly useful, dispensing as it does with the necessity of depending entirely upon the whims of the weather. Water from a pool close by can conveniently be drawn upon by means of these *Lâthas*, and poured on the land. The experiments answered the highest expectations. The yield was 32½ maunds* per bigah,† while the amount of seed used was four maunds per bigah. After deducting all possible expenses the nett profit, per bigah, was found to be Rs. 43. With justifiable pride it has been noticed that the villagers round about have since begun to cultivate the Naini Tal potatoes. It was also found on experiment that the method of

* About 82 lbs. = 1 maund. † 3⅓ bigahs = 1 acre.

hanging them in baskets from the ceiling of the first floor of the house, and taking care to pick out the rotten ones, was the most convenient means of preserving the seed potatoes from one season to another.

This enterprising farmer also planted cassava* in accordance with the directions contained in Mr. N. G. Mukherji's lecture on cassava cultivation, with promise of success. The cassava flour and the Brazilian arrowroot made from the crop were sent to the Director of Land Records and Agriculture for inspection, and were pronounced "very fair." He, however, suggested that *márkin*, or some other comparatively thicker cloth, should be used for straining the arrowroot. The cuttings for seed purposes were obtained from the Shibpur Agricultural Farm. It is intended to extend the scope of this branch of agriculture, and to obtain more tangible and direct profits, so as to induce the peasants to grow this profitable and interesting crop on patches of land as a set-off against the consequences of bad seasons.

Experiments with other valuable crops, which are not generally cultivated in this part of the district, have been tried, and the reports on the results of such operations have drawn the following remarks from the Director of Land Records and Agriculture to the Government of Bengal:—

"Babu Charu K. Mojumdar, a leading Zemindar of Islampur, in Murshidabad, made some interesting experiments with potatoes, cassava, sugar-cane, and other crops, and has favoured me with a report on the results attained by him. This gentleman has cultivated his potatoes at a profit, and has done much to encourage their cultivation in the neighbourhood. He has also contrived to preserve seed potatoes of the Naini Tal variety through the hot weather and the 'rains,' a matter of considerable difficulty. The further developments of this gentleman's experiments will be awaited with much interest."—*Extract from the Report of the Director of the Department of Land Records and Agriculture, Bengal, for the year* 1899-1900.

* *Manihot utilissima*, from which tapioca is obtained.

PRIYA KRISHNA MOJUMDAR.

HOUSE OF KUNJAGHATTA FAMILY.
ONCE THE HOUSE OF MAHARAJA NUNDA KUMAR.

BABU PULIN BIHARI SEN AND HIS RESIDENCE IN BERHAMPUR.

XXVI.

THE SEN FAMILY OF BERHAMPUR.

ONE of the most distinguished families in the Murshidabad district is that of the Sens of Berhampur. The founder of the family was Krista Kanta Sen, a Kayastha by "caste," who was born about the middle of the eighteenth century, and amassed great wealth in the service of the Government, as Diwan to the Salt Board, under Mr. Colbert. He had an elder brother, Krishna Govinda Sen, to whom he made over the family dwelling-house at Berhampur, together with large estates, while he himself finally settled in Calcutta, where his house is still well known by the name of the "Diwan's House." It is on record that he had acquired landed property before the "Permanent Settlement" of 1793 A.D. Krista Kanta died, leaving no issue, but his brother, Krishna Govinda, had six sons, Guru Das, Shiva Prosad, Radha Mohun, Madan Mohun, Bhuban Mohun, and Lal Mohun; and the present members of the family are descended from this line. Krishna Govinda dedicated a temple to the god Radha Govindaji at Berhampur, together with a property returning an annual income of four thousand rupees. His eldest son, Guru Das Sen, held the high, and responsible, post of Provincial Diwan under the Honourable East India Company, in the district of Moinpur in the N.W. Provinces, and greatly increased the family prestige. Radha Mohun Sen established a temple to the god Bala-Deviji, together with a *dharmasala*, or rest-house, for travellers, at Brindaban, and endowed them with a property yielding a yearly income of five thousand rupees. He also excavated at the same place several wells for the use of the public. He is still remembered at Brindaban with esteem for his great learning and piety.

Bhuban Mohun Sen founded a *sadabrata* (almshouse for the poor, without distinction of caste or creed), an *atibhisala* (or guest-house for Hindus), and a *dharmasala* at Berhampur, which are still fully maintained by his descendants, and are resorted to, not only by Asiatics, but also by persons of a better class from all parts of the country, who are all carefully attended to, fed, and lodged. He allotted an annual sum of six thousand rupees for the support of these institutions.

Shiva Prosad left a son, Biswanbhar Sen; Madan Mohun a son, Pulin Bihari Sen; and Lal Mohun a son, Ram Das Sen; who were all known throughout the province for their generosity and public spirit.

Babu Pulin Bihari Sen was a favourite with the European community of the Station, and was a particular friend of the eminent Captain Layard, after whose design his *boitokkhana* (house) on the Strand Road was built.

Dr. Ram Das Sen highly distinguished himself during his short life by his attainments as a scholar and antiquarian of world-wide fame, and also by his philanthropy and his encouragement of learning; a combination which is rare among the landed aristocracy of Bengal. He was the author of several well-known Bengali works, for which he was honoured with the title of "Doctor" from Italy. He also visited Europe with his cousin's son, Babu Nitai Charan Sen, and has left behind an extensive collection of manuscripts and books, in English, Bengali, and Sanskrit, which, perhaps, forms one of the most splendid private libraries in India.

A bust of the doctor has been erected from public subscriptions by the people of the Murshidabad district, in recognition of his public and private virtues and literary services. It was unveiled on the 1st of August, 1899, by the Honourable Sir John Woodburn, K.C.S.I., the Lieut.-Governor of Bengal, and is outside the compound of the Berhampur College.

Babu Ram Das Sen was born on December the 10th, 1845. Ram Das had the misfortune to lose his father when he was still an infant, and his early education was therefore somewhat neglected. But as he grew in years he began gradually to acquire a taste for learning, which induced those habits of industry and study that enabled him, while still a young man, to take rank among the literary celebrities of his time. He now entered upon those antiquarian and philosophical researches which attracted the notice of European scholars, and won for him the admiration of, among others, Professor Max Müller, Dr. Weber, and Count Angelo De Gubernatis. In the prosecution of these researches, he visited Europe, in the year 1885. He was an indefatigable collector of old and rare books, both Sanskrit and Bengali, and his library is still one of the best owned by a private gentleman. His Bengali poems and his contributions to the principal Bengali journals of the country are a rich mine of thought and information. Indeed, they were so highly appreciated that they earned him the sobriquet of the "Literary Zemindar."

Ram Das published several works, a list of which is appended—the most renowned of which, "The Aitihasic Rahasya" was dedicated to Professor Max Müller. The learned Professor, in his address to the Oriental Congress of London, spoke very highly of this book. In the course of the same address, he further remarked:—"In the *Antiquary*, a paper very ably conducted by M. Barges, we meet with contributions from Ram Das Sen and several other learned Indians, which are read with the greatest interest and advantage by European scholars."

Dr. Ram Das Sen was a distinguished member of the "Asiatic Society" of Bengal, the "Agricultural and Horticultural Society" of India, the "Sanskrit Text Society" of London, the Oriental Academy of Florence, the "British Indian Association" of Bengal, the "Societa Asiatica Italiana" of Italy, and the "Royal Asiatic Society" of Great Britain, and he received the title of "Doctor" from the Oriental Academy of Florence.

Sir Richard Temple, while Lieutenant-Governor of Bengal, conferred upon him a certificate of honour, in recognition of his loyalty to Government, the services rendered by him to the public, and the interest taken by him in educational matters and in pursuit of literature. Sir Alexander Mackenzie also, when visiting Berhampur, spoke of Dr. Ram Das Sen as an ornament to the district.

In her book of travels, Mrs. Mitchell, wife of Dr. Murray Mitchell, thus speaks of Dr. Ram Das Sen:—"We found him a very intelligent, well educated, modest man. Dr. Murray Mitchell had much interesting conversation with this young Zemindar, and found him to be a very good Sanskrit scholar."

But his literary and philosophical acquirements were not his only title to distinction. He was a sincere and sympathetic friend to poor Indian scholars, and a warm philanthropist. Nor must it be forgotten that, as an Honorary Magistrate of the Local Bench, as a Commissioner of the local Municipality, and also as a member of the Board of Trustees of the local College, he rendered very excellent services both to the Government and the community at large.

He died on August the 19th, 1887, leaving his country to mourn the loss of one of her ablest and worthiest sons.

The following is a list of the books written by Dr. Ram Das Sen:—

(1) Kusumamala

(2) Tatwasangit Lahari

DR. RAM DAS SEN.

(3) Chaturdaspadi Kabitamala
(4) Kabitalahari
(5) A lecture on modern Buddhistic Researches delivered at the Berhampur Literary Society (in English)
(6) Aitihasic Rahasya
(7) Bharat Rahasya
(8) Ratna Rahasya
(9) Bangalir Europe Darsan
(10) Buddhadeb, a work published after the death of the author.

The following note of the ceremony of unveiling the bust of Ram Das Sen is of some interest:—

"On the morning of August 1st, 1899, Maharaja Manindra Chandra Nandy, Secretary and Treasurer of the "Ram Das Sen Memorial Committee," after reading a short account of Dr. Ram Das Sen and the proceedings of the Memorial Committee, requested the Honourable Sir John Woodburn to unveil the bust. The Lieutenant-Governor, after a short speech, opened (*sic*) it. Then Babu Radhika Charan Sen, senior member of the Berhampur Sen Zemindar family, and then president of the "Murshidabad Association," thanked his Honour for this singular act of kindness displayed towards the family of the deceased Doctor, and introduced to him the three sons of Dr. Sen, Babus Mani Mohun Sen, Hiranmoy Sen, and Bodhisattwa Sen, and other members of the family, Babus Vishnu Charan Sen, Nitai Charan Sen, and Srivan Bihari Sen. It goes without saying that this kind act of his Honour has endeared him the more to the people in general, as the lamented Dr. Sen was universally popular here."

The following inscription appears on the tablet, below the bust:—

TO THE MEMORY
OF
DR. RAM DAS SEN,
Born Dec. 10th, 1845. *Died Aug. 19th*, 1887,

An eminent Oriental scholar, a learned antiquarian, and a staunch friend of education.
This bust is raised by his admiring and grateful friends, the people of the district of Murshidabad.

August 1st, 1899.

Babu Biswambhar Sen left three sons, Radhika Charan Sen, Vishnu Charan Sen, and Nitai Charan Sen. Babu Srivan Bihari Sen is the son of Babu Pulin Bihari Sen. Dr. Ram Das Sen's sons are Mani Mohun Sen, Hiranmoy Sen, and Bodhisattwa Sen. Babu Radhika Charan Sen, who died lately, was well known throughout the district as an intelligent and public-spirited zemindar. The members of the Sen family possess landed property in the districts of Murshidabad (including some in the town of Berhampur), Nadia, Birbhum, Hughli, Jessore, Midnapur, Dinajpur, the twenty-four Pergunnahs, and also in the town of Calcutta.

XXVII.

RADHIKA CHARAN SEN.

THE late Babu Radhika Charan Sen, a great-grandson of the Diwan, was a distinguished member of Berhampur local society. He was educated in the local College, and possessed a very fair knowledge of the English language, and history. He was a man of good natural parts, thoroughly understood Zemindari business, and was universally loved and respected for his gentlemanly manners and hospitable disposition. He was once an assessor and deputy Collector of Income Tax, under Mr. Hankey, the then Magistrate of this district; and in that capacity obtained a considerable reputation for his industry and efficiency, as may be seen from his many certificates from the Commissioner of the Rajshaye Division, and from the Magistrates. He was for many years a Municipal Commissioner, and from the beginning of the Berhampur Bench, an Honorary Magistrate, with second-class power, and a member of the Board of Trustees of the local College. As Vice-President of the "Murshidabad Association," he very ably managed the affairs of that important institution. He was pre-eminently the amateur horticulturist of the district, and had a first-class garden at Badarpur, a mile and a half distant from the town of Berhampur, where there were many good roses, and fruit trees, brought from various parts of India. The garden was often visited by the European officers and non-officials of the district. He was the head of the Sen family, and had some connection with every public service. He died in 1899, at the age of fifty-eight, leaving two sons behind him, named Jogesh Charan Sen, and Satya Charan Sen, who are the only heirs to his Zemindaries in Calcutta, Hughli, the twenty-four Pergunnahs, Midnapur, Jessore, Birbhum, Nadia, and Murshidabad. Mr. Kennedy, a Magistrate and Collector of Murshidabad, paid the following tribute to the late Deputy-Magistrate's memory:—"His quiet, unassuming character, and lovely garden, were always admired by me. His place in society will be very difficult to fill up. His sad death is not only a great loss to the town, but also to the whole district."

BABU RADHIKA CHARAN SEN.

THE HON. BABU BAIKANTA NATH SEN.

XXVIII.

BABU BAIKANTA NATH SEN.

BORN in 1843, of an old and respectable family, in the village of Alumpur, in the sub-division of Cutwah, in the district of Burdwan, Baikanta Babu's father was an officer in the District Judge's Court at Murshidabad, holding a responsible post, and respected by all who knew him as a pious, orthodox, Hindu gentleman.

Baikanta Nath Sen came to Berhampur when about five years old, and was admitted into the Saidabad "Hardinge Vernacular School," where he prosecuted his studies till the time when the Berhampur College was established, in 1853.

In 1859 he passed the Entrance Examination of the Calcutta University from the Berhampur College, was placed in the first division, and secured a scholarship of Rs. 8 a month, which scholarship was then known by the name of "The Junior Scholarship." He continued his studies in the Berhampur College until 1861, when he passed the "Senior Scholarship" Examination, and secured a scholarship worth Rs. 20 a month.

After securing the "Senior Scholarship" he had to join the Presidency College at Calcutta in the third-year class, from which class he was, according to the University rules, obliged to appear in the F.A. Examination, which he passed in the year 1862. He took his B.A. degree in 1863 and the B.L. degree in 1864, heading the list of successful candidates, and securing the University Law Gold Medal. In March, 1864, he was enrolled as a *vakeel* (Barrister) of the Calcutta High Court, and since then he has been practising at the Bar.

For about two years after his enrolment he practised at the Purnea Bar, with a view to learning *Urdu*, to prepare himself for the Agra High Court, and he would have joined the Agra Bar but for the death of a younger brother. His mother wished him to live with her and practise at the Berhampur Bar. He had the greatest affection and veneration for his mother, and he used in all matters to carry out her wishes. He therefore gave up the idea of joining the Agra Bar, and commenced practising at Berhampur from the year 1866, and he is now the recognised leader of the local Bar. His practice is not confined, however, to Berhampur alone, but he accepts briefs and conducts cases in many other districts.

He was appointed an Honorary Magistrate in 1873, a few years after he came to Berhampur, and was elected a Municipal Commissioner. He was also appointed a member of the Road Cess Committee. He resigned his post of Honorary Magistrate in 1899.

In 1877, on the occasion of the assumption of the title of "Empress of India" by her late Majesty Queen Victoria, he was granted a certificate of honour to the following effect:—

"By command of his Excellency the Viceroy and Governor-General, this certificate is presented in the name of Her Most Gracious Majesty Victoria, Empress of India, to Babu Baikanta Nath Sen, Honorary Magistrate of Murshidabad, in recognition of his loyalty to Government, his unselfish devotion to public duty, and his services to the cause of vernacular education.

"*January 1st*, 1877." *(Signed)* "RICHARD TEMPLE.

Sir Alexander Mackenzie (then Mr. Mackenzie, the District Magistrate of Murshidabad), in presenting the Certificate of Honour, addressed a note to him to the following effect:—

"BABU BAIKANTA NATH SEN.

"To you also, my friend, I have much pleasure in making over this token of the Queen's approval. Your special merit lies perhaps in this—that your brilliant natural abilities have not been blighted by conceit, and are not likely so to be. A hard-working Magistrate, a steady frequenter of the dullest Municipal Committees, and still the foremost ornament of your District Bar, you are a bright example to the other rising lawyers of Bengal."

(*Signed*) "A. MACKENZIE, *Magistrate*.

"BERHAMPUR, *January* 1st, 1877."

In 1885 Babu B. N. Sen was elected Chairman of the Berhampur Municipality, and he was re-elected Chairman in the following years, and served as Chairman of the Berhampur Municipality from 1885 to 1894.

In 1888 he was appointed a Visitor of the Berhampur Jail, and in 1888 he was appointed a Visitor of the Berhampur Lunatic Asylum. These two offices he still has the honour of holding. He is a staunch advocate and supporter of the Indian National Congress, and he is the Secretary to the Standing Congress Committee of the Murshidabad district. He takes keen interest in the "Murshidabad Association," of which he was the President from 1885 to 1894, and of which he is still a Vice-President. He takes active and sympathetic interest in all public constitutional movements in the district.

He is a member of the Board of Trustees for the management of the Berhampur College, and he takes great interest in matters educational, and still acts as Secretary to the Saidabad "Hardinge Vernacular School," where he commenced his education.

Though residing for the greater part of the year in the district of Murshidabad, his family residence is at his birthplace, where some members of his family live, with a regular establishment and considerable landed property. Every year he goes to his native village, with all the members of his family, during the *Durga Puja* vacation, and holds the *Pujas* there.

The District Boards of the Burdwan division elected him and recommended him to the Bengal Government for a seat in the Bengal Legislative Council, and he was appointed a member by H.H. the Lieutenant-Governor of Bengal, with the previous sanction of the Government of India, in July, 1899. His term expired in July, 1901.

He is the chief legal adviser of most of the local zemindars of the district, and was for about ten years the chief adviser of the late Maharani Surnamoyi, C.I., of Kasimbazar, and it was during that period that the coal fields, belonging to the Kasimbazar Raj estate, and lying in the district of Burdwan, were opened. He enjoys the confidence of, and gets retainers from, many of the local European firms.

In his own family he is joint, in food, with his brothers and cousin, but he bears the whole of the family expenses and maintains a large establishment; his brothers, and cousin, like himself, acquiring property for themselves from their individual earnings.

He has, living, a wife, four sons, and two daughters. The eldest boy went up for the B.A. examination in 1901.

Rai Sitab Chand Bahadur

THE NAHAR FAMILY.

THE following pages contain extracts from a translation, more or less free, of a Bengali book entitled, "Nahar Vansa Brittanta" (Hare Press, 1895). The "Brittanta," was compiled at the instance of Rai Sitab Chand, Bahadur, and his son, Babu Rai Mani Lal Nahar Bahadur, of Azimganj. Any merit in this work as regards the collection and arrangement of materials, etc., must belong exclusively to Babu Abinash Chandra Das, M.A., B.L., author of the original. March 11th, 1896.

THE NAHAR FAMILY, OF AZIMGANJ.

The Nahars belong to the Oswal* sect of the Jains. Their ancestors, before they embraced Jainism, are said to have been *Kshatriyas* of the Pramar line, having its founder in Pramar. Counting from him, Rai Sitab Chand Nahar, Bahadur of Azimganj, stands eighty-first in descent.

It will not be out of place here, perhaps, to inquire into the personality and historical importance of Pramar. He was a descendant of the *Agni-Kula* (literally, a race of fire), which had its origin in the defence of Hinduism against the Jains.

"There are four races to which the Hindu genealogists have given the name 'Agni,' or the element of fire, as progenitor. The Agni-Kulas are, therefore, the sons of *Vulcan*, as the others are of *Sol*, *Mercury*, and *Terra*. These four *Agni-Kulas* are: the *Pramara*, the *Purihara*, the *Chalook* or *Solanki*, and the *Chohan*.†

"That these races, the sons of Agni, were but regenerated and converted by the Brahmins to fight their battles, the interpretation of their allegorical history will disclose; and as the most ancient of their inscriptions are in *Pali* character, discovered wherever the Buddhist religion prevailed, their being declared of the race of Tusta or Tukshac (figuratively, the serpent) warrants our asserting the *Agni-Kulas* to be of the same race which invaded India about two centuries before Christ. It was about this period that Parswa, the twenty-third Buddha, appeared."

* An ancient lay explains the origin of the *Oswals* in the following manner:—Ratna Prabhu Swie, the twelfth preceptor from the Jain Saint Mahabir (*Bardhaman*), after he had assumed the chief priesthood, came to Osia in Jodhpur. Chammeda, the presiding goddess of the city, was his first convert, whose name he changed into Sanchal, or Sackcha (literally, follower of the true religion). Of the Rajputs, he converted as many as 484,000 to his own religion; and, all of them being citizens of Osia, were thenceforth called the Oswals. Uppálor Utpál, the then Raja of Osia, together with his family, was among the converts. Thus arose the five hundred *gotras* (groups) among the Oswals, corresponding to the five hundred heads of families initiated into the Jain religion at that time. To these Rajputs the Hindu Brahmins would no longer act as priests, and those consenting to do so were afterwards known as Bhojak Brahmins, who, in their turn, accepted gifts from none but the Jains.

† "The Annals and Antiquities of Rajásthán," by Lieutenant-Colonel James Tod, Vol. i., Chap. vii., pp. 85-87. (Unno Purna Printing Works, 1895.)

Many of the princes professed the Buddhist, or Jain faith, up to periods so late as the Mahomedan invasion.

The Pramara, though not, as his name implies, the "chief warrior," was the most potent of the *Agni-Kulas*. He sent forth thirty-five branches, several of whom enjoyed extensive sovereignties. "The world is the Pramara's," is an ancient saying, denoting their extensive sway; and the *Nau-Koti Marusthali* signified the nine divisions into which the country, from the river Sutlij to the ocean, was partitioned amongst them.

Maheswar, Dhar, Mandu, Oojein, Chandrabhaga, Cheetore, Abor, Chandravati, Mohun, Maidana, Parmavati, Omrakoti, Bekher, Loduvna, and Puthen, are the most conspicuous of the capitals they conquered, or founded.

Strange that Ashadharji, descended from a race, owing its very origin to the defence of Hinduism, should renounce his own religion in favour of Jainism! Yet such was the fact. The Nahar family chronicle represents Anar Kunda as the original abode of Pramar, probably Anal-Kunda. In course of time the Pramar family divided itself into various branches. Dhirraoji, the ninth in descent from Pramar, the branch from which the Nahars sprang, lived at Dhara Nagari. The seventeenth descendant, Premraoji, assumed the title of Chakraváti (head of a number of chiefs), and lived at Garkhambaj, which he very probably ruled as King. We find the same title borne by all the ten descendants that follow him, there being only one exception. We find it again in Vijay Pal, the thirty-first in descent from Pramar, who left Garkhambaj, and ruled at Kuopnagar. The Nahar family chronicle mentions, after him, no other name bearing the royal title.

Ashadharji (the thirty-fifth descendant) was the first to bear the title of Nahar (literally signifying a tiger). Tradition explains its origin as follows:—The goddess Bhagabati, disguised as a tigress, stole Asdharji from his mother's arms, when an infant, and nursed him with her own milk in the forest. The boy, when he grew up, came out of the forest into the world of men, and, on reaching maturity, distinguished himself by the title of Nahar. It was about the same time that he was, on his renunciation of Hinduism, converted by a Jain missionary, Maundes Suri of Mahanagar (660 A.D.).

For some time after the death of Ashadharji, the Nahars continued to live at Mahanagar, but we find the forty-seventh descendant, Ajeshiji, dwelling in Marwar. Sansamalji, the fiftieth descendant, came from Marwar to Bhilmar.

Kamarmalji (the seventy-third descendant), moved from Bhilmar to Radhria Delbna, and Tej Karanji (next in descent) again passed from the latter place to Degan, in Bikanir. Kharga Sinha (son of the seventy-seventh descendant, Prithvisingh), left Degan and set up his abode at Matikatra in Agra. He was afterwards invited to come to Bengal, and opened his firm at Azimganj, Dinajpur, and Calcutta. Azimganj is at present the home of the Nahars, Dinajpur being a place of business only.

KHARGA SINHA.

Kharga Sinha was born at Degan, in Bikanir, where the Nahars seem to have been wealthy and influential people. Kharga married a maid of his own village. It is a custom among the Jains to touch the gate of the bride's house on the eve of marriage. On such occasions the bridegroom, richly arrayed, and accompanied by his friends and relations, rides with great pomp on horseback: kings and nobles of the royal family alone enjoy the special privilege of riding on an elephant. Kharga Sinha, though not a king himself, was of royal blood, and, blessed with wealth and valour, he was bent on reinstating the royal custom in his own family, instead of tamely following his ancestors, who had cast, as he thought, a slur on their kingly descent by riding on horseback. The ceremony of "gate-touching" was accordingly performed on the back of an elephant with the greatest possible pomp. The marriage, too, seemed to go off smoothly enough after this ceremony. But all this coming to the ear of the ruler of the province, he burned with anger to think that the royal privilege and royal honours should have thus been insulted by one who, he thought, had not the slightest claim to royal descent. Forthwith he ordered his armed followers to bring him the heads of the audacious Kharga Sinha and his father.

The armed followers set out, but, on reaching the house of Kharga, they found it already deserted, the inmates having an inkling of their danger. Kharga Sinha came to Agra and took up his abode at Matikatra. The city, though shorn of much of its former splendour, had still a busy commerce, and it was quite natural for Kharga to adopt the mercantile profession. Already wealthy, he was soon regarded as one of the principal *seths*, or merchants, of the city. While at Agra it was his misfortune to lose his father.

The Jain banker, Jaggat Seth, of Murshidabad, was at this time the foremost in wealth, honour, and rank among his fellow-countrymen. On his way to Delhi, on some royal errand, he stopped at Agra and formed an acquaintance with Kharga Sinha, who was himself a banker, and professed the same religion as Jaggat Seth. Delighted beyond measure with the amiable manners of Kharga, and feeling a lack of members in the Jain community at Murshidabad, he pressed him to come and live with him in Bengal. He had also another reason for making this request. In Kharga Sinha he found the means of fulfilling a promise he had made to the Maharaja Radhanath, of Dinajpur, that he would give his town a wealthy banker, want of which was a subject of complaint with the Maharaja. Kharga Sinha was now asked to open a firm at Dinajpur, and he came to Bengal in the year 1766 or 1767 A.D. The Jain bankers resided and carried on their business chiefly at Azimganj, Baluchar, Mahinapur, Mahajantuli, and Kasimbazar, all lying close to one another on either side of the Bhagirathi. From amongst these towns Kharga Sinha chose Azimganj for his future home.

After he had settled at Azimganj, Kharga Sinha opened a firm at Dinajpur (1769). At Azimganj and Calcutta were also established branches of the main firm, where money-lending, combined with other business, was carried on. Fortune smiled on Kharga Sinha. Maharaja Radhanath and the officials of the East India Company treated him with marked respect.

But Kharga was too sagacious and far-sighted not to see that trade, however lucrative at first, was a most unsafe thing to rely upon. It involved risks of the most serious kind, and to fail in trade once was very often to fail for ever. The possession of landed property alone could counteract, to a certain extent, the fickleness of fortune, and would effectually remove all anxiety. He accordingly bought at public auction, between the years 1796 and 1797 A.D., a part of the estate of Maharaja Radhanath, which was put up for sale for arrears of revenue. This was the beginning of the zemindari of the Nahar family. Kharga Sinha now turned his attention towards the safe keeping of his newly acquired land. He won the hearts of all his tenants by his kindness and affability. This was a natural consequence following from his extreme devotion to his own creed, which inculcates upon its followers the duty of universal kindness as one of its first principles. During one of the great famines in Bengal, the sufferings of the people exceeded all anticipation. Kharga took compassion on his own tenants, absolved them from payment of rent for a few years, and paid the Government revenues.

He was loved, not only by his tenants, but by all who were in any way connected with him. Jaggat Seth extended to him the hand of warm friendship. The officials of the East India Company, too, treated him with respect, and were always careful to inform him whenever an estate was on the point of being sold at auction, for what buyer could be found better than Kharga?

Kharga Sinha was now blessed with wealth, honour, rank—with everything desirable, except a son. Uttam Chand, the only son he ever had, was born late in his life (1789). He had, previous to this, been bringing up, with a father's love, a youth, named Moti Chand, though he did not adopt him according to strict legal form.

Kharga's deep affection for Moti, however, still continued unchanged. In 1802 he became seriously ill at Dinajpur, and, perceiving that death was not far off, told Moti and Uttam to share his possessions equally. To this Moti did not consent, Uttam being yet too young to look after his own affairs. Kharga Sinha removed to Azimganj, and died shortly afterwards.

Kharga Sinha could not be characterised as a handsome man. He had marks of small-pox on his face, was of a dark complexion, middle-sized, and wore a beard. But he had a nature which charmed everyone who came in contact with him, and that more than atoned for the peculiarity of his external appearance, by which an old adage tells us not to judge. Deeply attached to his own religion, he built a fine temple to Swami Chanda Prabhu, still to be seen at Dinajpur; and he founded a *dharmasala*.

Uttam Chand and Moti Chand jointly inherited the estate of Kharga Sinha after his death. Moti, being the eldest of the two, took the management of affairs into his own hands. These two loved each other with all the depth of paternal affection, and Uttam was guided in everything by Moti's will. While yet a boy, Uttam succeeded in winning the love of all. But death had marked him out as an early victim, and, when only seventeen, he fell ill at Dinajpur (July, 1806), and passed away, leaving a young widow and family to mourn his loss. The obsequies of Uttam over, Moti Chand tried to keep the management of the estate to himself, as Uttam, on the eve of his death, had executed a will which made Moti the guardian of his widow and her estate. There was in it also an authority of adoption granted to his widow. By virtue of this deed, Moti Chand obtained a certificate from the Court (August, 1806). In the meanwhile, Babu Meghraj, father of the widow, had, for his daughter, taken possession of the firms at Calcutta and Azimganj. This was resented by Moti Chand, and he went at once to law. But the quarrel, as well as the lawsuit, was brought to a sudden end by the death of Moti, which took place unexpectedly in 1808.* Uttam's widow became, on his death, the sole and undisputed possessor of the estate.

BABU MEGHRAJ AND BIBI MAYA KUMAR.

Bibi Maya Kumar married Uttam when ten, was a widow in her fifteenth year, and succeeded to the Nahar estate at seventeen years of age. Lest his young daughter, having no experience in business, should be unable to manage things for herself, Babu Meghraj took the management of her estate in his own hands. The firm at Calcutta and the money-lending business at Dinajpur were now closed, and the Bibi was left with her zemindari only.

Before entering into a detailed account of her own life, we may pause here to give a short

* Out of extreme piety and a disregard of all wordly good, Moti Chand never married.

account of the life of her father, a most remarkable character. He was without a rival in wealth, honour, and liberality, as also in extravagance. His father, the well-known Bula Saha, left him, when a youth of sixteen, a legacy of forty or fifty lakhs of rupees. No wonder that Meghraj, master of such vast wealth at that susceptible age, should give himself up to pleasure. He was excessively fond of music and other amusements, and his house, with singing and dancing almost continually going on, wore a festive appearance all the year round. He could not even sleep, it is said, without the help of music. From among the many stories relating to his extravagance, we select one or two. Once a seller of *attar* came from a distant part to sell the most costly *attars* at Murshidabad. Finding none ready to buy his *attar* at the fabulous rate of Rs. 700 a *tolah*, he was returning to his own country, and passed through Azimganj. The luxurious habits of Babu Meghraj coming to his ears, he saw him, and laid his grievance before him. The Babu, hearing of *attar* at Rs. 700 a *tolah*, asked to see what it was like, and emptied the phial on the tail of a favourite horse that was standing by. The attar-seller was, of course, taken aback, but all his fears were effectually laid to rest by the Babu paying him Rs. 3,500 on the spot. Another story relates how Babu Meghraj, fond of flying kites, used gold or silver thread instead of the ordinary cotton thread, cut it off after a little while, and was delighted to see, from the roof of his house, the crowd scrambling to obtain the kite and its precious thread. His liberality knew no bounds; he spent lavishly and unceasingly to feed the poor, to relieve the distressed, and to provide for the treatment of the sick. To the sick he used to go personally, and arrange for their proper treatment, and sometimes even put under their pillow the money they might need. He engaged four native doctors, who regularly visited the sick, their attendants carrying with them all the necessaries for the patients, and administering to each the medicine and food prescribed.*

The gates of his house, it is said, stood open to all comers day and night, so that anyone and everyone might make his wants known to Babu Meghraj. He was also the founder of a *sadabrata* (for the charitable feeding of all comers), by which a good many men were fed daily. For the convenience of the public, he had a bathing-ghat built on the Bhagirathi; with a *dharmasala* close by, over both of which now flow the waters of the river.

Meanwhile, fortune had been busy turning her wheel, and Babu Meghraj was on the brink of ruin. Reckless extravagance had drained all his wealth, and what wealth could withstand it? He was now over head and ears in debt, and was involved in difficulties, from which he had no hope of extricating himself.

It was precisely at this time that Bibi Maya Kumar, his only daughter, lost her husband. Babu Meghraj forgot his own troubles in those of his widowed daughter, and exerted himself to the utmost to provide for the security and proper management of her estate.

There was a boy, Golab Chand by name, brought up in the family of Babu Meghraj. Born of a family of high rank, he was, in his eighteenth year, adopted by Bibi Maya Kumar, in pursuance of her father's wishes (1815). Golab Chand now undertook to manage everything for the Bibi. The extravagant habits of Babu Meghraj were yet strong, and he spent his daughter's money much in the same way as he had done his own. On one occasion, Maya Kumar took the liberty of openly contradicting her father. Taking it as a most cruel insult, the indignant father left her house, never more to return. Intending to recruit his shattered health, he was on his way to Behar, when he died at Maur (1822).

Babu Meghraj had numerous creditors. His death was, therefore, the signal for an immediate attack on his property at Azimganj. Much of it went into other hands without the knowledge of

* The system of medicine practised was the old Hindu system.

Bibi Maya Kumar, who was then absent at Dinajpur. She came to Azimganj just in time to see her father's dwelling-house on the point of being sold, and lost no time in buying it for herself. This fine mansion, called Aina-Mahál (house of glass), is at present the family residence of the Nahars.

On the death of Babu Meghraj, the management of affairs fell entirely on the shoulders of Bibi Maya Kumar, and it was not long before she involved herself in a domestic quarrel of a most serious kind. In an evil hour Golab Chand was adopted by her. He was disliked by her family priest, Man Sinha, and soon, to crown all, the Bibi herself felt a bitter dislike for her adopted son. Though born of poor parents, Golab Chand was a truly noble soul; he had a keen intellect and a pure character, and it was but natural that, coming of age, he should regard himself as the rightful possessor of the Nahar estate. But this sudden advancement of a nameless youth to so high a position, and his assuming the authority which properly belonged to him, was ill-borne by those placed under him, and they tried to work his ruin. The family priest, Man Sinha, left no stone unturned to poison the mother's mind against the son, till at last the Bibi's dislike for her adopted son rose to such a pitch that she was resolved to turn him out of the house.

Accordingly, one morning, returning from his daily bath in the river, Golab Chand found, to his surprise, the gates of the house shut against him. The porter, in explanation of his conduct, merely said that he had been strictly enjoined by the Bibi, not to let Golab in, so that he was but obeying her commands. He left the place without ceremony, but he knew not where to turn for help. Maya Kumar was a name dreaded throughout Azimganj; and who would dare shelter one that had been refused shelter by her, one especially, whose sole wealth consisted in the single piece of cloth he wore, a bathing towel, and a gold necklace? After long and weary deliberation, he bent his steps towards the house of his old friend, Babu Dharam Chand Srimal, a local zemindar of repute, who did not stand much in fear of others, one of the truest and most beloved of Golab's friends. The Babu* received him with open arms. Golab Chand had now some solid ground to stand upon, and had leisure to take counsel with his friend how best to tide over his difficulties. These events occurred about 1823. An amicable settlement was out of the question. Bibi Maya Kumar denied that she had ever adopted Golab Chand, and, though earnestly requested by many to relent, she insisted on keeping him out of the house. Golab Chand resolved to make his own way back into the house, and establish his claim to the property, or live and die poor. There would be no more stooping, no more reconciliation from his side. He next went to Berhampur, to lay his cause before the law courts. Through the influence of his friend Srimal, many of the rich and powerful at Berhampur lent a willing ear to his complaints, and even offered him loans to conduct the lawsuit. Golab Chand was supplied with the necessary funds by Babu Lalit Mohun Sen, and Babu Lal Mohun Sen (father of the celebrated Dr. Ram Das Sen); Babu Nimai Charan Sen using his influence with them. Babu Nimai Charan promised to conduct the suit on behalf of Golab Chand, provided he would give him a three-thirty-second share of the whole property in case he won, and a deed of contract was executed accordingly.†

In 1826 the suit was formally brought against the Bibi. All the time that the suit was being carried on, Golab Chand applied himself to zemindari business, acting as an apprentice in the zemindari office of Nimai Babu, who had a little land of his own. This part of Golab's training stood him in good stead afterwards. Meanwhile Bibi Maya Kumar had tendered a written statement disowning Golab Chand, and the lawsuit was continued with vigour, on both sides, causing, of course, a great waste of money. The adoption of Golab Chand was at last proved, and the Court,

* Babu is a title like Mr.; but also means gentleman as here used.

† This is not an uncommon practice in India, but such speculative legal work is not regarded with favour in England.

deciding in his favour, declared him to be the rightful owner of the Nahar estate, Maya Kumar being entitled to maintenance only. Against this decision, the Bibi appealed to the Supreme Court, which confirmed the decree of the lower Court, and an appeal to the Privy Council was in contemplation, when the quarrel between the mother and the adopted son was brought to an end through the exertions and mediation of Jaggat Seth, and many other persons of eminence. It involved a sacrifice on the part of Golab, for he had to give up the estate for the use of the Bibi during her lifetime. Golab Chand did, however, keep his word, and did make his own way into the house from which he had once been ejected with so much ignominy. But the proud Bibi, unwilling that the same house should contain them both, withdrew to a house built, close by the river, by her father, Babu Meghraj.

According to his former compact, Babu Golab Chand had to give away a three-thirty-second share of the whole property to Nimai Babu. Bibi Maya Kumar, to facilitate the management of business, gave up her claim to half the property, in favour of Golab Chand, on condition that she should receive a few thousand rupees every year. Babu Nimai Charan, too, gave up his share to Golab Chand, in return for a separate zemindari given to him. Babu Golab Chand thus became again the sole master of the estate.

In 1843 Bibi Maya Kumar went on a pilgrimage, returning after an interval of a year and a half. She built a temple at Azimganj in 1855, and died in her sixty-eighth year, August, 1859.

Golab Chand, as sole master of the estate, turned his attention towards its management. His object was to devise some means by which to relieve his tenants from the oppression of his officers, to prevent himself from being overreached by them, and to provide for a speedy clearance of the debts which weighed so heavily on him. Of the changes introduced by him in the management of his estate, one was particularly liked by the Government officials of the time. There were sixteen different *abwabs* (imposts), imposed upon the tenants of Dinajpur and its neighbourhood. These irregular cesses did not profit the zemindar in any way, but they were a source of income to the *Gomastahs* and *Tasildars* (zemindar's agents and rent collectors), who made them an excuse for much oppression. Babu Golab Chand made direct arrangements with his tenants, by which they were to pay him an extra five-pice* for every rupee of their rent, and were, in return, to enjoy common rights over the village trees, commons, and ponds, belonging to the zemindar. Thus the tenants were set free from the power of grasping officials, and, at the same time, Babu Golab Chand increased his income. It was this kind of practical sagacity and far-sighted policy alone that enabled Golab Chand to lighten the heavy burden of debt incurred by the protracted lawsuit against Bibi Maya Kumar. The debt entailed, in fact, life-long misery upon him.

He had to pass the greater part of his time at Dinajpur, as Azimganj was full of his creditors. But he always intended to act honourably, and if he did not pay off his debts at once, it was because he could not. Golab Chand owed a heavy debt to Babu Lal Mohun of Berhampur; but by the time that the latter sued Golab, the claims had been barred by limitation. Lal Mohun was accordingly worsted in the suit. This defeat greatly disgusted him, and not a doubt remained in his mind about Golab Chand being a most accomplished double-dealer. Golab was in reality so impecunious at the time, that it was quite impossible for him to repay the loan, but he appeared unexpectedly one day, later on, at the house of Babu Lal Mohun, who, as might be expected, gave him the cold shoulder. Babu Golab Chand then said, "I am not come, sir, to beg fresh favours from you. To-day, I have brought with me some valuable ornaments, and I shall deem it a great favour if you will accept them in lieu of cash payment."

* Four pice to an anna.

Golab Chand possessed a strong constitution, and a fearlessness that defied dangers of the most serious kind. On a certain occasion, a band of dacoits was routed by Golab Chand alone. He was journeying by boat to Dinajpur, in company with his young wife, Bibi Pran Kumari. Besides the barge, there were four other boats, and an escort, including his attendants and the boatmen. The boats were moored to a *chur* (sand bank), near Gerriah, about twenty miles from Azimganj. It was an April afternoon, verging on evening, and the men were busily engaged preparing their food, when Babu Golab Chand was informed that a gang of robbers had formed a plan of plundering the boats that very night. All his men, except an officer, Umedmal Dugar, and a faithful *Khansama* (butler), took alarm and fled, leaving Golab Chand to his fate. After nightfall, about ten o'clock, the further part of the *chur* was illumined with numerous torches, borne by men, who, with terrifying shouts, were steadily advancing towards the boats. There could be no mistake about them; they were the dacoits of whom he had heard, and Babu Golab Chand lost no time in preparing himself for defence. He first made his wife promise that, in case he were killed in the contest, she should save her honour by drowning herself in the river, with all her valuables. The wife having taken a solemn oath to keep her promise, the husband rushed out of the boat towards the approaching dacoits, having no fear of death. Umedmal Dugar and the faithful *Khansama*, armed with muskets, followed him. On the approach of the dacoits, Babu Golab Chand fired at them, and at the same time gave vent to shouts, which were echoed by the river banks. Umedmal and the Khansama also shouted in response, and it seemed to the dacoits as if a whole host had gathered to fight against them. Babu Golab Chand had to spend the whole night defending himself. The suspense was over at last. To avoid discovery, the robbers found it to their own interest to retire; the day was dawning, and one or two passenger boats were seen sailing on the river. When morning came, not a single creature was to be seen on the wide *chur*. This exciting event took place in the year 1848. Babu Golab Chand was an extremely handsome man. He was tall and well built, with a fair complexion, large expressive eyes, and an intelligent countenance, indicative of strength and decision. He was fond of playing chess, rowing, and riding. He married twice. His first wife was Bibi Patas Kumari, whom he had married before his expulsion from the house of Bibi Maya Kumar. Patas Kumari was the daughter of a rich man, and the splendour of her marriage ceremony is said to have surpassed anything of the kind in the district. This Patas Kumari was a good woman, endowed with the noblest qualities of womankind. It is not too much to say that she stood almost alone in her wifely devotion, her patience, and her kindness. When Golab Chand was turned out homeless by Bibi Maya Kumar, the wife went to live in her father's house, and passed her days mournfully, never ceasing to feel for her husband. Religious penances and fasts were her constant occupations. No amount of hardship was too much for her, if it promised in any way the blessing of a male child. But this was a fortune never granted her. The only son, born in 1833, died an infant. Her life, so full of trials, had at last one happy passage in it—she saw her husband regain his former possessions, but she was not long the partner of his happier days. This excellent woman passed away in November, 1846.

In February, the next year, Babu Golab Chand married Bibi Pran Kumari, who, born in 1836, was at this time a girl of eleven. In 1849 she gave birth to a son, who survived a few days only.

While residing at Dinajpur, Babu Golab Chand was attacked with fever and diarrhoea.

His health was already impaired by worldly cares and anxieties, and he lost all hope of recovery. He wrote to his wife's mother and brother to come to him at Dinajpur. The mother started at once, and came just in time to have a last look at her son-in-law. Golab Chand died May,

1850, leaving a young widow. His brother-in-law, Bhairabdan Lunaot, arrived at Dinajpur shortly after his death.

By a will, executed before his death, Babu Golab Chand had granted his wife authority of adoption and appointed his wife, her brother, and a faithful officer, the trustees of his estate. There was also an arrangement made in the will which secured a monthly allowance to some of his trusted officials.

The obsequies of her husband over, Bibi Pran Kumari returned with her brother and mother to Azimganj. Her brother Bhairabdan, an intelligent man, undertook to manage the zemindari for his sister. They were eager to adopt a suitable boy, and Bhairabdan thought it best to adopt one who would be able to look after business affairs in a short time. As none, answering to this description, could be found in this part of the country, a youth, named Iswardas, was brought from the west. This Iswardas was older than Bibi Pran Kumari, and it seemed to her quite improper to adopt one older than herself. The proposal to adopt Iswardas was accordingly set aside. There was at this time, at Azimganj, one Kshetsinha Patwari, who traded at Janaki Nagar, in the district of Purnea. He had a son, Gopi Chand,* who was taken from time to time to the house of Babu Golab Chand by his nurse. Golab Chand, a great lover of children, took a particular fancy to this boy and even expressed a wish to adopt him. But the idea of adoption was taken very ill at the time by the parents of Gopi. Afterwards, while living at Janaki Nagar, Gopi Chand suffered from small-pox, of a serious type. One of his elder brothers having died previously of an incurable disease, the illness of Gopi caused his parents much anxiety, and, though he recovered, they lived in constant alarm for his life. About the time that Golab Chand died there came a Sunyasi (hermit), who said to the parents that their boy was a fortunate one, but that they should give him away to some rich man, as their own ill-starred fate would not suffer the boy to live long, if kept to themselves. Bhairabdan Lunaot wrote to Kshetsinha again, offering to adopt Gopi Chand, and the father made up his mind to act on the advice of the Sunyasi. Accompanied by his wife and children, he came to Azimganj (September 1850), and Bibi Pran Kumari adopted Gopi, born in April, 1847, and at this time a child of three years and a half. After adoption, the child's name was changed to Sitab Chand.

Bibi Maya Kumari mourned the loss of her adopted son, and, when Babu Sitab Chand was adopted in the family, she became excessively fond of him. The boy, too, became strongly attached to his grandmother, and any chastisement on the part of Bibi Pran Kumari was resented by the old lady. On her death-bed, she imparted to Babu Sitab Chand advice of priceless worth, which every member of the Nahar family would do well to treasure up in his memory. "Keep away, my darling," she said, "from domestic quarrels of every kind, it is these which have wrought the ruin of our family; never contradict your mother, nay, even if she is in the wrong." It is to the credit of Babu Sitab Chand, that, throughout his life, he has not, for a single moment, forgotten the last words of his beloved grandmother.

Bibi Pran Kumar was born in July, 1836. She was married to Babu Golab Chand in February, 1847, gave birth to a child, which died an infant, in 1849, and was a widow in 1850, at the tender age of fourteen. Babu Sitab Chand was adopted by her the same year. Her brother, Bhairabdan Lunaot, continued to manage her business affairs until his death (1855). From that time she had to look after her own affairs, and had also to act as guardian of her adopted son, Sitab Chand, who was yet a minor.

Having ability and sagacity quite beyond her years, she managed her business matters so wisely that her tact excited the surprise of many. She had a splendid intellect and very great powers of

* Mahatab Chand, otherwise called Jhabu Babu, was another son of Kshetsinha Patwari.

decision. On all important matters people eagerly sought her advice. A determined enemy of falsehood, she would not even condescend to speak to any person whom she had reason to believe was not veracious. She was a capital judge of character, and it was impossible to deceive her by any exercise of cunning, however skilful. Kindness was another important feature of her character. To relieve the distressed, her purse was always open, and a certain sum of money was, every month, regularly spent in charity: the strict secrecy she observed in giving aid showing the true spirit that dictated it. Under her wise management, too, the material prosperity of the Nahars increased appreciably. All the debts contracted by Babu Golab Chand were paid, and the Nahar family was restored to its former flourishing state.

Bibi Pran Kumari was thoroughly versed in the Bengali language; she could read and talk Bengali with ease. All communications on business matters had to be read out to her, and she was always ready with her wise counsels, according to which everything was done.

Babu Sitab Chand was married in May, 1859, and in September of the same year Bibi Pran Kumari went on a pilgrimage, accompanied by her family. On this occasion she went only as far as Behar and returned home.

In 1869 they went again on pilgrimage to Mount Paresnath in the district of Hazaribagh. A great many of the inhabitants of Azimganj were their fellow-pilgrims, in all, two hundred and seventy-five persons. While returning home they met with a serious accident, which, but for the intervention of rare good fortune, would have ended fatally, bringing to extinction all the Oswal families of Azimganj.

It was a wintry night. The face of the moon, though full, was hidden by an eclipse and shed only a dismal light. In an evil hour the railway train in which they were, left Barakar Station, and was running at a great speed towards Sitarampur. Most of the passengers were Oswals of Azimganj, returning home from pilgrimage. The train travelled at such a high rate of speed that the passengers were unable to keep their seats, while the luggage was tossed about in all directions. Every minute they expected some serious disaster, and they had not long to wait in suspense. All of a sudden the train came to a standstill with a terrible crash, heightened by the piercing cries of the affrighted passengers. In a moment the passengers leaped out of the carriages, and found that the engine and its driver had been smashed to pieces. It was a singular piece of good fortune, however, that none of the passengers were killed. Bibi Pran Kumari, along with the rest, were more than grateful that they had been spared.

The Nahars were out on pilgrimage several times afterwards. In 1873 they travelled as far as Delhi. They left again in September, 1879, returning home in July, 1882. During the pilgrimage they undertook in 1889, they visited Guzrat, Katiwar, and other distant provinces of India, and, while stopping in her father's house at Jeypur, Bibi Pran Kumari was suddenly taken ill and died (October, 1889).

Babu Sitab Chand, born on the 17th of April, 1847, was adopted, as we have said, by Bibi Pran Kumari at the early age of three. When of age, he became a useful helper to her in the management of business affairs. To his adopted mother he tendered implicit obedience. The Bibi did, indeed, sometimes take him to task, which severity, on certain occasions, was enough to send him away from home, but, however rough her outward conduct might sometimes appear to be, the Bibi loved him at heart. In April, 1859, Babu Sitab Chand was married to the eldest daughter of Joy Chand Bayed, of Azimganj. The bride, born March 31st, 1851, was at the time a girl of eight.

In his boyhood, Babu Sitab Chand had to pass through a number of ordeals. He was attacked

RAI MANILAL NAHAR BAHADUR.

several times with serious illness, and was more than once within a hair's breadth of death. Before his adoption by Bibi Pran Kumari, he was attacked with small-pox, the terrible malady leaving its marks on his face. After his recovery, when his parents were taking him to Azimganj to give him away in adoption, the boat which contained them ran foul of a sunken rock in the river Kusi, and it was only due to the shallowness of the river that his life was saved. He was dangerously ill in his eighth year; and a year after his marriage, again, he became so seriously ill that his friends and relations gave him up for lost. On reaching maturity, however, he showed signs of great ability, but he did not act without the advice of Bibi Pran Kumari. The attaining of his majority was the occasion of many of the poorer tenants and debtors being absolved from the payment of their dues. He arranged wisely for the good management of his estate, and, through him, the Nahar family has recovered, in a short space of time, the high position it formerly occupied in the social scale.

A series of praiseworthy deeds have earned for Babu Sitab Chand the sincere esteem of society and special commendation from the Government of Bengal. He helped materially towards relieving the famine-stricken population of Bengal in 1873. In appreciation of his benevolence and liberality, the Government honoured him, in public Durbar, with the title of "Rai Bahadur" (March 12th, 1875). He was also granted a certificate of honour on the occasion of her Majesty assuming the title of "Empress of India," on the 1st of January, 1877.

Babu Sitab Chand has been the founder of a number of useful public institutions. On the occasion of the jubilee of her late Majesty Queen Victoria's record reign he founded a free English High School, which, we regret to say, has since been closed for want of a sufficient number of students, and for lack of sympathy on the part of the public. The system of feeding all comers—a custom instituted by Kharga Sinha at Siddhachala—has been kept up in the family of Babu Sitab Chand to the present day. To him also are due several gifts made by his mother, Bibi Pran Kumari. She established a charitable *serai* at Kasimbazar, and, in the jubilee year, gave away a garden and well to be used by the public at Baidyanath.

To the Jain god at Siddhachala she presented, in 1881, a massive throne of silver. Her crowning gift was a princely donation of sixteen thousand rupees for the construction of the temple at Bithora. Babu Sitab Chand has set up a charitable hospital at Sitabganj, in the district of Dinajpur, and has promised a permanent endowment for its support. There are two charitable *serais* founded by him, one at Hastinapur, near Meerut, and the other on the ancient road to Mount Abu.

Babu Sitab Chand and Babu Manilal, his eldest son, are both remarkable for their public spirit. They are both members of the Local and the District Boards of Murshidabad, Honorary Magistrates of the Lalbagh Bench, and commissioners of the Azimganj Municipality. Since his appointment, in 1883, Babu Sitab Chand has ably discharged his duties as Honorary Magistrate. Babu Manilal, also appointed an Honorary Magistrate in 1893, is a man of education, of cultivated taste, and zealous in everything calculated to promote the public good. He was educated in English by two English gentlemen, Mr. C. J. Owens and Mr. J. R. D. Fox, both of them teachers of great ability. Babu Sitab Chand has published several books,* more or less pertaining to the Jain religion. He is also the composer of a number of songs. He has a spotless character, and is piously devoted to his own religion. Babu Manilal emulates his father's excellent character.

Among the Jains of Baluchar and Azimganj, Babu Sitab Chand's family have accorded the

* These are "Jaina Stabanabali," "Jaina Juanabali," "Nirastha Tamonidhi," "Nemanathjir Baramasa," "Prasnotharmala," "Nrisinha Champu Kavya," "Sugam Chhatrishi," "Dadhilila," "Dadajika-stabanabali," "Snatra-bidhi," "Dharmalaoni," and "Atmanushasan." Under his auspices was also started a fortnightly magazine called *Uchit-Bakta.*

warmest welcome to education and culture, and the first graduate among the Jains of Bengal was Babu Puran Chand (second son of Babu Sitab Chand), who took his B.A. degree at the Presidency College, Calcutta.

The estates of the family lie mainly in the districts of Dinajpur, Murshidabad, and the Santal Pergunnahs.

Babu Sitab Chand is the father of a large family, whose names, with dates of birth, etc., are given below:—

(1) Manilal Nahar, born April 7th, 1865; married the daughter of Rai Budhsingh Dudhoria, Bahadur of Azimganj, June, 1878. His children are:—(*a*) Bhamarsingh, son, born December 6th, 1883; (*b*) Bahadur Singh, son, born July 23rd, 1885; (*c*) Chand Kumari, daughter, born March 10th, 1887; (*d*) Khudi Singh, son, born April 30th, 1893.

(2) A daughter, born July, 1866, survived only a month. (3) Bibi Phul Kumari, born July 11th 1868; married Bahu Narapat Singh, the second son of Rai Dhanapat Singh Bahadur, January, 1877. They have two sons and three daughters.

(4) A daughter, born October, 1871, is now dead. (5) Bibi Indra Kumari, born July 4th, 1873; married Babu Indra Chand Dudhoria Bahadur, November, 1881. They have a son and two daughters. Babu Indra Chand went to England in June, 1889, returning in October of the same year.

(6) Puran Chand Nahar, B.A., born May 15th, 1875; married the grand-daughter of Rai Meghraj Bahadur, February, 1888. They have two daughters and a son:—(*a*) Tara Kumari, daughter, born May 2nd, 1892; (*b*) Mina Kumari, daughter, born Deeember 6th, 1893; (*c*) Keshari Singh, son, born July 21st, 1895. (7) A son, born November, 1876; died the same month.

(8) Prasama Chand Nahar, born November 30th, 1878; died December 25th, 1891. He was a promising, intelligent boy.

(9) Fateh Singh Nahar, born October 10th, 1881; married the grand-daughter of the late Harek Chand Golecha of Azimganj, March 3rd, 1894.

(10) Kumar Singh Nahar, born October 8th, 1883.

GENEALOGICAL TABLE.*

Through the favour of Goddess Shakti, were born :—

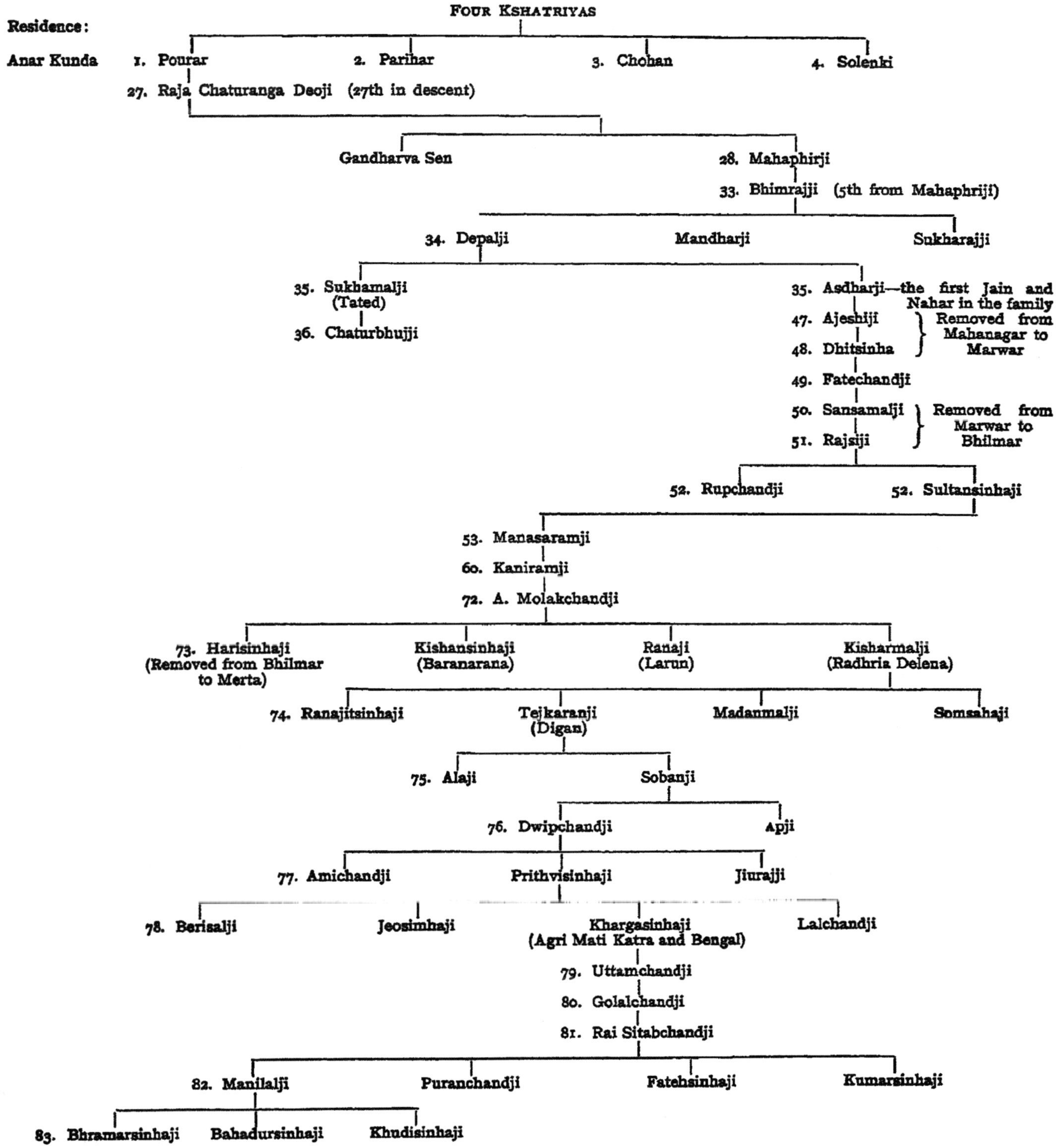

* Want of space has necessitated the omission of many intermediate names in the earlier part of the table. The spelling of names has been left as in the original.

XXX.

THE DUDHORIA FAMILY.

ABOUT the year 1774, the family first settled in Azimganj, having moved from Rajaldesar, in Bikanir, Rajputana. The first to emigrate were Harjimal Dudhoria and his two sons, Sabai Singh and Maujiram.

The following genealogical table will show the descent of the present heads of the family, viz. Rai Budh Singh Dudhoria Bahadur and Babu Bijoy Singh Dudhoria :—

HARJIMAL DUDHORIA (emigrated 1774)

- Sabai Singh
  - Mul Chand
  - Nem Chand
  - Baij Nath
  - Harek Chand
    - Rai Budh Singh Dudhoria Bahadur (Born 1847)
      - Indra Chand (Born 1868. Died 1899)
        - Jaggat Singh (Born 1886)
        - Ranjit Singh (Born 1898)
      - Ajit Singh (Born 1887)
      - Kuwar Singh (Born 1890)
    - Rai Bissen Chand Dudhoria Bahadur (Born 1852. Died 1894)
      - Bijoy Singh (Born 1879)
  - Jalim Singh
- Maujiram
  - Rup Chand

The history of the family affords a capital example of how one may attain to wealth, power, and position in society by dint of sheer perseverance, patient industry, and honest labour. Harjimal and his two sons started life at Azimganj as dealers in country-made cloths, and they were so industrious that they prospered in their trade within a short time. The real prosperity of the family, however, began with Babu Harek Chand Dudhoria, who became, not only a big cloth merchant, but also opened a money-lending business in Calcutta, Surajganj, Azimganj, Jangipur, and Mymensing. He died in 1862, a comparatively rich man, leaving behind a good name and two sons, Babus Budh Singh and Bissen Chand.

The sons, who were quite young at the time, succeeded to their father's wealth and flourishing business, and, as they grew up, joined their combined talent and energy to make a further move towards prosperity. Babu Budh Singh was patient, amiable, and industrious, while Babu Bissen Chand, who displayed wonderful business capacities from his boyhood, was distinguished by a versatile intellect, keen penetration, firm grasp of details, and quick decision. The two brothers lived harmoniously, and were not long in making their mark in the world. They extended their money-lending business to several districts, and opened banks at Calcutta, Surajganj, Mymensing, Jangipur,

RAI BUDH SINGH DUDHORIA BAHADUR.

and Azimganj. People had unbounded faith and confidence in the honest dealings of the bankers, in consequence of which they ran a very successful business. Gradually, they began to invest money in landed property, and ultimately became big Zemindars, owning lands in the districts of Murshidabad, Mymensing, Birbhum, Burdwan, Nadia, Faridpur, Purnea, Dinajpur, and Rajshaye. The brothers were bent, not merely upon amassing wealth, but upon making a proper use of it as well. They helped the poor members of their community, fed thousands of the needy and hungry in times of famine by opening *annachatras* (poor-houses), clothed the poor, contributed to charitable and other funds, constructed, or caused the ladies of their family to construct, *dharmasalas* and temples in several parts of India, for the use of their co-religionists, and did sundry other works of public good, too numerous to mention here. Their good name and fame spread far and wide, so that when Sir Ashley Eden, the then Lieutenant-Governor of Bengal, visited Jangipur (the scene of his early labours in another capacity), he was pleased to honour the brothers by paying them a visit. The Bengal Government was so pleased with their liberality and public services that it conferred on both of them, on January 2nd, 1888, the title of "Rai Bahadur," as a personal distinction. They were also appointed Honorary Magistrates of the Lalbagh Bench in Murshidabad, which Bench they adorned for several years.

Their banking and money-lending business having attained vast proportions, the brothers separated in 1877, and from that time carried on business under separate names. Their landed property remained joint property, and is even now, in part, managed jointly. Though separated in business, they remained united in heart, and prospered each in his own line. In 1894 Rai Bissen Chand Bahadur, after a short illness, died, leaving behind his only son and heir, Babu Bijoy Singh Dudhoria, who was then a promising lad of about fourteen years of age. Rai Budh Singh Bahadur had to take the minor, and the vast estates left by his father, under his charge, having been appointed guardian of the minor's person and property by the District Judge of Murshidabad. Though the management of two estates now devolved upon him, he ably discharged his onerous duties, and increased his nephew's wealth during his minority. He also gave Bijoy a sound and liberal education at home, under the tuition of Babu Abinash Chandra Das, M.A., B.L., a distinguished scholar. Babu Bijoy Singh attained his majority on the 22nd of December, 1900, and assumed direct charge of his estates and banking business. He is an intelligent young man of great promise, of amiable disposition, and strong common-sense, and seems to have inherited the firm grasp and quick decision of his father. He married the youngest daughter of the late Rai Dhunpat Singh, Bahadur of Baluchar.

The members of the Dudhoria family are known to be pious Jains, and have founded *dharmasalas* on Mount Abu, on the Parasnath Hill in Hazaribagh, at Azimganj, and in Bombay. They have also constructed a temple at Giridhi, and one at Jangipur, and a *dharmasala* at Poua Puri near Behar, also a charitable dispensary and hospital at Jangipur. They have maintained for a long time a school for Bengali girls at Azimganj, and Jain *patshalas** for the boys of their co-religionists at Azimganj, Palitana, and Dhoraji. The total amount of their many donations and contributions, for public and charitable purposes, reaches a very high figure.

Rai Budh Singh Bahadur obtained a Certificate of Honour on June the 20th, 1897, on the occasion of the Diamond Jubilee of her late Majesty Queen-Empress Victoria, "in recognition of his liberality and public spirit."

Rai Budh Singh Bahadur has been twice married. Babu Indra Chand was his eldest son by his first wife. This young gentleman, when receiving English education under Messrs. C. J. Owens and J. R. D. Fox, was led by youthful curiosity and the attractions of the Paris Exhibition, to

* Schools.

make a journey to Europe, and visited England in 1889. He undertook this journey to Europe without the consent or knowledge of his father and uncle. Indra Babu was married to a daughter of Rai Sitab Chand, Bahadur of Azimganj, and died in 1899, leaving behind him two sons, Jaggat Singh and Ranajit Singh, minors, under the guardianship of their paternal grandfather. Rai Budh Singh Bahadur has two sons by his second wife, Ajit Singh and Kuwar Singh, the first of whom has been married to a daughter of Babu Narpat Singh, Zemindar of Harwat.

Rai Budh Singh Bahadur is a typical gentleman of the old style of Jains, which is passing away. He is kind, affable, and generous, and, in his dealings, straightforward and honest. He is looked upon by the members of his community with just veneration and respect.

The family residences of both Rai Budh Singh Bahadur and Babu Bijoy Singh Dudhoria are stately structures and richly furnished. The latter's residence is called "Riverside," from its situation on the bank of the Bhagirathi. The collections of jewellery in both the families are rich and rare.

The Dudhoria family is counted among the aristocratic families of the district. His Highness the Nawab Bahadur of Murshidabad and his sons, the princes, have honoured the family by gracing certain festivities held from time to time in the handsome mansions at Azimganj.*

* For brief general remarks concerning the Jains see p. 61.

Babu Bijoy Singh Dudhoria.

BABU AJIT SINGH (DUDHORIA).

XXXI.

THE KHONDKARS OF PERGUNNAH FATEHSINGH, IN THE DISTRICT OF MURSHIDABAD.

ONE of the oldest Mahomedan families of Murshidabad is that of the Khondkars, descendants of the first Kaliph, Abu Bakr, through his son Mahomed, who was, at one time, the Governor of Egypt. One of Mahomed's descendants, Khwaja Mahomed Sharif, left Arabia, and settled in Khorassan. Shah Rustum, a descendant of Khwaja Mahomed Shareh, was compelled to leave Khorassan for India on account of the oppression of the famous Khanghiz Khan. Shah Rustum was well known in his time as a saint. The Emperor Shah Alum fixed a handsome allowance for the expenses of his tomb. The Emperor's *firman* to this effect is still in possession of the family. The son and grandson of Shah Rustum, named Shah Zeza-ud-Din and Shah Suraj-ud-Din respectively, are well known in the history of this country.

Suraj-ud-Din held the honourable post of Kazi-ul-Kuzzat (head of the Civil and Criminal Courts), in the reign of Sultan Ghias-ud-Din, son of Sultan Sikundar, independent ruler of Bengal between 1367 and 1373 A.D.

A curious story regarding Kazi Suraj-ud-Din's impartial justice is related in the histories of Bengal by Mr. Stewart and others, and runs as follows:—

"One day, while Sultan Ghias-ud-Din was practising archery, he accidentally killed a boy, the son of a widow. The woman demanded justice from Kazi Suraj-ud-Din, who was confounded, and said to himself: 'If I summon the King to my Court, I shall run the risk of being disobeyed, and if I pass over his transgression I shall be one day summoned before the Court of God to answer for my neglect of duty.' After much reflection he ordered one of his officers to go and summon the King to answer the complaint of the poor woman. The officer, after some difficulty, gained admittance into the presence of the King, and served the summons.

"The King instantly arose, and, concealing a dagger under his garment, went before the Kazi, who, far from paying him any mark of respect, said to him with a tone of authority: 'You have wounded and killed the son of this widow. You must, therefore, immediately make her adequate reparation or suffer the sentence of the law.'

"The King made a bow, and, turning to the woman, gave her such a sum of money as satisfied her, after which he said: 'Worthy Judge, the complainant has forgiven me.' The Kazi asked the woman if such was the fact, and if she was satisfied, and the woman having assented, was dismissed. The Kazi then came down from his tribunal, and made his obeisance to the King, who, drawing the dagger from beneath his garment, said: 'Kazi, if you had slightly deviated from the path of justice I would have at once taken off your head with this dagger. I return thanks to God that I have in my dominions a Judge who acknowledges no authority superior to the law.' The judge, taking up the scourge, said: 'I swear, by the Almighty God, that if you had not complied with the injunctions of the law, this scourge would have made your back black and blue. It has been a day of trial for us both.' The King was much pleased, and handsomely rewarded the upright judge."

Shah Azizulla, the grandson of Kazi Suraj-ud-Din, succeeded to the *Kaliphate* of Nur Kulbal-Alum, a celebrated Mahomedan saint and spiritual guide to the Kings of Bengal and its people. (*Vide* Stewart's "History of Bengal" and the "Ain-i-Akbari.")

It was Shah Azizulla to whose name the title of "Khondkar" was first added, and the sacred functions of spiritual leadership came down to his descendants. From the time of Khondkar Shah Azizulla, the members of this Khondkar family, generation after generation, held the above functions, namely, of leading the people to the path of righteousness, and to the ways of God and His prophet. Still a branch of this family, namely, the Khondkars of Benodia, in the district of Murshidabad, adheres to the duties of their forefathers, counting many disciples in the following twelve districts of Bengal:—Murshidabad, Rajshaye, Jessore, Faridpur, Nadia, Bogra, Rungpur, Dinajpur, Malda, Pabna, Khulna, and the twenty-four Pergunnahs.

The Khondkars obtained many *aimas* (quit-rent tenures) and *Lakhiraj* (rent-free) estates from the Kings of Gour and Subahs of Bengal for their maintenance, some of which are still in the possession of their descendants. [*Sanads* (viz.:—of Shah Sujah, Shahzada Mahomed Azim, Shaistah Khan, and Murshid Kuli Khan, dated 1639, 1680, 1665, and 1718 A.D. respectively), granting the above, are still in the possession of the family.] In the time of the Mahomedan Government, the family was generally maintained by the above-mentioned grants. The Khondkars scarcely accepted any service under the Government, and if some of them did so at all it was only in the position of Kazi, and this very occasionally.

In the early part of the British rule in this country, several members of this family were obliged to take service under the Government. Among these the first was Moulvi Fasuah, who was appointed by Sir John Shore, during his Governor-Generalship, Mufti of the Sudder Diwanni Adalut (High Court) at Calcutta. Mufti Rashid was, at first, Moulvi of the Supreme Court, and in 1805 was appointed Mufti of the Sudder Diwanni Adalut, and afterwards he became Kazi-ul-Kuzzat of the Sudder Diwanni Adalut in Calcutta. He translated "Hidaya" (Mahomedan Law) into Persian, from Arabic, by the order of Government.

Mufti Moez was appointed to the post of Mufti of Dayer-i-Sayer (circuit) during the administration of the Marquis of Hastings, and afterwards he was appointed by Government guardian and tutor to H.H. Nawab Nazim Humayun Jah, the Nawab Nazim of Bengal, during his minority. Mufti Suraj-ul-Huk was first made Moulvi Adalut of Murshidabad, and was then promoted to the post of Mufti of Dayer-i-Sayer in the time of the same Governor-General. Moulvi Gholam Shah was a Munsif of Rungpur in 1824, and subsequent years. Moulvi Mohsin Ali Khan Bahadur first held the post of Mir Munshi during the administration of Lord Amherst, and afterwards became Diwan to the Nawab Nazim's grandmother, and also a member of the Council for the management of Nizamat affairs during the minority of H.H. Nawab Feradun Jah. Moulvi Mozzam Hussain Khan Bahadur was first appointed Moulvi Adalut of Murshidabad in 1825, and then from 1842 to 1853 Sudder Amin of Maldah and Purnea, and Sudder-i-Ala of Bhagalpur. Moulvi Faizullah was Moulvi Adalut of Birbhum in the middle of the last century.

Several other members of this family held good and respectable posts under the British Government; but no sooner did the Persian language give way to the English language in the Courts than they, as well as other Mahomedans, having failed to take betimes to the study of English, partly in consequence of their superstitious notions, and partly in consequence of their circumstances, became deprived wholly of the "loaves and fishes" of Government service. Nowadays many a young Khondkar is studying English, and is succeeding in getting appointments under the Government, while some, not acquainted with English, are well versed in Persian and Arabic, and follow the profession of their forefathers, namely, that of spiritual leadership. They also possess landed property, which they have inherited. They have kept up their family usages and social rites up to this time, and no perversion has yet occurred in their family. They never marry into any family except their own.

For some time the ancestors of the Khondkars lived at Gour; they left it during its downfall, and settled in Fatehsing, Sarkar Sharifabad. Their descendants, namely, the Khondkars, now live in the following villages of Fatehsingh, in the district of Murshidabad:—Salar, Bharatpur, Shijgaon, Talibpur, Shahpur, Benodia, Mansurpur, Saidkuluthea, Talgaon, and Jagan. Those prominent among them now are:—Shah Abul Huk Saheb, of Benodia, Sajjadanashin; Moulvi Moh-ud-Din Hassan and his brother, Moulvi Mehdi Hussain, Zemindars of Shijgaon; Moulvi Fuzul Huk, Deputy Magistrate of Bharatpur, and Diwan Fuzli Rubbee Khan Bahadur and Shah Farhad Ali, Zemindars of Salar.

Khondkar Fuzli Rubbee, Diwan of Murshidabad, was born at Salar on the 13th of August, 1848. He is the son of Moulvi Obed-ul-Akbar, late Mir Munshi of the last Nawab Nazim of Bengal. Moulvi Obed-ul-Akbar was a man of great learning and piety, and was held in great esteem by his co-religionists and others. Mr. Clarke, late Secretary to the Bengal Chamber of Commerce, wrote to Fuzli Rubbee, Khan Bahadur, on the occasion of this old man's death:—"I, who know as a son what it is to lose a father, offer you now my truest sympathy for your loss of that venerable old man, your father. I feel his loss deeply, and I, therefore, can measure to some extent what you must suffer and must feel. I had a great regard and friendship for your father, because I found him true and faithful to the Murshidabad house, and just and upright in all his dealings. He had great learning and great wisdom, and yet he was simple as a child and as pure in heart. Such men, whatever their religion may be, are loved by God, for they are His servants. This may be some consolation to you to know that I, who am a Christian, respected and envied the earnest belief and the manly faith which made your father seem to me the best Mussulman I have ever known."

Fuzli Rubbee, at the age of twenty-one went to England, in November, 1869, being called by H.H. the last Nawab Nazim of Bengal to act there as the superintendent of his affairs. He accompanied his Highness on all his tours to the principal places in England. In the beginning of the year 1874 he was granted leave for six months by his Highness the Nawab Nazim to come back to India. When he reached Murshidabad he found that the Nizamat Commission had been appointed to clear off the Nizamat debts. At that time there was no man here with his Highness, the present Nawab Bahadur, in whom he could place implicit confidence; consequently he proposed to detain Fuzli Rubbee in his own interest, and wrote to this effect to H.H. the Nawab Nazim, who permitted him to do so. The Nawab Bahadur now made him Amin of Mahalat (manager of estates), the affairs relating to which were then in a chaotic condition. Under him the "Mahalat" showed a marked improvement, and its income rapidly increased. After Nawab Mansur Ali's relinquishment of his title of Nawab Nazim, in 1881, his eldest son became Nawab Bahadur of Murshidabad, and new schemes for the management of the Nizamat affairs were formulated. Babu Bangsi Dhur Roy, the then Naib Diwan, resigned his post, and was made a Deputy Magistrate. The Nawab Bahadur put Fuzli Rubbee into the vacant post of Naib Diwan. Later on, he was promoted to the Diwanship, which had remained vacant since the removal of the last Diwan, Raj Prosonna Narain. In all the reforms Fuzli Rubbee has carried out he has had the approval of an appreciating master. The faithful discharge of his duties strengthened his master's confidence in him, and the Nawab wrote to the District Magistrate:—

"MY DEAR MR. KENNEDY.

"I would solicit permission to bring the life-long services of Munshi Fuzli Rubbee to the notice of Government, as deserving of some recognition. In times of great difficulty and stress he has been my right hand, and has given me effectual aid in placing the affairs of my family on a sound and satisfactory basis. At the same he has given much time and considerable labour to public work in the Municipality and otherwise. I would trust he is already favourably known to yourself and to Government, and any mark of honour bestowed on him would greatly gratify me.

"Yours sincerely,

(Signed) "HASSAN ALI MIRZA."

In spite of his responsibilities as Diwan of the Nizamat, Fuzli Rubbee found time to devote his energies to the service of the public. As an Honorary Magistrate and Municipal Commissioner he did eminent service.

The few spare moments he could snatch, Fuzli Rubbee utilised in the study of historical works and in prosecuting historical researches. As the result of his labours, he has written lots of manuscript, which, if he had the inclination to publish, would be a valuable contribution to history. The only work which has seen the light of day is his history of the origin of the Mussulmans in Bengal, which has been very well received.*

Owing to the Nawab Bahadur's letter to Mr. Kennedy and his historical work, Fuzli Rubbee was made "Khan Bahadur" in 1896. At the Belvedere Durbar, Sir Alex. Mackenzie handed him the *sanad* with these words:—"Khondkar Fuzli Rubbee, Diwan of my old friend the Nawab of Murshidabad, is distinguished not only by his social position, but also by his historical work, 'Origin of the Mussulmans in Bengal.'" In 1897, on the occasion of the Diamond Jubilee of the late Empress of India, a Certificate of Honour was presented to him in recognition of his position and character.

* The Editor records his indebtedness to the Khondkar for much help with the present work.

KHONDKAR FUZLI RUBBEE KHAN BAHADUR.

The following is the Genealogy of the Khondkar Family, showing the principal branches:—

- ABU BAKR (the first Caliph)
- Mahomed
- Kasim
- Abdur Rahaman
- Abdur Rahim
- Ahmad
- Amjed
- Asid
- Asghur (Came to Persia from Arabia)
  - Rahullah (called Mahomed Shareb)
    - Zahed
    - Mahomed
    - Mahomed Wais
    - Nasir-ud-Din
    - Ahmed (Called Khwaja Khorassan)
    - Rustum (Came from Persia to Hindustan)
    - Zain-ud-Din Zahed
    - Kazi Suraj-ud-Din (Came to Bengal)
    - Shah Hidayetullah
    - Shah Azizullah
      - Abdullah Ilias Shah Mea
        - Kutub-ud-Din Hakkani
          - Shah Mansur
            - Shah Mahomed
            - Shah Taher
            - Shah Mahomed
            - Nasib-ud-Din
            - Abdul Muktadir
            - Nasir
            - Gholam Shah
            - Obidul Akber
              - Fuzli Rubbee
              - Ali Hyder
                - Ind Mokim
                  - Said-ud-Din
                  - Ind Kafi
                  - Golam Nabi
                  - Abdul Razzack
                  - Abdul Wahab
                  - Abdul Kasim
                - Rafik
                  - Mahomed
                  - Ishaqe
                  - Ind Afzul
                  - Ind Nasim
                  - Hafizul Huk
                    - Azizul Huk
                    - Fuzhul Huk
          - Shah Idris
            - Shah Hidayetullah
              - Serajul Areffun (line joins Ali Hyder's descendants)
            - Nasurulla
              - Khalilnddin
                - Ind Taki
                - Sukerullah
                - Mufti Frasih
              - Ali Mohomud
                - Ind Safi
                - Ind Mabih
                - Tofail Ali
                - Mehr Ali
                - Mohoun Ali
                - Ind Ahsan
                  - Moazam Hussain Khan
                    - Mehhi Hassan
                    - Mohi Uddin Hussain
                  - Shah Abdul Awol
                  - Shah Abdul Baki
                    - Oli Mohummud
                    - Abdul ola
                    - Imamuddin
                    - Abu Turab
                    - Abil Laio
                    - Abul Khair
                      - Abul Fuzl
                        - Abidul Huk, present Saffada Nassen of this family
                      - Saheb Uddin
                        - Yusuf Ali
                        - Furhad Ali
            - Reer Mohommud
              - Abdul Bakr
              - Shaulffuddin
              - Ziauddin
              - Mufti Rashid
      - Kazi Khondkar
        - Shah Hussain
        - Osman Ali (line joins Ind Ahsan's descendants)
  - Khwaja Abu Ishaq

XXXII.

THE SETHS.*

NO record of Murshidabad would be complete without some account of the Seths. So far as the motive power of money goes, they had undoubtedly a share in shaping the events of our local history. Nor did their power act only within our boundaries. They stretched out commercial tentacles, having a vast banking business in Calcutta and Dacca. Of Rajput descent, the family is probably very ancient, but the earliest records are destroyed.†

For more than two hundred years these "Rothschilds" of the East can, however, give some account of themselves. Marwaris by "caste," they travelled from western and central India, devotees to commerce, and its pioneers. By religion they were Jains and in part founders of the Jain community which is now so largely represented in Azimganj. Among all religious bodies there is dissent, and the Seths belonged to the sect known as *Svetembara*. The home of the "Jaggat Seths'" ancestors was in Nagar near Jodhpur. About 1695, Hira Nand Saha, the stock from which our Seths claim descent, stirred by the migratory impulse which drives every Marwari to try his luck in new centres of commerce, began his travels. When Hira Nand got as far as Patna he was attracted by that bustling city and its great wealth. This pioneer of the Seths was not long before he had amassed a considerable fortune which left him with few rivals in Patna. Fortune must have favoured him also in his choice of a wife. This lady bore him seven sons, and all seven, when they arrived at manhood, became bankers, scattering themselves over India.

The son whose career is of interest to us was Manick Chand. He settled in Dacca, then the capital of Bengal, and the home of the Nawab ruling as *Subah* of Bengal, Behar, and Orissa. Thus it remained until 1704. In that year Murshid Kuli Khan made Muxsudabad his capital, changing the name, as we have seen, to Murshidabad. Naturally enough Manick Chand moved with the court. He is said to have been in favour with Murshid Kuli Khan, who promoted the Seth to be one of his advisers as well as his banker. The word banker as applied to Manick Chand conveys only a half-truth, since the native banker is generally more a money-lender. He has not generally depositors' money to work with. However, Manick Chand seems to have advised his patron wisely and to have financed him with excellent judgement. One of the results of this combination of brains and money was the Murshidabad mint.

To Manick Chand was given a post something like that of the Chancellor of the Exchequer, with the duties of a collector of revenue. That Manick Chand must have found his post no sinecure we may judge from the fact that the Emperor of Delhi required his *Subah* to pay one

* This biography has been mainly compiled by the Editor from books noted in the Bibliography and papers from the Nizamat library.

† Fire, elephants, termites (white ants), and indifference to the value of records, have left the origin of many other families doubtful, and have deprived the historian of material of untold value. In every branch I touch, be it history, art, folk-lore, or industries, I have met with gaps and fresh beginnings, as though history, and things in general, had suddenly sprung from nothing, from nowhere; "Sans père et sans proches." This is convenient, or inconvenient, as the case may be with regard to individuals; but an irreparable loss to the historian. Of late years, however, the supreme government of India has been really awakened to the loss sustained by careless or routine destruction of records, the possession of which would have made the patient labours of Wilson, and Forrest (see Bibliography) of even greater value than they undoubtedly are.

crore and fifty lakhs of rupees annually. Of this enormous sum a large part was paid by the Delhi Marwaris on *Handis* (payment notes), which pass current between one native banker and another. In addition we learn that Manick Chand was keeper of the Nawab's purse and treasure. It is not unlikely therefore that, if he was so minded, he had always money at hand to speculate with or to lend out to high-born paupers such as are to be found in the *entourage* of every eastern court.

When Murshid Kuli Khan died, no doubt Manick Chand claimed, and obtained, the major portion of the Nawab's fortune.

The man with money has the means of success, but the man with money and brains is certain to go far. We are not surprised, therefore, to learn that Manick Chand was regarded as "one having authority." The title "Seth" was conferred upon the Marwari by Furrakshah in 1715. In Manick Chand we thus find the founder of the *Seths* of Murshidabad, men who, perhaps with no more exceptions than are found in most families, have prospered and earned a well-merited respect.

Manick Chand, having no son, adopted a nephew, one Fateh Chand Seth, chief partner in a firm in Delhi. The Emperor was under many obligations to this firm, so that there was no difficulty in obtaining for the adopted son the position of trust, formerly filled by Manick Chand, who died in 1722 A.D. It is said that when Fateh Chand established himself in Murshidabad he was the richest man in India.

The title "Jaggat Seth" ("banker of the world"), was conferred on Fateh Chand at his first visit to the Emperor, Mahomed Shah, in 1724. The rumour that Fateh Chand interceded for Murshid Kuli Khan into whose shoes he might possibly have stepped has no historical foundation. There is no doubt that Fateh Chand was a power, and when a "Khilat" (present of honour) was sent to the Nazim, a similar favour was shown to the banker, and, among other presents, he received an emerald seal bearing the title "Jaggat Seth." When Sujah-u-Dowlah succeeded Murshid Kuli Khan in 1728, Fateh Chand was one of his four councillors. Fateh Chand found favour with each ruling Nawab, and the succession of Serfiraz Khan, in 1739, made no change in his position. That a breach occurred, was due, it is said, to the lust of the Nazim who, hearing of the great beauty of the wife of Fateh Chand's son, sought to see her. How great an insult such suggestion conveyed can only be understood by a dweller in the East. Jaggat Seth, burning with hatred towards his oppressor, entered into communication with Ali Verdi Khan. Carried back to honour and power after the successful revolt of Ali Verdi Khan, Fateh Chand lived in luxury until 1744, when he died, leaving his riches and honours to "Jaggat Seth" Madhab Rai, his grandson, son of his eldest son. His second son's child, Swarup Chand, received the title of "Raja," which his wealth enabled him to maintain. The fortune of the two Seths is said to have been equal to £10,000,000.

We have seen that in 1742 the Mahrattas had partially plundered the outskirts of Murshidabad and it is reported, that the Seths suffered considerable loss.* Local legend, with its fondness for hyperbole, tells us that the wealth of the Seths would have blocked the entrance of the Bhagirathi river, at Suti, with rupees. As collectors of the revenue their opportunities for making money were numerous. At the *Punya* (rent day) the zemindars poured treasure into the Seths' coffers, and the discount on advances, or on exchange, went into their private purse. Jaggat Seth was also the source of supply to Europeans who needed advances for the purchase of silk, etc., and the interest on these loans formed another addition to his income. According to Orme, the French in Chandernagore owed the Seths one and a half million rupees.† The East India Company had resorted also to the Seth brothers for the sinews of war, needed to carry out the operations which ended with the battle of Plassy.

* Stewart: 3 lakhs. Others put the figure higher. † Orme (42) ii., p. 138.

In 1749 the Armenians had complained to Ali Verdi Khan of tyrannies on the part of the English at Kasimbazar. The Nawab Nazim seeing a source of profit to himself, blockaded the factory at Kasimbazar, demanding compensation. The claim, Rs. 1,200,000, was only settled by the help of the Seths, who no doubt advanced the greater part of the money. When the East India Company's Directors suggested a mint in Calcutta, the Council pointed out that it would be hopeless, as against the interest of the Seths.

In 1756 Ali Verdi Khan died, and Suraj-u-Dowlah employed the Seths in his transactions with the English. On June 22nd, and August 22nd, the East India Company's scattered Council met at Fultah, and sent a letter to the Jaggat Seth, asking him to intercede with the Nawab. The fate of this letter was to be detained by Omichand. In the meanwhile, Suraj-u-Dowlah, hated by all, quarrelled with the Jaggat Seth, who protested against being the means of wringing more money from the Nawab's oppressed subjects. It is said that the enraged Nawab struck the banker, and caused him to be imprisoned. This treatment of the Seth further estranged Mir Jaffer, who was already smarting under his own grievances.

On the 23rd of November, the Fultah Council sent a letter, written by Major Kilpatrick, to Jaggat Seth.

The arrival of Clive and his victorious progress, rendered the assistance of the Seth of less importance. The cousins, through their agent, Ranjit Rai, had a share in framing the treaty of 1757, by which Suraj-u-Dowlah granted the wishes of the English, and again they tried to pour oil on the troubled waters, when the Nawab was again incensed by the taking of the French settlement Chandernagore.

On April the 23rd, 1757, Yar Luteef Khan, commanding the Nawab's cavalry, and also the bodyguard of the Seths, who paid the commander extra for his protection, came to Mr. Watts at the factory at Kasimbazar. At the instigation of the Seths, he was to betray the city to the English, and give material assistance. This plot was the one which, afterwards, by the adherence of Mir Jaffer, became the means by which Lord Clive was able to overthrow the Nawab at Plassy. Thus again the Seths secured their safety and position under Mir Jaffer.

In 1759, Jaggat Seth accompanied the Nawab Nazim, and, with him, was the guest of the East India Company. But the pinnacle of prosperity was reached, and the fall came. Mir Jaffer had to produce money to satisfy the East India Company and Lord Clive's troops, officers, and men. Money, too, went to compensate those who had suffered loss at the "sack" of Calcutta, and at the spoiliation of the Kasimbazar factory. To the members of council, Mir Jaffer also gave presents. It is evident that the amount of money in the Murshidabad treasure chest has been over-rated, for even the Seths could not comply with the calls for ready money.*

This was the moment for their enemies. The cousins had hardly set out on a pilgrimage to Parasnath, when a rumour was circulated that they were financing the Shahzada, who was preparing to invade Behar. True or false, Mir Jaffer believed the story, and sent to recall the Seths. They had a strong escort of two thousand men, and trusting to this, they refused to return to Murshidabad. They secured the allegiance of the soldiers by promise of pay, to include all arrears. Mir Jaffer was too wise to insist, and the subsequent course of events served to contradict the evil rumour concerning the Seths.

The ill-fortune of the Seths followed them, and Mir Kasim, who was in 1763 at loggerheads with the English, seized and imprisoned Jaggat Seth and Raja Swarup Chand. The Governor and Council, always on good terms with the Seths, at once remonstrated.

* *Vide* "Life of Clive."

The Governor wrote, April 24th, 1763, as follows:—

"I am just informed, by a letter from Mr. Amyatt, that, 'Mahomed Taki Khan went on the 21st inst., at night, to the house of Jaggat Seth and Swarup Chand, and carried them to Hirajhil, where he keeps them under a guard. This affair surprises me greatly. When your Excellency took the Government upon yourself, you and I, and the Seths being assembled together, it was agreed that as they are men of high rank in the country, you shall make use of their assistance in managing your affairs, and never consent that they should be injured; and when I had the pleasure of seeing you at Monghyr, I then likewise spoke to you about them, and you set my heart at ease by assuring me that you would on no account do them any injury. The taking men of their rank in such an injurious manner out of their home, is extremely improper, and is disgracing them in the highest degree. It is, moreover, a violation of our agreement, and therefore reflects dishonour upon you and me, and will be the means of acquiring us an ill name from everybody. The above-mentioned gentlemen were never thus disgraced in the time of any former Nazims." As is well known, this remonstrance was unavailing. Mir Kasim took no notice of the letter, and after the defeat at Udai Nala, he carried off the Seths with him to Monghyr, where they were murdered. They were thrown from one of the bastions of the fort into the Ganges.

Jaggat Seth and Raja Swarup Chand were succeeded by their sons. These two Seths, Khushal Chand, eldest son of Madhab Rai, and Udwat Chand, eldest son of the Raja, revived the family fortunes, and in 1766 the Emperor Shah Alum conferred the title of "Jaggat Seth" on Khushal Chand, while the title of "Maharaja" was granted to Udwat Chand. In 1765 they had petitioned Lord Clive for favours on their own behalf, and on behalf of their brothers, Seth Golab Chand, and Babu Mir Chand. The new heads of the Jaggat Seth firm had been in Monghyr, where their fathers were killed, but from there they had been sent to Oude.

When Mir Jaffer was re-instated as Nawab Nazim, one of his first acts was to ask that the Seths should be made over to him. Sujah-u-Dowlah, Subah of Oude, claimed a ransom, which was paid, and the cousins again joined their families at Murshidabad.

In their petition to Lord Clive, in May, 1765, the Seths had pleaded great poverty; but Lord Clive, when replying, in November, makes no allowance for what may be called "the petitioners' licence." His letter in reply was as follows:—

"You are not ignorant what attention and support I always showed to your father, and how cordially I have continued it to you, and the remainder of the family. It cannot, therefore, but be matter of great concern to me to learn that you do not seriously consider what part you ought to act, to establish your own credit and the public interest. Instead of keeping up to the original intention and necessity of having the treasury under three separate keys, I find all the money has been lodged with your family, in your own house, and that you have been consenting at least to the farming of the Bengal province under the rents I am assured it will bear. I am informed also that you have been pressing the zemindars to discharge their debts to your fathers, at a time when they are five months in arrears to the Government. This is a step I can by no means approve of, or allow. You are still a very rich house; but I greatly fear that the tendency you seem to have to avarice will not only turn greatly to your disadvantage, but will, at the same time, destroy that opinion I had of your inclination and disposition to promote the public good."

In 1766 Jaggat Seth sent in a claim for fifty-sixty lakhs of rupees. Of this sum he said that twenty-one lakhs had been advanced to Mir Jaffer, to enable him to fulfil all his promises to the British after the battle of Plassy, and to pay for his troops, and those under Lord Clive.

Lord Clive admitted the claim for the twenty-one lakhs, and suggested that one half should be paid by the Nawab, and the other half by the Company. It does not seem likely that the East India Company paid their portion, as at that very time they were about to apply to the Seths for a loan of one and a half lakhs. Lord Clive appointed Khushal Chand, "Jaggat Seth," to be the treasurer to the East India Company, and to manage the newly acquired receipts from the provincial revenues.

The treaties of 1766 and 1770 included Jaggat Seth's name as manager of financial affairs. This was a great honour and responsibility for a youth, only twenty years of age when first appointed. For his duties Lord Clive offered him a salary of three lakhs of rupees. This the Seth refused, hoping, no doubt, to be allowed to make for himself a greater fortune from loan advances, and discount, as his ancestors had done.

After nineteen years' work, Khushal Chand died. He is reported to have been very generous to his own family, and to have given large sums to the priests in charge of the temples on Parasnath hill. One of these temples, built in 1768, by Seths, Sunogal Chand, and Hoshiyal Chand, is still supported by the Jain community. The family of the "Jaggat Seth" bears the expenses of a temple erected by Rup Chand, "Jaggat Seth."

The fortune of the Seths, from one cause and another, began to dwindle away at this time. They spent money with a lavish hand, but it was the check on the income that ultimately reduced them, from the highest position to one of very minor importance, among the merchants of the district. Tradition tells that Khushal Chand buried much money and treasure. Where this is, no one knows, as Khushal died suddenly, without revealing the secret. Khushal Chand, having no son, adopted a nephew, Harek Chand.

The coveted title of "Jaggat Seth" was conferred on him by the English without any reference to Delhi.* To the historian this act is of great political importance, as showing that the English felt confident in their position as rulers of Bengal. Perhaps the Seth lost some prestige among the Jains and traders generally by changing his religion. Giving up the Jain tenets, Harek Chand became a follower of Vishnu.

The reason given in Hunter's "Gazetteer" is, that, wishing for a son, he carried out the ceremonial enjoined by the Jain religion. No son came, and Harek Chand lost faith in gods that absorbed so much money and gave nothing in return. In a moment of *pique* he turned from his deities, and on "the advice of a Bairagi," became a follower of Vishnu. That this apostasy was justified must be taken as proved, otherwise how are we to account for the son his wife bore him after his intercession with Vishnu?

Showing a proper spirit of gratitude, the Seths have remained Vashnavs. Reciprocity seems to be one of Vishnu's attributes, for a second son appeared in due course. These two sons, appropriately named Indra Chand, and Vishnu Chand, received equal shares of their father's property.

Indra Chand received the title of "Jaggat Seth," and, according to Hunter,† it became extinct when he died. Indra Chand's son, Gobind, inherited his father's fortune. Whatever this amounted to, Gobind Chand was not long in spending it. He then parted with the family jewels, and lived on the money realized by their sale. Lastly, when all was gone, he turned to the East India Company. The Council granted him a pension of £1,200 a year, as a recognition of the services rendered to the English by his ancestors. The pension descended to Krishna Chand, and when he died his wife received Rs. 300. With her death the pension ceased. The son Golab Chand still lives in Murshidabad, in a house almost opposite the dilapidated family mansion of the founder.

* W. W. Hunter (17). † "Gazetteer," p. 265. The title by right, or by courtesy, is still used.

XXXIII.

THE SUBADHICARI FAMILY.

THE founder of the Subadhicari family was Sureshwar, who was appointed, in the beginning of the fifteenth century, Diwan of Orissa. Sureshwar administered that province very successfully under the Imperial Court of Delhi. He received the hereditary title of "Subadhicari," which means the "head of all classes" in point of wealth, rank, "caste," and descent, from the Emperor of Delhi, Mahomed Shah,* in consideration of his political position as Diwan, or Governor, of Orissa. To support the dignity of the title, he was allowed a princely Jaghir in the well-known Zemindari of Orissa named Raganathpur, that gave a yearly income of about two lakhs of rupees. It was under Sureshwar's administration that the celebrated temple of Jagannath was walled up, and that various improvements were made in the management connected with the worship of the sacred shrine of Jagannath (Puri). He was allowed also the exceptional privilege of entering the temple of Jagannath at any time he liked, with an umbrella carried over his head (a sign of honour), whereas, according to ordinary practice and custom, the temple of Jagannath could only be opened to the general public at certain prescribed times. This privilege was not only granted to Sureshwar, as a personal distinction, but was made hereditary in the male line. Sureshwar subsequently transferred the seat of Government to his Raganathpur estate, where his descendants lived and flourished for a long series of years. Sureshwar's younger brother, Eshaneswhar, was the Vizier of the Emperor of Delhi at that time (1409, *circa*), and as such commanded a very high political influence all over India.

It was not an easy task to trace the successive migrations and movements of Sureshwar's descendants, which may number more than two thousand, now scattered all over the country. Several branches sprung from the main line are living. When Murshidabad became the capital of Bengal, in the very early part of the eighteenth century (1704), a branch of this family came to this district and settled at Dahapura and Choa.

Choa was then a very important place, and one of the most populous villages of Bengal, about fourteen miles distant from Murshidabad. It was a military station under the Nawabs of Bengal. Raja Mahendra Narain was a Revenue Minister of Nawab Ali Verdi Khan, and as such had great influence at the Court of Murshidabad. He had substantial dealings with the East India Company's silk *Concern* at Kasimbazar. He helped the East India Company during their troublous days, and rendered signal service to Lord Clive in the negotiations that preceded the battle of Plassy. His descendant, Raja Bubhan Mohun, was a great Persian scholar, and a Minister of the Emperor Shah Alum. He was also a Diwan, under the East India Company. When the Company had the monopoly of the salt business, Bubhan Mohun's son, Raja Hari Prosad, *alias* Raja Kishori, was Diwan of the East India Company's entire silk *Concern* in Bengal. When the Company had the monopoly of that trade, this appointment was considered to be the prize appointment, considering the princely salary

* The contributor of these notes gives the name *Toghluk;* but he was much earlier, 1340.

attached to the office. The Diwans amassed a colossal fortune, and added to their extensive zemindaries. Their charities were very large, and to do good to others was the motto of their lives. They expended lakhs of rupees on the occasion of their mother's "shradh" (funeral ceremony).

A cousin, Ram Narain, who lived at Khanacool, got the title of "Munshi" for his proficiency in Persian. He established a Persian school at Radhagaon for the free education of the poor; and he constructed a road, costing about a lakh of rupees, running from Khidderpur Watganj, Calcutta, to Munshi's garden, and declined to accept the cost, which was offered to him by the Government.

Ram Narain's son, Madhan Mohun, was the first native appointed a Subordinate Judge, the highest judicial appointment then open to a native. Hari Prosad's sons, Joy Narain and Kala Chand, were widely distinguished for various public services rendered to the Government and the public. Kala Chand took a substantial part in founding the Berhampur College at the instance of Sir Cecil Beadon, the then Lieutenant-Governor of Bengal. His son, Ashutosh, too, made a free gift of land to the Government at the instance of the District Magistrate of Murshidabad, which Mr. Wavel and his successors required for the construction of a public road from Berhampur to Patkabari when the *Road Cess Act* came into operation. Ashutosh was a member of the newly created Road Cess Committee. Their descendant, Raja Sitanath, was Diwan to the Viceroy, and subsequently Diwan to Nawab Nazim Humayun Jah, during the minority of his son, Munsur Ali.

One of Sitanath's descendants is S. B. Subadhicari, a barrister-at-law, who is practising in the Allahabad High Court, and has acquired an European education by travelling in America and Europe. He wrote a book, "Sojourn in the West," which has been favourably reviewed by the newspapers of America.

It may not be out of place to note that Mr. S. B. Subadhicari has been addressed by the present Secretary of State for India, Lord George Hamilton, through his Private Secretary, Mr. Richmond Ritchie, saying that "he fully appreciates the services of his forefathers, who helped Lord Clive in holding the thread of the negotiations between the English and the Government of the Nawab."

Sitanath's other successful descendants were Prosonna Kumar, Anunda Kumar, Surya Kumar, Raj Kumar. Prosonna Kumar is now dead; he was truly a great man, *great* and *noble* in the true sense of the word. He was a member of the Bengal Legislative Council. He was an eminent scholar, of European fame in his time; he was held in such high estimation by all classes of the people, both European and native, official and unofficial, not only for his eminent scholarship and invaluable services rendered to the Government, and the people, his capacity as an inspector of schools in the Presidency Circle, and as principal of the Berhampur Sanskrit Colleges, as a professor at the Presidency College, Calcutta, a leading member of the Syndicate of the Calcutta University, and author of several works of public celebrity, and as a trusted and recognised leader of all the public movements connected with the advancement of education, but also for his rare social virtues, as evidenced by his expending most of his earnings throughout the period of half a century, for all sorts of public good in establishing schools, feeding the poor, mitigating the sufferings of the people in various ways, and in doing all that lay in his power to advance the cause of humanity by every means. In order to commemorate him, a portrait and bust were raised by public subscriptions, and unveiled by the late Chief Secretary to the Government, the Hon. Mr. C. W. Bolton. In the public meeting held to celebrate the unveiling ceremony, Mr. Bolton paid a well-deserved tribute of respect to the real worth and character of Prosonna Kumar, and exhorted his countrymen to follow his noble example.

Anunda Kumar was a successful Subordinate Judge of Bengal. He has now retired on pension, and has a worthy son, Joytish Prosad, who is a rising pleader of the High Court, Calcutta. Upon Surya Kumar has been conferred the title of "Rai Bahadur" by the Government, in consideration of his success in the medical profession, and of his high social position. He has been a very successful medical practitioner in Calcutta for forty years; respected equally by Europeans and natives, and was at one time President of the Faculty of Medicine of the Syndicate of the Calcutta University.

Raj Kumar has also been invested with the title and dignity of "Rai Bahadur" by the Government. He is a Fellow of the Calcutta University, the very successful editor of the "*Hindu Patriot*," a Presidency Magistrate of Calcutta, and the secretary of the first political association of India, viz., the "British Indian Association." He was the author of "Law Lectures on Hindu Law of Inheritance."

Dr. Surya Kumar Bahadur's son, Dr. Satyacharan, is a Presidency Magistrate in Calcutta, and Davi Prosad is a successful attorney of the High Court, a Fellow of the Calcutta University, and a prominent member of the "National Congress." Dr. Suresh Prosad is in the medical profession.